Lady Bird

A BIOGRAPHY OF MRS. JOHNSON

Jan Jarboe Russell

A LISA DREW BOOK

SCRIBNER

SCRIBNER
1230 Avenue of the Americas
New York, NY 10020

SCRIBNER and design are trademarks of Jossey-Bass, Inc.,
used under license by Simon & Schuster,
the publisher of this work.

Designed by Colin Joh

Set in Goudy Old Style

Manufactured in the United States of America

1 3 5 7 9 10 8 6 4 2

Library of Congress Cataloging-in-Publication Data
Russell, Jan Jarboe [date].
Lady Bird : a biography of Mrs. Johnson/Jan Jarboe Russell.
p. cm.
"A Lisa Drew Book."
Includes bibliographical references (p. 318) and index.
(hc.: alk. paper)
1. Johnson, Lady Bird, 1912– .
2. Presidents' spouses—United States biography.
I. Title.
E848.J64R87   1999
973.923'092—dc21
[B]   99-27544
CIP
ISBN 0-684-81480-3

In memory of my mother, Laverne Pope Jarboe, who,
like Lady Bird, sacrificed her own wishes and desires for her family,
and for my husband, Lucky Russell,
who requires no such sacrifice.

Contents

❧

Lady
Bird

INTRODUCTION

Lady Bird's Red Shoes

> I stand in the ring
> in the dead city
> and tie on the red shoes . . .
> They are not mine,
> They are my mother's,
> Her mother's before,
> Handed down like an heirloom
> But hidden like shameful letters.
> —Anne Sexton

On a long and rainy day in November 1994, I spent eight hours with Lady Bird Johnson, talking to history. The interview was for an article that was to appear in *Texas Monthly* magazine. Lady Bird, then eighty-one years old, met me in the kitchen of her house, which is located on the side of a steep hill in northwest Austin. Standing at her stove, dressed in a pleated navy skirt, cotton blouse, and black lace-up shoes, Lady Bird leaned against a steel cane and fired the first question.

"Do you take your coffee black or with sugah?" she asked, rolling her "r" like a big old Southern marble in her mouth. I recognized that I was on familiar terrain. I could feel the past rising up between us, like the steam from the kettle that she picked up from her back burner. Internally the landscape that we shared was the American South, our motherland.

All through that day, we talked about the major events of the Cold War era, when her husband, Lyndon Baines Johnson, wielded power ferociously like the American equivalent of the Greek god Zeus, and Lady Bird stood resolutely by his side, like Zeus's ambitious wife, Hera, who achieved immortality through the power of marriage. We talked about civil rights, Vietnam, his efforts to end poverty, their disparate upbringings. Naturally, we talked, as well, about wildflowers and her own individual path to serenity: the planting of peaceful gardens. "If we can get people to see the beauty of the native flora of their own corner of the world with caring eyes," she said, rooting herself in the pleasures of the soil, "then I'd be real happy."

In that first interview, we also touched on the darker parallels between Johnson and Zeus: their pride, their petulance, their philandering, and all of the manners of tricks they used to hide their infidelity from their wives.

When I asked how she handled her husband's indiscretions, Lady Bird, who was legally blind in one eye and had very little vision in the other due to a condition called macular degeneration, yanked a pair of sunglasses from her eyes, looked straight at me, and said in a firm, Hera-like voice: "When people ask me these sort of things, I just say, 'Look to your own lives. Look to yourself, everybody. Fix yourselves, and keep your problems to yourself.' The public should weigh what public servants are doing, not their private, innermost feelings. I think we are getting into such a state of intimacy of everyone's lives that we don't judge people by what they are able to do for the country."

She was speaking from high atop her throne as Lyndon Johnson's queen. However, she was also speaking for history's line of long-suffering First Ladies, who have borne similar indiscretions and humiliations— those "shameful letters" as the poet Anne Sexton called them— by tying on "red shoes," the conventional expectations of the culture that the way to handle such matters is to persevere and keep your problems to yourself.

Lady Bird issued that declaration of warning for the country not to delve too deeply into a President's "intimate feelings" four years before President Bill Clinton, another Southerner, was acquitted of impeachment charges over a sex scandal and his wife and co-sovereign, Hillary Rodham, would remake herself in Lady Bird's image by stoically refusing to vent her humiliations in public.

In the process of trying to count the cost of such stubborn fidelity, I inevitably encountered resistance from Lady Bird herself. Three years into the research of the book, Lady Bird abruptly ended our series of interviews. Her decision came after I asked questions about Johnson's key relationships with other women and published an essay in *Slate,* an on-line magazine, about the public release of Johnson's private telephone calls of 1964. In a letter written on December 5, 1997, Lady Bird brought her participation in the book to an end. ". . . Your conclusion about me may well come at Lyndon's expense. . . ." she wrote, ". . . there is no way to separate us and our roles in each other's lives."

The tone of the letter was icy and final. By the time she wrote it, Lyndon Johnson had been dead almost twenty-five years, but Lady Bird was still functioning as his chief defender. Who could blame her? Like Hera, her identity and power came solely from her husband. I remembered a comment she had made near the end of our first day together. The conversation had turned to death, and I asked Mrs. Johnson if she believed in heaven.

"Oh yes, I do," she said. "I do know that there is something hereafter, because all this has been too significant, too magnificent, for there not to be something after. Heaven, to me, is a mystery, a place I'll know what all this—the events of my life—meant."

History, too, is that kind of place. This book, then, is an effort to examine what the life of Lady Bird Johnson has meant, to her and to all those who have followed in her red shoes.

CHAPTER ONE

❧

Marriage, the Ultimatum

ady Bird Taylor's life with Lyndon Johnson began with an ultimatum. "Let's get married," an overwrought twenty-six-year-old Lyndon wrote her from Washington shortly after the two met on a date in Austin on August 1, 1934. "If you say no, it just proves that you don't love me enough to dare to marry me. We either do it now, or we never will." It wasn't that Lady Bird didn't love him. She loved him at first sight.

A few days after they met, she visited a friend, Emily Crow Selden, in Dallas and took a large photograph of Lyndon with her. Lady Bird pointed out Lyndon's good features, noting his exceptional height, his slim frame, his thick, wavy hair, his rakish good looks. "Well, his ears are a little too long," acknowledged Lady Bird. "But he doesn't take a good picture."

Later that night, after the two girls had gone to bed, Lady Bird told her friend that she was crazy about Lyndon Johnson, that she loved his drive, his directness, his ability to take charge. She confided that he had asked her to marry him on their first date. There was something about Johnson that drew him to her.

At the time, Johnson was working as an administrative aid to U.S. Congressman Richard Kleberg, heir to the fabled King Ranch. Kleberg was a rich playboy who left the day-to-day running of his office to Johnson, who in effect served as the district's surrogate congressman. While Kleberg played poker, went to horse races, and traveled to Mexico, Johnson made speeches on his behalf, handled constituent complaints, ran the office, and instructed Kleberg, whom he called "Chief," how to vote. Johnson's willingness to fill a void, to take charge, was part of what attracted Lady Bird.

From the beginning, Lady Bird recognized Johnson had the two qualities she most admired in a man: ambition and perseverance. She had never met anyone who asked such personal, probing questions, who looked her straight in the eye, and who exuded such energy. Lyndon seemed, she told her friend, as if he were headed straight to the top.

Emily was flabbergasted. Lady Bird had always been so sensible and solid. Unlike her other college friends, Lady Bird had never skipped a test to go shopping for a new dress or indulged in angel food cake with whipped cream.

The idea of judicious, obedient Lady Bird doing anything sudden or on impulse, especially marrying a complete stranger who had no money, seemed inconceivable to Emily. Even then, Lady Bird was the kind of person who could size up a situation quickly, especially her own place in it, and not be immobilized by indecision. This quality stood her in good stead at that moment and many others in her thirty-nine-year marriage to Lyndon Johnson.

In the fall of 1934, Lady Bird Taylor found herself standing at a crossroads that would have paralyzed most young women of her generation. At twenty-one years of age, she had graduated cum laude from the University of Texas at Austin with not one but two degrees, in history and journalism. A pragmatist to the core, she had also earned a teacher's certificate, and knew shorthand as well.

When friends asked her what she wanted to do, Lady Bird told them that she was considering applying for teaching jobs in Hawaii or Alaska, the most glamorous places the soft-spoken Texas native could envision.

Her aunt Effie Pattillo, a Southern spinster who had raised Lady Bird after her mother died in 1918, had urged her down an unbeaten path. Effie wanted Lady Bird to become a reporter for the *Washington Post*, or failing that, a drama critic for the *New York Times*, maybe even a ballerina.

Effie was one of those prototypical women from the Old South, so gentle in spirit that she wouldn't crush a violet or kill a fly, but at the same time so infirm of body that she spent her evenings sipping medicine from small brown bottles to quell the pain of migraines and ulcers.

All Effie's hopes and dreams were concentrated on Lady Bird. She encouraged her niece to think first of a career, not a family.

The other path was well worn and traditional: she could do as her father expected and stay in Karnack, a small East Texas town located in a narrow, dense pine forest on the edge of a wide swamp, and continue to supervise the redecoration of her family's two-story Southern mansion, which had been built by slaves on a six-hundred-acre plantation in 1843.

However, at that moment, the Brick House was the last place on earth Lady Bird wanted to be. Though Lady Bird kept it a secret from her friends, her father, Thomas Jefferson Taylor, a tenant farmer, country merchant, and the richest man in Harrison County, was ending his second marriage. The stout, domineering Taylor, then a sixty-year-old patriarch with a legendary reputation as a philanderer, had married a much younger woman, Beulah Wisdom.

Miss Beulah, as she was known in Karnack, had short black hair that she wore in a 1930s bob and was so high-spirited that she was often seen speeding through the hills of East Texas in Taylor's old Desoto, leaving a cloud of red dust behind her. "Miss Beulah was one fine-lookin' woman," said Dorsey Jones, an old Black man who lived near the Brick House. "She was full of spit and vinegar, the kind of woman only a rich man could have."

Like almost everyone in Karnack, Beulah worked for Taylor. She was his bookkeeper. Beulah's father also worked for him as the manager of one of his cotton gins. Not long after she married Taylor, Beulah fell in love with one of his hired hands, and ran off with him. Taylor, who was not the kind of man to restrain his own passion or forgive anyone else's, flew into a rage. "I threw $5,000 at the two of 'em and sent 'em packin'," Taylor boasted some years later to a relative. "It was the best $5,000 I've ever spent." His divorce was finalized in September 1934.

Miss Beulah presented Lady Bird with still another option that may not have otherwise occurred to her, that of fleeing her father's control. Two months after the divorce, on the morning of November 17, 1934, as the sun streamed through a grove of ancient cedars and a flock of guineas scattered noisily on the Brick House's front lawn, Lady Bird left her father's home in Lyndon Johnson's Ford roadster convertible.

Originally they were headed for Austin, a four-and-a-half-hour drive away, but an hour out of Karnack, Lady Bird found herself unable to resist Johnson's constant avowals of love. "I guess what settled it is when Lyndon really made me understand that he had done all he could to persuade me to marry him, and he just couldn't stand to live in a state of uncertainty," said Lady Bird, indicating that she knew that Johnson would end the relationship if she continued to make him wait. "I just couldn't envision going on without him," she recalled mournfully.

As a young woman, Lady Bird felt different with Lyndon Johnson, happy, free, as though she really were a bird and finally flying. Somewhere on the edge of East Texas, Lady Bird finally agreed to marry him.

"When?" she asked him.

"Tonight," he said, without hesitation.

Johnson pulled off the road, stopped the car, and telephoned a political crony, Dan Quill, who was then the postmaster of San Antonio. In his rapid-fire voice, Johnson explained that he and Lady Bird wanted to be married that night at St. Mark's Episcopal Church in downtown San Antonio.

They had decided on San Antonio, rather than Austin, because Lady Bird didn't want to offend her many friends from college by not inviting them to what amounted to an elopement. "Austin was my past," she explained. "Austin had too many ghosts of old dreams. I needed to break from it—everything was going to be different from now on."

The man Johnson put in charge of the ceremony, Dan Quill, was short, stocky, and constantly chewed on a cigar. Like Johnson, Quill was committed to Roosevelt's New Deal. He had helped Johnson run Kleberg's campaign in the special election to Congress earlier that year, and was accustomed to Johnson's habit of giving orders and expecting instant action.

"Fix everything up!" Johnson barked. Then the telephone went silent. Quill knew he wouldn't hear from Johnson again until nightfall, and that he better get busy.

All through the fall day, as Lady Bird and Lyndon drove across 425 miles of Texas, Quill hastily planned Lady Bird's wedding. There were many problems to solve, but Quill found solutions—political solutions—for all of them.

In those days couples had to be physically examined before getting a marriage license. Since there was no time for either Lady Bird or Lyndon to visit a doctor, Quill wrote the license himself and convinced the chief deputy clerk at the courthouse to sign it. Quill's next hurdle was to persuade the Reverend Arthur R. McKinstry, a high church Episcopalian who presided over the wealthiest pulpit in town, to marry two strangers on short notice. McKinstry was adamant: he would not do it.

In his most unctuous voice, the rector explained to Quill that holy matrimony was a very serious matter, and he needed time to counsel the young couple about the gravity of their commitment. "I simply can't do it," the minister said.

"Well, this young man is in a hurry," snapped Quill. "He has to get back to Washington. There's no reason why you can't marry them legally. I'll never do this to you again, but they want to be married in your church this evening at 8:00 P.M. Please do this for me!"

McKinstry might have held firm, but he owed Quill a favor. A few months earlier, Quill, although a Catholic, had nonetheless pulled some strings in Washington and arranged for St. Mark's to have a second-class mail permit, which saved the church $12 a month—not an inconsiderable sum in 1934. McKinstry was indebted to Quill, and on this particular day Quill called in his marker. Reluctantly, the minister agreed.

At about 6:00 P.M. that evening, Lady Bird and Lyndon arrived at the Plaza St. Anthony Hotel in downtown San Antonio and rented two rooms, side by side. Lyndon went off in one room with Quill and a couple of lawyers, Henry Hirshberg and Oscar Powell, who wandered over from the courthouse down Presa Street. Lady Bird retired to the room next door by herself. She telephoned Cecille Harrison, a college roommate who lived in San Antonio, and asked if she could drive downtown and be the maid of honor at her wedding.

"I'm getting married at 8:00 P.M.," Lady Bird told her friend, in a voice that Cecille later described as suppressed excitement. "Will you come stand up with me?"

Cecille, a thin, airy blond, was thrilled by the idea of a spur-of-the-moment wedding. It sounded like an adventure to her. She grabbed a black satin cocktail dress from the back of her closet, and hurried down to the hotel, where she found her friend seated by a window gazing down at the San Antonio River. Cecille had always thought of Lady Bird as self-contained, someone who kept her own private counsel, but never more than at that moment.

As Cecille recalled, Lady Bird seemed serene and absolutely sure of what she was about to do, yet she was not giddy or excited, as one would expect a bride to be. Rather, an air of poignancy surrounded Lady Bird like gauze. In fact, she was terrified.

"If you give me a quarter," the bride-to-be told her friend, "I'll jump out of this window."

Lady Bird had good reason to be scared. She was being given what the whole world would one day recognize as the "Johnson treatment." From the moment he met Lady Bird, Lyndon Johnson had carried on a relentless campaign to get her to marry him on his terms and his timetable. Take me or leave me, he told her. As a bachelor who was about to run for a seat in the U.S. Congress, Johnson needed a wife and he recognized that Lady Bird—shy, intelligent, and rich—was a good choice. Their courtship and marriage established the dominant pattern of their relationship. No matter what happened, the focus was always on him.

However, the directness of Lady Bird's gaze out the hotel window and her confession of fear to her college roommate indicated that the twenty-one-year-old woman understood the exact nature of the bargain she was making. Many years later, others would speculate that Lyndon had married Lady Bird for her father's money, and that the moment the wedding was over, she became his full-time servant.

While it's true Lady Bird adapted her life to his—filling his ink pens and his lighter, laying out his clothes, suffering his wrath, and ignoring his indiscretions—it's also true that she never considered herself a servant, or a victim, not then and not later in her life.

In fact, she viewed herself in the opposite way: as a woman strong enough to control and contain an ego as colossal as Lyndon Johnson's. On the eve of her eighty-second birthday, she sat on her porch in Austin, Texas, and said, "Ours was a compelling love. Lyndon bullied me, coaxed me, at times even ridiculed me, but he made me more than I would have been. I offered him some peace and quiet, maybe a little judgment."

In love and life, Lady Bird Taylor Johnson has always been a realist: she understood early that she brought to her marriage what Johnson most needed and was unable to give—loyalty. Simultaneously, she also understood what he offered her: freedom, a way out of the lonely, isolated world of her childhood. "We were a good match," she said. "I guess you could sum it up by saying we were better together than apart."

The land that formed Lady Bird is dark, wooded, secretive—hermetically sealed from the outside world by tall stands of trees that form a barrier to intruders. The people of deep East Texas have always mistrusted outsiders, while to the west, Texans like Johnson thrive on the raw energy of newcomers. The Johnson home in the Texas Hill Country is open, a gentle progression of hills and draws set against the long, flat line of the horizon.

By contrast, the view from Lady Bird's upstairs bedroom at the Brick House was completely blocked by trees. The feeling in that high-ceilinged, drafty room is of living in quarantine. As a girl, Lady Bird grew up behind a wall of hedges, swamps, and virgin forests. From her bedroom window, the horizon was invisible and the light was refracted. The light on the land shines down in thin, timorous streams, fighting its way to the ground through layers of trees.

Temperamentally, Lady Bird is like her favorite tree, the mesquite, which grows in the Hill Country, not East Texas. She is strong, resilient, immovable, capable of extracting all that she needs from the harshest of environments—water, air, sun, and light—in order to survive.

Her wedding day was chaotic and hurried, but nothing she saw from her window at the Plaza Hotel made her flinch. Unrest and chaos were not new to Lady Bird. She had known them all her life. For Southern women born in the early 1900s, a fundamental fact about life was that it was not rational. Southern women carried within them the history of defeat, the scars of slavery, and the imperceptible cycles of nature. There were two common ways for Southern women to deal with the inherent irrationality of their lives: one was to escape into the realm of dreams, maybe even madness, as did Lady Bird's mother and some of her other relatives. The other was to do what Lady Bird has done: accept things as they are, bury your grief in the ground, and concentrate on what has to be done next, on behalf of the survivors.

Like all Southern women, Lady Bird must be understood in relation to the bonds of her kin and her place. What she suffered in private as the wife of Lyndon Johnson—his violent mood swings and his endless betrayals—she suffered not because it was reasonable but because she loved him and believed that she could care for him and control whatever chaos he created.

If Franklin Roosevelt was Johnson's role model, Eleanor was Lady Bird's. Like Lady Bird, Eleanor was also a motherless child. Lady Bird lost her mother when she was five years and nine months old, and Eleanor's mother died when she was eight.

There were also similarities between the two women's marriages. Both of their husbands were unfaithful, and both women endured the betrayal by looking the other way and becoming involved in inspirational projects that had the effect of lifting them out of the depths of their own private misery. When news of FDR's affair with Lucy Mercer was first published, Lady Bird downplayed its importance by telling Nancy Dickerson, then a correspondent for NBC, that FDR's affair was like "a fly on the wedding cake." She dismissed Johnson's affairs in a like-minded way.

Historically, Lady Bird has benefited from comparisons to Lyndon. He was considered ham-fisted, gruff, and amazingly awkward for a man reputed to be so persuasive, while she is regarded as calm, gracious, understated, firmly rooted in nature. He gave us Vietnam, riots in the streets over civil rights, and the war on poverty. She championed an unlikely cause—wildflowers—that helped give birth to the American environmental movement.

But Lady Bird herself has always insisted that she and her late husband's fortunes—like their initials—be exactly the same. Her willingness to bear anything on behalf of her husband and her husband's memory has given her mythic importance in American life. Even now, friends and family members talk about the way he treated her with embarrassment. "Everyone felt sorry for her," said Virginia Durr, the liberal Alabamian who was the sister-in-law of Supreme Court Justice Hugo Black. "He yelled at her. He ordered her around. He left her alone at the most important times of her life, and made no secret of his affairs. Still, she stayed loyal." Even former Texas governor John Connally, one of Johnson's oldest friends, wrote before he died of LBJ's affair with Alice Glass, the mistress and later wife of one of Johnson's biggest supporters. Of Lady Bird's reaction, Connally wrote, "She handled the affair, I suppose, as well as such things can be handled: by behaving as if there were nothing to handle."

Lady Bird has always refused to play the role of the wronged wife. "I am not a saint," sighed Lady Bird during an interview, implying that she bears some responsibility for the problems in her marriage. "All I can say is I had a great love affair. No matter what, I knew he loved me best."

Behind the myth was the marriage, and, as Lady Bird implied, it was a complicated relationship. She knew about his affairs, but kept her stoic silence. The mystery is, Why, having made her bed, did she never publicly complain about it? LBJ's friends explain that Lady Bird understood Johnson's limitations as well as his greatness, and accepted him as he was. She would not do his enemies the favor of sharing her pain in public.

Theirs was a marriage of opposites. Lyndon Johnson was the embodiment of her own denied ambition. Over the years, it became clear that she could be as ruthless and savvy in business, love, and politics as he could be. What seemed like countless efforts to please him also had the effect of exerting her own control. Laying out his clothes for a trip, for instance, was her way of knowing about and subtly influencing his schedule. In the end, her bargain, difficult as it may have been at times, paid off. Lady Bird wound up with it all—their family, their vast fortune, even the admiration that the public has denied her husband.

Johnson, on the other hand, saw in Lady Bird the answer to his own inconsolable need for comfort, and for unconditional love. She was the repository of his emotion and ideals. This is how Doris Kearns Goodwin put it in *Lyndon Johnson and the American Dream*: "Amid the most complicated intrigues and struggles of her husband's career she remained outwardly composed and reasonable. If his incessant demands and orders . . . or his occasional abuse in front of company became too much to bear, she possessed, or soon developed, a strange ability to take psychic leave. . . . 'Bird,' Johnson would call out at such moments, 'are you with me?' And straight off, her accustomed alertness and competence reappeared."

What Lady Bird offered then was balance. Her ability to take momentary leave from her husband and then return, no matter how great his abuse, gave him the inner strength to continue his drive for power, a drive he made for both of them. She was as fascinated by power as he was, and she had the added advantage of being utterly self-reliant. "Are you with me?" he asked, over and over in many forms and many places. Her reply was always and obsessively the same: "Yes."

On the day their life together began—their wedding day—Lady Bird was an orphan bride. There was no relative to see her to the altar. In fact, not a single member of her family or any of her friends, except Cecille, even knew that she was about to be married.

After the ceremony, she telephoned one friend and told her, "Lyndon and I committed matrimony last night," as if, the friend later recalled, "it was a little bit of a crime." No invitations were sent. There were no flowers on the altar, no music at the ceremony.

She didn't even have time to buy a traditional white wedding gown. The dress she wore was a lavender silk sheath that had appliquéd flowers on each shoulder. She had purchased it a few weeks earlier in a dress shop in Shreveport because it was frillier than most of her other clothes. Johnson had already lectured her on the need to choose more flattering dresses. He wanted to see her in lace and bows. Her silk wedding dress, slinky to the touch, was an early effort to accommodate him.

A few minutes before she left the hotel to drive over to the church, Lyndon turned to Dan Quill and asked him, "Did you get the ring?" Quill was speechless. Lady Bird and Lyndon had driven past jewelry stores all day long. Quill assumed Johnson would have at least thought to buy his wife a wedding ring. But already Johnson was not paying attention.

"Go get a ring," Johnson ordered Quill, who grabbed his hat, ran out the door, and walked across the street to a Sears, Roebuck store. Since he didn't know Lady Bird's size, he bought a dozen rings and placed them on a wooden stick and took them over to the hotel. One by one, Lady Bird tried them all on, until she found one that fit. Quill returned to Sears, Roebuck and paid $2.50 for the ring, returning the rest. "The dime-store ring answered the purpose," Quill later said. "I don't think Lady Bird or Lyndon were much concerned about the quality."

Still, no one asked Lady Bird what kind of wedding ring she wanted, not Johnson, not Quill, not even Lady Bird herself. Her feelings about an article of jewelry that she would wear for the rest of her life went unnoticed.

The ceremony itself was decorous and brief. There were only twelve people present, and it took fifteen minutes from start to finish. When the vows had been said, Lyndon led Lady Bird to one side of the church for a private embrace. At the altar, Reverend McKinstry shook his head and told the members of the wedding party, "I doubt this marriage will ever last."

What McKinstry and Johnson did not know is that Lady Bird had read the wedding vows before she took them. She had not only read them, but had also committed them to memory and had made up her mind to do whatever was necessary to make this marriage work.

"Have you read the vows?" she asked Lyndon before they were married. "Yes," he told her, somewhat sheepishly. "Well, I have, too, and I want to make sure you understand what's in them," she told him.

Over the years, the way Lady Bird would sustain herself in the hard periods of her marriage was to perform a solitary, private ritual. When she was alone, at night or in the early morning, she would take out her Episcopal prayer book, read the vows, and recommit herself to love Johnson, to honor him, to keep him, in sickness and in health, forsaking all others, keeping only unto him. She trained herself not to think about or notice whether he was honoring his vows.

After the wedding, Lyndon, Lady Bird, and their friends had dinner at the roof garden of the Plaza St. Anthony Hotel. Before dinner was served, Henry Hirshberg, one of the guests, sent his brother-in-law to his house with the keys to a special wine locker that contained five bottles of sparkling Burgundy. As the members of the wedding party sipped the wine, Hirshberg, a stranger to Lady Bird, toasted the bride, who settled herself in a chair and listened to the music of a small combo and enjoyed the view of San Antonio's skyline.

It was a cool, clear night, and Cecille later remembered that Lady Bird and Lyndon started dancing the two-step and continued long past midnight. Everyone agreed they made a nice-looking pair. At six feet, three inches tall, Johnson towered over Lady Bird, whose head fit right into the crook of Lyndon's shoulder. She drew close to him on the dance floor as if she were nesting in his body.

However, as she moved across the roof of the Plaza St. Anthony Hotel in her lavender sheath, Lady Bird had no way of knowing that the nest she had just made was very much like the one she had fled. Although she did not realize it, there was a reason why she felt so instantly comfortable with Lyndon Johnson. He was a larger, more ambitious, more extreme version of her father, Boss Taylor.

CHAPTER TWO

Gone to Texas

The seventeen-room Southern mansion where Claudia Alta Taylor was born on December 22, 1912, is a house of spirits. The two-story antebellum house, with a pair of thirty-foot-high white columns on the front porch, sits on an isolated rise in East Texas, facing a narrow road that winds through a double wall of trees toward the border of Louisiana, fifteen miles to the east.

Only a mile down the road lies the small community of Karnack, a town of fewer than four hundred people. C. C. Baker, a postmaster who made an error in spelling, had grandly named it at the turn of the century for the temples in Egypt—"Karnak." As former Texas governor John Connally once said of Lady Bird's birthplace, "You could pass through Karnack and not be at all reminded of Karnak on the Nile." Baker had calculated that the tiny town was the same distance from Port Caddo, the port of entry for the Republic of Texas, that ancient Karnack was from the Thebes.

It was here, however, that Lady Bird's father, Thomas Jefferson Taylor, Jr., a six-foot-two, heavy-framed man, came to Texas in 1899 with her mother, Minnie. Taylor, like thousands of other poor Southerners, fled his native Alabama and its soil, depleted by cotton growing, in search of the inexpensive, plentiful land on the frontiers of East Texas.

The land and culture the pair found in Texas was remarkably similar to those of their native Alabama. Like Alabama, the land around Karnack is heavily timbered with pines and surrounded by swamps. Taylor opened a general store in Karnack in 1899, bearing a sign that spelled out his enormous ambition: "T. J. Taylor—Dealer in Everything."

By the time Lady Bird was born thirteen years later, Taylor had lived up to the grandiosity of his own expectations and become rich. A tireless, domineering man who woke up every morning at 4:00 A.M. to get to work, Taylor presided over a fifteen-thousand-acre cotton empire, two general stores—the one in Karnack and another one down the road in Leigh—two cotton gins, and a fishing business on nearby Caddo Lake. He loved the feel of money and habitually rolled dollar bills through his fingers while grinning and humming softly and ominously, "Mmmmm, boy!"

"My father was a very strong character, to put it mildly," recalled Lady Bird. "He lived by his own rules. It was a whole feudal way of life, really." The Negroes of the county, who comprised more than 50 percent of the population and toiled long hours in servitude, called him "Mister Boss."

They worked his land, raised his cotton, charged groceries and clothing at his store for twice the prices asked of larger stores in nearby Marshall, and borrowed money from him to buy cars or pay medical bills. "I worked for him sunup to sunset for 50 cents a day," said Dorsey Jones, one of the oldest living Black people in Harrison County. "Everyone in Karnack—white and Black—depended on him for everything we had."

Whites in the area acknowledged his authority by calling him "Cap'n." "He was the law around here," recalled Diane Taylor, a neighbor. "As a child growing up, I was taught there were three things you never questioned—God, country, and Mister Cap'n."

As a young girl growing up in the ten-room house, Lady Bird always felt uneasy because the Brick House was rumored to be haunted. The Black servants who raised Lady Bird told her that she was never to go into the rear bedroom on the second floor, the one just down the hall from her own cheerful, high-ceilinged room where she slept in a large, four-poster bed, listening to the sound of crepe myrtle branches scratching across her windows.

That other bedroom was known as "Miss Eunice's room," for it was said that a "girl ghost," the spirit of a nineteen-year-old girl named Eunice Andrews, lived there. Eunice Andrews was the daughter of Confederate colonel Milt Andrews, the original owner of the Brick House, who supervised eighty slaves in the construction of the house built out of red bricks that were fired in a large kiln on site.

The remains of the slaves' kiln still exist. As a child, Lady Bird played hide-and-seek among the broken pieces of clay. The kiln was part of her familiar world, as much as the six hundred acres of pasture that immediately surrounded the house and the giant, sixteen-pane encased windows that ran from floor to ceiling. In order to be opened or closed, the windows were raised and lowered by pulleys, which made a shrill, screeching noise. The squeaking of the windows and the whining of the wind contributed to Lady Bird's childhood fears, as did the repeated telling of the story of Miss Eunice's death.

Sometime after the start of the Civil War in 1861, Miss Eunice was supposedly seated alone in a rocking chair near the fireplace in her bedroom when a thunderstorm blew through the forest of pine, oaks, and cypress trees. A bolt of lightning hit the chimney, raced down the fireplace, and struck Miss Eunice, who fell forward to a fiery death. Periodically a servant in the house or one of Lady Bird's relatives from Alabama would see her ghost and describe their visions to Lady Bird, who listened with her large brown eyes rounded in terror. According to the descriptions, when Miss Eunice showed up in two-dimensional form, she did not look decayed or gray at all, but was said to be an ethereal, light-filled being, a slightly built girl dressed in a white dress with long sleeves. Miss Eunice's most distinguishing feature was her freakish blond hair that stood up from her head, glinted and charged by lightning.

Lady Bird never saw the girl ghost herself, but she believed that others did. The fear still had her in its grip, even in old age. "I felt quite likely that ghosts did exist and I was scared," she later recalled, with a physical shudder. "I would not even now, at this age, feel comfortable being alone in that house by myself."

These were the stories Lady Bird grew up with: of burning women and the lost Civil War. Like all of us, Lady Bird was a child of her heritage. She comes from a long line of female martyrs and male tyrants. The women in her family all learned to suffer well and in silence, while the men fought against poverty and pursued power.

Like many old Southern families, Lady Bird's has concurrent strains of triumph and tragedy. Great fortunes were built, but in their shadow many have battled depression and suicide. Her father's half-brother, Leo Howard, committed suicide, and his namesake son also killed himself. Her maternal grandmother as well as her mother, Minnie, and her aunt Effie all suffered from what was then called "melancholy." She had two sisters-in-law who were diagnosed with mental illness. As recently as 1995, one of her grandnieces committed suicide at thirty-nine years of age after a long battle with depression. The woman's mother, Diana MacArthur, Lady Bird's niece, acknowledged her own problems with depression. "It's like the family curse," acknowledged Mrs. MacArthur. "It goes from generation to generation."

The remnants of the world her ancestors built are still in place in Autauga County, Alabama, which even today is no more than a collection of small towns strung together on Alabama's Highway 14. There are no big cities in the county. The closest—Selma and Montgomery—are located thirty miles away in separate counties. A car trip to either city is considered a full day's journey. The land and local people have won, over time, what they lost in the Civil War: a chance to be left alone.

From this land Lady Bird has derived a chief feature of her personality—her remoteness. J. B. West, former chief usher at the White House, has said that when President Johnson would lose his temper, Lady Bird would never respond in anger. Instead, when faced with criticism or unpleasantness, she would simply slip into a trance and "tune it all out."

Her ability to bury anger beneath a calm, cool veneer is part of her heritage as a Southern woman. From her mother and grandmothers, Lady Bird learned that wars come and go, as do husbands and children. In the end, the only true consolation is the retreat that nature and the imagination can sometimes provide.

It is no accident that her favorite writer is Mississippi's famous son, William Faulkner, because Faulkner describes a South saddled with its history, where people struggle to exist between the extremes of hospitality and cruelty, wealth and poverty, education and ignorance—a crucible Lady Bird understands. "He describes a South I'm somewhat acquainted with," Lady Bird has said. "It has a dark side. It's shadowy but yet it speaks to a world I know."

She knew it because her parents, who were born and raised in the red-clay hills of Alabama in Autauga County, came from opposite ends of the South's extremes. They grew up on farms physically separated by bayous and gullies and also segregated by fundamental differences in class. Her mother was part of the gentry, while her father was extremely poor. "My parents came from different worlds," she acknowledged. "It made for a stressful situation."

Lady Bird's mother, Minnie Lee Pattillo, was descended from George Pattillo, who came to America from Dundee, Scotland, in 1740. The Pattillos were all farmers, merchants, and ministers. One of them, Henry Pattillo, a Presbyterian minister, published the first textbook in the state of North Carolina in 1787. He described the book, which was circulated throughout the South, as a "geographical catechism" to assist travelers who had no maps. In the book, Pattillo gives a physical description of the land, noting major rivers and passable streams, as well as providing excerpts from his sermons collected throughout his thirty years in the pulpit.

In one passage, he warns women that the world is a place of pain and misery and that they can never be happy outside of God. "How often is the preacher's heart grieved when his eye informs him that the irreligious of your sex is the most careless and giddy part of his audience," wrote Pattillo.

In another passage, he offers what he calls a "Negro's catechism," a litany of questions and answers later used by whites as a method for controlling the behavior of their slaves. The prayers of the litany were intended to be spoken with "slow solemnity," according to the preface written by Pattillo.

The minister would face the Black members of the congregation and ask, "When Negroes become religious, how must they behave to their masters?" To which the Negro was supposed to respond: "The scriptures in many places command them to be honest, diligent, and faithful in all things and not to give saucy answers, and even when they were whipt for doing well to take it patiently and look to God for their reward."

Women and Blacks, according to Pattillo, were supposed to be diligent, faithful, not giddy or given to emotion, and to await their reward in heaven. Their goal was distant and invisible, literally in another world. An independent life could only be achieved through exile or death. They carried the burden of what Mrs. Johnson referred to as the South's shadowy side.

In Pattillo's sermons, the husband was described in the traditional language of the Bible as the "head of the household," from whom all domestic power flowed. This doctrine was a literal interpretation of a passage of scripture in Ephesians 5, which warns that women should submit to their husband's authority, no matter what. Men had a biblical imperative to rule. In the cultural hierarchy of power, authority flowed downward from God to husbands, then to wives and children, and finally to slaves. It was a culture that forced the union of opposites: powerful men required sacrificial wives, masters required slaves, and the absolutism of Pattillo's religion required not only faith but fear.

When Lady Bird described her parents' marriage as "stressful," she acknowledged the strain of such a union, the same one that defined the marriage of her maternal grandparents, as well as her parents, a pattern of domination and submission that she inherited from her deep Southern roots and played out in her own marriage on a world stage.

By the time Lady Bird's mother was born in 1874, her father, Luther, had become the wealthiest member of Autauga County's planter class. From the Pattillos, Lady Bird inherited her love of nature and books, as well as her tendency toward introspection. When she was only six years old, Lady Bird went to Alabama to visit one of her aunts, who was struck by how solitary she seemed. "She was a quiet little thing," recalled Ellen Taylor, the wife of her father's brother. "When we went to the farm, she sat on the back seat of the car with her skirts spread primly on the seat, read a book, and nibbled on dried fruit."

This was unusual behavior for her father's people, who were uneducated. Lady Bird did not know her father could read until she was a teenager. The Taylors were poor tenant farmers who eked out a living near the banks of Mulberry Creek. Meals consisted largely of what they could fish out of the creek or hunt in the woods.

Physically, Lady Bird favors her father's side of the family. She has their black hair, their brown eyes, the trademark Taylor hook nose, and their terror of scarcity. All her life Lady Bird has pinched pennies. Her father's fear of poverty is part of her psychic makeup. Even as First Lady, she often shopped at December sales to fill out her wardrobe.

Yet she has never lacked for money. The origin of her wealth can be traced to Luther Pattillo, her mother's father, the first of the big men in Lady Bird's life. At six feet, three inches tall and over two hundred pounds, Pattillo grew up in Alabama, one of seven sons of a yeoman farmer.

In 1861, when Alabama became the third state in the South after Mississippi and Florida to secede from the Union, Luther Pattillo, whose nickname was Luke, joined a group of ninety Autauga County men and quickly went to war. He fought four years, a period of time in which nearly one third of the South's soldiers were killed and another third were wounded in battle. Pattillo fought at the battle of Shiloh, where he saw most of his company killed. Afterward, he joined another Alabama regiment and finally arrived home in Autauga County in 1865, a defeated and penniless Confederate officer.

According to James Cato Pattillo, his nephew, the only thing Luke owned at the end of the war was the horse that carried him home. He used it to farm part of his brother's land, but after working a few days, he hired other men to do his plowing for between 35 and 55 cents a day, and then went into business for himself as a peddler. First he gathered, split, and sold kindling wood, carrying it by horse and wagon to Montgomery to sell. Demand for commercial goods was high in the city, which was rebuilding from the war. Next he invested in wool, hides, and other necessities to sell in Montgomery.

In time, he accumulated enough money to open a two-story general merchandise store in Billingsley, where he and his brothers lived. There were few banks or lending institutions left after the Civil War, so Pattillo stepped forward to gain financial advantage in the small town. "My grandfather used to do something that is so obvious," Lady Bird said. "He would just go down to the courthouse whenever there was a sale of land on which people had not paid taxes. And he just bought anything that was for sale for a pittance, like a dollar an acre." Within a few years after the war was over, he had bought more than 8,000 acres in Autauga and Chilton counties, 3,800 of which Lady Bird inherited in 1947.

Once Pattillo owned the land, he then advanced the former owners, who were now his tenants, everything they needed to farm—the land itself, seed, equipment, fertilizer, shotgun shells, groceries, and dry goods. After the crops had been harvested in the fall, the tenants turned over their crops, primarily cotton, to Pattillo, who would subtract what they owed him and return what was due them, if anything. Often their debt was carried over from year to year.

Luke Pattillo had a reputation for being both mean and shrewd. As an old man, Pattillo told his nephew James about meeting a Black man who did not recognize him by sight. "Do you know who I am?" Pattillo asked the man, who replied that he did not. "Well," asked Pattillo, "who's the meanest man in Autauga and Chilton counties?"

The Black man did not hesitate. "That's Mr. Pattillo," he said.

From the perspective of the local Blacks and the tenant farmers, Pattillo was an extortionist, a boss, a master. He profited by keeping other people in debt.

One day a Black man who had a headache came into Pattillo's store and wanted to purchase medicine. Pattillo told him he could not sell him anything else because his account was past due. The man said he didn't have any money, and rubbed his head in pain. "Here, I'll give you a pill," Pattillo told the man, as he took a single pill from a large bottle on the counter. "That'll be a nickel."

Later that night Pattillo and a clerk who worked for him were asleep in the room above the store. Pattillo woke up with a start and shook the clerk awake. "Did you ever charge that pill to that nigger?" demanded Pattillo. "No," replied the sleepy clerk. "I haven't yet, but I will." Pattillo ordered him to do it first thing in the morning. It wasn't the nickel that was important to Pattillo, but advancing debt, however small, on the books. His rule of economics was simple: great fortunes are built from small debts. It was a rule passed through the family, and one that Lady Bird took to heart.

He did not marry until after the Civil War. When he did, he wed a widow, Sarah Jane Myrick Lewis, who had two small daughters from her previous marriage to a man who died in the Civil War. After her marriage to Pattillo, Sarah had four additional children. Claud, the eldest, was born in 1872. Lady Bird's mother, Minnie, was born two years later, followed by her spinster aunt Effie, born in 1879, and Harry, who came along in 1882.

The marriage was burdened, however, by Sarah's grief over her first husband's death and the long hours Luke put in at the store. Luke's lack of affection for his stepchildren also created conflict in the marriage. When Luke died in 1913, he left one of his stepdaughters $500 and the other $1,000, while each of his other four children or their heirs received large, equal shares of his vast estate.

Sarah, hardened by years of anger and grief, had died a year earlier and so there was no one to advocate for the stepdaughters' finances. One of Lady Bird's cousins said her most vivid memory of her grandmother was that of Sarah in the last years of her life seated on the back porch of the family home in Billingsley. Rocking in her chair, Sarah would gaze bitterly at the cemetery below, hum hymns softly to herself, and talk about how much she longed for the day when she could take her place there among the graves. At the end of her life, death was her only imaginable reward.

The conflict between Sarah and Luke Pattillo left its mark on each of the children. Of the four they shared, Harry, the youngest, was the only one to marry successfully. He married a woman from Montgomery named Belle, moved there, and prospered in the grocery business. Effie, who studied piano at the Juilliard School in New York, had the first of a series of nervous breakdowns in 1912. She never married. Claud, the oldest, and for whom Lady Bird was named, was once engaged but was left at the altar, and remained a bachelor. Apparently his unrequited love was never discussed by his family. It is from the Pattillos that Lady Bird learned to guard her emotions, to hide them behind a veil of stoicism and the righteousness of work. "Uncle Claud took care of his emotions by himself," said Lucille Pattillo Thomas, one of his nieces who still lives in Selma. "I guess it broke his heart, but such things were never talked about out loud in the family. If it was bad, we just didn't talk about it."

Claud owned the family store in Milton, which was located about a mile from where T. J. Taylor, Jr., was born on August 29, 1874, the fifth child of Emma Louisa and Thomas Jefferson Taylor. T.J. never knew his father, who died one month before his last child was born. Shortly thereafter, his mother remarried Reuben J. Bishop and had eight more children. They settled on the banks of a creek on a small piece of farmland that was owned by Claud Pattillo and there they lived the hard life of tenant farmers.

One Friday in February 1885, when T.J. was only eleven years old, his older brother Preston, then twelve, came in from hunting, went into the dining room, and shot himself in the face while cleaning his gun. T.J. was in the front yard. When he heard the shot, he followed his mother into the room where his brother lay dying. What he saw, as reported a few days later in the local newspaper, the *Prattville Progress*, was so imprinted in his mind that it haunted him the rest of his life. As a grown man, T.J. had a phobia about guns. He sold them in his stores in Karnack, but did not own one himself and did not like for others to bring them into the Brick House. "The gun discharged its contents of powder directly into his face, blowing off the fleshy part of his nose, together with his entire upper lip," reported the newspaper. T.J.'s mother rushed to her son's side and frantically "reached forth her hand to assist her struggling but speechless son," but could do nothing except turn him on his side and watch him die.

After the accident, T.J. and his two remaining brothers, William Thomas Taylor and Walter Bates Taylor, vowed to make a new life for themselves—far away from Alabama. They did not get along with their stepfather and wanted to escape his farm and hard way of life. T.J. told Lady Bird and other relatives that Bishop worked him and his brothers like field hands. He saw his future in grander terms.

It's easy to see why Taylor was attracted to Minnie Pattillo. She and her family represented everything he wanted—cash, power, a place of respect within the community. As an old man, he told one of his grand-daughters, Susan Taylor, about the first moment he saw Minnie. "He told me that one day he was plowing his grandfather's field. He remembered that he was barefoot because he could feel the dirt between his toes," she recalled. "When he looked up, he saw my grandmother Minnie riding a horse. He watched her jump a fence and decided right then to get to know her."

Taylor had never seen a woman like Minnie, a woman who was not working the fields or behind a stove, but strong, powerful, and privileged, sailing through the air astride a horse. Not long after, he saw her again riding her horse, Nell, and watched as she was thrown to the ground. It was Taylor's big chance, and he seized it. Minnie's leg was hurt, so Taylor bandaged it and took her home to her father's house. After that, Minnie and T.J. began meeting in secret.

Often they met behind Claud's store in nearby Milton. As Claud worked at the counter, Minnie sat outside beneath a tree and read books, including the poetry of Robert and Elizabeth Browning.

Poetry fired her imagination for romance. By the time she met Taylor, she was twenty-five years old and must have wondered if she would ever know the kind of all-consuming love described in the Brownings' poetry. She had an unfortunate combination of characteristics for a Southern woman in the 1880s. She was smart, well read, and rich, but not beautiful. In the South, beauty was the only true coin of the realm, and a lack of it translated into a kind of poverty that became its own exile.

The word that people commonly used to describe Minnie was "handsome," which has a masculine implication, probably due to her interest in books. She was about five feet, five inches tall and stout, with thin, blond and reddish brown hair that she wore parted on the side. Her face is remembered by relatives as angular, with faintly drawn eyebrows set over a wide forehead, green eyes, and a thin, worried mouth. She was so self-conscious about her looks that she never allowed anyone to take her photograph. Lady Bird has no memory of her mother's face.

"Miss Minnie was a big woman," said Dorsey Jones. All of the Pattillo women have a weakness for sweets, including Lady Bird, who has watched her weight her whole life, often on Johnson's orders. During private dinners she often has complained to family members over dessert, "Oh please! Don't give me another piece of pie no matter how much I beg!"

Intellectually, however, Minnie Pattillo could hold her own. On Sundays after lunch, the Pattillos gathered on Luke's front porch to talk about politics, business, or news from Chicago or New York. During these family discussions, Minnie compared the ups and downs of the commodities market with her brother Claud, and in the next instant swapped opera news with her sister, Effie. She did not keep silent. "Unlike Effie or her mother, Aunt Minnie said what was on her mind—she had a lot of spirit," said Nettie Pattillo Woodyard, her niece who still lives in Autaugaville.

That feisty spirit led her to T. J. Taylor, who at twenty-five was a tall, black-headed, and strong man with large dark eyes and the kind of silent, brooding style that could communicate a lot with a tuck of the lip or a nod of the head. He was a rebel—a fact that Minnie's father disliked but made him more attractive to Minnie. Pattillo's rejection exacerbated Taylor's insecurities and made him angry. Years later, Taylor told Susan, his granddaughter, that in the summer of 1899 Pattillo called him "white trash" and forbade him from seeing Minnie.

Naturally, the two young people ignored his demand. When Taylor asked Pattillo for permission to marry Minnie, Luke laughed in his face and told him he wasn't good enough for her. "You'll see," Taylor told the old man. "I'm going to make a lot of money and I'll be back. And when I come, you'll beg me to marry your daughter."

At the end of that summer, T.J. abruptly left Alabama for Texas. Through the years, his reasons for leaving were shrouded in a mystery of his own making. The only official story he ever gave was apocryphal. In 1951, he told a reporter for the *Marshall News*, his hometown newspaper, that when he was still living in Alabama he saw a man drive by his house in a wagon. He started following the wagon on foot because he wanted to see if the larger back wheels would ever catch up with the front wheels. They didn't. By then, he'd walked so far he was afraid to return home.

There was another, less flattering explanation for his leaving that circulated within the family, a common reason why many others posted signs on their doors in the late 1800s that said "GTT" (Gone to Texas) and struck out for a new life on the frontier. Three family sources say they had always heard that Taylor was fleeing a crime. In the summer of 1899, a train was robbed on the Southern line near Burnsville, one of the tiny communities in Autauga County. T.J. and his brother Walter were said to have been suspects in the train robbery. They left Alabama shortly afterward and came to Texas. Neither was ever charged with the crime, but the shadow of scandal stayed with T.J.

Taylor's stepfather had begged him to stay and help him farm his land with a mule. "Give me another year," Bishop pleaded. "The crops look good this year." But Taylor had made up his mind to leave. Nothing could stop him. "If I don't have a sign up on a store in a year in Texas," Taylor told his stepfather, "I'll come back and help you farm."

Privately, however, Taylor had no intention of ever coming back. Upon his arrival in Karnack, he paid $500 for a piece of land at the intersection of two trails, a crossroads well known to hunters in the area. The landscape was fitting because Taylor himself was at a personal crossroads. He lived in a rooming house, paid $5 a week for both room and board, and made plans to open a country store, which he hoped would give him a foothold on the frontier.

Within a matter of weeks, he had his sign up—"Dealer in Everything"—and was making plans to stock his store. His days of tenant farming were at an end.

From Taylor's perspective, Karnack seemed like paradise. The environment was much like his native Alabama. It was on the same parallel of latitude and had the same kind of heavily timbered land, the same rolling hills, and the same rural way of life. Cotton was the cash crop. The best land in Harrison County yielded about one bale per acre, a respectable rate even by Alabama standards.

Geographically, Harrison County was blessed in a way in which Alabama was not. It had a thriving port at the mouth of Caddo Lake and provided a water route, navigable by steamboats, for shipping cotton and other goods, first to Shreveport and then on to New Orleans by way of the Red and Mississippi rivers.

The port was a vital transportation link on the frontier. Life grew up around it. By 1850, the port had made Harrison County the busiest and most populated county in the state. There were a total of 11,822 residents, more than 50 percent of whom were slaves. By comparison, Houston had only 4,668 residents and San Antonio 6,052. Ten years later, on the eve of the Civil War, Harrison had more slaves than any other county in the state. Moreover, they sold for twice what they had the decade before, a fact that local newspapers regarded as proof of the area's productivity and prosperity.

In 1860, Robert W. Lougherty, editor of the *Texas Republican,* told his readers, "The South has never been pecuniary in so prosperous a condition as at the present time. Last Tuesday, a number of Negroes were sold for cash at public auction. One man, a carpenter, brought $2,755, and a boy, 11 years old, was knocked off at $900." Those prices continued until after the war ended. When Taylor arrived in 1899, slavery was gone, but the Old South's way of life continued. Landowners depended on Blacks for agriculture's hard labor.

The talk that first summer in Karnack was familiar to Taylor. Cotton plants bloomed in early June, and though the small farmers were able to clean their fields in a month or less, the picking season of the larger planters began in August and continued for six days a week from sunup to sundown into the late fall. Once picked, the fiber from the cotton had to be separated from the seeds, a process known as ginning, and pressed into bales weighing about five hundred pounds each.

Taylor bought a gin for his store, which meant that the farmers around Karnack no longer had to transport their cotton to Marshall or nearby Jefferson for ginning and baling. He was pleased, and had good reason to be optimistic about Karnack's future. "Real estate is advancing," wrote the Marshall newspaper that summer, "and it is believed Karnack will be a safe place for investment."

In the fall of the year, confident of his financial success, T.J. returned home to Alabama and asked Minnie Lee Pattillo to marry him. She immediately said yes. Her father was outraged, and her sister, Effie, who would soon be left at home alone, took to her bed, sick with grief.

Given the family tensions, Minnie and T.J. decided to marry quickly.

None of her family came to the wedding. Just as her daughter Lady Bird would one day marry alone, Minnie was also an orphan bride. Minnie wasn't even married in a church, but at the home of T.J.'s older brother William.

On December 14, 1900, the *Prattville Progress* carried the official notice of the wedding, carefully noting the distinctions between the two families. "The bride is the daughter of one of Autauga's most esteemed citizens, Mr. Luther Pattillo," wrote the newspaper. "The groom is an old Autauga boy and a young man of great promise."

Two days later, Taylor and his new bride left Alabama for their new home in Karnack. They were united by a common desire to put their past behind them. In effect, they were both on the lam. T.J. was fleeing rumors of scandal, and Minnie was in full flight from her father's unhappy home.

On the journey to Texas, T.J. called her "dearie" and tried to put aside his own fear that Minnie might have trouble adapting to her new environment. She brought with her the things that had nourished her in Alabama—several crates of books. The newlyweds arrived in Karnack near the end of the year, jubilant about having successfully GTT, and joyfully blind to her father's warnings about how ill-suited they were for marriage.

CHAPTER THREE

Motherless Child

While Texas gave Lady Bird's father the second chance he needed, the eighteen years Minnie lived in Karnack were a lonely exile. From the moment they arrived, Taylor focused on his business, while Minnie struggled to get her bearings.

They moved into a simple frame house that was designed around a long L-shaped hall, with the kitchen and dining room on one side and two bedrooms on the other. Taylor built the house directly next to his store, so that he could work round-the-clock.

Minnie was a dreamy, cultured woman in a raw land. The dirt roads around the tiny village of Karnack were crudely constructed and often impassable, but Minnie refused to stay at home. With money from her father, she bought a Hudson Super Six, a heavy, long automobile often used in funerals, and hired a chauffeur named Ransom Horne to drive her around the maze of bayous, forests, and cypress swamps.

In the summer, Ransom raced through the woods in the Hudson. Occasionally he drove the car into a bed of sand and was stopped dead. While Ransom dug the car out of its rut, Minnie sat in the Hudson's jump seat, her face hidden behind large hats, batting flies. In the winter, rain and mud closed the roads and confined Minnie to her home.

Day-to-day life was more isolated and harder than it had been in Alabama. Her first tablecloth in Texas was dingy and made of oilcloth, unlike the hand-pressed linens she used in her mother's house. Her husband offered little companionship. "My father was a very busy man," recalled his younger son, Antonio. "He worked all the time. He had few interests or hobbies outside his business and his little world."

Minnie, on the other hand, had unlimited interest and curiosities, which took her far from Karnack. She was not constrained by the traditional nineteenth-century view of women as primarily domestic creatures. She did not like housework and soon hired maids to do it for her. As often as possible, Minnie traveled to Chicago with her sister, Effie, to attend the opera. When she was home, she read widely, often speaking the words of novels or poetry out loud to herself.

Diana MacArthur, one of Antonio Taylor's two daughters, said her grandmother Minnie avidly collected books. Through the mail, she kept in touch with New York publishers and ordered many first editions, both biographies and novels. She also bought classics, such as Gibbon's *History of the World,* the legends of Greece and Rome, and expensive leather-bound travel books about places such as the lakes of Italy and the silk routes of China, faraway places that fed her imagination.

One of her favorite books was *My Ántonia* by Willa Cather, a novel about a heroic young girl who lived at the turn of the century in Nebraska. Minnie must have identified with Ántonia, because she named her second son for her. Cather's Ántonia is a bohemian spirit who follows a ruthless man, away from her frontier homeland; he later betrays her. At the end of the novel, Ántonia commits suicide. Like Ántonia, Minnie was always looking for some new ideas or piece of knowledge to lift her from the constraints of her time, her place, and the bounds of marriage.

Lady Bird's primary memory of her mother is of her books. "My mother had an enormous supply of books, mostly history and biographies," she said. One that she remembered especially was *The Book of Knowledge,* a collection of spiritual essays. Minnie owned other spiritual books that Lady Bird said "dipped into the occult and beyond the fringe."

In Alabama, the Pattillos were Southern Baptist, but Minnie attended the Methodist church in Karnack, located three quarters of a mile from the Brick House. Yet she doesn't appear to have been comforted or consoled by either her church or her readings on spirituality.

She was a perpetual seeker. Her choice of books reflects her longing to make some kind of connection to a larger world. For instance, one of the people she read was Emanuel Swedenborg, a Swedish scientist and mystic who wrote in the late 1700s about heaven and hell and the presence of other unseen worlds.

There weren't many people in Karnack reading Swedenborg. Minnie's bookish nature, combined with her preoccupation with matters beyond the fringe, had the effect of placing her in a social quarantine. "A lot of people didn't like her because she was aloof and a little strange," recalled Cameron McElroy, one of her neighbors. Her granddaughter Diana MacArthur put it more succinctly: "My grandmother was viewed as eccentric, possibly even mad."

Her appearance also set her apart. "I remember that she wore this large hat with a veil, and her carriage was excellent," said McElroy's wife, Lucille. Minnie wore the veils because she suffered from migraine headaches. Every morning, she tied one scarf tightly around her forehead, then veiled herself with additional scarves to diffuse the light, which she found painful. The Black people in Karnack spoke with fear about "Miss Minnie's skullcaps."

Even now, more than eighty years after her death, they remember her as if she were an apparition, like the daughter of the Confederate colonel who was consumed by fire at the Brick House. "We never saw her face," said Dorsey Jones. "Sometimes she just laid in bed for days in the dark. Miss Minnie didn't want no noise. She didn't want no light either."

Lady Bird's own memories of her mother are equally elusive. She remembers that her mother read to her, primarily Greek and Roman myths, but not much more. "I wish I knew more about her," she said, closing her eyes, as if trying to bring a concrete image to mind.

Lady Bird was five years and nine months old when Minnie died. Her mother's death became the primary lens through which Lady Bird saw the world. It marked the end of her brief childhood. As a child and adolescent, the fact that she was motherless was never forgotten. In fact, her motherless status constituted her initial identity. Friends and relatives pointed to her and said, behind her back, "Poor Lady Bird. She has no mother." Still, her loss was not something discussed out loud—by her or anyone else—but treated as an open secret. Over time, her mother's death became a kind of emotional prison, a life-changing event that she was never allowed to talk about. "No one dared say a word about it—including me," said Lady Bird.

When in a crowd of girls she never knew what to say when they talked about their mothers, so she often kept silent. This silence distanced her from her peers. Her tendency to stay to herself was interpreted by Lady Bird and others as shyness. Her mother's death left a psychic scar. No one—not her father, her relatives, or her friends—empathized with Lady Bird in her time of childhood despair. She was left to cope with that loss alone, a fact that affected her ability to relate to others for the rest of her life. The way she dealt with her loss was to comfort others, primarily her father and later her brothers. The earliest lesson of her life was that she had no one to rely on but herself and that there was power in comforting others.

Later, when she had become the wife of Lyndon Johnson, she drew from this deep internal well of self-reliance to bear any difficulty with a determination that amazed even Johnson. "I was one of five children and I thought my mother was the greatest woman in the world," Johnson said in 1963. "But I think Lady Bird spills out a great deal more of herself."

Although Lady Bird's memories of her mother are hazy, the few visual images she's managed to remember constitute a fragile mother-daughter bond. "My memory of her is being tall and moving around very fast and dressing a lot in white. And yes, there is something on her head," said Lady Bird, as she traced her index finger across her lined forehead.

This uncertainty about what lay behind her mother's veils has been the central mystery lodged at the core of Lady Bird's life. It kept her in a constant state of yearning. "I sometimes try to imagine how my life would have been different if my mother lived, if I would have had a life like other little girls. I think about whether she would have been there when I came home from school or for my graduations or for the birth of my children," said Lady Bird. "I cannot imagine."

Many of the details of her mother's life in Texas had been told to Lady Bird by Dorris Powell, who was twelve years older and whose mother, Mrs. John Odam, was one of Minnie's few friends in Karnack. Mrs. Odam and Dorris lived down the road from the Brick House in Karnack.

According to Dorris, when Minnie first arrived in Karnack in 1900, she was fresh, enthusiastic, and in love with her husband. As a young girl, Mrs. Powell once watched Minnie walk barefoot in the woods to meet T.J. as he came home from the store. "I remember how she looked as she came in because we were concerned that her feet were wet with dew and her skirts were damp and bedraggled," said Dorris, referring to her mother and herself. "But Minnie looked happy and carefree. She had a bunch of wildflowers in her hand."

This vignette about her mother—walking through the woods to meet her husband with wildflowers in her hand—became a defining one for Lady Bird. On her seventieth birthday, when she founded the National Wildflower Research Center on sixty acres in Austin, Lady Bird memorialized the image and supported it with $9.5 million for research about how native plants can thrive in their own habitat. During her remarks, it was clear how completely Lady Bird transferred her need for affection from her own mother to Mother Nature. She talked about the sensory qualities of wildflowers in such an overtly emotional way, that she could have been describing the qualities that children want from their mothers.

"Almost every person, from childhood on, has been touched by the untamed beauty of wildflowers," said Lady Bird. "Buttercup gold under a childish chin, the single drop of exquisite sweetness in the blossom of wild honeysuckle, the love-me, love-me-not philosophy of daisy petals."

Her concern for the environment is part of her emotional inheritance from her mother. After Taylor purchased the Brick House, Minnie built a birdbath in her front yard and fed the birds all year round. Sometime around 1910 she became concerned that the local quail population was being endangered by hunters and sponsored a Save the Quail Society. To protect them, she posted "no hunting" signs on several thousand acres of her husband's property, and only allowed hunters on her land at the end of the season to trim the size of the coveys in order to prevent starvation.

Lady Bird's first connection to political campaigns was also through her mother. Minnie believed that women should have the right to vote. She participated in local elections and followed national politics through newspapers and magazines. One of Minnie's granddaughters, Susan Taylor, of Shreveport, Louisiana, said Lady Bird lived the kind of life Minnie Pattillo Taylor would have loved to live. "My grandmother loved politics and wanted nothing more than for women to be able to vote," said Taylor. "Here Aunt Lady Bird came along and campaigned in every state of the union and wound up living in the White House. She fulfilled my grandmother's wildest dreams."

Lady Bird does not know where her mother got her ideas about voting rights for women and saving quail. "I know she must have been somewhere between greatly respected and being laughed at in the community. But she was Cap'n Taylor's wife and that would keep bounds on any ridicule," she recalled.

Minnie gave birth to her first son, Thomas Taylor, Jr., on October 20, 1901, in the house next to the store. Antonio J. Taylor was born three years later in the same house on August 29, 1904. The pregnancies and births of her children sapped her strength. Antonio's daughter Diana MacArthur said that her father's primary memories of his mother were of a melancholy woman who was ill-suited in every way for the demands of a normal household.

The family never established any sort of routine domestic life, a pattern that Lady Bird in time repeated in her own family. The Taylor family ate few meals together, shared no common hobbies, and rarely even lived under the same roof—like the Johnsons during LBJ's busiest times in politics.

When Antonio was still an infant, Minnie took her two sons and went home to Alabama to live with her parents. "Our mother was in bad health," Antonio explained in his oral history. He indicated that Minnie was also fleeing his father and the problems in the marriage. Of his father, Antonio said: "We were doomed to scatter like frightened quail before the hunter."

The separation lasted several years. Naturally the family wanted to know why Minnie had left Texas. The explanation that she offered to her family was that Taylor had become involved with another woman. "He simply lost all affection for Miss Minnie, and took up with someone else," said Nettie Pattillo Woodyard, one of Lady Bird's Alabama cousins. "Minnie told her family that she had no choice but to come home."

Back in Billingsley, Luke Pattillo now found himself living with two emotionally distraught daughters—Minnie and her unmarried sister, Effie. For help, he turned to Dr. John Kellogg, a physician and health reformer who operated a sanitarium in Battle Creek, Michigan.

The sanitarium, founded in 1866, was a haven for America's upper class, who used it as a combination spa, rehabilitation facility for alcoholism, and a hospital where routine surgeries were performed. Each week one thousand patients checked into the six-story sanitarium. They heard Dr. Kellogg, a short, mustachioed man who dressed theatrically in white suits, lecture on the importance of a strict vegetarian diet comprised mainly of bulky vegetables and grains. He also advocated plenty of exercise, sweat baths, regular enemas, and complete abstinence from alcohol, caffeine, and cola products.

Kellogg's sanitarium, which was advertised in the *Saturday Evening Post* and the leading newspapers of the day, was particularly popular with businessmen, which may have been why it had credibility with Luke Pattillo. Edgar Welch, the grape juice producer, visited twice; a textile manufacturer Joseph Cannon and W. A. Cannon, the treasurer of the United States, each came to the sanitarium twenty-two times. C. W. Barron, the founder of the *Wall Street Journal,* made annual pilgrimages to Battle Creek from New York. Alfred DuPont and John D. Rockefeller were also among Kellogg's famous clients.

Though Luke was the first of the Pattillos to go to Battle Creek, in time all of the family, including Lady Bird and her brother Antonio, became devotees of Dr. Kellogg. In addition to practicing medicine, Kellogg was an inventor. He devised the process of flaking grains, which was later used for manufacturing Cornflakes by the company that bears his name. He also invented other health food products, which he sold through a mail-order business. From Kellogg, the Pattillos ordered granola; Paramels, a mineral oil preparation in the form of chocolate-covered caramels; and L.D. Lax, a derivative of psyllium seed.

Kellogg's remedies had a lasting impact on the family. As an adult living in Santa Fe, New Mexico, Antonio liked to sunbathe and then walk to the top of the mountains and roll in the snow. He believed that this was good for his circulation. On Dr. Kellogg's recommendation, Antonio drank hot water and lemon juice, and in the evening he drank lukewarm water from a pottery jar that he kept by his bed.

One of Lady Bird's early memories is climbing the stairs of her grandfather's store to find her namesake uncle, Claud, eating Paramels in his office above the family store in Billingsley. Whenever anyone in the family had any kind of pain or ailment, the cure of choice was laxatives. The family discussed the movement of their bowels as frequently as they discussed the ups and downs of the stock market.

"It's fair to say that the entire family enjoyed their poor health to the hilt," said Lucille Pattillo Thomas. According to Lucille, Effie's collapses were blamed on her failed career as a pianist, while Minnie's were blamed on her unfortunate decision to marry Taylor and move to Texas.

For escape, the two sisters went to the sanitarium, where they heard Kellogg's lectures on the importance of chewing food slowly and thoroughly, his theory that overeating led to alcoholism, and his repeated, evangelical diatribes against eating meat. During one famous lecture, Kellogg placed a beefsteak under one microscope and a pile of manure under another, and announced with great fanfare that there were more harmful germs in steak than in manure.

Such tactics earned notoriety for Kellogg and his sanitarium, and Lady Bird grew up with stories of his eccentricities. In 1916 alone, a year that both Effie and Minnie visited the sanitarium, Kellogg treated seven thousand patients at a cost of $30 per week. In the morning, all the patients did physical exercises on the veranda overlooking a large lake or in the large indoor gymnasium. Kellogg believed everyone should regularly perform calisthenics, such as jumping jacks, push-ups, and sit-ups, long enough to break a sweat and to feel physically tired.

For the "neurasthenia," or nervous exhaustion, the condition that troubled both Minnie and her sister, Kellogg recommended long, soothing baths with the temperature of the water kept at 92 to 96 degrees. He sometimes wrapped patients in cold wet sheets, which he said calmed the nerves.

While Minnie followed Kellogg's health regimen, T.J. focused on his obsession—to become richer and more powerful than Old Man Pattillo. Looking back on it as an adult, Lady Bird described the relationship between her father and maternal grandfather as follows: "There was sort of an old bull, young bull situation. My father judged himself by my grandfather's standard."

The business Taylor built in Karnack was modeled directly after Pattillo's in Billingsley. In the store, Taylor sold everything the people of Karnack needed—spools of thread, patent medicines, clothes, school supplies, farm tools, food—at higher prices than they could buy the same items in Marshall, the county seat. Unlike other men, Taylor did not hunt or fish. His sole interest in life was making money. Three or four times a day, Taylor would get up from his desk and walk to the front of the store and check the cash register near the door. Then he would stroll the length of the store to collect money from the register near the meat market.

Like Pattillo, Taylor made most of his money advancing land, seed, and equipment to tenant farmers in the spring, and getting back his investment and profit in the early fall after the cotton was ginned and sold. White men viewed him as a generous caretaker. "He took farmhands in when they had no place to stay and loaned them money and gave them a wagon and a pair of mules," recalled Jack Hayner, whose father worked for Taylor. "He took care of everybody around here."

In the woods around Caddo Lake, where the people in Harrison County lived, it was understood that most everyone had two jobs, their day jobs as farmers and their night jobs as moonshiners. Deep in the woods were carefully hidden stills where liquor was illegally distilled. When men who worked for Taylor were arrested, he would bail them out of jail so they could return to their fields.

There was no escape from his power, not even in church. Taylor paid the full salary of the Methodist minister, where he went to church on Sundays, and half the salary of the Baptist minister. One Sunday the Methodist minister made the mistake of asking Taylor to pray aloud in church. From his place in the pew, Taylor shook his head and refused. "I pay," he told the minister quietly in front of the entire congregation. "You pray."

In East Texas in the early 1900s, Blacks were dependent on white men with money. "This is the way it used to be around here," said Dorsey Jones, who lived near the Brick House. "You were nobody in this world without a white man standin' behind you. Boss Taylor was a good stand-behind man." Without money to buy cotton seed or groceries, the only way Black families could survive was to borrow money from Taylor for what they needed, a practice that kept them in debt. As Wyatt Moore, a lawyer from Waco, once said, "Communism ain't nothing new. It's the system of letting bad debt carry good. Old Cap'n Taylor's been doing it since I was a boy." Some families deeded over their land to him as repayment for bad debts.

The records of the Harrison County courthouse contain lawsuits filed by Black families who lost their land to Taylor in just this manner. For instance, one Black man, Nathaniel Haggerty, had a one-hundred-acre farm but gave half of it to Taylor as repayment for his debts. When Haggerty went to Marshall to arrange for a new deed, he told the abstractor who handled the transaction that Taylor was due sixty acres and he was to keep forty. When the abstractor asked why it wasn't a straight fifty-fifty split, Haggerty replied, "You don't understand. When you deal to Boss Taylor, he takes a bit."

The Haggertys were the largest Black family in Harrison County. In 1914, Taylor bought their original family homestead, a five-thousand-acre tract of rich cotton land. Years later several members of the family sued Taylor in an attempt to recover a portion of their land, but they did not prevail. Records on file at the courthouse reveal how Taylor amassed his fortune. In 1918, he had twenty-six tenants working on the one thousand acres of the Haggertys' homestead that was cultivated land. On seven hundred acres, he grew 233 bales of cotton that sold for 30 cents a pound and 3,750 bushels of corn at $2.25 per bushel, which give him $43,387.50 for the sale of cotton and corn alone. He also made money selling leftover cotton seed, as well as from the sale of horses, cattle, and hogs that tenants raised in the pasture. At the time, this tract represented less than one third of Taylor's holdings in the county.

He was rich and wanted everyone to know it. One morning, according to Jack Hayner's memory, Taylor arrived early at the store to find two Black men waiting outside to talk to him about some business. Hayner, who was only a boy at the time, was there. "Old Cap'n dropped 50 cents on the ground," said Hayner. "When one of the men reached down to pick it up, Taylor stopped him." He told the man to leave the money on the ground, and then, according to Hayner, Taylor said, "Nigger, don't you know if my money stays in one place very long, it grows." Taylor had remade himself in the image of Luke Pattillo.

Lady Bird's father was no different from most white men in East Texas. Racism was a way of life, and the Ku Klux Klan was an accepted part of society. Like many others, Taylor joked in the crudest possible ways about Blacks, particularly Black women. Hayner said one morning he had been out hunting with a dog and stopped by the store to see Taylor. The dog sniffed repeatedly in the area of Taylor's groin. When Hayner asked why, Taylor told him, "I've been out with a nigger woman this morning. The dog's got her scent."

Taylor made no secret of the fact that he was a ladies' man. In fact, people, both Black and white, in Karnack gossiped openly that Taylor had at least one son by a Black woman. According to the tale, the son carried the nickname of Sugar because he often came by the store and Taylor gave him free sacks of sugar.

Nonetheless, in 1910, six years after Antonio was born, Minnie and T. J. Taylor reconciled. As a peace offering, he bought her the Brick House, as fine as any in Alabama, and traveled to Billingsley to persuade her to come home. "Perhaps he wanted to anchor her or to give her an interest," Lady Bird explained. "Something to hold on to."

For a while, the family was reunited. Tommy and Tony, who had rarely lived in Texas, started studying at the Fern School, a one-room schoolhouse located about one-half mile from the Brick House. Minnie attempted to adapt to her role as wife and mother. She volunteered for the local Red Cross and entertained more at home.

The Brick House had a large dining room with a stone fireplace at one end. Minnie covered the floor with bearskin rugs. At Christmas, she put up a tree in the dining room and invited all the Blacks who worked for her to a party. They came—with their children—and ate a large turkey dinner, and after dinner rolled up the rugs and danced. Fifty years after the end of the Civil War, social life had not changed at all in East Texas. Minnie's Christmas parties were patterned after the way plantation owners entertained slaves.

Minnie struggled to maintain her strength in Karnack. On the back porch of the Brick House was a well filled with fresh springwater that was always ice-cold. From it Minnie drank the enormous amounts of water that Kellogg suggested for flushing out her system. Kellogg recommended that patients drink forty glasses of water a day. She even convinced her husband to follow one of Kellogg's pieces of advice. Every morning, Taylor went out to the back porch, shed his pajamas, and took a brisk, cold shower from the well, which Kellogg said stimulated circulation. "He would stand there buck naked, and pour cold water over his whole body and then shake like a wet dog," said Jerry Jones, Taylor's nephew by a later marriage.

Despite Kellogg's remedies, however, nothing restored Minnie's health or strength. After she returned to Karnack, she suffered two miscarriages. The closest hospital was in Marshall, and Minnie relied on a local doctor, Philip Baldwin, a tall, slim man who lived in a grove about a mile up the road from the Brick House, for medical care. After one of the miscarriages, Baldwin operated on Minnie on her dining room table.

In March 1912, when Minnie was forty-four years old, she again became pregnant. This time Minnie carried the baby to full term. On the afternoon of December 21, she went into labor. Baldwin was sent for, and he came by horse and carriage to the Brick House. The two boys, Tommy and Tony, were sent to a friend's house to spend the night. Baldwin stayed with Minnie all night. Every fireplace in the Brick House was lit. Early in the morning, in a bedroom upstairs at the Brick House, Minnie gave birth to a little girl. She named her Claudia Alta Taylor after her brother Claud.

Taylor wrote a letter to Effie in Billingsley dated January 8, 1913, telling her that Minnie had given birth to a daughter. The letter was written on his stationery, which describes him as a "dealer in merchandise, shipper of fresh water fish." "We have a little girl, born Sunday morning, 5:32 o'clock, December 22," Taylor wrote. He then wrote "name" and left it blank, but put the birth weight at six and one-half pounds. "She really is very pretty, and Minnie is very proud of her. She had a remarkably easy time. We had, though, the best doctor in Marshall and a trained nurse. The nurse is still with us, though Minnie is up, and I believe and hope that she is going to be better than she ever was."

Lady Bird has always said that she got her nickname at age two from her Black nurse, Alice Tittle, who pronounced her "purty as a lady bird." Tittle lived in the servants' quarters behind the Brick House, along with a rotund cook, Cindy Gibson, and several other Black servants.

However, according to one of Lady Bird's Alabama cousins, it was T. J. Taylor who gave Claudia her nickname, not the child's nurse. When his daughter was born, Taylor repeated the nursery rhyme, "Lady Bird, Lady Bird, fly away home, your house is on fire and your children will burn."

Metaphorically, Taylor's house was on fire. Contrary to the hope Taylor expressed in his letter to Effie, Minnie's health did not become better than it ever was. She didn't feel strong enough to care for three children. Tommy was eleven when Lady Bird was born and Antonio was eight. Shortly thereafter, both boys were sent away to the Raymond Riordan School for Boys, located in the Catskills of New York. Minnie had wanted her sons to be stretched physically and mentally in ways that Karnack could not provide. Minnie also wanted a different kind of life for her daughter. When Lady Bird was still an infant, Minnie wrote for brochures about girls' boarding schools for Lady Bird, including one that Lady Bird later visited as an adult in Washington, D.C. The message that all three children received from their mother was to get an education and to get out of Karnack.

"My mother pinned all her hopes on education," said Lady Bird, who acknowledged that her mother's ambition drove a wedge between her and her husband. "There is no doubt she wanted a bigger life. She did not want to leave Daddy, but she did aspire to a broader field."

The first Christmas of Lady Bird's memory was when she was five years old. Her two best friends at the time were Doodle Bug and Stuff, children of Black servants who worked at the Brick House. When Lady Bird came downstairs on Christmas morning, she saw a white wicker rocking chair with a nice doll seated in it and a teddy bear beside her. Her stocking was full of oranges, walnuts, and firecrackers. She rushed over to see what Santa had left for Doodle Bug and Stuff.

Instead of toys, they got underpants, socks, and other clothing essentials. She asked her mother, "Why did Santa not bring Doodle Bug a doll?" She doesn't remember that her mother gave her a direct answer. It was the first time Lady Bird realized that there was a difference between how Blacks and whites lived in Karnack.

Later she had a harsher lesson. "I remember once when I was a little girl that a group of white men cornered a Black man in the middle of the night and accused him of some crime," said Lady Bird. "The poor man was so terrified that he just took off running. The white men shot him in the back." The incident happened in the woods near Karnack. Lady Bird heard about it the following morning at her father's store. She was a little girl, with an unformed social conscience, but she remembered thinking, "This isn't right. Somebody ought to change this." This incident stayed with her for as long as she lived. In time it became her own private motivation for supporting civil rights.

Despite her ill health, Minnie's interest in politics continued. In the summer of 1918, Minnie loaded her daughter up in the Hudson Super Six and went door to door campaigning against Robert Hope, a candidate for county commissioner, because she questioned the man's patriotism. "She got out and electioneered against him because she thought he was a slacker," said Dorris Powell. "In fact, she called him a slacker. That was a term they used for young men who didn't go into the service when they were qualified." Hope had stayed home from World War I to work on his father's cotton farm. He was a popular candidate, a man that Cap'n Taylor supported, but, in this case at least, Minnie's influence helped determine the outcome. The slacker lost the election.

This act was a defiant effort to assert her independence. She took a stand that was opposite that of her husband and prevailed. It was all the more remarkable given the fact that Minnie was fifty years old and pregnant again. Two months later, in September 1918, she fell down a circular staircase in the living room and was taken to a hospital in Marshall, where on September 14, 1918, she died. The circumstances are mysterious. There is no death certificate on file at the Harrison County courthouse, which would have listed an official cause. Other family members say that Minnie died of complications resulting from a tubal pregnancy, but there is no way to know for sure.

Lady Bird was always told that her mother tripped over the family's collie while descending the staircase. She has no memory of the accident. After Minnie was taken to the hospital in Marshall, Alice, Lady Bird's nurse, took her to visit. The clearest memory she has of her mother was at her deathbed.

"She looked over at me and said, 'My poor little girl, her face is dirty,' " said Lady Bird. In a childlike voice, Lady Bird recalled that her mother asked Alice Tittle for a washcloth and then slowly and carefully wiped Lady Bird's face. She knew she was dying. She rubbed her daughter's face until it was clean, and then she fell back into bed and cried. "Nobody at home to care for you but the Black nurse," said Minnie. "Poor child."

Lady Bird stared at her mother numbly. A few moments later Alice took Lady Bird's hand and led her from her mother's room. Minnie died shortly thereafter.

Taylor did not notify either of his sons in New York about their mother's illness. Tony was by then thirteen years old and Tommy was sixteen. They did not know how sick she had been until after she died, an omission that Antonio, who had his mother's sensitive temperament, held against his father for the rest of his life. "There was a vacant place in his heart at her loss and also anger at my daddy, who didn't face up to that right," said Lady Bird. "People must be given the opportunity to hurt out loud."

Taylor did not tell the boys about their mother's death for almost a year. In fact, he asked the officials at Los Alamos, the summer camp where Tommy and Tony were enrolled, not to tell them that their mother was dead. The boys stayed away at school all through the next fall and winter.

Immediately after Minnie's death, Taylor had her body taken to the Methodist parsonage in Karnack, where the neighbors viewed her body in an open casket. The service was held at the Methodist church. Afterward, she was buried in a cemetery dedicated to the memory of the Confederate war dead, located in a pine forest near the small community of Scottsville. Some time later, it was Tommy who wrote her epitaph. "Forgetful of self," says the small, unadorned marker. "She lived only for others." In death, she achieved her rightful legacy: a martyr's epitaph, etched in stone.

Lady Bird did not attend the funeral. A few days after the service, the Methodist minister came to the Brick House to comfort her father. He told Taylor that Minnie was better off in heaven than on earth. Taylor exploded in front of Lady Bird, who was frightened. "I had never seen my father lose his temper," she said. The sight of him angry and out of control terrified her.

Taylor asked the minister how he could say such a thing and then pointed at Lady Bird, who stood quietly, astonished by her father's display of emotion. Part of Taylor's outburst was directed not at the loss of Minnie but at the burden she had left behind, meaning Lady Bird. "Who is going to take care of that little girl?" Taylor demanded. "I ask you, who is going to take care of her?"

Lady Bird was shaken to see her father in such a vulnerable state. Her loyalty shifted from her mother to him. She made up her mind not to be the burden he feared. "I just felt so sorry for him," recalled Lady Bird. "I had no feelings at all for myself."

Her mother's death came at her father's busiest time of the year. From September through December, tenants brought their bales of cotton to Taylor's two gins to be processed. Taylor had to be at the store in order to see that everything went as it should and to collect money from the Blacks who came in during that time of year to pay up their accounts. Minnie's death did not slow Taylor's pace.

Taylor took Lady Bird with him to the store. At night he made a bed for her on the second floor, near the coffins. One night after he put her to bed, Lady Bird asked her father, "What are those long boxes?" Taylor looked at the coffins, hesitated a moment and then answered, "Dry goods, honey, just dry goods."

It's difficult to imagine that Taylor would have been so insensitive to his daughter's feelings that he would have made a bed for her near a coffin in the first few weeks after her mother's death. Yet that is what he did. As a matter of survival, she learned early on to keep her emotions buried, symbolically locked in a coffin in her soul.

In the first few months after her mother died, she told herself her mother hadn't really passed away. "I was incensed that people thought she wasn't coming back," she said. Then, in later years, she pretended to see her in the clouds, racing across the sky in a chariot. Her mother's death gave her a mystical perspective, and she soon found her comfort in nature, not in other people. "Often, when there were clouds or sunset or something dramatic in the sky, I would somewhat expect that if I looked at it in the right angle, I might indeed see her," said Lady Bird. "But I never did."

A few months after her mother died, Taylor put his only daughter on a train in Karnack bound for Alabama. He dressed her in a nice dress, tied a bonnet around her head, and put a sign around her neck, "Deliver this child to John Will Pattillo," who was her mother's uncle. Lady Bird has no memory of being afraid to travel such a long distance by herself. All her life she had been cared for by servants. "I knew the conductors and porters would take care of me," said Lady Bird. "I thought it was an exciting trip."

By then, Effie was sick with worry about Lady Bird. John Will had a daughter, Nettie, Lady Bird's second cousin, who was roughly Lady Bird's age. Nettie went with her father and aunt to the station to meet Lady Bird but was instructed not to talk about her dead mother. "We were told not to mention it," recalled Nettie, "but I could tell how much she missed her mother." Nettie and Lady Bird went on picnics and went swimming, but Nettie was always careful to avoid any mention of grief.

The Pattillos were frankly surprised that Taylor had sought out their help. The mistrust between the family and Taylor was apparently mutual, but Taylor realized he needed them. His sons' prolonged stay at the Los Alamos Ranch continued. A year after Minnie's death, on September 16, 1919, Tony wrote his father a letter about a long hike he and

Tommy had taken through the mountains of New Mexico. The letter described peaks almost three miles high. "We could see it raining down below us while it was snowing up there. There were snow banks 10 feet deep. We made some snow ice cream on the 23rd of August," Tony wrote. He also described other adventures. For instance, one night a bear wandered into camp and frightened the horses.

About that same time, Lady Bird and Minnie's sister, Effie, arrived back at the Brick House so that Lady Bird could start school. Effie was polite to Taylor but kept her distance. She did not call her niece Lady Bird, but "Bammy." Privately, whether fairly or not, Effie blamed Taylor for her sister's death.

"What precisely happened Effie did not know," said one of Effie's nieces. "Whatever happened, we all knew that Effie blamed Mr. Taylor." Effie also believed that the ghost of Minnie lived in the Brick House. Some nights she would wake up in a cold sweat, convinced that Minnie had visited her to tell her to clean the grime off the windows or to make sure Lady Bird received some kind of consolation. It was a poisonous, otherworldly atmosphere for a child. For all practical purposes, Lady Bird was an orphan with an orphan's mentality.

Taylor continued to nurse his own private wounds and focused on his business. Years later, after Lady Bird had married Lyndon Johnson, Taylor sat on the porch at the Brick House with his shoes off, dug his toes in the black soil of East Texas, and told his granddaughter Susan Taylor, "Old Man Pattillo was wrong about me. He thought I wasn't good enough for his daughter. Now I'm richer than he ever was."

CHAPTER FOUR

❧

First Flight

In July 1923, when Lady Bird was eleven years old, she traveled by train with her aunt Effie to Dr. Kellogg's sanitarium in Battle Creek, Michigan. Effie went in search of treatment for her ulcers and her nervous condition. Lady Bird sought adventure. The trip was Lady Bird's first journey out of the South and memorable because everything about it was new and strange.

Her visit to Battle Creek coincided with Dr. Kellogg's annual Fourth of July celebration, a festival of fireworks. In East Texas and Alabama, where ties to the Union were tenuous, the country's independence was not a matter of celebration. Lady Bird had never seen a Fourth of July fireworks show. As a Southerner, she associated fireworks with Christmas, not summer. "Those strange Yankee people," she said to herself as she watched Roman candles explode and light up the Michigan night sky.

She was the only child in residence and enjoyed her privileged status. The atmosphere at the sanitarium was heady and elegant. It was the first place she had ever encountered finger bowls. Dinner was served on starched white tablecloths, and full silver service was used at every meal. She dressed for dinner in a Sunday dress and ate the vegetarian meals that were served to adults. Like an actress in a play, she pretended as though she routinely ate entrées made of beans and ground nuts and drank many glasses of water each day. Asked if she felt out of place, Lady Bird insisted that she did not. In fact, she liked the attention.

It was in the dining room at Battle Creek that she saw her first U.S. senator. From her place at Effie's side, she watched as Robert La Follette, the legendary progressive from Wisconsin, strolled through the dining room. "I remember the flurry of excitement that went through the room," Lady Bird recalled. "All eyes followed him." She recognized that he was powerful and that people respected him.

In the mornings, Lady Bird rose early to watch Dr. Kellogg conduct calisthenics classes on the front lawn. "He had white hair and a white mustache, and he would wear white knickers and a shirt," said Lady Bird. Kellogg lifted his arms, touched his toes, jogged in place, all the while yelling to the members of his exercise class, "Breathe deeply!" Kellogg reminded her of an aging cherub, something not of this world. He was eccentric and spontaneous, the antithesis of her hardworking father.

Lady Bird liked him because he offered Effie what she most needed—the promise of strength. "Aunt Effie was always seeking for something that was going to make her stronger," said Lady Bird, with a mixture of pity and sadness.

In Lady Bird's eyes, Effie was an invalid. Unlike her mother, who was active even when ill, Effie lived a cauterized life, cut off from her own ambitions as an artist. Yet it took a certain amount of strength for Effie, a woman from a small Southern town in the early part of the century, to have had a clear vision of herself as an artist at all. The fact that she failed to sustain this sense of herself and develop a career was not surprising. Her family and her culture expected her to have a family, not play the piano and paint. Their expectations put her at odds with her own nature. Even as a grown woman, Lady Bird herself dismissed Effie's interest in art as ridiculous. "I remember that she painted some. I don't remember how well," she said. "I think she did it for her own pleasure."

One of Effie's nieces, Nettie Pattillo Woodyard, has a painting in her living room in Billingsley, Alabama, that Effie did in the 1930s. The painting is of a slim woman with a tiny waist dressed in a long white dress walking by herself down a winding path through a snowy forest. The style of the painting is airy and romantic and reveals a glimpse of how Effie must have seen herself in her own imagination: a woman alone in nature.

At an early age, Lady Bird resolved not to follow Effie down the path she perceived as weak and dependent. "I saw that her poor health made her dependent on Daddy and other relatives," said Lady Bird. "She depended on them for money and for a place to live. I didn't want to be like that."

By the time Lady Bird was an adolescent, Effie had abandoned both her piano and her easel in order to care for Lady Bird. When Effie died in 1947, her self-sacrifice was complete. The epitaph on Effie's tombstone in Billingsley is remarkably similar to the one on Minnie's. It reads, "A truer, nobler trustier heart, more loving or more loyal, never did beat within a human breast." Both women paid a high price for female acceptance. They lived their lives for others. (Effie's epitaph was written by a third woman who paid the same price—Rebekah Johnson, the mother of Lyndon Johnson.)

This, too, was part of Lady Bird's female inheritance. She was expected to do what Effie and her mother had done—put others ahead of herself—without clear direction from either one of them. In Lady Bird's mind, her mother was lost forever, somewhere in the clouds. Effie was someone to be loved, cared for, and pitied, but not imitated. Neither woman could be depended on. As for her father, he was to be feared, placated, and pleased. Her only way to defend herself was to put on the armor of self-reliance. She slipped it on easily.

Even when her niece was eleven, Effie had no real authority over Lady Bird. In fact, it was the other way around. "Somehow, instead of Aunt Effie taking care of Lady Bird, I think more it was Lady Bird taking care of Effie," said Dorris Powell, her mother's friend from Karnack. According to Mrs. Powell, when Lady Bird went to Marshall on errands, she always remembered to bring Effie's list of medicines from the drugstore. "The list came first," recalled Mrs. Powell. In the evenings, she read to Effie aloud or tuned in her favorite operas on the radio. She accompanied her on car rides through nature. Lady Bird resented Effie's neediness, which triggered her own sense of guilt. "I was her reason for being," she said. "I felt that I must carry that weight, but I always wanted to be free and be myself."

In Battle Creek, the responsibility of caring for Effie was given over to a staff of professionals, and Lady Bird could do as she pleased. She indulged herself in adultlike ways. She had massages, took regular mineral baths, and was rubbed down by nurses who scrubbed her skin with straw mittens until her whole body tingled. It must have felt good for an eleven-year-old who hadn't felt the touch of a mother in five years to surrender to the sensation of her own flesh. "I liked it just fine," recalled Mrs. Johnson.

But the most important thing that happened to her in Battle Creek was that she took a ride in a biplane. One day a patient, a female pilot who was in her twenties, buzzed over the sanitarium in an airplane and landed in a nearby field. Lady Bird had never seen a plane, but she was aware that pilots like this woman were setting flying records all over America. She stood in the center of the field, watched the plane circle above her, and knew instinctively that she wanted to go up. She asked permission, but Effie said no. "It's too dangerous," Effie told her.

Lady Bird decided to go anyway. She gave the pilot $2.50, threw her legs into the back seat, and strapped herself into place. To her, the female pilot was a heroine—the embodiment of a risk worth taking. As the engines roared and the pilot prepared to take the plane off the ground, Lady Bird peered out the window and noticed that the wings looked as if they were held together by thin baling wire. She didn't care. In her mind, she was already flying. "It was a lark," said Lady Bird, "an adventure, the most exciting ride of my young life."

In the sky, she found the freedom she craved. She lay her head back in the rear seat of the plane and floated in the clouds. She was literally above it all. The eleven-year-old who flew that clear July day was not yet weighed down by convention. It wasn't romance that captivated Lady Bird's imagination, nor Effie's artistic sensibilities. Her quest was the same as her mother's—what she wanted was freedom and adventure.

Back home in Karnack, however, Lady Bird was earthbound, as tied to her place as the pine trees were rooted in the land. She started elementary school in the first grade at a one-room school, the Fern School No. 14, located on top of a red-clay hill by a cemetery on the outskirts of Karnack. Only a handful of other students attended the school in any given year. The class size never exceeded fourteen students, all whites. Blacks went to a separate school or didn't go at all.

The teacher, Nancy Lawrence, was a friend of her mother's. Lady Bird's father paid her salary. Yet Lady Bird doesn't appear to have received special treatment from Miss Lawrence, who was busy with the responsibility of teaching seven grades in a single room. Lady Bird brought her lunch to the school every day in a tin pail, like all the other students, and shared her books with them.

The highlight of Lady Bird's regular week at the Fern School came on Friday afternoon when they had what were called "exercises." All of the students lined up in a row and sang two or three patriotic songs. Years later when Lady Bird sang "America the Beautiful" or "Columbia, the Gem of the Ocean" on endless campaign stops, she remembered the songs line for line because she had memorized them that way when she was a young girl at the Fern School.

By the time Lady Bird reached the seventh-grade level, most of the other students, who were the children of tenant farmers, had moved away. The school was closed, and Miss Lawrence moved to the Brick House, where Lady Bird finished her studies in a room adjacent to her bedroom on the second floor. That year, caught in the hazy twilight period between childhood and adolescence, she alternated her time between books and dolls.

With few friends to play with, Lady Bird filled her emptiness as her father did, with work. She found that working kept her from thinking too much. Once she told Dorris Powell, "Well, I don't want to work but I must." Sometimes when she did take breaks from her studies for picnics or a swim in Caddo Lake, she would criticize herself out loud. "Oh that's pure self-indulgence," she would say, giving voice to her father's view of life.

Taylor left the Brick House every morning before dawn. On his way to the store, he would pass rows of darkened houses. Years later, when Jerry Jones, his nephew by marriage, drove him to work, Taylor would say, "Everybody around here is still asleep. Guess I'm the only man in Karnack who has to work for a livin'."

Lady Bird's playmates were the Black children whose parents worked at the Brick House. On Sundays, she sometimes attended services at the Black church and enjoyed the free-flowing style of the service, particularly the singing of hymns.

The emotion in the music reminded her of the dramatic operas her mother had listened to on the radio. Her own preference was for more cheerful songs. At home in the Brick House she played with one of the few gifts that her mother had given her, a small harp, and tried to make lighter, sweeter music than the plaintive sounds she heard in church.

Every summer, Dorris Powell took her to weeklong revival meetings, which were held in cavernous tents near Karnack. The revivals were held in the dog days of summer, after all the fields had been plowed but before the cotton had been picked. It was a time when families, exhausted from their labor, gathered to be with their friends and to hear the out-of-town preacher, who was treated as a celebrity, remind them of their need for salvation.

Lady Bird listened to the hellfire and brimstone sermons, but already she had too many questions to take everything the minister said on faith. She found herself wondering, for instance, how the Bible story about Jonah living in the belly of a whale for three days could be literally true. How could a man stay alive if he had been swallowed by a whale?

Such questions sharpened her powers of observation. At the conclusion of the weeklong revivals, Powell took her to baptism ceremonies that were held on a creek bed called Mount Sinai. Some years there would be as many as fifty candidates for baptism. After the singing of hymns, the candidates were led, one by one, into the river where the preacher slowly immersed their whole bodies in the water. "Sometimes they'd be very happy when they came out of the water," recalled Mrs. Powell. "Other times they would come out sobbing. It affected them differently."

For a child, especially one who was hiding an inconsolable grief, the display of emotion must have been a vicarious experience. It brought her close to her own inner world. Religion, however, was one of the many matters she did not discuss at home.

Everyday life at the Brick House was too fraught with conflict for Lady Bird to add to the fray. In 1920, two years after Minnie died, Taylor married Beulah Wisdom. According to Sylvia Bishop, Beulah's niece, Wisdom had attended business school in Tyler and was a valuable employee to Taylor. After the marriage, Beulah continued to work for Taylor at the store. Taylor kept the territory of the women in his life well divided. Beulah's place was at the store, while Effie and Lady Bird held sway at home.

Lady Bird privately regarded Beulah as a pariah, a dangerous rival for both her father's attention and her mother's memory. "Effie and I were the ones who belonged," said Lady Bird. "Beulah was the outsider." Beulah's presence in the Brick House was one of the traumas in Lady Bird's life—it aroused feelings of both jealousy and her mother's abandonment—but she did not confront her father or Beulah.

The irony, however, was that in Beulah, Lady Bird found a flesh-and-

blood female role model, a woman who demonstrated how women traditionally attract men. Beulah, who was only a few years older than
Lady Bird, wore her hair in a short bob with bangs. She wore short
dresses that she bought at Perkins Brothers in Marshall for less than a
dollar, and long strings of beads around her neck. She flaunted her sex-
uality by living with an older, rich man, and she worked full-time out of
the house. Lady Bird was both fascinated and repelled by her. When
asked as an adult if Beulah was pretty, Lady Bird replied, "Yes, in a
coarse and crude sort of way."

As an adolescent, however, Lady Bird could not keep from interact-
ing with, and even imitating, Beulah. Who else was she going to emu-
late? Not Effie, and there were few girls her age in Karnack. In a
photograph taken on a picnic in the late 1920s, Beulah struck a coy
pose in front of one of Taylor's large cars. In another photograph taken
at roughly the same time, Lady Bird wore her hair in the same style.

She learned other lessons from Beulah as well. Years later Lady Bird
would be confronted with women who were typed similarly to Beulah,
flirtatious women who had careers and who competed for her husband's attention. Her reaction to these rivals was the same as her initial
reaction to Beulah. She distanced them in her mind as "outsiders" and
assumed a façade of aloofness.

Throughout the time of her father's marriage to Beulah, the atmosphere in the Brick House was sexually charged. Effie was particularly
hostile to the younger woman who had taken her sister's place as the
rightful mistress of the Brick House. However, sex was another issue,
like her mother's death, that was not directly addressed. Lady Bird was
left alone with her own private questions about why her father had
married Beulah and why the marriage was so stormy. When the marriage ended in 1934, Lady Bird blamed herself and her two brothers at
least in part. "Daddy didn't tell Beulah that he didn't want any more
children," said Lady Bird. "That really wasn't fair of him."

The truth was more straightforward. Beulah may have been the only
woman in Taylor's life who gave him a taste of his own medicine. In
1934, Taylor discovered that Beulah had become involved with another
man and divorced her, a fact that Lady Bird knew and that seems to
have suited her just fine. At some level, it verified her own low opinion
of Beulah. Nonetheless, in the face of her first encounter with sexual

betrayal, Lady Bird's anger failed her. "In the end, Beulah had to seek solace somewhere," said Lady Bird, with a shrug. "I didn't blame her."

When Lady Bird was thirteen, Taylor sent Lady Bird and Effie to Jefferson, located thirteen miles from Karnack, so that Lady Bird could start high school. By then, Tommy, her oldest brother, had opened a general store in Jefferson. That same year Tommy, who had their father's handsome features, married Mary Wright. But Tommy's marriage was troubled, too. According to the Taylor side of the story, Mary suffered from mental illness. In 1933, shortly before T. J. Taylor divorced Beulah, Tommy and his wife were also divorced.

Lady Bird wrote to her brother Antonio, who was then a grown man living in Santa Fe, and announced in a self-righteous tone that Tommy had lost "very little" when he lost his wife. In his reply to Lady Bird, Antonio wrote: "He seems to have always picked the wrong woman to love, strangely enough, too." He mentioned that Tommy had been left at the altar by one woman, and "now he had to marry that schizophrenic," speaking of Mary. Antonio concluded his letter about his brother as follows: "If I were he, I would take my female companionship free after this."

Given the fact that there were two divorces in her family within a year of each other, it was natural that Lady Bird felt awkward about relating to boys when she first arrived in Jefferson. The difficulties surfaced in her insecurities over matters of cosmetics and personal style.

Though her father was rich, Lady Bird did not own many shoes or clothes and didn't know about the practical aspects of life that other girls talked about. She was a country girl, but she didn't know how to cook, sew, or shop. What she did know how to do—read books and roam through nature—were activities that most girls her age did not share and that did not attract boys. Her family considered her a tomboy.

Her father believed Jefferson was the perfect place for Lady Bird to learn how to be a Southern lady. The women of pedigree had run the city since the late 1800s. At that time, Jefferson was a thriving inland port, the second largest city in Texas, following Galveston. The railroad baron Jay Gould had come to Jefferson and demanded that the city grant him right-of-way to build his Texas and Pacific railroad line. The city refused, so Gould built the railroad around Jefferson, which in effect destroyed the town's economy. The port city quickly dwindled to a town of 2,600 and was managed almost entirely by the ladies of the Jessie Allen Wise Garden Club, who restored many of the town's old buildings.

Effie and Lady Bird moved into the house of Miss Bernice Emmett, one of the leaders of the garden club. Effie felt at home in Jefferson, surrounded by the old houses fronted by roses and crepe myrtles, and it was there that Lady Bird acquired the thickness of her Southern drawl, her habit of saying "mah" instead of "my," "yew-nited" instead of "united," and of rolling her r's. Jefferson is also where she tried to put into practice the subconscious lessons she had observed from Beulah. She learned to smile, to slick back her dark black hair, to open her brown eyes widely, and to allow her eyebrows to rise and fall, while feigning interest.

Before she moved to Jefferson, she had gone on picnics and explored Caddo Lake with Karl Boehringer, whose older sister, Eugenia, was the friend who later introduced Lady Bird to Lyndon Johnson and whose other sister, Emma, was Lady Bird's age. The Boehringers lived not far from the Brick House in Port Caddo. Lady Bird remembers that Boehringer was her first boyfriend. "He was funny and good-looking," said Lady Bird of Karl. "But he was never in love with me, nor I with him."

In Jefferson, she had her first real romance. J. H. Benefield, the son of a member of the garden club, asked her to several dances, called Germans, that were held at a private club in Jefferson. The dances were elaborate rituals, the biggest social events of the year. At home in Karnack, she typically wore pants that looked like knickers, with white cotton camp shirts and long white socks. The Germans were her first occasion to wear party clothes.

On the afternoon of the first party, she and Effie went to the Benefield home, had an early supper and took a nap, then Lady Bird worried about whether she had the right dress and what she would talk about. Soon Benefield arrived and they went to the dance, which started at 11:00 P.M. and lasted all night.

She described her feelings for Benefield as more frightened than excited. She was attracted to him, in part, because he had an aunt who was the high school superintendent. "This woman had suffered a lot from being a woman in a time when men were expected to do everything," recalled Lady Bird. "It was not accepted if women were active, held good jobs. They were considered bossy."

She talked to Benefield about his aunt in ways that made him believe that Lady Bird, too, was a little bossy. Later Benefield described her as "one of the most determined persons I met in my life, one of the most ambitious and able. She confided in me her wish to excel."

Another early boyfriend, Thomas C. Soloman, said Lady Bird allowed him to believe he was in control, but later he realized that they had been doing exactly what Lady Bird wanted to do, down to the last detail. "Even when we went on a picnic, it was she who thought up the idea. This convinced me it would take a strong man to be the boss," Soloman said.

When it came to getting around in East Texas, Lady Bird was remarkably self-reliant. In the society in which she lived, her father was a king, and she understood that his power translated to her. If she wanted something—a soda, candy, or dry goods—she simply took it from her father's store. She felt safe to walk or drive alone in the woods because she knew if she got lost, someone would help her find her way to the Brick House. "I was Cap'n Taylor's daughter," she recalled. "That gave me a certain amount of freedom."

For instance, the summer she was fourteen, her cousin Nettie visited Lady Bird at the Brick House. Effie was already back in Billingsley for her annual summer visit. By then, the routine was that she and Lady Bird spent nine months in Karnack and the three months of summer in Alabama.

This particular year Lady Bird had Effie's car in Karnack. Her father allowed her and Nettie, two teenage girls, to make the long drive from Karnack to Billingsley by themselves. Lady Bird took the wheel, driving to Shreveport the first night, where they checked into the best hotel in town and treated themselves to a nice dinner.

The next morning, Lady Bird filled the car with gasoline. When she paid the bill, she realized that she didn't have enough money to get all the way to Billingsley. She drove as far as Jackson, Mississippi, checked into a hotel, and sent a telegram to her father asking for more money, confident that the money would arrive.

Twenty-four hours later, Taylor still hadn't sent the money, so Nettie wired her father, her uncle, and Aunt Effie. About an hour later, Taylor telephoned the hotel. Lady Bird explained that she and Nettie had been held up, and her father misunderstood and thought she had been robbed. She continued to talk and was finally able to make him understand her true situation. Taylor wired more money, as did all the relatives from Alabama. Suddenly flush, Lady Bird and Nettie left Jackson that night and drove all the way to Autauga County, arriving at 2:30 A.M. at the home of one of Lady Bird's aunts.

Her summers in Alabama were full of freedom. She and Nettie took the car and visited relatives. They once drove all the way to Birmingham to hear a concert by the yodeler Jimmie Rodgers. They swam in Mulberry Creek and went on hayrides. One night Lady Bird and Nettie stole a few watermelons from a neighbor's patch. They were so noisy about it that the neighbor recognized their voices. The next morning Nettie's father went over and paid for the watermelons they had eaten.

In September 1926, Lady Bird moved back to the Brick House and she enrolled in high school at Marshall, the county seat of Harrison County, which had a population of fifteen thousand. At the start of the school year, her father had someone from the store—a clerk or a butcher—drive Lady Bird to the high school in a pickup truck that was sometimes used to carry cowhides. Lady Bird didn't like the smell of the truck and usually asked the driver to let her out several blocks from the school so none of her friends would see her arrive in the truck. She was afraid her friends would make fun of her about the cowhides and preferred to walk the last few blocks on her own. Finally, her father decided he couldn't spare anyone from the store to take her to school, so he bought Lady Bird her first car, a Chevrolet coupé.

When it rained and the roads to Karnack were too muddy to drive, she stayed the night at the home of Helen Bird, the daughter of an Episcopal priest, or Emma Boehringer, who was both her friend and rival. There were eighteen girls in her class, and Boehringer was the prettiest and most popular, the leader of the clique that sometimes excluded Lady Bird.

"I had two heavy crosses to bear in my early teens," she once said. "One was my nickname and the other was my hook nose, which at one time I seriously tried to have bobbed." She tried to get Emma and the others to call her by her given name, Claudia, instead of her nickname, which she considered "absurd," but often the girls would call her "Bird" to taunt her.

She began to think of herself as two people: Claudia, her true self, and Bird, her persona. Claudia Taylor rode in airplanes, walked in the woods, and drove across the South by herself. She was a heroine. Bird Taylor was teased by her friends because of her nose and her baggy, drab clothes. Her senior year, the *Parrot*, the high school newspaper, printed that Lady Bird's ambition was to be an old maid, which must have stung, given the example of Effie in her own life.

Her father's money and her mother's absence made her an outsider, the subject of both envy and pity by her friends. One day she offered Emma a ride home, and Emma told her that she would prefer to ride home with another girl. Later Emma's mother forced her to write Lady Bird a letter of apology. "I have come to realize how bad I treat you," wrote the then fourteen-year-old Emma on Valentine's Day. "I just feel awful, and want to beg your pardon."

Lady Bird nursed her hurt feelings by retreating to the place she always went for consolation—nature. Sometimes she took long boat trips on Caddo Lake by herself, shielding herself from the outside world in the drapes of moss that hung from the cypress trees. She invented imaginary solitary rituals to connect herself with nature. In the spring, when the first daffodils bloomed, she had a secret ceremony that served as her own private theater. She named the first daffodil of spring "queen," which is what she most wanted to be. Even as a girl, the great paradox of life was already firmly established. Claudia, the girl who loved flowers, saw her other self, Bird, as a wallflower.

On the other hand, she realized that her father's money was also a shield. Her relationship to it was secret. On a scrap piece of paper from one of her school notebooks in 1928, Lady Bird kept a running tab of the monthly sales in her father's store, all written in her own hand. For instance, in January, she noted that he sold $16,427.85 worth of clothing. December was naturally the most profitable month—$28,693.72 was sold during December that year. By year's end, she calculated that her father had made $212,127.45 in his retail business alone. Her father's money was the source of her ambition, but there was something miserly about the way she related to it, noting every penny in a back page of her school notebook.

She excelled in school. In high school, she took only a half-credit of home economics and preferred instead to concentrate on more substantial subjects, such as physics, communications, law, both solid and plane geometry, and Latin. Near the end of her senior year, Lady Bird realized that she had the highest grades in the class, even higher than Emma's.

Her report cards from that year, each signed by her father, are all straight A's, except in Latin and law, courses where her marks were A+s. As graduation approached, she purposely allowed her grades to slip so that she would not be the valedictorian or salutatorian of the class. In her own mind, she had two good reasons for not wanting to win—first, she didn't want to make a public speech, and second, she wanted Emma to win instead. The two girls crammed together for English finals at Emma's house.

When the final grades for the whole year were tallied Emma Boehringer was first at 95, Maurine Cranson was second at 94½, and Claudia Taylor's grades were 94, a safe third.

Lady Bird felt nothing but relief—by coming in third, she had avoided making a speech and had not risked the loss of Emma's friendship. Before the grades were posted, she prayed that if she came in first or second in her class that she would be struck by smallpox. "I had enough pride to want to amount to something," she recalled, "but not enough to pay the price to make a speech."

The night of her graduation, she went to the dance and banquet with another classmate's boyfriend. Naomi Bell's mother had arranged the date out of pity for Lady Bird. Naomi went with someone else. Nevertheless, on that May evening in 1928, Lady Bird did not seem to care. She was looking ahead, not behind.

One of the graduation day customs at Marshall High was that seniors tried to guess one another's futures. Some of the standard ones for girls were predictions about careers as movie stars or fashion designers. Lady Bird took comfort in the prophecy that had been written anonymously about her. The prediction for Claudia Taylor's future was that she would become a "second Halliburton, poking her nose in unknown places in Asia." Years later, when as First Lady she poked her nose in just those kinds of foreign places, she remembered that prophecy with enormous satisfaction.

First, however, she had to get out of Karnack. After graduation from high school at fifteen, she went to summer school at the University of Alabama, where she took four hours of history and two hours of journalism. She missed Texas, however, and her friends, and tried to figure out a way to get back home. Helen Bird, her high school friend, was planning to attend St. Mary's Episcopal School for Girls, a junior college in Dallas, and suggested that Lady Bird apply.

Her father opposed the idea, but Lady Bird was insistent. She and her father drove to Dallas to look at the school. Taylor could not understand why Lady Bird would want to go there. It was a proper, old-fashioned girls school. She would have to be a boarder, since there was nowhere else in Dallas for her to live. Boarders had strict curfews and weren't allowed to leave the campus without a chaperone. Taylor didn't think it was a likely place for Lady Bird to find a husband.

"I'm not in favor of this," he told Lady Bird flat out. "I don't think it's going to be good."

In addition, she didn't find support from her namesake uncle, Claud Pattillo, who questioned the value of a college education. In a letter from Billingsley, Pattillo asked Lady Bird, "Does [sic] all these fine colleges and schools, with their wonderful, comparatively, equipment and paraphernalia, gotten up at so much cost of outlay of money and time, really contribute very largely to making real men and women of the children and youths who attend them?" He advised his niece that if she did go to college to remember, "You must not depend on them for the best part of your education."

Even at fifteen, she had a strong enough sense of self not to allow herself to be dictated to by either her father or her favorite uncle. She told them both that she was going to Dallas. In the fall of 1928, she left Karnack in a Buick that her father had given her, with her monthly allowance and purse full of charge cards, and enrolled at St. Mary's. She and Helen Bird were roommates.

The most lasting influence of St. Mary's on her life was that while she was a student, she converted to the Episcopal faith. Every morning she was required to go to chapel, and Sunday services were also mandatory. The routine became part of a lifelong habit.

The school had a reputation for attracting pious young girls. One song that the girls sang while Lady Bird was in residence had the following lyrics: "Root-a-toot-toot, root-a-toot-toot, we're the girls from the institute. We don't smoke and we don't chew, and we don't go with boys who do."

Her Bible teacher at St. Mary's was known as Little Miss Voice—as opposed to Big Miss Voice who taught English—and it was in her class that Lady Bird found an alternative to the narrow interpretation of the Bible that she was familiar with in Karnack. "God didn't seem less real or awesome to me," reflected Lady Bird, "just bigger and more complex." Although she began her studies of the Episcopal Church that first semester at St. Mary's, she was not formally confirmed until five years later, at St. David's Episcopal Church in Austin.

Lady Bird earned fifty-two hours of college credits in her two years at St. Mary's and did well. She made straight A's in almost every subject. Science, however, was a blank page for her. One semester, she made a D in chemistry. She pushed herself to improve, telling herself, "This must be important. I just don't know why."

She took French, and a drama course from a teacher named May Davis-Moore. Lady Bird and the other girls at St. Mary's thought it was extremely affected for the drama teacher to hyphenate her name. Nonetheless, drama was her favorite class at St. Mary's.

She was in two plays. Since St. Mary's had no male students, girls had to play the parts of men. Lady Bird played a butler in *The Importance of Being Earnest,* and later she played Sir Toby Belch, Olivia's uncle, in Shakespeare's *Twelfth Night.* In Dallas she saw her first professional play, *Liliom,* at the Dallas Little Theater. She discovered that when she was playing a role or watching someone else play a role, she felt somehow bigger, less insulated.

In April 1930, the month before she was scheduled to graduate from St. Mary's, Lady Bird faced a decision about where to go for her last two years of college. By then, she was tired of the all-girl environment and wanted to go to a coed school. She considered the University of Alabama, but by then Emma's older sister, Eugenia (Gene), was a student at the University of Texas in Austin and persuaded Lady Bird to consider Austin as an alternative. Lady Bird decided to go.

Dallas is about two hundred miles north of Austin, a distance that could easily have been traveled in four hours by car in 1930. However, Lady Bird decided to fly, not drive, to investigate her future. She went alone—without her father or Aunt Effie—on a chartered flight.

As the plane landed on a dusty airstrip on the edge of Austin, Lady Bird looked out her window. She could see the horizon, and on the side of the control tower, she saw a field of bluebonnets in full bloom. She had never seen so many bluebonnets in one space before, and it was the sight of the field of flowers set against the brushy range that made her want to move to Austin. "It was as though the gates of the world flung open for me," she said. "I felt in love with life itself."

CHAPTER FIVE

❧

The Moth Finds the Flame

hen Lady Bird Taylor stepped from the plane at the rangy Austin airport, she was met by Emma's sister, Gene Boehringer. By then, the romance with their brother, Bo, was off because, as Lady Bird later told friends, she had concluded, "Bo never would amount to anything."

She regarded the Boehringer girls in a more positive light. As she had with Emma, Lady Bird saw in Gene a reflection of everything she wanted to be. In her eyes, the Boehringer sisters were funny, charming, lighthearted, while she saw herself as moody and dark.

"Most girls are in full bloom at that age," an elderly Lady Bird said of her seventeen-year-old self. "I have to say my bloom was not accompanied by much." In fact, the two years in Dallas at the all-girls' school had made Lady Bird look more of a small-town girl, not less. On the day she arrived in Austin, she wore a baggy dress that made her look pudgier and plainer than she in fact was. The face she caught sight of in the airport rest room as she hurriedly doused it with cool water was small and round. For as long as she could remember, she had looked into the mirror and regretted her olive skin, dark eyes, and large nose. Like her mother, Minnie, Lady Bird was a bookish, plain woman, not a great beauty.

Gene, on the other hand, was pretty and easygoing. She was a slim and stylish secretary who worked for C. V. Terrell, chairman of the Texas Railroad Commission and one of the most powerful men in Austin. In addition to railroads, the commission regulated the production and price of the state's supply of oil and gas, which meant that Terrell was in a position to determine whether oil prices—and the fortunes of many wealthy Texans—soared or dropped.

Even in 1930, as the South sank into the depths of the Depression and Texas wildcatters desperately looked for oil, Gene was well paid and could afford to buy high heels, stockings, and attractive dresses. Through Terrell, Gene got to know the important people in Austin. She was good friends with the governor's secretary, knew the newspapermen who covered the state capital, and was friendly with ambitious political staffers, including Lyndon Baines Johnson, then a slender young secretary to U.S. Representative Dick Kleberg from Kingsville. Gene was the first person to mention Johnson's name to Lady Bird. She mentioned him at least two years before arranging for the two to meet.

On the day that Lady Bird arrived in Austin, Gene met her at the airport in her own car. As the two young women drove downtown, Lady Bird saw the pink granite dome of the Texas capitol, the seat of the state government where Gene worked. The view Lady Bird saw out her window was dramatically different from the land she grew up on in East Texas. There was no veil of Spanish moss and pine trees; everything was out in the open.

Austin sits on a large escarpment of stone, called the Balcones Fault, and is fed by a series of underground springs and rivers, which burst forth from the limestone in deep pools and eddies. Visually, the city is a luminous collection of pink buildings set among sand-colored stones.

Here was a rosy-hued city set on a series of low-lying hills, a city of books and ideas, of people and politics. Her suffocating Southern nostalgia was behind her. Austin would require more of Lady Bird than Karnack, but Lady Bird was ready to leave her dwarfed and insular world behind. She glanced over at Gene, who was four years older than Lady Bird, and marveled at her own good fortune. Gene, who was animated by self-confidence, was in the driver's seat, and Gene gave her courage. "She was one of those tremendously outgoing people who made everyone around her feel a little more alive," Lady Bird recalled.

By then, Gene had lived for four years at the Austin Woman's Club, an elegant two-story frame house on the corner of Eighth and San Antonio, near the center of downtown. Over that weekend, Gene pointed out the city's landmarks—Barton Springs, a large, blue-green pool of bracing cold water; the glitzy Paramount Theater on Congress

Avenue; the capitol, seat of power; and the University of Texas, which was expanding in every direction from its original forty-two acres. By the end of the weekend Lady Bird decided to apply to the state's largest university. "I fell in love with Austin the first moment I laid eyes on it," she said. "I had to go there."

At first her father refused to let her go. Taylor encouraged his daughter to choose instead the University of Alabama at Tuscaloosa to be near her grandparents and cousins, but Lady Bird wanted to move forward in time, not backward. She pressed for Austin.

During a trip home to Karnack, it was Gene who interceded on Lady Bird's behalf. Gene, not Lady Bird, found the words to tell Taylor what his daughter desired. "You should let Bird come to the University of Texas," she told Taylor. "If she plans to live in Texas, she should have Texas friends and not have to go way back to Alabama."

"All right," Taylor told Gene, "as long as you take care of her."

The following fall Lady Bird enrolled. As for many other small-town boys and girls, UT was a natural magnet for Lady Bird. In 1930, as now, education was the way up and out of parochialism and poverty, the great social engine of the early twentieth century, the ticket to the larger world.

The University of Texas was founded by the state legislature in 1853 and conceived of as a broad, democratic institution that was paid for by public funds. The goal, as defined by the original charge, was "to place within the reach of our people, whether rich or poor . . . a thorough education." When it opened in the fall of 1883, the first catalogue described it as an open door "to male or female on equal terms, without charge for admission." Blacks, however, were barred from entering that open door. Segregation was so deep and virulent a strain within the state that Blacks would not be allowed at UT for another half century.

By the time Lady Bird arrived in 1930, tuition was $25 a year, and the annual cost of unlimited use of the library was a mere $7. For $10.50 a year, students were given a "blanket tax," which allowed them admission to all sports and cultural events. The enrollment that year was 6,652 students. Despite the high-minded goal of gender equality, male students outnumbered females four to one. Demographically at least, the university was a wallflower's dream. Even though Lady Bird had serious scholastic aspirations, UT was still a difficult place for a girl to get a serious education.

The expectations for girls were primarily social. "Most girls at that time were majoring in a Mrs." said Margaret Berry, a UT historian. "They were looking for husbands." The Scottish Rite Dormitory, a large and imposing building, was considered the good address for women on campus. Lady Bird investigated it, but decided to move into a much smaller two-story boardinghouse at 301 West Twenty-first Street owned by Mrs. Matthews, a tidy French woman. Mrs. Matthews rented the three upstairs bedrooms to college girls. "I liked the thought of the six girls at Mrs. Matthews's more than the six hundred at Scottish Rite," Lady Bird recalled.

Lady Bird was determined to fit in at UT. In a formally posed photograph taken of her that year, Lady Bird's oval face is staring directly and somewhat resolutely into the camera, as though resolved to stare down her own timidity. She is wearing a fedora hat, cocked over her right eyebrow. The only hair that is showing in the photograph is a single dramatic curl—what used to be called "spit curls" in Texas—plastered against her left cheek. Her lips are turned in a demure flapper's smile.

One detail spoils her allure. In the photograph, Lady Bird is wearing a wool coat, a hand-me-down that had belonged to her aunt Effie. It wasn't that Lady Bird could not afford to buy her own coat. Before she left the Brick House to go to St. Mary's in Dallas, her father had given her a charge account at Neiman-Marcus. She could have bought any coat she wanted—in any size or color—but the fact is, the coat she chose to take to Austin was the hand-me-down from Effie.

The photograph reveals Lady Bird's inner conflict at seventeen. "I was determined to let go of the old business of being shy," Lady Bird recalled. She wanted to be the outgoing flapper, popular and vibrant like her friend Gene. The other part, the smart freshman, was hidden under wraps beneath the coat of her emotionally fragile aunt.

The first person Lady Bird met on the steps of Mrs. Matthews's boardinghouse was Cecille Harrison, an outgoing blond from San Antonio who had gone to Brenau College in Georgia for her first year. That fall, Cecille entered UT as a sophomore. Her mother, a divorced woman who worked as a legal secretary, had driven Cecille up to Austin. In August 1930, Cecille, dressed in a tailored Sunday suit and high heels, her mother, and Lady Bird collided on the front porch.

"Hi, I'm Bird Taylor," said Lady Bird, dressed in a sensible light summer dress. By then, she had given up her name of preference, Claudia. On the way upstairs, Cecille explained that she had brought plenty of sheets and towels, but it was Bird who took charge. "You're not going to need that bedding," Lady Bird said proudly.

Once in their room, Lady Bird pulled out a brand-new down comforter, a luxury in the Depression, and the two girls shook it high in the air and let it fall over their double bed. Cecille, who had slept with her mother since she was two years old, was accustomed to sharing a bed. Lady Bird, who had lived a solitary life, was at first taken aback at the idea of sleeping with another person, but she liked Cecille right off. Each had a missing parent, and both girls believed that may have been part of their unspoken bond.

There were two other bedrooms upstairs, both rented by college girls. Mrs. Matthews's family lived downstairs. Breakfast was served off the parlor in a dining room. Lady Bird and Cecille ate lunch and dinner in a restaurant about half a block from Mrs. Matthews's house called Wukasch's, which served mostly Southern-style food, such as fried chicken, mashed potatoes, soft lima beans, and cornbread. According to Cecille, Lady Bird ate just like she dressed, sensibly. "She took what she learned from Battle Creek with her to Austin," recalled Cecille. "She ate lots of vegetables. For her, a splurge was lamb chops. For me, a splurge was angel food cake smothered in whipped cream."

There were other differences between Cecille and Lady Bird. Cecille loved clothes. Once, she skipped classes in order to buy a red-and-white striped evening gown made of taffeta for Lady Bird's birthday party. The party was a progressive event: they had cocktails at one friend's house, dinner at another's, and dessert somewhere else. Even though the party was for her, Bird didn't bother to buy a new dress. She instead wore what she already had, a beige dress with lace shoulders.

Clothes just weren't that important to her. To classes, she wore oxford shoes and simple blouses and skirts. "We all knew that Bird could buy anything she wanted, but shopping never much interested her," said her friend Cecille. As Lady Bird explained it, she had the idea that people should like her for who she was—for being a "bright, cheerful person out to learn a lot"—not for what she wore.

She took her classes seriously. She worked quietly but diligently, often late into the night at the library. A friend from St. Mary's, Emily Crow, who followed her to UT, had this to say about Lady Bird's academic life: "She was very conscientious about her studies, a lot more than Cecille and I."

For a girl at UT in the 1930s, intellectual curiosity was as much a curse as a blessing, just as it had been for her mother two decades before in East Texas. Lady Bird must have realized this, because like most things that really mattered to her, she kept her academic life to herself. "She was quiet about it," recalled Cecille, "but we always knew she had come to college for an education, not just for the romance of it, like I did. Bird wanted to make something of herself."

Where was a girl like Lady Bird to safely put her desire to make something of herself? There was no one to talk to about these desires. Gene, her friend from home, was working as a secretary, and Cecille, by her own admission, wasn't interested in school, only in having fun. Lady Bird's wider world, the student population of UT, was a mixture of Baptist and Methodist farm boys and girls who had been reared to believe, like her uncle Claud, that too much knowledge was a bad thing.

One anonymous publication of the time described the student population as follows: "It is populated, yearly, by some six thousand bewildered boys and girls who are far less interested in the chase after Higher Learning than in the pursuit of their own adolescent amours. Plucked from the bayous, the buck-brush, and the bulrushes of this far-flung commonwealth and dispatched to the Pierian Spring, they decline almost unanimously to drink of the founts of learning. They would rather see a football game. They would rather go to a movie. They would rather make passes at their girlfriends."

In such an environment, a secretly ambitious girl, like Lady Bird, who was plucked from the bayous and was in fact interested in the chase of higher learning, was bound to be plagued with the old feelings of insecurity. Wherever she went—in East Texas, in Dallas, and now in Austin—she was faced with a limited image of what a girl should be. In Austin in the 1930s it was that a girl wasn't really a girl unless a boy found her attractive and interesting.

"She was a little dowdy, nice-looking in a ladylike way," recalled Gordon Abney, a college friend who shared a few journalism classes with Lady Bird. Abney said she always looked a little "thrown together, verging on tacky." One particular day Abney got an A on a journalism test, and Lady Bird pulled a rare B. Proud of himself, Abney raced straight over to Mrs. Matthews's house to show his A to Cecille Harrison. "Get this," he told her, showing off his grade, "this is hot news."

To Abney and others, Lady Bird's intelligence obscured rather than revealed her femininity. Not only was she brainy, she was rich and therefore independent. She had her own car, a black Buick, and that meant she didn't have to rely on boyfriends for transportation. Most students either got around on foot or rode the streetcar, but Lady Bird went where she wanted to go. C. V. Terrell, Gene's boss, teased Lady Bird about her car because it was always littered with candy wrappers. "If you don't clean up this car," the powerful Terrell told her, "you'll never find a husband."

Though she never talked about money, everyone knew that Claudia Taylor was a special case. If Cecille or Emily needed to go somewhere, both knew they could borrow Lady Bird's car. "She had more money than anybody, and she was always generous," said Cecille.

In the fall of her freshman year, she and her friend Emily Crow were both invited to join Alpha Phi sorority. It was not the best sorority on campus (the most beautiful girls joined the Pi Phis or the Kappas), but it offered Lady Bird a sense of belonging. At a practical level, membership in a sorority placed girls in the dating pool for fraternity boys. It meant that a girl was officially not a wallflower.

Crow declined to join because she didn't think her family could afford it. Lady Bird was flattered and surprised when the Alpha Phis asked her to pledge, and was initially enthusiastic about the idea.

She quickly telephoned her father in Karnack to give him the good news. Taylor told her a sorority was a waste of money. He thought it was a bad idea and ridiculed her for even suggesting it. "I think he just plain told her that if she joined, he'd take her out of school," said Emily Crow. On this issue, Lady Bird did not argue with her father.

Emily and Cecille both thought Lady Bird's father was being unfair. One of Lady Bird's cousins Winston Taylor was a student at UT and was in a fraternity. The girls thought Bird was being held to a different standard and were angry about it. Lady Bird was disappointed, but she did not challenge her father's will.

The following morning she broke her pledge, which infuriated the members of the Alpha Phis. Years later Lady Bird suggested that she could have changed her father's mind, if she had really tried. "I don't think I behaved very well and I think I should have gone on and sold Daddy on the business of the sorority," said Lady Bird. "The fact is I liked those girls, but I didn't like them any better than I did lots of other girls. It was not inclusive. It was exclusive, and I really didn't feel comfortable with that."

For whatever reason, the decision to break her pledge freed her to spend time with her trio of friends—Emily, Cecille, and Gene—and put her on a less advantageous social track at UT. Weekends were spent riding around the Austin countryside in her black Buick. They drove up and down Guadalupe Street, known then and now as the Drag. Often they parked at a drive-in restaurant, ordered Coca-Colas laced with lime or cherry juice, and then circled the quiet streets of the capital, before heading into the hills west of Austin, where they picnicked on sandwiches made of cream cheese and pineapples. "Bird was crazy about bluebonnets and wildflowers, and we loved to go on long walks in the woods," recalled Emily Crow.

One of the places they went was called Dillingham's Pasture, a field eight miles north of Austin where students went for what they called "Navajo parties." They took Navajo blankets and alarm clocks and drove out to the pasture, where a farmer, D. H. Dillingham, charged 25 cents a car for students to park.

On some nights, Lady Bird and her friends paired off with dates and spread their blankets in the pasture for what they called "heavy petting." As a matter of practice, they set their alarm, so that they would know when it was time to head back to Mrs. Matthews's boardinghouse. Curfew was 11:00 P.M. on the weekdays and midnight on weekends. On at least one occasion, Cecille and Lady Bird missed Mrs. Matthews's curfew and spent the night in Lady Bird's car, parked in front of the boardinghouse. Cecille took the back seat; Lady Bird got the front.

Other than necking in a pasture, the sexual atmosphere at the university was officially sheltered. Sex was more of a social prohibition than the legal one against the drinking of liquor that was ratified on February 28, 1918, by the Texas legislature. In small-town Texas, ministers routinely admonished young people to stay away from both sex and alcohol under threat of all kinds of ruination. Nowhere did this battle between minds and hormones rage more fiercely than on blankets under the night sky of Dillingham's Pasture.

Amid such tensions, Lady Bird, Cecille, and Emily talked ambiguously about sex. After her first day in an English history class, Lady Bird came back to Mrs. Matthews's house and reported that the professor had described Anne Boleyn, the second of King Henry VIII's six wives, as "not beautiful, but oh those eyes," and then outlined the shape of a woman's body with his hands. Lady Bird repeated the gesture for Cecille, and they both collapsed on the bed in laughter. It was innocent girl talk; as Cecille put it, "just crazy fun."

To Lady Bird and her friends, sex was strictly taboo, but sentimentality was perfectly acceptable. "I fell in love every April," said Lady Bird when she was in her eighties. She spoke in a voice that was wispy and naive, just as she must have been at seventeen, as if the sexual revolution of the 1960s had never happened. Mother Nature had given Lady Bird many gifts, but somehow nature failed to reveal herself in her most fecund, primitive state. "We talked a lot about boys and romance," said Cecille, with a grimace, "never sex."

There were a lot of boys to talk about. Despite her reputation as a wallflower, Lady Bird had many boyfriends from a variety of circles. She attended a heavily chaperoned formal dance in Gregory Gym with Chilton O'Brien, the president of the student body at UT. She had a long romance with Victor McRea, a serious-minded student at the law school, and was particularly interested in Jack Mayfield, a premed student who later became a well-known surgeon in Houston. All of these boys had one quality in common—ambition.

One suitor Lady Bird recalled was Wayne Livergood, a wealthy blond boy from Houston who drove a new Chevrolet with a rumble seat. "He reminded me of a pixie because he was short and liked to do wild, giddy things," Lady Bird said. One night she and Wayne double-dated with Emily and a boy with a common Texas nickname, Bubba.

The four of them drove from Austin to Laredo and crossed the bridge of the muddy, caramel-colored Rio Grande to Nuevo Laredo, Mexico. They spent the night drinking gin and dancing beneath a revolving multicolored globe at a nightclub called the Bohemian Club. At 3:00 A.M., the club closed and they stumbled out into the streets of Nuevo Laredo in search of other bars. As their money and the night ran out, they finally found their way into one final bar, the last one open in town, a cantina off a deserted street that was about the size of a large closet.

Near the bar sat a piano player, a Mexican boy in his twenties who loved American music. He kept playing two jazz tunes—"St. Louis Blues" and "Minnie the Moocher"—over and over. The two couples held on to one another and staggered around the tiny dance floor until dawn, when they headed back to Austin. That night Lady Bird danced all night.

Among the influential men that Gene introduced her to were Hiram King, a vice president of Sinclair Oil Company in Houston. Emily, Cecille, and Lady Bird often rented horses and rode to Mount Bonnell, the highest point in Austin, near where King lived, and had supper. King mixed the girls a cocktail—they liked Tom Collinses with extra lime juice—and then ordered steaks from Hillsboro, a local steakhouse.

King was a married man, older, powerful, and savvy. Emily expressed her concern about spending so much time with King and wondered in particular about the attention he paid Lady Bird. "That's just one side of him," Lady Bird told Emily, and then confided she liked him. There was nothing wrong with their relationship, but it revealed Lady Bird's vulnerability.

Wherever she turned around, she seemed to bump into men whose style and personality resembled that of her father. Gene also introduced her to Jack Aldridge, a former captain of the famed Texas Rangers, who lived in a rambling colonial-style house near the present-day Austin airport. Aldridge was a huge, elderly man who wore khakis and a cowboy hat; he was so old that he had lost his teeth. He told Lady Bird, Cecille, and Emily he didn't need teeth, that he could gum his food as well as most people could chew.

One room of Aldridge's house was lined with books, including erotic literature. Aldridge proudly showed Lady Bird and her friends his collection of books and read to them risqué Mother Goose rhymes that seemed, at least to Emily, "very, very naughty." Aldridge may have seemed like a dirty old man, but Cecille, Emily, and Lady Bird found him larger than life, an authentic Texas character. "We didn't think of him as a dirty old man," recalled Cecille. "When he would read those nursery rhymes, all three of us would just have laughing fits."

Like most seventeen-year-olds, Lady Bird wasn't asking any big questions of herself. She had no role model to help her fashion an identity for herself. That would have involved asking such questions as, What do I want my life to be like? What do I want from men? What do they want from me? If I choose not to be a spinster like my aunt Effie, does that mean I have to be like Beulah? She did not know how to frame her life as a series of questions; instead she was carried along by a series of experiences.

What drew her to Aldridge were the stories he told about life on the early Texas frontier, tales about how the Rangers protected the border between Mexico and the United States against Indian raids and Mexican bandits. "He seemed to me," she said, "to be the very embodiment of the Old West."

Gene continued to manage her off-campus social life. She introduced her to Duncan Dawson, a reporter for the *Dallas Morning News* who covered the capital. Lady Bird and Duncan dated for much of Lady Bird's last two years at the university. "Dawson was a handsome, smart man, who was absolutely smitten with Lady Bird," recalled Margaret Mayer, a reporter for the *Austin American-Statesman* who was friends with both Duncan and Lady Bird. Duncan inspired Lady Bird to pursue an interest in journalism. She noticed that Duncan and his friends, Charlie Green and Dick West, two other reporters, were always in the center of things and yet one step removed from the action.

Unsure of her own role, Lady Bird liked the idea of playing the part of the detached observer. Journalist, she thought, was a practical substitute for explorer. It was not a typical woman's job—not a secretary, teacher, or nurse—but not out of her reach. "I saw journalism as an outlet, a safe outlet, to be a little bit more aggressive," she explained.

She finished her bachelor's degree in arts in May 1933, graduating with honors, and stayed on another year so that she could take a second degree in journalism. She fell under the tutelage of DeWitt Reddick, a sandy-haired journalism professor who wore owlish glasses and took a special interest in her.

In Reddick's class she wrote a feature story about Captain Aldridge and the Texas Rangers. That year she joined Theta Sigma Phi, a society for women journalists, and told Effie that her long-term goal was to become a newspaper reporter. Career-wise, she felt her course was set.

At UT, she was also interested in intramural athletics. In her junior year, she was president of the UT Women's Intramural Sports Association. She also continued to pursue her interest in drama. She and her friends went to all the plays on campus and drove the ninety-two miles to San Antonio once with Gene to see a patriotic play called *Of Thee I Sing*. After that, Lady Bird talked idly about wanting to become a drama critic for a major newspaper, an idea that Effie seized on and encouraged.

On January 18, 1933, her byline appeared on the front page of the *Daily Texan,* the university's school newspaper, above a story about a gift to the UT library of first edition copies of some of the poems of John Keats, the great English Romantic. Here is how she started the story:

> In Leigh Hunt's old stone house on Hampstead Heath, where tobacco and ale mugs went the rounds and a spirit of intellectual camaraderie and good fellowship prevailed in the air, a convivial company of England's most ardent spirits, the painter Haydon, Joseph Severn, Percy Shelley, John Keats, and Leigh Hunt, and the host were gathered to celebrate an important event. The proof sheets of John Keats's first volume of poetry had just come from the printer, and Leigh Hunt with his pervasive enthusiasm was reading them to the young poet's assembled friends.

To Lady Bird, Keats was a soul mate. She viewed her life in Austin as an imitation of the life he described—full of camaraderie. Like Keats, who lived amid the ashes of Great Britain's colonialism, Lady Bird found herself surrounded by the dying remnants of an established order. Life on the cotton farm and cattle ranches was being replaced by the arrival of the Texas oil age.

Lady Bird viewed the frenzied search for oil and the new big money that came with it as a mixed blessing. The kind of slow, rambling talks she had overheard her father carry on in his store about cotton seed, ginning, and the price of bologna and cheese had vanished by now. The talk was of mineral rights and drilling bits and how many wells could be fit in which pasture.

One weekend she and Emily went home to Karnack, and she stood near a dormant cotton field where her father planned to drill for oil. "They say there's a possibility that they'll discover oil here on Daddy's property," Lady Bird told her friend sadly. "I hope to heaven they don't. It would just ruin everything, all these growing things." She pointed to a lake on the property. "That's liable to be ruined," she said. "Everything that I love will be gone." When it came to the land, Lady Bird was a purist.

They did discover oil on Taylor's property in Karnack, although not in large quantities. At the time of his death in 1960, about a third of the hard cash he had on hand, a little less than $100,000, came from royalties and lease income from oil and gas wells.

"I literally saw oil and gas flare into importance in Texas," Lady Bird recalled. "Flaring is the correct word, because when I drove across Texas, all I could see were the tall stacks where gas was being burned off. It burned red and blue from those stacks and looked just like hell when you drove through. The land itself looked like it was on fire."

As a student at UT during the Depression, Lady Bird was on the periphery of great social tumult. Everywhere she looked on campus she could see how tax income from the production of oil was being put to use. A new student union was under construction, as was a physics and chemistry lab and many other classrooms, yet there were also hundreds of unemployed people standing in bread lines on Congress Avenue.

In effect, Texas was between two worlds. Though a majority of people still lived in rural areas, many others moved to cities in search of work. The same day Lady Bird's story on Keats appeared in the *Daily Texan*, fifty-seven-year-old Miriam Amanda Ferguson, whose nickname was Ma, was sworn in for a second term as governor of Texas. Her husband, Farmer Jim, was a former governor who had first been elected in 1914 on an anti-prohibition platform. Though Ferguson had a strong base of support among small farmers in Texas and was considered a populist, he was impeached and removed from office in 1917. LBJ's father, Sam, had served in the Texas legislature while Ferguson was governor and considered himself a "Ferguson man," as did Lyndon Johnson. After Ferguson was impeached, small farmers began to lose political sway in Texas. His wife, Ma, ran for governor ten years later and was the first woman to be elected governor in the United States. Though she functioned as a figurehead for her husband, Ma was also a populist herself. She attacked the Ku Klux Klan and authorized $20 million in "bread bonds" to feed the hungry, but she was best known for forcing through a repeal of prohibition.

At the end of Ma Ferguson's second term, adults could buy beer and wine in Texas, as long as the alcohol content did not exceed 3.2 percent. Full repeal of prohibition did not come until two years later. At a practical level, prohibition had kept Texans from drinking in public. Lady Bird's own views about alcohol were generally liberal. At home in Karnack, Lady Bird and her friends drank homemade whiskey out of

Mason jars. Her father used to brag that "the best farmers make the best bootleggers." The end of prohibition meant that people could buy liquor legally in the store instead of brewing their own in the woods.

At UT, according to Lady Bird's friend Cecille, the repeal of prohibition was like the popping of a long-corked bottle of champagne. "There seemed to us to be nothing quite as delicious as gin and grapefruit juice or gin and cherry juice," Cecille recalled.

Politically, Lady Bird and her friends all supported Governor Ma Ferguson. Through Gene, Lady Bird got to know Gladys Little, who was Ma Ferguson's personal secretary, and Duncan Dawson, who was still Lady Bird's boyfriend, covered the governor as a newspaperman. The news of the day—prohibition, the Klan, FDR, bread lines at home, and the rise of communism abroad—was part of her everyday conversation.

Through her connections at the capitol, Gene arranged for perks for Lady Bird and others. In 1933, Lady Bird and Emily went on a private tour of a series of underground caves, called the Longhorn Caverns, which had been opened by the state's parks department. When the two of them arrived at the caves, it was almost time for lunch. They sat down at a large picnic table with several convicts from a nearby state prison who were working inside the caverns. They ate lunch on a tin tray, and afterward one of the younger prisoners brought out a deck of cards and suggested a game.

"Sure," said Emily. The convict dealt the hand, and they all played a game of cards. After the game ended, another prisoner arrived and took the girls on a tour of the caverns. Emily felt claustrophobic and a little afraid, but Lady Bird, the explorer, was fascinated by the caves. On their way out, Lady Bird and Emily thought to ask what crime their guide had committed. They were told he was in jail for murdering his wife after finding her in bed with another man.

Both of the girls reacted to the murderer with something approaching glee. "He was extremely nice to us and even after we found out that he'd killed his wife, we weren't the least bit concerned," recalled Emily. They left the caverns and headed home for Austin, feeling strangely alive.

Her brush with the convict was an odd moment of synchronicity for Lady Bird. The convict's story was close to the drama that was in progress at the Brick House. It was about the same time period that stepmother Beulah had become involved with another man and fled

Taylor's home. Taylor later said he had caught the two of them in bed, bragging that he had picked up a large shovel from the front yard and threw it at Beulah and her lover, before he ordered them both to leave the Brick House. "I'm surprised old man Taylor didn't kill 'em both," said Jack Hayner, who lived a quarter mile from them in Karnack.

Lady Bird distanced herself from the trouble at home by staying in Austin as long as possible. However, by the end of May 1934, most of her friends were leaving to find jobs and Lady Bird was restless, unsure of her future. Duncan, according to Mayer, was serious about Lady Bird, but Lady Bird resisted making a commitment to him and continued to see other men.

A transcript of her grades from UT shows that once again she had performed reasonably well. In the sixteen grades she earned for her bachelor of journalism degree, she had A's and B's in ten of them. She earned six C's, one for a half-semester of philosophy, another in sociology, and two in a journalism course. She also earned a second-grade teacher's certificate "just to be on the safe side," as she put it.

By then, she had written for information about teaching positions in Hawaii and Alaska. She also knew typing and shorthand and told herself that she might find work as a secretary and work her way toward a career in business. She wanted to be a reporter, but she also knew that most girls from wealthy families did not have careers in 1934. That expectation thwarted her ambition.

She also felt responsible for her father. With Beulah gone, she told her friends she believed she should return to Karnack and spend a year or two restoring the Brick House. The house needed repairs. At the time, the electricity was run by a Delco battery, which was noisy and inefficient. The upstairs rooms were filthy, and some of their doors had been boarded up. The plumbing was old, and visitors recalled the persistent stench of sewage.

Lady Bird wanted the old place restored to its antebellum grandeur. "Even though I know it's hopeless," she told her friend Emily. "Whatever I decide to do to the house, Dad will just send old Jack Moore down from the store with a couple of buckets of paint and that will be the end of it."

Lady Bird decided to postpone a final decision about her future and take a trip. Her father agreed to pay for it as a graduation present. Lady Bird, Emily, and Cecille wanted to go out west to California, but when

Emily decided not to go, Lady Bird and Cecille changed their plans and decided to go first to Washington and then to New York. It was Lady Bird who suggested Washington. She wanted to see the White House and the Capitol, and Effie wanted her to consider seeking a job at the *Washington Post*.

In June she wore a black cap and gown and graduated cum laude from UT with her second degree in journalism. She and Cecille made plans to sail from Galveston in August 1954.

When Lady Bird told Gene she was going to Washington on her graduation trip, Gene immediately took charge. "Oh wonderful!" she told Lady Bird. "I know just the very young man that you must meet. He's a good friend of mine, and I will write him that you're coming."

Gene's friend was Lyndon Johnson, then twenty-six years old and working in Washington for Kleberg, who was known as "Mr. Dick" at his ranch and the capital. Johnson was living in the basement of the Dodge Hotel, an eight-story redbrick building just south of the Capitol, in one of twelve cubicles that rented for $20 a month. Gene wrote down Johnson's telephone number and told Lady Bird to call him as soon as she got to Washington.

"All right," Lady Bird told her, as she placed his number in her purse.

But Lady Bird had no intention of telephoning Lyndon Johnson on that trip. It wasn't that she was too shy, but the reverse. Lyndon Johnson wasn't the romantic suitor she had in mind. She was going to Washington to visit McRea, who was a native of the small West Texas town of Roby, founded by his grandfather L. H. McRea, a country lawyer. McRea was a good-looking boy who was five feet, six inches tall, almost the same height as Lady Bird, with black hair. He had just taken his first job as a young lawyer for the postmaster general's office.

At the port of Galveston, Lady Bird and Cecille struggled to load nine pieces of luggage—most of it Cecille's—onto the boat. There were hat boxes, shoe boxes, all shapes of luggage, and it was a chore to get them stowed away, especially since the weather was disagreeable. As they got on board, it started to rain and the wind whipped the Gulf Coast waves against the boat. Lady Bird and Cecille worried that their trip might be canceled, but, a few hours later than planned, they did finally set sail.

The sea journey was neither as serene nor as romantic as they had hoped. Lady Bird became ill with motion sickness. She spent most of the first leg of the trip—the seven-hour sail from Houston to Miami—inside her cabin, feeling as sickly as Effie, fragile as a spun-glass bird. In Miami, both Cecille and Lady Bird left the boat for a few hours and did some shopping. When they returned, both the weather and their stomachs had settled. Two days later, their boat lapped up to the port of New York.

Hiram King, the oil lobbyist, had advised them on their travel arrangements. On his recommendation, they checked into the Taft Hotel, located near Times Square. He had also helped them get tickets to several Broadway shows.

Of her first trip to New York, Lady Bird remembers long night rides in taxi cabs and spending her days as a tourist. She had plenty of time to herself because Cecille had reconnected with an old beau from the University of North Carolina. At twenty-one, Lady Bird had good theater tickets and plenty of money to explore the galleries and museums. "Life," she said, "seemed very full."

After a few days in New York, she and Cecille took the bus to Washington and stayed at the Wardman-Park Hotel. McRea met them there, and over the course of the next four days, McRea showed her the sights of Washington. He took her to the Washington, Lincoln, and Jefferson monuments, and Lady Bird decided on that trip that the Jefferson Memorial, which McRea showed her at night, was her favorite. They went to the Supreme Court, where she and Cecille took turns sitting in the justices' large chairs, and took the standard tour of the U.S. Capitol, where Johnson was putting in twelve hours a day for Kleberg in Room 258, which faced the inner court of the Old House, now the Cannon Office Building.

Lady Bird thought briefly of Johnson while she was in the Capitol but again decided not to call him. "I just had enough to do," she said. "Victor and I were having a good time. I didn't see any need of introducing a stranger into it."

One hot and muggy afternoon, McRea took Lady Bird and Cecille to the White House. The two girls peered through the railings at the green lawn and the house where, thirty years later, Lady Bird would live. That night McRea took her to the Cotton Club, a nightclub where they had cocktails and danced. She felt her wallflower days were behind her.

Two weeks later, Lady Bird was back in Austin and went by Gene's office at the Texas Railroad Commission near the end of the workday.

Lyndon Johnson stopped by to keep a date with another girl, Dorothy Muckleroy, who had roomed with Gene in Austin. Johnson immediately asked all three girls—Gene, Dorothy, and Lady Bird—out for a drink. All three said yes.

For several months, Gene had been trying to get Johnson and Lady Bird together. Now they had bumped into each other by accident. Since they both knew a lot of basic information about each other through Gene, their conversation over drinks was easy. The attraction—at least on Lady Bird's part—was instantaneous.

"He was very, very good-looking," she recalled. "Lots of hair, quite black and wavy, and the most outspoken, straightforward, determined young man I'd ever met. I knew I had met someone remarkable, but I didn't know quite who."

Watching him hold court with three woman at once, Lady Bird recognized Johnson as her opposite; he was confident, extroverted, loud, and had a hunger for glory. He seemed to look directly at all three women at once, and he did not just hold his drink in his large hands, he mauled it. Everything about him—his body, his voice, his ears—seemed outsized. "I had a sort of queer moth-in-the-flame feeling," she later said.

That first night Lyndon had a date with Dorothy, but before he left, he leaned over toward Lady Bird's chair and asked her to have breakfast with him the next morning. Her initial instinct was to refuse, but she did not.

"Meet me in the dining room of the Driskill Hotel," he told her. Before she could stop herself, she said, "Okay." In that instant, Lady Bird leaped into the flame.

CHAPTER SIX

❧

A Ten-Week Affair

At 8:00 the following morning, August 31, 1934, Lyndon Johnson took a window seat in the coffee shop of the Driskill Hotel in downtown Austin, ordered breakfast, and nervously scanned the room, looking for Lady Bird to walk through the door. She made him wait.

That particular hour, Lady Bird was meeting next door with Hugo Cuney, an architect whom she had retained to redesign the Brick House. She was now the woman in charge of her childhood home. Taylor's divorce from his second wife, Beulah, would be final in only a few weeks.

Taylor assigned his daughter a wifely duty: he told her to spend whatever money she needed to fix up the Brick House. Such generosity was unusual for Taylor, and Lady Bird didn't really believe he meant it. She knew her father was, by nature, frugal. "He always used to lecture me about the valueofadollar," recalled Lady Bird. "He rattled off that phrase as if it were one word."

She felt pressure to come to her father's aid, but restoring the Brick House was not exactly Lady Bird's idea of a dream job. She was anxious to strike out on her own. With the full weight of Southern womanly duty on her shoulders, Lady Bird went to see Cuney about what to do to shore up her father's sagging house.

The Driskill's dining room was located next door to Cuney's office. On the way upstairs, Lady Bird saw, through the corner of her eye, Johnson seated by the window, but she hurried up the stairs without stopping. She wasn't yet ready to meet his gaze. She felt conflicted, simultaneously excited and afraid. "He was so dynamic and so insistent," she recalled. His aggression made her cautious. "He came on very strong and my first instinct was to withdraw," she added.

As she left the architect's office, she intended to keep walking, without joining Johnson at the table, but by now he was frantic. He stood to his feet and waved both arms, throwing himself in her path. Only when she sat down at his table was he momentarily quieted. She liked the fact that her presence seemed to calm him. It filled a need in her as well.

Thirty years later, Johnson told an interviewer that if he had not waved her down, Lady Bird would have walked out the door of the hotel without acknowledging his presence. He couldn't bear the idea of being ignored. "I've always doubted whether she would have really walked in that dining room," Johnson said.

Once she was seated over a cup of coffee, Johnson began talking as fast as he could. He assaulted her with many questions, asking her about what she had majored in at college, about her family, about her plans for the future. "He seemed on fire," Lady Bird recalled, again evoking the image of the flame.

Before she answered any of the questions, he shifted the focus to himself. He told her about his work in Washington as a secretary for Kleberg, providing her with such details as how much money he made and how much insurance he had, all information that Lady Bird found uncomfortably personal. "It was just as if he was ready to give me a picture of his life and what he might be capable of doing," Lady Bird said.

By the time breakfast was over, Lady Bird was swept up in Johnson's larger world. All her life Lady Bird had felt isolated, first by the stultifying nature of her physical surroundings in East Texas, then by her repressed grief over her mother's death, and more recently by her lack of options after graduation from college. She was accustomed to being alone, even preferred to live her life that way, but now she was at a crossroads and wanted to become part of something bigger, either a career or marriage.

Suddenly—directly across the table—sat Lyndon Johnson, talking with enthusiasm about President Roosevelt and the New Deal, about pending legislation to curb poverty and unemployment and to reduce the number of farm foreclosures. She saw in him a man who was exactly where she wanted to be—powerfully situated in the middle of things. So she settled back in her coffee shop chair and listened to him talk.

Only a few months before, in March 1933, Johnson had attended Roosevelt's inauguration. Johnson described to Lady Bird how that "great man" Roosevelt had stood behind the podium and quoted from Proverbs: "Where there is no vision, the people perish." He was a New Deal man, thoroughly absorbed by Roosevelt. He told Lady Bird that he hated poverty and bragged that he had persuaded Kleberg to vote to raise crop prices, despite the conservative congressman's feelings that many of Roosevelt's programs were socialistic. "It was just like finding yourself in the middle of a whirlwind," said Lady Bird of her breakfast conversation. "I just had not met up with that kind of vitality before."

After breakfast, he invited her to take a drive in a Ford convertible with leather seats that had the King Ranch brand stamped into them. The car was showy and ostentatious, finer than anything twenty-six-year-old Lyndon Johnson could afford. He had gone to work for Kleberg in November 1931, three years before, and was making less than $4,000 a year.

While Johnson considered himself underpaid, that salary was more than most Americans were making at that time. It was, after all, the second winter of the Great Depression. Ten million Americans had lost their jobs and millions more worked fifty to sixty hours a week for literally pennies. In Washington, Johnson lived a spartan life, but he still managed to send money home to his parents, who depended on him. His close association with Kleberg, a multimillionaire who lived at the other end of the extreme in a suite at the Shoreham, Washington's most expensive hotel, was a window into the world of the rich and powerful.

He was living between two worlds and wanted it both ways. He wanted to be a champion of the poor—to stamp out the poverty that he had grown up with—but he also wanted a secure place in Kleberg's higher realm. He confided this dream to Lady Bird as they drove around the hills west of Austin during their first day together.

"He talked a great deal about his job, about wanting to be best at whatever he did, about all the things he wanted to do," said Lady Bird. All day long he talked and talked, and by day's end he was practically intoxicated with his own words. From his place behind the steering wheel, he leaned over and told Lady Bird that he wanted to marry her. She thought she had misheard him.

"You must be joking," she told him.

"Listen, you're seeing the best side of me," Johnson acknowledged.

Though Lady Bird did not realize it, Johnson was telling her the truth. She was seeing his best, most heroic side. Johnson had a strong, valiant image of himself—one given to him at birth by his mother—but he also was haunted by feelings of insecurity, shadow feelings that sometimes overwhelmed him.

As most biographers of Johnson have noted, his attraction to Lady Bird followed a set pattern: he pursued daughters of rich men. In the spring of 1924, when Johnson was only fifteen, he told friends and family that he had "fallen in love" with Kitty Clyde, one of the six members of his high school graduating class. Kitty was Johnson's first girlfriend. Her father, E. P. Ross, was the owner of the general merchandising store in Johnson City and the richest man in Johnson's hometown.

By then, Lyndon's father, Sam Johnson, a gregarious lawyer who served six terms in the Texas legislature, was broke. In the dry, hot summer of 1920, cotton production at his family farm near Stonewall fell off at exactly the same time cotton prices fell from 40 cents to 8 cents a pound. In September 1922, Sam Johnson was forced to sell his family's 443-acre farm in Stonewall and move into Johnson City, where the unpaid bills mounted year after year in Ross's store. Lyndon's attraction for Ross's daughter came at an auspicious time, at the precise moment that his father was in debt to hers.

Ross thought Lyndon was too much like his father—an idealist who was unlikely to make much money. Ross ordered his daughter not to spend time with Lyndon. She did as she was told and broke up with Johnson. Even after the breakup, Lyndon continued to pursue the relationship. He asked Kitty for a date to a local baseball game, but Kitty said she first had to ask her parents, who again told her no. Johnson went to visit his two favorite female cousins, Ava and Margaret, who described him as devastated. He could not bear rejection.

The pattern continued when Johnson was a student at Southwest Texas State Teachers College in nearby San Marcos. Johnson had many girlfriends and often bragged to his brother and others about his many sexual conquests. His next serious romantic interest, Carol Davis, was the daughter of a former mayor who owned a successful wholesale grocery company.

A. L. Davis was the richest man in San Marcos, and there was bad blood between Davis and Lyndon's father. Sam Johnson had once been engaged to Davis's wife. Johnson had unpaid bills in Davis's store, as he had in Ross's store. Carol drove a white convertible, and she often picked up the check when she and Lyndon went out on dates. Lyndon visited Davis often at his home and tried to win him over, but he failed to succeed. Davis, too, believed Lyndon wasn't good enough for his daughter.

All through the summer of 1928, Carol and Lyndon continued to see each other, despite her father's objections. After graduation, Carol went to work as a schoolteacher in the small town of Pearsall, and John-son tried to persuade her to marry him. But Carol was beginning to have her own doubts about Lyndon. She liked opera and movies, and Johnson was already set on politics. In June 1929, she broke up with Johnson and became engaged to Harold Smith, a quiet postal worker whom her father liked. Once again, Johnson was rejected and devastated.

During their first day together, he told Lady Bird about his failed romance with Carol Davis and stories of other girlfriends as well. She felt sympathy for him and proud that someone who had so much expe-rience with women was now focused on her. "My feeling was here was a very attractive man, who had all kinds of women interested in him. I was a little amazed that he was at all interested in me," she recalled.

Lady Bird knew that she completed the trilogy of rich men's daugh-ters in Johnson's life, but she did not question whether her money was part of the reason for his interest. He told her that he liked the fact that she was smart and self-reliant, which appealed to Lady Bird. At least she wouldn't have to appear to be uninterested in books or current events. A man as self-focused as Johnson would need someone who could take care of herself, and Lady Bird—who had in effect raised her-self—knew that she could keep herself occupied.

From the beginning, Johnson told Lady Bird that she reminded him of his mother, Rebekah Baines Johnson, whom he idealized. There were similarities between the two women. Lady Bird's Southern manners, her love of words, her romantic nature, her willingness to put Johnson on center stage and keep him there, her endless desire to gratify his every wish—all were characteristics she had in common with Johnson's mother.

Johnson expected her to fulfill the same role that his mother had: to believe in him and make sacrifices on his behalf. Of Lady Bird's capac-ity for self-denial, Lyndon once said admiringly, "She won't admit pain or ask for any mercy. I remember one time she was running a high temperature but she said it was all right for me to go on to the office. The minute I was out of the room, she called the doctor." In return for putting his needs ahead of her own, Lady Bird earned a high place on Johnson's pedestal.

However, she shared that pedestal with his mother. In conversation, Johnson often compared Lady Bird and his mother. For instance, he told one interviewer in 1963, "I was one of five children and I thought my mother was the greatest woman in the world. But I think Lady Bird spills out a great deal more of herself. I know a lot about mothers. I thought I had the best one in the world, but I never knew one [i.e., Lady Bird] I thought was more devoted yet more reserved, not gushy."

His relationship with his mother was conflicted. He both idolized Rebekah and felt dominated by her. "My mother was everything—religion, character, and right and wrong," he told Ronnie Dugger, one of his biographers, in 1967. She was not, however, particularly warm or nurturing. One longtime staff member described her as "overbearing and opinionated." Another put it this way: "The only words to describe her were that she was damn mean."

The seeds of Johnson's narcissism—his desire to be first, go further, and dominate others at all costs—are found in his mother's unmet ambition. After her son became famous, Rebekah wrote these words: "We welcomed you—Daddy and I—with great hope. We felt that in you we would realize our dreams, cherished ambitions, and fond hopes."

Rebekah had been raised in a Southern mansion, a large two-story stone house in the Texas Hill Country near the small town of Blanco. When she was older, Rebekah described her childhood home in idealistic language, as set among "perfectly spaced trees, terraced flower beds, and broad walks." She also described the "purple plumbed wisteria climbing to the roof" and "fragrant honeysuckle at the dining room windows."

Rebekah came from a long line of Baptist ministers and had a strict, narrow view of God. Her memories of her home were all wrapped up in a heavy package of spiritual idealism. What she remembered most of her childhood, she later said, was "the gracious hospitality, the love and trust, the fear of God and the beautiful ideals." Those are all attributes that she sought to pass on to her children.

Claudia Alta Taylor with her nurse, Alice Tittle,
who gave her the nickname "Lady Bird."
(Taylor family photo, LBJ Library collection)

Lady Bird's father, T. J. Taylor, about the time he met her mother, Minnie. *(Susan Taylor)*

Lady Bird's father, T. J. Taylor, after she married Lyndon Johnson. *(Susan Taylor)*

Lady Bird, an East Texas tomboy.
(Taylor family photo, LBJ Library collection)

Tommy Taylor, Lady Bird's brother; Lady Bird;
and a cousin, Leo Howard. *(Susan Taylor)*

Her father's store in Karnack. *(Taylor family photo, LBJ Library collection)*

Lady Bird and her second stepmother, Ruth Scoggins. *(Taylor family photo, LBJ Library collection)*

Lady Bird *(left)* during her first flight.
(Taylor family photo, LBJ Library collection)

Cap'n Taylor, on the steps of the Brick House,
Lady Bird's childhood home.
(Taylor family photo, LBJ Library collection)

Lady Bird in a field of bluebonnets in Austin. *(Taylor family photo, LBJ Library collection)*

Lady Bird *(left)* and
Gene Boehringer, who introduced
Lady Bird to Lyndon Johnson.
(Taylor family photo, LBJ Library collection)

Lady Bird and Duncan Dawson, an early beau, in Austin.
(Taylor family photo, LBJ Library collection)

Lady Bird, June 19, 1941.
(Austin Statesman)

Lady Bird and Lyndon with Lynda Bird and Lucy, 1948.
(LBJ Library collection)

Lady Bird Johnson, Jackie Kennedy, and Nellie Connally (walking
behind them) all shared a common political frame in November 1963.
Their job was to go to Texas to raise money for the Kennedy-Johnson
ticket. *(John F. Kennedy Library collection)*

November 22, 1963, aboard Air Force One. *(Cecil Stoughton)*

Lady Bird and daughter Lynda on the Lady Bird Special. *(Frank Muto)*

On board the Lady Bird Special. *(Frank Muto)*

Lyndon and Lady Bird united in New Orleans, October 1964.
(Cecil Stoughton)

Lynda, Luci, Lyndon, and Lady Bird in the White House.
(LBJ Library collection)

An inaugural dance, January 1965.
(Yoichi R. Okamato)

Liz Carpenter, Lady Bird, Bess Abell, and Ashton Gonella,
January 1969. *(Yoichi R. Okamato)*

Eartha Kitt confronts the President with Lady Bird *(left)*,
January 18, 1968. *(Yoichi R. Okamato)*

May 8, 1968. *(Robert Knudse*

March 8, 1968. *(Robert Knudsen)*

Lynda Johnson Robb, Luci Johnson, and Lady Bird, December 22, 1982.
(LBJ Library collection)

Queen Elizabeth, Lady Bird, and Lynda Johnson Robb at the LBJ Library, May 20, 1991.
(LBJ Library collection)

Lady Bird at the National Wildflower Center in
Austin, still hugging trees, January 1, 1991.
(Frank Wolfe)

Her paternal grandfather, the Reverend George Washington Baines, organized a Baptist church in Marshall, Texas, in 1850, and later converted Sam Houston, president of the Republic of Texas, to the Baptist faith. Later Baines became president of Baylor University, the state's largest Baptist college, and was eulogized at his death as "a figure among prophets."

Rebekah talked of Baines often and held him up to her children as the ideal of a good and moral man. She also glorified her own father, Joseph Wilson Baines, who fought as a Southerner in the Civil War, attended Baylor University, and studied law. As a young man, he founded a Democratic newspaper, the *McKinney Advocate,* in a town north of Dallas, where Rebekah was born on June 26, 1881.

Six years later, Joseph moved his family to Blanco in the Texas Hill Country and began the practice of law. For a while, he thrived economically and was elected in 1900 to one term in the Texas legislature. He held the seat that Johnson's father, Sam Johnson, later held.

In 1902, however, the Hill Country suffered a four-year drought that brought ruin to Baines's large farming operation. He was forced to sell his family's home and move to nearby Fredericksburg, where he failed to recover his fortune. In contrast to Rebekah's sentimental memories of her childhood, the hard reality was that her father was, spiritually and financially, a badly beaten man. He died in November 1906 after a long depression. After that, her mother took in boarders to support her family.

Despite his economic failures, Joseph Baines remained a towering, idealized figure in Rebekah's mind. As she later told her son, her father was the embodiment of all that was good and right in the world, all that she expected Lyndon Johnson to become. "He taught me the beauty of simple things," she later wrote. "He taught me that a lie is an abomination to the Lord." At a practical level, he also taught her to read, which made her less lonely and gave her self-confidence.

His death came during her final year at Baylor University. The following year, Rebekah returned to Fredericksburg, where she taught elocution and wrote for the newspapers. She was one of the best-educated women in the county.

The photographs of her then are of a slender light-haired woman with her hair swept off her face and piled on top of her head beneath a bow. She preferred lace to cotton. Her most striking features were her large eyes, and she exuded an air of privilege. This was a woman who wanted more from life than she would get.

In the spring of 1907, when she was twenty-six years old, she went to Austin and interviewed Sam Johnson, a tall, lanky thirty-year-old legislator who held her father's former seat. Sam was delighted to find a girl with a strong interest in politics, and the two began what she later called a "whirlwind romance."

Though she felt Sam had her father's "principles," she was worried because Johnson had no formal education and did not abstain from alcohol, as many of her Southern Baptist relatives did. Her father had only been dead a year. Rebekah was lonely, poor, and in need of solace. The fact that Johnson reminded her of her father was enough to provoke her interest. When Johnson asked her to marry him, she hesitated only briefly before saying yes.

They were married on August 20, 1907, and moved to a three-bedroom house on the north banks of the Pedernales near Stonewall that had no indoor plumbing or electricity. It was there on the Texas frontier that Rebekah's dreams ended and she began a steep descent into bitterness. In time, she repeated her mother's pattern of losing financial stability and having to take in boarders.

Although Sam had, according to his wife, "the type of mind for law" and preferred to be in Austin at the legislature, he was not a reliable wage earner. Ultimately, he was forced to work his father's farm on the Pedernales, just to put food on the table. While neither Sam nor Rebekah was happy on the farm, Rebekah particularly hated her life, which consisted of nothing but hard work.

The college graduate who loved poetry soon found herself cooking three meals a day outdoors over an open fire, kneeling over scrubboards on wash days, and pumping water from a back-porch pump. "Normally the first year of marriage is a period of readjustment," she later wrote. "In this case, I was confronted not only by the problem of adjustment to a completely opposite personality, but also to a strange and new way of life. At last I realized that life is real and earnest and not the charming fairy tale of which I had so long dreamed."

A little more than a year later, on August 27, 1908, Rebekah gave birth to her firstborn son, Lyndon Johnson, in the house at Stonewall. Though she was unhappy in her marriage, she remembered none of the physical pain of his birth but described it as a religious experience. "It was daybreak," she wrote. "Now the light came in from the East, bringing a stillness so profound and so pervasive that it seemed as if the earth itself were listening."

The reality was less profound. Her labor pains started at 5:00 A.M. and her father-in-law had to go by horseback in search of a midwife, who delivered the baby. The doctor did not arrive until several hours later, a fact that Rebekah Johnson was ashamed of all her life. She thought that only women from the lower classes had their children delivered by midwives.

Nonetheless, Johnson accepted his mother's view of his birth as nothing short of a miracle. It is one of the reasons he felt entitled to power. Years later, Johnson told an interviewer, "The first year of her marriage was the worst year of her life. Then I came along and suddenly everything was all right again. I could do all the things she never did." Those are the words of a mother-bound man.

Two years after Johnson was born, Rebekah gave birth to a daughter named Rebekah. Over the course of the next six years, she had three other children: Josefa was born in 1912, Sam Houston in 1914, and Lucia in 1916. In letters to her mother, Rebekah complained in a child-like way about her day-to-day chores. Duties such as cooking, cleaning, washing, and making clothes for the children seemed too much for her. In one letter that she wrote when Lyndon was eighteen months old, Rebekah told her mother, "LB was playing Sunday week and threw an empty ink bottle so that it struck me full force under my right eye. The eye has been black and bruised ever since . . . and it certainly hurt." In her letters, it was hard to tell who was the child and who was the parent.

Johnson's earliest memory was when he was four years old and saw his mother standing near a water pump outside their house, crying at night. His father, Sam, was not home. By that time, he was drinking to excess, and Rebekah considered him an alcoholic. When Lyndon walked over to the water pump to console his mother, she confided she was afraid to be alone, a fear he would later inherit from her. "Don't worry," the four-year-old told his mother, "I'll take care of you."

Johnson's world might have been different if he had had a chance as a baby to command and receive her attention without having to take on the responsibility of caring for her. Such infantile needs were never met in him. From the beginning, his ideas about love were confused.

Early on, it meant being strong and powerful enough to take care of his needy mother.

In July 1924, his father, then forty-six years old, was forced to give up his seat in the Texas legislature and come home to Johnson City a penniless man. Rebekah had borrowed money from her mother to help make ends meet. Things were so bad that she considered leaving him.

In a letter to her mother, Rebekah apologized for not being able to send her any of the money she owed and complained that Sam was too proud to buy anything less than the best breed of cattle. Of some less expensive cattle that were available, Rebekah said, "He [Sam] doesn't want to get any but good stock but if I get a separation I might get them myself. I don't know yet whether I'll get one or not, but I surely want to."

For a pious, Southern Baptist woman of her day and age to tell her mother that she was even thinking of separating from her husband was an indication of how badly the marriage was frayed. At the time, Southern Baptists were socially exiled for dancing in public, much less for marital separations. Rebekah was vocal in her misery. "Sam has been having a fever," she wrote in the same letter. "It looks like we will never be well again."

LBJ's father's illness was undefined, but he spent a lot of time in bed. Lyndon was then in the eleventh grade and had become increasingly defiant to both of his parents. He had mostly B's in school, did not want to go to college, and had joined the Christian Church to spite his mother, a proud Southern Baptist. "That really hurt his mother," recalled Wilma Green Fawcett, a contemporary of his in Johnson City.

A recurring dream that he had during this period is an indication of Johnson's fragile inner state. In his dream, he was a boy of fifteen seated alone in a small cage in front of a stone bench piled high with dark books. As he bent down to pick up the books, an old lady—a hag—with a mirror in her hand walked in front of the cage. It was then that he caught sight of himself in the mirror and found that he had been transformed into an old man, twisted and bent with long, silver hair and skin with dark blotches. He pleaded with the old woman to let him out, but she turned and walked away.

He had this dream many times, and each time he awoke drenched in sweat and muttering, "I must get away."

The dream turned out to be prophetic. It showed how caged he felt by his father's financial failures and his mother's unhappiness. In the dream, Johnson saw the mirror image his mother held up for him: do what I say or you'll amount to nothing, like your father. Deep within the boy's psyche, Rebekah reigned from her pedestal as both a loving mother and evil witch. He loved her but couldn't wait to get away from her, a pattern of behavior he would carry within him into marriage.

Shortly after he had this dream, he did in fact run away, not to college as Rebekah had hoped, but to California, where he stayed for a year working for a cousin who was a lawyer. One way or another, he continued to run from her the rest of his life.

In Lady Bird, Lyndon Johnson found his mother in a younger form. Their marriage was similar to his relationship to his mother. In return for her satisfying his incessant demands for attention, he lived up to her expectations of success. Having put Lady Bird on the same pedestal on which he had placed his mother, he spent the whole of their married life fleeing her as well. All his life he wanted out of his cage, but he never made it, which fueled his sense of inner desperation. When he died, Johnson was in fact an old man, twisted by the failure of the Vietnam War and the chaos of civil unrest, his hair long and with speckled brown spots on his flesh. He had become his worst nightmare.

Even late in his life, when Johnson was majority leader of the Senate and seemingly one of the most powerful men in the country, he felt paralyzed by insecurities and sought his mother's pity and attention, as he often sought Lady Bird's. "So often in my life, I have felt misunderstood," he wrote his mother on July 16, 1958. "I need the inspiration and strength that comes from a mind and heart as rich and deep and profound as yours."

To get that inspiration, he flattered her, using the kind of sentimental language he had learned from hearing her talk. A few days earlier, on July 12, 1958, he wrote to her. "All my life I have marveled at the way you have borne with grace, discipline and immense dignity the abundant difficulties and hardships that have filled your life. That's the reason you are who you are and when the balance sheet is totaled up it will be said of you that you are a great woman and the most wonderful mother a man ever had." Those phrases—"great woman . . . most wonderful mother"—are the exact words he later used to describe Lady Bird to the press when he became President.

It came as no surprise, then, that the moment Johnson met Lady

Bird, he was desperate for her to meet his mother. The day after their breakfast at the Driskill, Johnson drove from Austin to San Marcos, where his parents were then living.

Lady Bird got to see firsthand evidence of just how difficult Rebekah Johnson's life had been. "My first impression of her," said Lady Bird of her future mother-in-law, "was that she was an elegant woman in less than elegant circumstances."

The house in San Marcos was small, obviously the home of a poor family. As she looked at the secondhand furniture and the meager surroundings, Lady Bird realized that Lyndon was seeing his family's poverty through her eyes. She knew he felt embarrassed and tried to put him at ease.

Rebekah explained that she had insisted that the family move to the rented house in San Marcos so that Lyndon could live at home and go to college at Southwest Texas State Teachers College. It was a sacrifice she had made for him. Sam spent most of his time in bed, nursing the illness that was sometimes called pneumonia and other times described as nervous exhaustion. When Lady Bird met him, Sam was white, gaunt, and weak, old before his time. She had the impression that "bad heart trouble had laid its hand on him" and felt sorry for him.

Her first visit to the Johnson home set the tone for Lady Bird's long relationship with Johnson's mother. Rebekah treated her with cool detachment, and Lady Bird treated Rebekah in a similar fashion. She never thought of Mrs. Johnson as a substitute mother. "I've never been one to claim intimacy when it wasn't present," Lady Bird explained.

In letters over the years, she always referred to Johnson's mother as "Mrs. Johnson," not mother or Mama Johnson, as was the custom in the Texas Hill Country. That first day, Lady Bird felt critically judged by Rebekah, as if the older woman were assessing her and thinking, "Is this young woman going to take my son away from me?"

She resisted the urge to pat Rebekah on the shoulder and say, "Don't you worry." It was only day two of her romance. Lady Bird had no intention of getting married. Her first thoughts were that the Johnson family was a bit strange, and she felt sorry for all of them.

By the time the visit was over, Lady Bird had a strong opinion of Mrs. Johnson. "I saw her as an absolutely lovely woman, who had given too much to her husband and family," recalled Lady Bird. She was staring at her future. That same statement would later be made many times by family and friends about Lady Bird herself.

Johnson was defensive about his family's circumstances. A few months later, in a letter to Lady Bird from Washington dated October 27, 1934, he alluded to how unhappy his parents' marriage had been because of his father's failure to make enough money. He did not want to repeat that pattern. "It is bad to fall in love with a girl who has had some comforts and advantages, but it is worse than bad to attempt to make her happy with a nominal salary after marriage," Johnson wrote. "Haven't learned that from marriage, but took a few lessons from a good teacher when I was only a youngster." He was describing his father's futile attempts to please his mother and his fear of repeating that failure.

To show Lady Bird the kind of life he envisioned for them, he left his parents' home in San Marcos and drove directly to Corpus Christi, where the next day he planned to give her a tour of the King Ranch. That night they had dinner with Ben Crider, an old friend from Johnson City, and since it was late, they checked into separate rooms in a hotel in the center of the city.

"I remember Lyndon was very respectful about just accompanying me to the door and saying good night," recalled Lady Bird. "However, when he lingered at the door to my room, I was very quick to shut the door."

That Lady Bird checked into a hotel with a man she had known for less than seventy-two hours is evidence of how thoroughly carried away she was with Johnson, and also of her own willingness to take a risk. The only friend who even knew she was with Johnson was Cecille Harrison, her roommate from the University of Texas, who was living in San Antonio with her mother at the time.

On the way to Corpus Christi, Lyndon and Lady Bird stopped by Cecille's house on the South Side of San Antonio, and Lyndon showed Cecille the upholstered leather in his car. "He seemed quite proud of that," recalled Cecille, who understood Lady Bird's attraction to Johnson. "There was something about Lyndon—his face was full of eagerness—he was impossible not to like."

The next day Lady Bird and Lyndon toured the King Ranch, where Dick Kleberg had an office. Kleberg's mother, Alice King Kleberg, the family matriarch, took Lyndon off to the side and told him, "Listen. Don't lose that girl. She's the best thing that could happen to you."

Lady Bird thought of Mrs. Kleberg as a duchess or queen and was a little afraid of her. Later she told her friends that the King Ranch was so large, ranch hands had to use compasses to find their way around. At the end of the visit, Mrs. Kleberg also gave her blessing to Lady Bird. "You should marry him," she told her, straight out.

As they drove away from the house, Lady Bird imagined what it would be like to be married to Lyndon Johnson. He soon filled in the details. Johnson thought of Kleberg's district as his own and told Lady Bird he thought it would be a good idea for her to start memorizing the names of all the counties and to acquaint herself with the problems in the area.

He then told her stories about constituents he knew, including one about a family that was fighting to make the loan payments on their farm. His own father had lost a farm, and Lady Bird could tell how frightened he was by the idea of anyone losing land. It was personal to him, not just political. To Johnson, a piece of land represented both security and identity. He explained how much he admired this particular family, all of whom were working from sunup to sunset to hold on to their land. The details of their life fascinated him.

One day he asked the farm wife how she woke up every morning at 6:00 since she went to bed every night long past midnight. She told him that she put her alarm clock under a dishpan so it would create a noisy clang in the morning. "He thought that woman was so clever," Lady Bird said. She, in turn, considered him clever for noticing the woman's resourcefulness.

On the way back from the King Ranch, Johnson told her that he had to go back to Washington. Again, he pressed her to marry him, but she told him it was ludicrous to make such a big decision after so short a time. Still, she invited him to stop in Karnack on the way and meet her father.

In San Antonio, they picked up Malcolm Baldwell, a secretary to Congressman Maury Maverick. The plan was for Johnson and Baldwell to drive back to Washington to go to work and make a detour in Karnack along the way.

After spending a single night under Taylor's roof, Lyndon was more certain than ever that Lady Bird was the perfect choice for a wife. He and Malcolm Baldwell were served a traditional Southern dinner, with plenty of biscuits, in Taylor's dining room. Johnson held forth with stories about his life in Washington.

After dinner, Lyndon and Baldwell went upstairs to bed and Taylor took his daughter aside and told her, "Hmmm, you've been bringing home a lot of boys. This one looks like a man."

Over the years, Lady Bird has repeated her father's line about Johnson to many reporters and biographers, without acknowledging the implied criticism of her. In her father's mind, the "boys" she had attracted before were nice but not manly enough. He thought of Johnson as a catch, and seemed a little surprised that his daughter had managed to catch Johnson's eye.

Taylor may have also been trying to get Lady Bird out of the way. By then, Taylor, sixty years old, had a new girlfriend, Ruth Scoggins, who was two years younger than Lady Bird. Three years later, on February 7, 1937, Scoggins became Taylor's third wife.

Soon it would be Ruth, not Lady Bird, who would supervise the remodeling of the Brick House, and not to Lady Bird's liking. Ruth would cover her mother's square-pegged floor with hardwood floors and replace the wooden banisters on the upstairs balcony with wrought iron. There was less reason than ever for Lady Bird to stay on in Karnack.

Besides, Johnson was determined not to lose Lady Bird. The following morning, Malcolm Baldwell wandered downstairs in his pajamas and told the cook what he wanted for breakfast. When Baldwell returned to the second-floor bedroom, Johnson chastised him for running around the house in his pajamas.

"I'm going to marry this girl. You're going to ruin my marriage if you run around that way," Johnson told Baldwell.

As an unofficial engagement present, Lyndon gave her a book called *Nazism: An Assault on Civilization*, which was a little-known collection of essays about the threat of Nazism written by German journalists. In it, he inscribed the following message: "To Bird, in the hope within these pages, she may realize some little entertainment and find reiterated here some of the principles in which she believes and which she has been taught to revere and respect." He signed it: "LBJ."

Already she thought of him as a Henry Higgins, instructing her on everything from farm foreclosures to foreign relations. She read the book immediately and wanted to give him one in return that would broaden his views.

She chose a classic, Voltaire's *Candide,* a novel about a voracious young traveler not unlike Lyndon Johnson who witnesses a series of catastrophes that challenge all his optimism. "To my knowledge," said Lady Bird, "he never read the novel." To Johnson, the world of books and ideas belonged exclusively to women. Voltaire had no value to him.

After he returned to Washington, he kept up the courtship by mail and over long-distance telephone lines. The tone of some of Johnson's letters are persistent, even angry, because Lady Bird believed they should wait a while, maybe even a year, before getting married. Any lapse in time between letters infuriated him.

On September 18, 1934, less than two weeks after kissing her good-bye on the steps of the Brick House, Johnson began his love letter by criticizing Lady Bird for not writing soon enough.

"My dear," began Johnson, "when it isn't indifference or independence that delays my mail, inefficiency presents itself and my disappointment is assured. For three days, I've watched and waited for your second letter. From your telephone conversation, I felt positive my letter would be at the office this morning when I came to work. It wasn't. The House post office in answer to my inquiry said the delivery was unavoidably delayed and now that it is almost time for lunch, I get my semi-weekly note. *Honey, don't be so long between notes.*" He underlined the last line for emphasis. Already he was issuing demands.

He then went on to paint a detailed picture of his life in Washington, much of which revolved around newly elected Congressman Maury Maverick, who took office in January 1935 and served two terms as one of the most liberal of the New Deal congressmen. Maverick was a rotund, quixotic man whose grandfather, Samuel Maverick, was a Yale graduate who came to Texas in 1835 as a founder of the Republic of Texas. The term "maverick" originated with Samuel Maverick's nonconformist practice of refusing to brand his cattle. His grandson Maury broadened its meaning to include dissent of all kinds when he went to Congress and formed a group of thirty-five young congressmen called the Mavericks who met weekly to advance liberal causes.

Johnson regarded Maverick as a mentor. He filled his love letters to Lady Bird with news of him. Wrote Lyndon, "Maury Maverick and Malcolm Baldwell have been with me all week and every day has been a busy day for me. We have visited dozens of departments to bring relief and satisfaction to some admiring, or to say the least believing, constituents."

Later in the letter, he wrote: "A night or two after he arrived in Washington, Maury insisted that we accompany him to hear the Negro preacher Elder Michaux. This was my first time to be in a Negro church, but there I learned the effectiveness of psychology. I heard some of the best singing to be heard anywhere. All of the Negroes [were] laughing, shouting and happy. Why can't we have more enjoyment and happiness?"

For the second time in the same letter he complained about her "aloofness, independence and indifference." He considered her aloof because she wouldn't marry him immediately, but pressed them to wait.

"Every interesting place I see, I make a mental reservation and tell myself that I should take you there when you are mine," he wrote. "I want to go through the museum, the Congressional library, the Smithsonian, the Civil War battlefields and all of these most interesting places. One week we must go over to New York together. Then we must visit Maryland and Virginia together. Why must we wait 12 long months to begin to do the things we want to do together forever and ever?"

From her place in the Brick House, the thought of traveling to such places must have seemed exciting, but Lady Bird's response was subdued. Her letter, written the night of October 1, was all about touring the countryside with Dorris Powell, her neighbor and good friend, but her descriptions of nature seem melancholy. Here is what she told him:

This morning, after breakfast I went down to Dorris' and we hied forth in search of cape jasmine bushes and a little magnolia and jonquil bulbs, me thinking I could find them somewhere, and in the florists' sketch they are quite numerous and expensive. We walked through the woods to the old Haggerty place—site of an old colonial mansion, now quite dilapidated and doleful looking.

It always gives me a very poignant feeling to go over there. It must have been a lovely place. There are the tallest magnolias I've ever seen, and great live oaks and myriads of crepe myrtle, and a carpet of jonquils and flags in the spring. But some of the trees have rotted and fallen down and there is a clutter of underbrush and only the bottom logs—an outline—of the house remains . . . there are some half dozen or more fine marble tombstones in disarray in the old family graveyard. Folks tell that old Spencer Haggerty buried gold in the vaults of the graves and I think they have been dug up and disturbed for that reason. . . .

It's getting quite cold. We [had] a fire tonight. It makes it cozy, but I mourn the passing of summer. I'm never completely happy from October until March.

While the bulk of the letter sounded like a nature and weather report, she ended on a more personal note. "In all sincerity, Lyndon, I believe I miss you more all the time," she scrawled and signed it, "Goodnight my dearest dear, I love you, Bird."

Five days later, however, Lady Bird wrote again, and this time it was she who felt rebuffed.

"No letter today!" she complained. "I wonder why you didn't write. I had no idea how peculiarly empty a day would be without a letter from you." She told him about taking some of the Black children—"Isabel and Nig"—who lived near the Brick House to a fair in Marshall. "They were as tickled over it as I'd be over seeing Broadway!" Lady Bird told him. While they went to the fair, Lady Bird went to see a movie based on Somerset Maugham's novel *Of Human Bondage.*

The movie reminded her of another favorite of hers, *The World Moves On,* and she told Johnson she felt sure he would like this particular movie. "The love-making is in the most flawless good taste I've ever seen on the screen," she told him. "It makes me feel very set up about the human race to watch them."

Set up for what? The display of passion on the screen seemed to confuse her, perhaps because she held her own passion on a tight leash. At any rate, she immediately turned to a safer topic: books. Johnson had sent her some books he wanted her to read, and she thanked him for them. "They are library books aren't they? Is the limit two weeks. I shall hurry!" she wrote.

Then she explained that she had been reading the novel *Early Autumn* and described herself as "enthralled." Wrote Lady Bird, "If we were together I'd read it to you. . . . There's nothing I like better than being comfortable in a nice cozy place and reading something amusing or well-written or interesting to someone I like. All good things are better shared, aren't they?"

Encouraged by her warmer tone, Johnson wrote on October 24 in a large, black scrawl that leaped off the page, "This morning I'm ambitious, proud, energetic and very madly in love with you. I want to see people. I want to walk through the throngs, want to do things with a drive. If I had a box I would almost make a speech this minute. Plans, ideas, hopes, I'm bubbling over with them."

A month before, he had enrolled in the Georgetown University law school and was attending classes at night. In the same letter, he complained to Lady Bird about his frustrations over law school, telling her that he worked such long hours, he didn't have time to prepare for class. A few sentences later, he came close to apologizing for bothering her. "You are apparently always so free from concern that when I feel as I do this morning, I think how cruel it was to even let you know how despondent I felt last week," he told her.

At the end of the letter, he asked, "How much a young man in law school can hope?" He then pleaded, "Tell me you love me if you want to and if you don't, I'll believe you do anyway and keep on loving you every minute."

Lady Bird painted a vivid picture of what life was like—how lonely and frightened she felt in Karnack—in a letter to him on September 17, 1934. She told him that the Delco that provided electricity to the Brick House had gone "pfft"—her made-up word for broken—and so, "I'm sitting here by a kerosene lamp and a candle. And feeling like one of the last outposts of civilization. When I come up the stairs the lamp makes the queerest shadows in the corners and I am very scared! . . . (I wish for you more than ever then)."

Later in the same letter, she told Johnson that she had discovered two of her mother's old stone flower pots on the property, "muchly covered with dirt and accumulation of years of debris." She scrubbed them clean and told him that she planned to use them to plant lavender hyacinths and red tulips. By this time, her mother had been dead twenty-two years, but Lady Bird soothed herself by recovering her flower pots and planting something new in them.

She also gave Johnson news of the favorable impression that he had made on her father, Boss Taylor, news that must have been a relief to LBJ. "Daddy expressed himself about you the other night and was I surprised—I mean because he is so seldom enthusiastic about any of the young men I bring around. And he thinks very highly of you! I surely was glad," Lady Bird wrote.

In response, Lady Bird received a letter on September 25 from Johnson that indicated that his mother had written to him with a generally favorable reaction to Lady Bird, but he hinted that his loyalty had passed from his mother to Lady Bird. "Destroy Mother's letter and write if you want to," he instructed Lady Bird. "All my love—lyndon."

Despite his pleas, she was still not sure it was wise to marry in such a hurry. Tormented by indecision, Lady Bird drove to Montgomery, Alabama, where Effie was hospitalized, to ask her for advice. Effie, who remembered her sister Minnie's hasty elopement and all the unhappiness that followed, begged Lady Bird to proceed with caution.

"If he really loves you as much as he says he does," Effie told her, "he'll wait for you." Lady Bird looked at her frail aunt, lying in a hospital bed, and realized that if she married Lyndon Johnson, she would hurt Effie, and she didn't want to do that. At the same time, she didn't want to end up where she had—an old maid, without a husband or children, and ill. "It was a fearsome thing to go against her," she recalled, "just like stepping on a cape jasmine or something."

On the same trip, she visited Ellen Cooper Taylor, the first wife of one of her father's brothers, and took a photograph of Johnson with her. "Aunt Ellen," she told her, "here is the picture of a man I met not long ago in Austin. He says he is in love with me, but I don't know whether I am in love with him or not." She told her all about his job and his family in Texas. Ellen then asked directly if Lady Bird loved him.

"I don't know, but I have never felt this before," Lady Bird replied.

"That's it," Ellen told her.

The fear of being an old maid was real to her, and it coincided with Johnson's fear that he would not be able to accumulate wealth and power fast enough to satisfy his own insatiable demands. Every day, over long-distance telephone lines, he talked to her about various jobs.

For a while, he thought of trying to become president of a small college of ten thousand students, Texas College of Arts and Industries, in Kingsville, and had the support of his boss, Dick Kleberg, who had influence in the college, which was located near his ranch headquarters. However, Johnson only had a bachelor of arts and wasn't really qualified for the job, and it didn't pay as much as he thought he needed, so he didn't pursue it.

On October 22, Lady Bird wrote him another letter, alluding to the college job in Kingsville. By this time, she had reversed herself, and seemed anxious to marry. "And so," she wrote on that Monday night, "something has happened which precludes all possibility of our marriage for four or five years? I believe it is something which will involve a much lower salary for a number of years and then chances of much greater advancement. Whatever will be better for you, Lyndon, I am for!"

A sentence or two later, she voiced her fears that he would meet someone else. "Of course there is the problem that in the meantime one of us may meet someone he or she likes better. I think, Lyndon, if we do, it will probably be you . . . you are the only person I've ever considered marrying. Besides, you are in a position to meet attractive and intelligent and charming young women. And I am rather on cold storage."

Her image of unmarried life was stark, and by then she was afraid of being trapped in Karnack. It was a fear real enough to provoke her to take a risk.

"Lyndon, please tell me as soon as you can what the deal is . . . I am afraid it's politics. Oh, I know I haven't any business—not any proprietary interest—but I would hate for you to go into politics. Don't let me get things any more muddled for you than they are though, dearest," she wrote, closing. "I still love you, Lyndon, I want to say it over and over, goodnight, not goodbye, Bird."

By now, she was willing to go to almost any lengths not to lose someone she thought she loved. All marriages are based to some degree on the fear of being alone and the illusion of romantic love. On this fall day in 1934, Lady Bird confronted two fears—that of being unmarried and her equal fear that Johnson's "deal" might be politics—and decided that even a life in politics was better than a life alone.

Four days later, he wrote back a clever letter, needling her on their different approaches to problems, differences that would persist throughout their lives. "I see something I know I want. I immediately exert efforts to get it. I do or I don't, but I try and do my best," said Johnson, adding, "You see something you might want. You tear it to pieces in an effort to determine if you should want it. Then you wonder why you want it, and conclude that maybe the desire isn't an 'everlasting' one and that the 'sane' thing to do is to wait a year or so, and then if you still want it, to decide at that time whether or not you should make an effort to get it."

He recognized his own impulsive nature and seemed to understand that her cautious nature could be valuable to him. At the end of the letter, he continued to tease her.

As to whether she should continue to write him so often, Johnson told her he "lived from one day to another" for her letters. "I realize," he wrote, "such a course would only be followed after due reflection and careful analysis upon the part of the sweetest, most deliberate little girl in all the world."

It was a grand seduction. Three weeks later, on November 16, Lyndon showed up at the Brick House unannounced. Lady Bird arrived back home from her trip to Alabama on that day and found him waiting for her in the front parlor. He told her that he had quit law school and come back to Texas to marry her. "We either do it now, or we never will," he told her.

On her way upstairs to her bedroom to pack her bag, she realized she had to marry him or run the risk of losing him. Twenty-four hours later, she was a married woman. Her ten-week affair was ended. She was the prize, and Johnson had won her. Almost instantly, he seemed to lose interest.

❧

CHAPTER SEVEN

A Life Behind Walls

The morning after their wedding, Lady Bird and Lyndon drove to Corpus Christi and boarded a train for Monterrey, Mexico. The decision to go there for a honeymoon was mutual, but it was perfectly suited to Lady Bird's taste. The heavy fragrance of red hibiscus blossoms, the broad-leafed banana trees, the impromptu serenades, not to mention the favorable exchange rate, making every purchase seem like a fantastic bargain, all combined to make Monterrey a natural place for Lady Bird's transition from life on her own to Johnson's strange new world.

They stayed the first night at the Grand Ancira Hotel, the largest hotel in Monterrey, where Lyndon scratched their names in his loping scrawl—Mr. and Mrs. Lyndon B. Johnson—into the hotel registry. The next morning they took a train to San Luis Potosí and stayed the night in a hotel room that had a small stucco fireplace built in a corner. As a Southerner, Lady Bird had seen plenty of fireplaces in bedrooms, including the ones at the Brick House, but never the small oven-style fireplaces called *hornos* that are built into corners of some Mexican homes. "I was charmed," she said. This is what made Lady Bird content—exploring foreign places, focusing on details of ordinary life.

The following day, they boarded another train to Mexico City. From the train, Lady Bird's eye was continually drawn to hundreds of shrines to the Virgin Mary that had been built along the winding roadways. As a Protestant, she was unfamiliar with the role that the Virgin Mary occupies as the embodiment of the ever-present merciful mother to

Roman Catholics. "Those places by the side of the road seemed strange to me," she recalled. "I don't know why, but the sight of little girls laying paper flowers at the shrines is one of the strongest memories I have of my honeymoon."

She tried to engage Johnson in conversation about the shrines, but he wasn't particularly interested in Mexico. Mentally, he was back in Washington. He spent most of their honeymoon talking about his work. "I heard a lot of big talk about how he wanted to be the best, hardest-working congressional secretary in Washington," she recalled. He missed his friends and the round-the-clock action on the Hill.

"I was a born sightseer," sighed Lady Bird, "but Lyndon was a born people-seer. He indulged me on that trip, but the truth is he wasn't much intrigued."

As she talked about their opposite natures, Lady Bird seemed almost preternaturally composed. Yet to meet her blank gaze was to see the fragility behind the pose. She couldn't acknowledge that it must have hurt to spend her honeymoon with a man who, in her words, was "not intrigued." Her inability to reflect on a small moment of feeling ignored is an indication of how quickly and thoroughly she identified with Johnson. As one of the long-term members of her staff put it, "Whenever she remembers something she doesn't like about him, the psychic wall just drops down, as if from out of the sky. Nothing can penetrate that wall."

In Mexico City, the newlyweds climbed the pyramids and visited the floating garden of Xochimilco, where vegetables and plants have been growing in an olive-colored watery pool since the time of the Aztecs. The only photograph of the trip is a posed shot taken on a gondola in those gardens. They are standing in front of a small arch of flowers in the hull of the boat. Lyndon, dressed formally in a double-breasted suit as though he were about to head off for work, has his arm draped over Lady Bird, who is wearing a dark dress and holding a nosegay of white flowers.

Although she is physically located in a natural setting—the middle of a garden—the expression on her face is completely unnatural. Her shoulders are hunched up between her ears, her smile strained. She doesn't look much like a blushing bride, but a startled one. As a child, Claudia was usually photographed hanging from a tree or jumping off a dock at Caddo Lake. Then she looked like what she was, a carefree tomboy. In college, the camera caught her with a wide grin, seated in an

open field of flowers, a hopeful ingenue. On her honeymoon, the camera captured her in Johnson's maw, holding on to some small aspect of
nature. The bouquet is a visual annunciation, proof of the change in
her identify. On a small wooden boat in the center of a foreign land,
Claudia Taylor, child of nature, was already well on her way to becoming Lady Bird Johnson, political wife.

They left Mexico City by train and picked up Johnson's car in Laredo
and then drove immediately to San Antonio, where Lady Bird made
hasty arrangements to visit a gynecologist. In the rush to get married,
there had been no time for a routine exam.

In Mexico, Lady Bird found herself confronted with an aggressive
husband with a priapic past and a need to brag about it. One of his college roommates, Willard (Bill) Deason, described him as being as hard-
driving and single-minded with women as he was with everything else.
"If he concentrated on a girl, he would concentrate pretty hard, but
then he would switch after a while," said Deason. Another longtime
aide described Johnson as a "sexual gorilla." Faced with the physical
realities of life with such a man, it's easy to understand why Lady Bird
felt stunned and sought out a doctor.

Nothing about marriage to Johnson was as Lady Bird expected. She
had thought that once they settled in Washington, they would go to
plays and concerts together and visit Mount Vernon and other tourist
sites, as Johnson had promised in his letters during the grand courtship.

Instead, when they returned to Washington, they spent about a
month in the basement of the Dodge Hotel where Lyndon had lived
out of a brown suitcase as a bachelor and where he continued to sur-
round himself with the other congressional secretaries on the Hill.

"Right away I learned how to live in the middle of a full working
house," Lady Bird recalled. Throughout their life, Johnson worked
round-the-clock. He explained that he expected her to function as the
chief-of-staff at home, no matter how meager or grand, providing Johnson and the members of his staff with whatever they needed—food,
supplies, time away from the telephone, personal items—in order to
work.

From the beginning, she had to snatch moments of privacy—time
and space to go to the bathroom, wash her face, or change her
clothes—whenever she could find them. Johnson had grown up in a
house in which everyone lived in everyone else's space. At various

times while growing up, he shared the same bed with his mother, his father, and all four of his siblings. He was a man who could not bear to be alone, even when he went to the bathroom.

He expected his wife to live as he lived. It was his habit to work from bed. Even as a congressional aide, Johnson rose early in the morning and conducted meetings there, while Lady Bird hid beneath the covers.

In January, she convinced him to move from the hotel into a modest one-bedroom furnished apartment at 1910 Kalorama Road. There, Lady Bird, who had never swept a floor or cooked a meal, set about trying to learn how to be a housewife. She, who had been waited on all her life by maids, now filled her days and nights waiting on Johnson.

He expected to be served coffee in bed every morning, along with the morning newspaper. He also expected her to pay the bills, to take care of his clothes, and to have meals ready at all hours of the day and night, in case he or any member of his staff showed up hungry. When asked if she resented doing any of these chores, Lady Bird said, "Heavens no. I was delighted to do it. I adored him."

She discovered that one domestic chore that gave her real satisfaction was handling the family money. Having grown up watching her father hovering over ledgers and cash registers, Lady Bird knew how to stretch a dollar, and the Johnsons needed every extra penny. Every month, Johnson kept $100 of his $267 paycheck and gave the rest to Lady Bird to pay all the bills. She started the habit of buying a U.S. savings bond—as her mother had with her own money from Alabama—every month at a cost of $18.75.

Then there were the payments she made to members of Johnson's family. She sent home money regularly to his mother, Rebekah, and also wrote checks to pay for Johnson's younger brother, Sam Houston, to go to law school. From time to time, she also wrote checks for Lyndon's three other siblings: Rebekah, two years younger than Johnson; Josefa, four years younger; and the baby, Lucia, eight years younger. Born frugal, Lady Bird resented the constant drain on her resources, and so, she said, did Johnson. "He spoke of himself as being a donkey—of trying to bear the burdens of anybody in the family that needed help," Lady Bird said. "I think the other children resented the fact Lyndon was his mother's favorite and was making something of himself."

Johnson's mother also placed demands on Lady Bird. Rebekah told Lady Bird that she had modeled herself after the biblical character of

Ruth, a martyr to her husband's family. Rebekah let Lady Bird know that she expected her daughter-in-law to live by Ruth's credo: "Thy people will be my people."

Two weeks into their marriage, Lady Bird and Lyndon received the following letter from Rebekah, which outlined how she viewed their common future:

My precious children,

Thinking of you, loving you, dreaming of a radiant future for you, I somehow find it difficult to express the depth and tenderness of my feelings. Often I have felt the utter futility of words, never more than now when I would wish my boy and his bride the highest and truest happiness together.

My dear Bird, I earnestly hope that you will love me as I do you. Lyndon has always held a very special place in my heart. Will you not share that place with him, dear child? It would make me very happy to have you for my very own, to have you turn to me in love and confidence, to let me mother you as I do my precious boy.

I hope, and hope as you know is composed of desire and expectation, that Lyndon will prove to be as true, as loyal, as loving and as faithful a husband as he has been a son.

My dear boy, I have always desired the best in life for you. Now that you have the love and companionship of the one and only girl I am sure you will go far. You are fortunate in finding and winning the girl you love and I am sure your love for each other will be an incentive to you to do all the great things of which you are capable. Sweet son, I am loving you and counting on you as never before.

My dearest love to you both,
Mamma.

Viewed at face value, the letter, written by a woman from the rural South, is a heartfelt expression of love and good wishes to her son and his new wife. She wrote in the vernacular of her time. Rebekah wanted her son to escape his family's circumstances and wanted to make sure her new daughter-in-law became an ally, not a foe.

Yet even the casual observer can see where Johnson got his drive, his ambition, his insatiable need for conquest. In a few paragraphs, his mother had revealed how she had confused maternal love with domination. At the time the letter was written, she had only met Lady Bird once, and yet she professed to love her. Her offer to "mother her" sounds more like a conquest than a consolation. In the last line of the letter, she revealed the depth of her unmet ambition. Of her son, she wrote that she was "counting on him as never before," depending on him to do "great things."

The message in the letter to Lady Bird is also mixed: in return for regarding Rebekah as a surrogate mother, Rebekah is willing to share in her son's glory. To Rebekah, Lady Bird is a prop in the large drama of her son's life, an instrument to propel her son to greatness. She sees her not as a person but merely as an "incentive" for Johnson to continue his rise—the same kind of aggressive incentive she had been in his life. Unconsciously, Rebekah was setting her son up to rebel. He might do her bidding, ascend as high as she could imagine, even to the presidency, but the pressure to succeed was constant and corrosive. In time, he would express his anger and frustration not at his mother but at his wife, a constant, loyal presence.

Lady Bird was extremely wise in handling her mother-in-law. She treated Rebekah as an ally but also kept her at a careful distance. "I felt it was important to maintain my independence," Lady Bird said.

She did accept Rebekah's challenge to be Lyndon's trophy and partner, to help him make his ascent. In order to do that, she had to align her priorities to his on issues large and small and to regard his family as part of the baggage she had assumed with marriage.

Lady Bird was particularly resentful of Sam Houston, an alcoholic, who often wound up sleeping on the roll-away bed in the living room of their apartment. Occasionally, both her brother-in-law and her own Aunt Effie would stay at the apartment at the same time. Effie exacerbated the situation by fixing Sam Houston highballs with the bottle of Scotch that she kept stashed in her closet. "I would get angry," acknowledged Lady Bird. "Alcoholism was not understood as a disease at the time. I thought with enough willpower that Sam Houston could change. He did not change."

One night Johnson himself came home drunk after playing a round of golf at a Washington country club. He arrived in the middle of a rainstorm and entered the apartment with his clothes and shoes soaked. He left puddles wherever he stepped and went straight to Sam Houston's bed, shook him by the shoulders until he was wide awake, splashing both his brother and the bed with water.

Lady Bird woke up to the sound of Lyndon yelling at his brother. "I want Sam Houston to look at me," he told her. "Yes, by God, I want you to take a damned good look at me, Sam Houston. Open your eyes and look at me. I'm drunk, and I want you to see how you look to me, Sam Houston, when you come home drunk."

"Okay, Lyndon," said Sam Houston, as he turned his back and hovered beneath the covers, frightened. But Lyndon kept up the tirade. It was Lady Bird who finally came to Sam Houston's defense. She physically pulled Johnson out of the room and tucked him into his own bed, assuming in that instant the only role that would allow her to survive her marriage: that of both wife and mother to Lyndon Johnson.

There were other rocky early moments. For instance, one day they decided to go horseback riding. Lyndon helped Lady Bird mount her horse, handed her the reins, and then slapped the horse—hard—on its hind flank. The horse lurched forward and was off in a full gallop, with Lady Bird struggling to stay on. After she managed to rein in the horse, she returned to the stable, jumped off, and ran up to her husband. "Damn you!" she shouted. "Don't ever do that to me again. I could have been killed."

The scene ended in a standoff. He did not apologize. Instead, he pushed her to be a more daring rider, but Lady Bird had drawn a line about behavior she would and would not accept, and he knew it. His reaction was to pretend to be amused, to pass it off as a prank. "He thought a lot of things were funny that I did not," Lady Bird said.

In public, Johnson often treated her as if she were invisible. Sometimes he would tell negative stories about her—about how she kept house or how she pinched pennies or mimicked her Southern drawl—in front of her in a group. "I thought if we went to a party, Lyndon would be with me the whole evening. He wasn't. At first I was incensed. I was left alone with a bunch of strangers," she recalled. Instead of showing her anger, Lady Bird realized that either she would have to work hard to win over Johnson's friends, to become part of the circle, or she would have to reconcile herself to staying on the fringe.

Early friends in Washington remembered how difficult it was for her to overcome her insecurities. Not long after she arrived in Washington, Lady Bird saw Dale and Virginia Miller outside of Kleberg's office. Dale had been at the University of Texas at the same time as Mrs. Johnson and was then working as a lobbyist for the Dallas Chamber of Commerce. He and his wife, Virginia, whose nickname was Scooter, helped organize the Texas State Society in Washington, an enormous network of Texans that eventually became the Johnsons' primary social outlet. "You probably don't remember me, but I'm Mrs. Lyndon Johnson," she told Dale Miller that first day in Washington, who in fact did not remember her.

It was just one awkward social moment among many, but it was typical of her struggle. As Scooter Miller put it, Lady Bird was married "to a man on his way, a man who physically dominated every room he entered." Lady Bird, a born introvert, was the opposite, easily overlooked.

Arthur E. "Tex" Goldschmidt, who worked in the Department of Interior under Harry Hopkins and helped Johnson build a series of public dams in the Texas Hill Country, recalled that Lady Bird was so successful at staying in the background he did not realize that Johnson had a wife until four years after they were married. In a letter he wrote from Texas to his wife, Elizabeth, at their house in Georgetown on August 2, 1938, Goldschmidt said, "Lyndon and his wife (I never knew there was one before—but there she was all the time) took me to a curb service place for a late meal after a day that started about 6:30 A.M."

In Mamie Kleberg, the wife of Johnson's boss, Congressman Dick Kleberg, Lady Bird found an example of the terrible fate that could befall a congressman's wife who stayed at home in Texas and refused to make a life for herself in Washington. According to Mamie's nephew B. K. Johnson, who is no relation to Lyndon, Mamie Kleberg was an "overbearing woman who had the idea that being the wife of a congressman was like being the wife of a prince consulate." She wanted to stay at the King Ranch, fly into Washington, be treated like royalty, and then fly back home to Texas when she grew tired or bored.

Meanwhile, her husband, the congressman, viewed himself as estranged from his wife and therefore felt free to spend time with other women. Mrs. Kleberg would call Lyndon Johnson to find out information about her husband's mistresses. Johnson even found himself in the position of parceling out money to Kleberg's wife, who came to blame Johnson for her husband's behavior. "It was an impossible situation," recalled Lady Bird, who tried but failed to soothe Mamie Kleberg's feelings. "Aunt Mamie may have been one of the few people in the world who didn't like Lady Bird Johnson," said her nephew B. K. Johnson. "It wasn't fair, but she took out her anger at Uncle Dick on both Lyndon and Lady Bird."

Looking for advice and a role model, Lady Bird turned to a more successful congressional wife, Terrell Maverick, a gregarious, cheerful woman. Not long after she arrived in Washington, Lyndon took Lady Bird to Maverick's congressional office, which was located near Kleberg's office on the ground floor of the Old House Office Building, and they found Terrell hard at work collecting press clippings about her husband, Maury, in a scrapbook.

Mrs. Maverick was a thin, wiry woman who trilled her voice and carried herself like an aristocrat, even though she was also from the woods of East Texas. Terrell immediately invited Lady Bird to the House members dining room and gave her some motherly advice. She told her to get involved in the issues of the day and to find a way to make her life in Washington fun. The alternative was to wind up like the Klebergs, who eventually divorced. "It was another one of those Washington situations that happen," said Mrs. Maverick of the Klebergs' problems. Terrell Maverick told Lady Bird that life in official Washington was so demanding that husbands and wives easily go their separate ways. Her advice was to get as involved in Lyndon's career as she could, as quickly as possible.

Lady Bird listened to Mrs. Maverick and resolved to follow her lead and involve herself in every aspect of her husband's political life. The first people she invited to dinner in her apartment at Number 401 on Kalorama Road were Maury and Terrell Maverick. She served baked ham, rice that Mrs. Maverick later said tasted like library paste, and lemon pie for dessert. The reason the rice was ruined was that she had prepared it ahead of time.

In fact, the whole menu was organized around the idea of having everything ready before the guests arrived so that she could stay in the living room and listen to Johnson talk to the Mavericks about what was going on in Congress. "I didn't want to be separated from the good talk too much," she recalled. Already she was following Terrell Maverick's advice by trying to be in two places—the kitchen and the living room—at once.

During the day, she worked hard to take care of the chores at home as quickly as possible so that she could explore Washington on her own, often with a camera. She still thought of herself as an explorer and wanted to document the places and events around her in photographs. Neither housework nor shopping held any interest at all for her.

As soon as she could afford it, she hired a maid to scrub the floors and do the major housework. Johnson's clothes posed a special challenge to her. Tall and skinny, Johnson had an extra-long torso. Lady Bird bought size-17 shirts and then had the tails extended in order to stay tucked inside his pants. Eventually she also had to have his ties lengthened so they would hit his belt in the right spot. These and a thousand other details preoccupied her in the early days of the marriage. As winter turned to spring and then summer, Lady Bird found herself standing in an apartment without air-conditioning, struggling over a hot iron to press shirts that seemed as big as tents. She resorted to a trick that she'd heard other Washington wives used in the summer of 1935: she stood in front of the open door of the refrigerator while ironing.

She continued to be ambivalent about her own wardrobe. Her lack of interest in clothes was one of the few concrete expressions of her desire for some degree of independence from Johnson, who pushed her to look a certain way—even to the point of humiliation. He wanted her to look respectable but sexy. He liked bold colors—red, blue, green, and black—and straight skirts, not flaired or pleated. If she walked into a room and she wasn't wearing lipstick, he would bark, "Put your lipstick on. You don't sell for what you're worth." If he thought her hair was too long or too short, he would order her to have it cut or let it grow. If some other woman was wearing a dress he liked, Johnson would point to her and ask, "Why can't you look like that?" It was just his bellicose way of talking—the kind of stereotypical, macho speech he had grown up with in Texas—and Lady Bird didn't take offense.

In fact, she even regarded Lyndon's admonitions on clothes as backhanded compliments. "He thought I was good-looking and he wanted others to see me that way," she explained. She viewed it as an indication that he was interested in her. Said Lady Bird: "I had the idea that people were supposed to love me because I had an interesting mind, a kind heart, and a warm smile. I thought that Lyndon's emphasis on clothes and appearance was the wrong system of values. He used to say that a lot of the people that I met would only see me once, and that the opinion they would form would persist. He wanted them to have a good opinion of me. By the world's rules, he was right. I was wrong."

Even as an old woman, her strongest need was for Johnson to have been right at all costs. She regretted that she had once felt a long time ago the natural desire of a young woman to be loved for who she was, not for how she presented herself, and that clothes had been such a sticking point in their marriage. The feelings she voiced were not her own; they belonged to Lyndon Johnson. This is the emotional wall that Lady Bird stands behind. By constantly adapting her feelings to those of her husband, Lady Bird does not have to experience her own. There are big payoffs for making this shift—she does not have to feel sad, lonely, shabby, humiliated, or abandoned because she sees the world through LBJ's perspective, not her own. Emotionally, she is bulletproof. By adjusting herself to him, Lady Bird can feel as powerful and ambitious as Lyndon Johnson.

The ability to take "psychic leave" or to just "emotionally vanish"— as her friends have called it—was one she had learned as a child. Johnson was merely the trigger. He constantly stirred up memories of how she had felt as a five-year-old when her dying mother looked at her from her hospital bed and wept because her soon-to-be-orphaned daughter had a dirty face and there was no one to take care of her. When she grew up, she married a man whose treatment reminded her of her mother's dying wish that the face she showed to the outside world not only be clean but also pretty, with a cheerful mouth and a fresh coat of lipstick.

By all accounts, the wall went up early in the marriage. "Bird was a sweet-looking, dark-haired, dark-eyed girl who seemed to adore her husband and let him have the floor," remembered Alabamian Virginia Durr, whose husband, Clifford Durr, came north to join Roosevelt's New Deal as one of three heads of the Federal Communications Commission. Cliff Durr later went back home to Alabama and became famous as the lawyer who represented Rosa Parks, the Black woman who helped usher in the civil rights movement by refusing to give up her seat in the front of a public bus to a white person. Parks's protest instigated a Black boycott of public buses that propelled Dr. Martin Luther King, Jr., to prominence.

The Durrs were frequent guests at the Johnsons' apartment on Kalorama Road. Virginia recalled how Johnson would hold forth with such passion about his ideas as to how to abolish poverty. And what of Lady Bird? "She just looked at him with worshipping eyes and let him hold the floor, and he did hold the floor and he held it very well," Durr said.

When Lady Bird remembers those days, a genuine softness falls over her. To hear her talk about Johnson is to understand how happy she was just to be in the same room with him, to listen to him talk long into the night with friends, to simply breathe the same air.

One evening in the late 1930s, they went to the movie version of John Steinbeck's novel *The Grapes of Wrath*. In the darkness of the theater, Lady Bird heard Johnson sniffling. Moments later she heard loud sobs. The story of the Joad family reminded him of his own family's poverty. Lady Bird was astonished that he was able to express such strong emotion over a movie. She grabbed his hand and squeezed it, both proud of him and puzzled. "He had a tender, sentimental side that he didn't show very often," she recalled.

She also remembers her long waits for him to come home. Night after night, she would stand by her kitchen window in their first Washington apartment, watching for the headlights of his car as he pulled in behind the apartment. "He would run through the door and grab me into his arms," Lady Bird recalled. "It was the highlight of my day."

All through the summer of 1935, the Johnsons, like the rest of America, worried about job security. Lyndon's relationship with Kleberg continued to sour. Mamie, playing the behind-the-scenes role of Lady Macbeth, continued to poison her husband against Johnson, telling him that Lyndon was so ambitious that if he didn't get rid of him he might one day run against him. Ultimately, Kleberg, anxious for peace at home, suggested Johnson find another job. Both Lyndon and Lady Bird were devastated.

In June 1935, President Roosevelt provided Johnson—and thousands of other unemployed young people—with a way out of their dilemma when he signed an executive order to create the National Youth Administration (NYA). Johnson immediately sought out Congressman Maverick, who had close ties to Roosevelt, and asked for his help in getting a job as NYA director of Texas. Maverick was worried that Johnson was too young, but told him he would help him anyway.

One day in early August, Johnson walked through the back door of the apartment and asked Lady Bird, "How would you like to live in Austin?"

At twenty-six, he had been named the youngest NYA director in the country at a salary of $7,500. Lady Bird recalled her feelings that night. She was so happy to be going home to Austin, she said, that Johnson might just as well have asked, "How would you like to go to heaven?"

Back in Austin, the Johnsons soon moved into a large two-story house in the 2800 block of San Gabriel Street that was owned by Bob Montgomery, who had taught Johnson math in high school. An economist by trade, Montgomery and his wife, Gladys, had moved to Washington to work for the Department of Agriculture. They rented their house to Johnson and two of his NYA aides, Luther Jones and Bill Deason, old college friends of Johnson's. Johnson wanted his NYA staff available to him at the office and at home, which had two bedrooms, two bathrooms, and a front porch large enough to accommodate everyone.

In addition to Deason and Jones, Effie lived with them on and off in the house as well. Johnson resented the demands that Effie placed on Lady Bird and didn't have much in common with her dreamy ways. By then, however, Lady Bird was Effie's primary caretaker. As Deason put it, "Effie thought she was taking care of Lady Bird and Lady Bird very graciously let her think that."

Montgomery knew Johnson well and recognized his ability to motivate others to achieve his own goals. As a high school student, Johnson had complimented him on what a good teacher he was, but then took him aside and said, "You could be so much better if you'd do just one thing." Naturally, Montgomery wanted to know what he could do to improve his teaching method. Johnson wasted no time telling him. "You just come in there and fire away!" he complained. "You ought to organize that course so we will know exactly where we are going next."

Now, as the new administrator for the NYA, it was Johnson who was preoccupied with problems of organization. He felt great pressure to do a good job, presenting his dilemma to Lady Bird in grandiose terms. He felt that thousands of young Texans were either going to eat or starve, depending on how he personally performed as director of the NYA.

One night Montgomery and his wife were at the house with the Johnsons. Lyndon asked all of them for help. "I need two things from you two," Johnson told them. "One thing I need is a plan of organization to salvage what we can of the younger generation of Texas." In addition to the plan, he asked for a list of tangible jobs unskilled workers could do.

Montgomery felt the desperation as well. He told Lyndon about how one of his closest friends, a well-to-do banker with a wife and two children, had lost his last dollar, his home, and even his car trying to salvage his bank for stockholders and depositors. He went in search of a job but couldn't find one and was ultimately forced to sell everything he had—his furniture, his wife's engagement and wedding rings—and still wound up on a bread line.

"How do we put these people to work?" Johnson demanded, this time turning to Lady Bird and Mrs. Montgomery, who responded by telling him of an accident that she had recently witnessed late one night on a two-lane Texas highway. A family from Mexico had parked a Model T Ford on the edge of the road. The father, mother, and several children were asleep on the ground behind the car. Two other cars, one traveling north and the other south, collided in front of the parked Model T, killing the entire family. Mrs. Montgomery, still haunted by the incident, suggested NYA workers might build small roadside parks along the highways of Texas, where people could pull over and have a safe place to change a flat tire or sleep for a few hours.

Lady Bird seized upon the idea, and encouraged Johnson to pursue it. Six months later, Johnson had put fifteen thousand unskilled young people to work constructing roadside parks, building public buildings, planting grass, laying bricks, and painting murals. His NYA experience influenced the way in which Johnson would later approach public policy issues, especially the war on poverty in the 1960s.

However, it influenced Lady Bird as well. The roadside parks were not only useful to those who traveled the highways, they were beautiful. Road crews cleared trees and shrubs from the sides of the highways and built adjoining parks, constructing picnic tables and large rest room facilities from native stone. It was Lady Bird's first opportunity to see how public resources could be used to improve the physical environment and formed the initial seeds of the beautification effort that later defined her role as First Lady.

According to Lady Bird, the year and a half that Johnson spent as director of the NYA was among the happiest and most productive times of her husband's career. Johnson was a brash young liberal, thoroughly identified with Roosevelt, and the NYA was "right down his alley," as Mrs. Johnson put it. With Johnson and the NYA, she said, "Man had found job."

But the pace that Johnson kept as NYA director placed a strain on the marriage. He was traveling across the state constantly and wanted Bird—as he called her—to go everywhere with him. He became frantic at the idea of traveling by himself. However, once they reached their destination, he would become so absorbed in his work that he wouldn't spend time with her. Lady Bird would feel at loose ends.

Usually she went with him, which eased his tension. On April 6, 1936, he wrote to Welly Hopkins, a former member of the Texas senate who was now working as a lawyer for the Justice Department in Washington. Hopkins and his wife, Alice, were two of the Johnsons' closest friends. Lady Bird had known Alice briefly at the University of Texas. In the letter, Johnson described the kind of life he and Bird were leading on the road:

> Bird left with me last week, and we visited El Paso, Lubbock, Amarillo, Abilene and Brownwood. We really had a very enjoyable trip. Spent two or three days in El Paso and several evenings across in Juarez. You, of course, know my thoughts turned to you and Alice when I crossed the bridge, and we could not enjoy our trip across the border as much as we should have because you all were not with us. For the last month things have slowed down considerably. Bird has been making all of the trips with me, and we are really enjoying ourselves much better.

There were other, far more overt strains on the marriage, tensions that Lady Bird could not alleviate. Around this period of time, Johnson began an affair with Alice Glass, whom Lady Bird had known briefly at the University of Texas and who was a cousin of Alice Hopkins. Born in the central Texas farming community of Marlin, Alice was almost six feet tall with honey-blond hair and blue eyes. Her long affair with Johnson has been written about by Robert Caro in *The Path to Power*, and also in a memoir published in 1993 by former Texas governor John Connally, Johnson's closest political adviser.

Like most affairs, the one between Alice Glass and Lyndon Johnson was a web of intrigue, fraught with peril. Glass was the mistress and later wife of Charles Marsh, the wealthy publisher of the *Austin American-Statesman* and one of Johnson's primary patrons. It had the potential to imperil Johnson's marriage and his political career, a risk that he seemed compelled to take. Like other Presidents before him and after, Johnson was a man who, even from a young age, was pulled in two different directions at once. Part of him wanted great power for the glory of helping others on a mass scale. Another part of him wanted power so that he could satisfy rawer instincts, including his desire for random, unlimited sex and the thrill of dominating others.

The affair with Alice Glass illustrates how power and sex were joined in Johnson's mind. The pursuit of the former seemed to justify his pleasure in the latter and vice versa. Connally first learned about the affair in 1937, not long after he had gone to work as Johnson's secretary. One particular weekend, Johnson told Connally he was going away and would be at the St. Regis Hotel in New York but left instructions not to tell anyone how to reach him. Connally agreed and followed Johnson's orders, until a call came into the office from Marsh, who insisted he had to speak to Johnson right away. Connally believed that his boss would not want to miss such an important call and gave Marsh his number at the St. Regis. Marsh placed the call, and fortunately Johnson answered the telephone in the hotel room, not Alice, Marsh's mistress.

Later that day, Johnson reached Connally by telephone. He was furious. "Do you have a brain in your head?" Johnson roared. "The next time I tell you not to let anyone know where I am, I mean exactly that." Connally and other key staff members were expected to indulge Johnson's vices.

Lady Bird indulged him in more subtle ways. On occasion, she was forced to deal with Alice Glass and Lyndon together. These meetings occurred after Alice had married Charles Marsh and moved to Longlea, an eight-hundred-acre horse farm set in the Blue Ridge Mountains in Virginia. From Lady Bird's point of view, it was difficult not to be intimidated by Alice. She was gregarious and openly seductive, the very embodiment of all that Bird had repressed in herself. "Alice had a great presence," said Frank Oltorf, a lobbyist for Brown & Root Construction Co. who knew both the Johnsons and Alice. "When she walked in a room, everyone looked at her. She was tall, slim, good-looking, and extremely smart. She had a voice that was both sexy and soothing." Oltorf believed that in Alice, Lyndon Johnson had found his match: a woman as smart and seductive as he was.

Though Lady Bird never voiced her feelings about the affair, those who were close to the situation are convinced she knew. "Everything about Longlea—Alice, the fine surroundings, the smart talk—all of it made Lady Bird feel real green," said one of her oldest friends. She was envious of Alice's knowledge of art and history, her good looks, her way with horses, her ability to attract bright people to her dinner table and then orchestrate the conversation. Connally believed she handled the affair by keeping quiet and hoping it would pass.

This is the standard male take on how Lady Bird handled Johnson's indiscretions, one that Lady Bird herself has perpetuated. Her reply when confronted with questions about Alice Glass has been not to reply at all and to take refuge behind her emotional wall. "I never saw that side of him," she has said repeatedly.

However, her actions—as opposed to her words—during the time that the affair was in progress indicate that Lady Bird was neither unaware nor passive about her situation. After all, her whole mission in life—to be a good wife—was under threat. In response, she did what women have done throughout the ages. First, she retreated. Her visits to Longlea became more infrequent, as she withdrew into a stubborn silence that seemed to those around her incomprehensible.

Next, she seemed to blame herself—at least in part—for her husband's infidelity. After the initial withdrawal, Lady Bird embarked on a frenzied self-improvement campaign, using Alice as an unconscious model for what she needed to become. She lost weight, getting down to about 115 pounds, a weight she maintained throughout Johnson's presidency. She started wearing the sexier clothes Johnson liked. She checked book after book—including *War and Peace*—out of the library, steeping herself in history and in the classics. She applied makeup and wore jewelry, as Alice did. She learned to drink champagne.

And she also played a card Alice could not play: she tried to become pregnant. Silently and swiftly, using every means at her disposal—her mind, her body, and her money—she fought for her marriage.

In February 1937, as the Glass affair lingered on, U.S. Representative James P. Buchanan, who had represented the Tenth Texas District for twenty-four years, which included Johnson's hometown, died of a heart attack at seventy. Johnson wanted badly to run but underestimated his chances. Blanco, the county seat of Johnson City, was the smallest of ten counties in the district, the majority of the votes coming from Austin. Then there was his age—he was only twenty-nine.

He used both of the women in his life—Alice and Lady Bird—to shorten his odds. Alice helped him by making sure her husband, Charles, raised money for his campaign and gave him the editorial backing of the largest and most influential paper in the district.

Lady Bird carved out an equally important role for herself. At this critical moment in Johnson's career, she placed herself in the center of his crucible. As she put it, "I pitched in." Her first act was to go see an even more crucial figure than Marsh in Johnson's life—former state senator Alvin Wirtz, an Austin lawyer and resident political wise man.

"I liked Senator Wirtz, and he liked me," recalled Lady Bird. She telephoned him and asked for his opinion on what Johnson's chances were for winning Buchanan's seat and what she could do to help. Wirtz came over to her house in Austin and the two went for a half-mile walk through the neighborhood. "He told me that Lyndon was a long shot because he was the least known of any of the people who were going to run, but that he thought Lyndon had a chance."

Then Lady Bird asked Wirtz outright what the race would cost. "About $10,000," Wirtz told her. Lady Bird assured Wirtz that she would find the money.

On a Sunday night after the walk, Lady Bird telephoned her father in Karnack. Johnson secretly listened on another extension as the telephone rang in the Brick House and Taylor came on the line. She knew how her father felt about politics: he hated the whole business. Nonetheless, she did not hesitate to ask him, the tightwad who had lectured her all her life about the careful use of money, for $10,000 so that her husband could run for Congress.

Taylor hesitated, and Lady Bird put it to him in terms she knew he could not refuse. For years, Taylor had been holding her portion of her mother's estate and she asked that he take $10,000 of her inheritance and deposit it in a bank in Austin. Lyndon kept quiet and allowed his wife to make the financial deal that would help send him to Congress, even as his mistress lobbied on his behalf from the bed of the publisher of the largest newspaper in Austin.

Taylor still balked, suggesting that $10,000 was too much. "What about $5,000 or $3,000," he asked his daughter. But Lady Bird stood her ground with her father. "It must be $10,000," she said flatly.

"Well, daughter, today's Sunday," she remembered Taylor telling her. "I don't think I could do it until in the morning, around nine o'clock."

Lady Bird told him that 9:00 A.M. would be soon enough.

With the money in the bank, Johnson became the first of eight candidates to announce in the special election. Wirtz orchestrated the campaign, in which Johnson supported Roosevelt's every move, including his controversial proposal to enlarge the Supreme Court to fifteen members to give the President a majority support. The campaign lasted only forty-two days. Johnson moved across the Tenth District like a man possessed. He limited his speeches to only five minutes so that he could shake more hands, and he went through half a dozen Arrow shirts in a day, all supplied by Lady Bird. "Lyndon was never so young, never so vigorous, and never so wonderful," Lady Bird recalled. She criticized herself for being too timid to get out and campaign with him, and pushed herself to work harder behind the scenes.

Two days before the election, Lyndon collapsed while giving a speech. He had appendicitis and was taken to an Austin hospital for emergency surgery. Lady Bird went to his side, but on election day she spent the day at his campaign headquarters, making telephone calls to ask people to get out to vote. She received letters from friends back in Washington, including one from Tex Goldschmidt. "I heard it straight that when Lyndon was opened up some time ago they found a couple of telephones inside. I hope the disease was not contagious and you fared better," Goldschmidt wrote.

The partnership worked. Johnson won the first race, with twice as many votes as the nearest contender, and Lady Bird won big as well. For better or worse, she had established herself in public and private as a political wife, an asset to her husband's future that he would find impossible to disregard.

After the election, Johnson dropped Lady Bird off in Karnack to rest. He went on to Washington, where he was sworn into Congress on May 13, 1937, and resumed his weekend visits to Longlea. In his congressional office, Johnson had a telephone in a bottom drawer of his desk that he left orders no one was to answer but himself. "When that telephone rang, you knew it was the Horse Lady calling," said O. J. Weber, then a young aide to Johnson. Weber and the other aides called Glass the Horse Lady.

Their relationship was common knowledge. Sometimes Lady Bird, Lyndon, and Alice would wind up attending the same cocktail party, and when that happened, Lady Bird would hold up her head and become extremely exaggerated in her graciousness, as if her good manners could make up for his bad behavior. "Everybody knew about the relationship with Alice," said one family member, "and everybody felt so sorry for Lady Bird."

Lady Bird did not want pity. What she wanted was to win the private war. In the end, the way Lady Bird triumphed over Alice Glass was to bide her time. Connally and Oltorf believed that during the height of the affair, Alice thought Johnson would one day leave politics and Lady Bird and marry her. If this is true, Alice not only misjudged Johnson but she underestimated Lady Bird's staying power.

In the early spring and summer of 1941, Johnson ran for the U.S. Senate in a special election to fill the vacated seat of Senator Morris Sheppard, who died on April 9. This time Johnson did not need Lady Bird's money. The Brown brothers—George and Herman—whose Houston-based construction company had attracted millions of dollars in government contracts since Johnson went to Congress, quickly contributed nearly $300,000, most of it hidden. Two hundred thousand dollars more came from other businessmen, including Charles Marsh.

Johnson's opponent in the Democratic primary was the sitting governor, Willie Lee "Pappy" O'Daniel, the wealthy owner of the Hillbilly Flour Company and leader of a country and western band that appeared weekly on a statewide radio show. Each week the announcer of the show introduced O'Daniel with the phrase, "Please pass the biscuits, Pappy."

O'Daniel was well known and popular. His style of politics was similar to his style of music—evangelical and sentimental. In 1940, he was elected governor with 54 percent of the vote. In May 1941, Johnson's own polls showed that O'Daniel was the odds-on favorite in the Senate race, even though the governor had yet to announce. An early poll showed 33 percent favored O'Daniel, compared to 9 percent for Johnson.

Johnson and Connally built an organization around young men of their generation, primarily men that Johnson had been in college with: Bill Deason, Sherman Birdwell, and Jesse Kellam, plus bright young lawyers that Connally knew, including Jake Pickle, Bob Strauss, John Peace, and others. These men viewed it as a contest between old and new Texas. O'Daniel had the backing of former governor Pa Ferguson, who had been the populist of his day but was discredited when he was impeached in

1917, as well as his own lieutenant governor, Coke Stevenson, who would run against Johnson for the U.S. Senate seven years later.

Lady Bird took home movies during the campaign and worked hard to soothe Johnson's shaken confidence. His early campaign appearances were disappointing. Johnson tried to appear "senatorial—statesmanlike and dignified"—but he fell flat. On May 10, he entered the Scott and White Clinic, a medical facility in Temple, sixty miles from Austin, for what Connally described as "pneumonia," but what Lady Bird thought was depression caused by fear of losing the election. "He was depressed and it was bad," she said. He stayed in the hospital nine days, threatening to drop out of the race, but Lady Bird, Connally, Charles Marsh, and others refused to let him quit.

This was the first of many dark, depressive bouts in Johnson's life that Lady Bird learned to manage. She learned that the best antidote to Johnson's depression was to appeal to his ambitious side and get him back to work. In the end, it was a poll, taken on May 19, that helped lift Johnson's spirits. The poll showed that Johnson's support had gone from 9 percent to 17.6 percent. Lady Bird used the poll as a carrot to get Johnson out of the hospital and back into the race. "He did get out," she said defiantly.

Johnson's depression was a precursor to the outcome of the election. Early results on June 28 showed that Johnson led O'Daniel by 5,150 votes out of 600,000 cast, but O'Daniel demanded a recount. At the time, there were few voting machines in rural Texas. It took time to hand-count the ballots, and there was plenty of room for tampering with the results, especially in East and South Texas. During the course of the next five days, the election hung in the balance as both sides maneuvered behind the scenes to sway the election in their favor. Each charged that the other side had stolen the election. In the final count, however, Johnson lost by 1,311 votes.

When he went back to Washington to resume his congressional duties, Lady Bird recalled that he was trying to look "very jolly and putting extra verve into walking, with his head up and just stepping along real spryly." But he was devastated and found it disheartening to go back to his House seat. He felt rejected and angry. He ranted and raved at his staff for letting O'Daniel steal the election out from under him. After each tantrum, Lady Bird went to each staff member and tried to smooth hurt feelings. Johnson could not be soothed. Not even a good-natured telephone call from President Roosevelt cheered him up.

Lady Bird then tried a firmer approach. She told him that he still had his House seat and lectured him that a "steady diet of success isn't good for anyone." He'd been in Washington for ten years, and won almost every victory. There would be other Senate races, Lady Bird assured him.

Her reaction was to work harder than ever to make up for his loss. When constituents came by Johnson's office, Lady Bird was often there and gave tours of the Capitol, Mount Vernon, and the White House. In the course of them, she talked to the people in Johnson's district—often the wives of the mayors of small towns, schoolteachers, and garden club members—about what was happening back home. She took Texas grade school children to the Smithsonian to see the plane in which Lindbergh had flown across the Atlantic and brought high school students to the National Gallery of Art. During every tour, she kept notes and lists of things to do for constituents, and later reported her conversations to Johnson. Slowly, Washington began to feel like home.

She also worked hard at learning the rules of social protocol. Like other congressional wives, every year Lady Bird purchased the *Green Book* written by Carolyn Hagner Shaw, an updated social guide to official Washington. "In those days, the wives of congressmen made official calls on other wives," recalled Lady Bird. "I had my calling cards printed up and every day I got dressed up in hats, gloves, and a nice dress and went out to make my calls. It was like a business."

She followed the rules to the letter and made the best of what was a constrained and constricted social life. On Mondays, she called on the wives of the Supreme Court justices. On Tuesdays, she went to visit other congressional wives. Wednesdays were reserved for cabinet wives, Thursdays for the Senate wives, and Fridays for the Diplomatic Corps. She went to the White House whenever invited. "I made the calls between 4:00 P.M. and 6:00 P.M., and usually I hoped the ladies weren't in, so I wouldn't have to stay. Most of them weren't, thank heaven," Lady Bird said. She left her card for the wife and Johnson's card for the husband.

Margaret Mayer, then a young reporter for the *Austin American-Statesman*, recalled how deftly Lady Bird navigated her way through the rigid social labyrinth. "One afternoon I was at her house for dinner and she had several important wives over. It was a mixed group: cabinet wives, Supreme Court justices' wives, and a few wives of congressmen, too. I served the tea and apparently I was supposed to serve the wives of the Supreme Court before anyone else. I didn't know the rules, and so I mistakenly offered the first cup of tea to a lowly congressional wife. Lady Bird walked over to me, took the tea away from me, and took it over to the most senior wife in the room, and asked her, 'Do you take sugar or lemon?' She knew exactly what to do."

In the summer of 1941, Johnson was anxious for the United States to enter the war in order to come to the aid of Britain. He received a letter from Charles Marsh advising him that if war was declared, he should immediately resign his House seat and go to war.

After the Japanese attacked Pearl Harbor on December 7, Johnson did as Marsh advised. He joined the Navy and was given the rank of lieutenant commander. Roosevelt assigned him to Secretary of Navy James Forrestal, and Johnson insisted that John Connally, his congressional aide, also be assigned to Forrestal. Lady Bird and Nellie, John's wife, were taken to the train station in Washington by Speaker of the House Sam Rayburn to see their husbands off to war.

At the time, the most senior member of the office staff was O. J. Weber, a twenty-one-year-old lawyer from Beaumont. Mary Rather, a secretary, was the only accomplished typist on staff. Before Johnson left on the train, he and Connally talked to Weber about who should be put in charge of the office in their absence. At first it was assumed that it would be Weber, but Johnson suggested that Lady Bird fill his place. "She carried the authority of his name," recalled Weber. "He thought it would look better to the people in the district if he put his wife in charge."

Lady Bird took over the office as Johnson's unpaid substitute. To save money, she moved into Nellie Connally's one-bedroom, one-bathroom apartment in Buckingham, Virginia. The rent was $60 a month. The year before, Nellie and Lady Bird had briefly taken a shorthand course in a nearby business school together. "I didn't want to learn shorthand because I didn't want to get stuck with secretarial duties, but Lady Bird worked hard and got real good at it," Nellie Connally recalled. Nellie had worked in Johnson's office before and didn't like it. "One day I didn't get a telephone number fast enough for Mr. Johnson, and he threw a book at me," said Nellie. "I was a little afraid of him after that."

In January 1942, Lady Bird took over the office. She learned to type her own letters to constituents, and she helped organize a petition drive in the summer of 1942, signed by 22,564 voters in the Tenth District, to have her husband reelected to Congress even though he was serving in the Navy. "The fact that Mrs. Johnson is carrying on the duties of the congressman's office was noted in the petition," the *Austin American-Statesman* reported that summer.

The following letter, written on March 2, 1942, to Ernest Pearcy, a constituent from the tiny town of Bastrop, was typical of hundreds that Lady Bird wrote while she was running her husband's office:

Dear Mr. Pearcy,

While Lyndon is in the Navy, and I am working here in the office, I want to do my best to carry out the program of operation he maintained when he was here in the office every day. I know, for I have often heard him say, how much he valued your opinion and how he counted on you for suggestions, so I am hoping you will drop me a note from time to time and tell me what I can do to serve the people during his absence.

Since Bastrop has become a boom town, I want you to keep me informed on all the problems arising and I'll certainly do my best to be of assistance. Also, I want to write little notes of condolences and congratulations to our friends. Of course, we will watch the papers we get up here, but I will appreciate your writing me these things, particularly if they do not appear in print.

With many, many thanks, I am,
Mrs. Lyndon B. Johnson

In the evening, Lady Bird and Nellie often invited staff members and constituents to their apartment for dinner. Neither were very good cooks, and so they confined themselves to two entrées: steak and fried chicken. "If it was chicken, I left early to start dinner," said Nellie. "If it was steak, we left together."

Both women were worried about their husbands' safety and waited anxiously for cables and letters. In May 1942, Lady Bird wrote a good-natured letter to her college friend Emily Crow, in which she tried to make light of the situation. "When I think of Lyndon's being captured by the Japs, I think of O. Henry's 'Ransom of Red Chief,'" she wrote, as if to suggest Johnson would cause so much trouble to the Japanese that they would soon be paying the United States to take him back.

Johnson's only close call came on June 9, 1942. He went on a bombing raid of the Japanese base at Lae, which was located on the northern side of New Guinea. At the time, the Japanese were winning the war in the Pacific. They planned to use Lae to get control of the southern side of New Guinea and then proceed against all of Australia. Johnson, dressed in his blue and white naval officer's uniform, flew in one of the twelve B-26 Marauders that attacked the Japanese base that day. During the course of the air battle, seven Japanese bombers pursued Johnson's plane. One U.S. plane, the *Wabash Cannonball,* was hit and plunged into the ocean. The plane that carried Johnson, the *Heckling Hare,* was fired on for about ten to fifteen minutes by the Japanese, took some hits in the wings and fuselage, but landed safely. For his time in combat, Johnson was awarded the Silver Star by General Douglas MacArthur, who was headquartered in Melbourne.

Afterward, he left on an inspection tour of various bases on the islands of the Pacific, and from May through July he kept a diary of that trip. The diary reveals not only how Johnson categorized the war, but also how he felt about the women in his life. For instance, after arriving in Palmyra, he had a fever, headache, and night sweats. The following evening he wrote, "As soon as we arrived went to see Dr. Mobley from Little Rock, Ark. Nice visit. Sprayed throat, nose, gave me ice water . . . Got pills tried to rest. Enima [sic] at 8: sleep at 9: up at 5:30 . . . Wrote Bird and left letter for Dr. Crain . . . only one woman on island, wife 60 years old of consular office. Only intercourse—social."

In the course of a single entry, he notes the time he had an enema, having written dutifully to his wife, and his despair over the fact that the only woman on the island was sixty years old, which precluded any other kind of intercourse other than social. Elsewhere in the diary, he refers many times to an unidentified woman that he calls "Miss Jesus." As he flew from base to base, he wrote, "Thought of Miss Jesus all day," and later, "Thought of Miss Jesus plenty."

The next day he left Sydney and described the countryside as a lot like the land around Johnson City. "Hills and draws. Had tea and fair lunch. Thought of Miss Jesus much. Muddy cow pasture field with green grass and a dozen B17s and 24s." Still later he wrote, "Had sent cables to Miss Jesus. Hope and pray for an answer." On Sunday, June 21, he was sick with the flu in Sydney and wrote: "Mother's birthday. Chills all night. Chest and hand hurt. Want coffee. Am constipated. Feel terrible." The diary reflects the tumult of Johnson's personality. He was ill, far away from home, a man totally at the mercy of his own needs, and completely incapable of offering himself any kind of relief.

Oltorf, who was Alice Glass's friend, believes that Johnson must have been referring to Alice when he wrote of "Miss Jesus," although Oltorf acknowledges it could have been a reference to someone else that Johnson might have casually picked up. While Johnson was at war, the affair continued. On June 1, 1942, Alice sent him a cable, urging him to run for the U.S. Senate in the regular election, which Johnson did not do. It said: "Charles believes you should file for Senate. Polls show you leading. No one else shares his opinion enthusiastically. If possible, telephone. Love, Alice Marsh."

Though the affair subsided after the war, Johnson and Glass continued to communicate with each other for the rest of their lives. Alice and Marsh divorced in the 1940s. She continued to live in Longlea but fell on hard times financially. When Diana MacArthur, Lady Bird's niece, visited her there in the 1950s, she said that Alice looked "a little frayed around the edges, as if she'd taken a beating."

She became a lost soul. In 1964, during a taped conversation in the White House, Johnson referred to a letter that she had written him and told an aide to write a "nice letter" back to her. "She's an old friend," said Johnson. "She's Charlie Marsh's ex-wife. She's alone—and an alcoholic."

Eventually she moved from Longlea and wrote in a letter to Johnson in 1971 that she didn't feel at home anywhere. "I just travel as much as I can. I have been to Greece, Turkey, Ethiopia, Ireland—name it—I have been there."

After Marsh, she married three other men, including Robert Lester, a soldier in the Korean War whom she told Oltorf she married because she was bored; Dagel Skolofski, a musician; and in 1959, she wed Colonel Richard J. Kirkpatrick, who died in 1974.

When Johnson was President, Alice, who had stayed a liberal, told mutual friends that she opposed his policies in Vietnam, but she never stopped pursuing him. On at least one occasion when he was majority leader, he drove to Longlea with a mutual friend for lunch. During the

1960s, she lobbied for ambassadorial appointments for a few of her acquaintances, and after he left the presidency, she encouraged him to speak out against then President Nixon. "You have no right to sit on the sidelines. You must get out, and you must speak," she wrote. Then she told him to think of himself as Winston Churchill did after the war. "He kept England together with pure courage during the war; the electorate threw him out in the next election. He did not desert his country because of his defeat."

Johnson wrote back on May 17, 1971, telling her, "I'm not as young as you think I am. Like you, Churchill is one of my heroes. It's true he didn't desert his country, but, I have not done that either." He signed the letter, "love, lbj."

On May 26, 1971, she sent Johnson an antique brass eagle mounted on a glass base, about nine inches high with a four-and-three-quarter-inch wingspan. The eagle had reportedly been made for Thomas Jefferson as a gift from the French when Jefferson was ambassador to France. Alice had owned it for thirty years and wanted Johnson to have it in his post-presidential years. On the card, she wrote of the eagle: "For Lyndon, From Alice. Feed him properly." She warned him not to use his initials but to sign his name. "I never did call you LBJ; it's too late to start now," she said.

In a response two days later, Johnson wrote, "The elegant eagle on the beautiful crystal has arrived and it is all you said and more. I am prouder than you will ever know that you wanted me to have it, after its long and illustrious history which, of course, includes its thirty years with you. And I will cherish it as I do your faith and friendship. Thank you so very much and do come to see us." He signed it "affectionately," but then closed the letter with his initials, as if trying to distance himself from her.

After Johnson died, Alice wrote a letter to Lady Bird and asked her to return the eagle. Mrs. Johnson responded in a letter dated October 16, 1973, in which she explained how the eagle was used at the LBJ Library. "Lyndon kept it on his desk at first and then we placed it in a glass and bronze cabinet in the corner of our living room," Lady Bird wrote, taking claim of her husband's former lover's possession.

Elsewhere in the letter she wrote, "I know how much you must treasure the eagle, because it has given us such pleasure." This is consistent with the pattern of how aides say Mrs. Johnson dealt with the other women in Johnson's life. Johnson tried to win over his political enemies by going overboard to be nice to them. Lady Bird adopted the same approach with her most intimate enemies: she wooed them, bringing them into her tent.

"I would love to have you come by the ranch and/or Austin and visit," she told Alice, but then ended the letter in an icy way that left no doubt that she really was not welcome. "Let me know ahead of time as I do travel a lot." She did not even bother signing her initials. The closing of the letter reads "Lady Bird (dictated, but not signed)."

Alice fired one last salvo. She let a member of Mrs. Johnson's staff know that the eagle had been a personal gift to Johnson, not Mrs. Johnson. She wanted it back. On November 16, 1973, Mrs. Johnson dictated another letter, telling Alice, "It will be on its way to you shortly," and sent it back.

Three years later, at the age of sixty-five, Alice died in Marlin, Texas, where she had moved to be near her sister and her close friend Frank Oltorf, who had been Brown & Root's lobbyist in Washington during her glory years. She left the eagle to Oltorf.

Mrs. Johnson maintained a lifetime of official silence about Alice Glass, although she told friends that she never really believed the rumors about Alice and Lyndon. "She was too plump for him," she told one friend. Still, Lady Bird never forgot that eagle and the betrayal that it represented.

Some years later, Oltorf was invited to the LBJ Ranch for a small dinner party. After dinner, Lady Bird pulled him aside. She had a question for him that she wanted to ask in private.

"How did Alice spend her last days?" Mrs. Johnson asked. Oltorf replied that Alice had died peacefully. "Good," said Lady Bird. "That's good."

"Tell me," she added, as an afterthought. "Whatever happened to that brass eagle of hers?"

Oltorf looked at her and smiled. "Don't worry, Mrs. Johnson," he told her. "The eagle landed safely on a tall bookshelf in my living room."

CHAPTER EIGHT

❧

Getting Rich

"I had a degree in journalism and planned to practice it," Lady Bird said of her decision on December 31, 1942, to buy KTBC, a small radio station in Austin. Her decision to go into business was driven as much by LBJ's agenda as her own. Johnson, then a thirty-four-year-old congressman, wanted to buy a business because his political career was under threat from charges that he had used his office to enrich his friends and family.

In September of that year, the Internal Revenue Service had begun a formal investigation into allegations that George and Herman Brown, owners of Brown & Root Construction, had funneled several hundred thousand dollars of contributions, disguised as "business expenses" and "employee bonuses," into Johnson's 1941 Senate race. Brown & Root had received millions in government contracts, including one to build a naval station at Corpus Christi, while Johnson was a member of the House Naval Affairs Committee. Johnson thought the investigation might ruin him and did all in his power to stop it.

Five months after it began, Johnson went to see President Roosevelt and the two talked privately. Shortly thereafter, the IRS settled the matter by ordering Brown & Root to pay $372,000 in back taxes.

The settlement did not ease either LBJ's or Lady Bird's mind about their future in politics. Johnson also faced similar criticism involving Lady Bird's father. Taylor had started a construction company when Johnson went to Congress and had earned several hundred thousand dollars building rural electrification systems—a legislative priority for Johnson.

Taylor's fortunes had increased dramatically as a result of his son-in-law's influence in other ways. In 1941, Taylor sold 7,804 acres of land near his store in Karnack to the federal government for a reported $70,000. There the government built a plant, Longhorn Ordnance, which produced explosives and ammunition from World War II through the Vietnam War. However, Cameron McElroy said in his oral history that Taylor received much more than that amount. McElroy said Taylor got "top dollar—about $22 an acre" for his land.

Against this backdrop of scandal and uncertainty, LBJ and Lady Bird searched for a path to their own financial stability. In their effort to build a fortune, the question was, Did Lyndon drive Lady Bird or was Lady Bird driving him? Nellie Connally, who watched the process first-hand, said that it was not so much that Lady Bird was loyal to Johnson in business or politics but that "they both wanted the same things and had the same goals." In other words, their ambition was mutual.

Throughout the 1940s and early 1950s, Lady Bird moved on three major fronts to bolster and sustain her marriage: she bought the radio station, she bought three houses, and she successfully waged what had become a battle to have children.

By 1942, Lady Bird had been pregnant three times—each time she suffered a miscarriage. As she endured the painful cycles of pregnancy, turmoil, and miscarriage, her maternal instinct grew stronger. "I felt a peculiar sense of failure, of not being a complete woman," she said of her inability to have children. "After each miscarriage, I felt the loss of a little being . . . of the potential for new life. It was a big psychological put-down as a woman."

Despite her melancholy, she understood that the way to cope was not to sit at home waiting for Johnson. If she was going to survive, she needed to carve out a secure life for herself within his larger world. Johnson returned to Washington on July 10, 1942 and resumed control of his office. The eight months Lady Bird had spent running LBJ's congressional office had given her practical skills. She'd learned how to type, how to manage an office, how to solve high-level problems, and how to manage large sums of money. She decided to put those skills to use to build her own business. As Lady Bird put it, "I learned while Lyndon was away in the Navy that I could make my own living without him. That increased my self-worth and gave me the courage to try to start a business of my own."

The story of the making of the Johnsons' fortune has often been cast as an example of LBJ's abilities as a wheeler-dealer, evidence of his ability to manipulate others for his own advancement in business as well as politics. While it is true that Johnson used his political connections to buy the KTBC radio station and to extract a series of favorable rulings from the Federal Communications Commission, Lady Bird's own role was equally important.

He had the influence, but she had the cash. Throughout their marriage, Lady Bird invested her time and money in helping to create a grand persona for LBJ. She helped build his reputation as a great man, a Texas rancher, a wealthy businessman, as well as a member of Congress—someone worthy of the whole nation's leadership. It was a vision that she could share as his wife. Socially, Lady Bird may have been bound to LBJ, but financially, it was he who was bound to her.

From 1937 to 1942, Lady Bird used $41,000 in inheritance from her mother's estate, paid in several installments, to lay the foundation for their family business, over which she presided as president and later chairman of the board. In time, she became a multimillionaire in her own right—the only First Lady in history to have built and retained a fortune with her own money.

Lady Bird viewed the business as an extension of the marriage. "We were a team," she said. "In a family-owned business, like ours, who cares most about your business? First, it's the husband and then it's the wife. At least that's the way it was with us."

Despite her drawl and her Southern ways, Lady Bird had little in common with most married women in Texas in the 1940s and 1950s. Rather than teaching her domestic skills, marriage had strengthened her capacity to be cool under political fire, as well as the ability to out-maneuver all kinds of competitors, both personal and in business. She viewed her marriage as a career as much as a relationship. "His life became my life. I respected it. I wanted to learn from it, excel in it," Lady Bird recalled. It was an odd frame in which to view marriage. Lady Bird described Johnson's life possessively as "hers" and emphasized she wanted to do well at his life—as if the relationship were an election she could win or lose.

While Johnson kept his eye on political prizes, Lady Bird focused on the accumulation of wealth. Privately he sometimes complained to aides that Lady Bird cared too much about money. "She has the first nickel she ever had tucked in her bra," he told his closest aides.

This characterization of Lady Bird as cold and tightfisted was one that Johnson shared with at least one of LBJ's detractors. In 1968, J. Evetts Haley, a Texas historian and rancher, suggested in his anti-Johnson tract, *A Texan Looks at Lyndon,* that Lady Bird had twin "obsessions"— money and politics—and argued that she was so shrewd that she might have been "the real mind behind the President." From Haley's perspective, Lady Bird was like Lady Macbeth, a schemer who manipulated her powerful husband as a way to acquire power for herself.

Another way to look at her role is that Lady Bird was a woman who throughout her life gravitated toward a long line of strong men, including her father, her husband, Sam Rayburn, John Connally, Alvin Wirtz, the Brown Brothers, and Adlai Stevenson. In business and politics, Lady Bird formed key alliances with strong men—alliances that gave her the means to compete in a male-dominated world.

Yet the image of her as a passive protégée is too narrow. Even in the initial stages of her business, Lady Bird had her own ideas. She suggested that she and Johnson buy a newspaper, not a radio station. "Newspapers were what I knew," she explained. "Radio was unfamiliar to me. I was a little afraid of it, more comfortable with the written word." She made inquiries about the newspaper in Jefferson, located not far from her hometown of Karnack, but soon realized the newspaper was so small "it would never satisfy our ambitions." Johnson then tried to buy the *Waco News-Tribune,* but a combination of factors killed the deal, including Lady Bird's unwillingness to pay the owner's asking price.

They soon set their sights on KTBC, a small radio station in Austin that had lost $7,500 in 1941 and had liabilities of roughly $19,000. KTBC had operational problems as well. It had a mere 250 watts of power and only broadcast during daytime hours. At night, it shared its frequency with Texas A&M, a college station that broadcast agricultural news and weather reports. "The little company was owned by three absentee owners," recalled Lady Bird. "It had a lot of debts. The management was inept. We had no network affiliation. The only thing of real value was the license."

The battle for the license was primarily a political one, a power play fought behind the scenes between New Dealers and anti–New Dealers. At the time the Johnsons negotiated for the station, KTBC was owned by a three-man group headed by Robert B. Anderson, a Roosevelt supporter who much later became secretary of the treasury. Anderson had offered the station to James West, who owned the *Austin Daily Tribune*, a conservative newspaper that was vocal in its opposition to Roosevelt.

When West attempted to exercise his option and get the Federal Communications Commission to increase KTBC's power, James Fly, the FCC's chairman, blocked his application. Fly, also a Texan, supported Roosevelt and did not want West to use KTBC as a political platform against FDR. When West died in 1942, his option passed to three people: his two sons, James and Wesley, and E. G. Kingsbery, another conservative Austin businessman.

His death created the opening the Johnsons needed to go after the station. Working behind the scenes, Herman and George Brown convinced the West brothers to sign over their options to Lady Bird. Over Christmas 1942, Johnson persuaded Kingsbery to do the same. Before anyone could change his mind, Lady Bird wrote out a check for $17,500 to the original three owners.

The application was submitted to the FCC. On it, Lady Bird listed her net worth as $64,322.50. Her namesake uncle, Claud Pattillo, had died the year before and had left her about $20,000. In addition to the cash, she also had about 3,800 acres in the heart of Alabama from Aunt Effie and her uncle Claud—land that earned money from tenant farmers as well as timber.

Like Johnson, Lady Bird was interested in the station as a political, as well as financial, vehicle. Clifford Durr, her friend from Alabama, was a member of the FCC at the time and recalled that Lady Bird went to see him to ask for his help with the application. During the conversation, she told him that she wanted to use the station to defend Homer Rainey, a New Dealer who was then president of the University of Texas, Lady Bird's alma mater. At the time, conservative UT regents were threatening to fire Rainey, and, according to Durr, Lady Bird was "hoping if they could get that station on its feet, they could give him a fair break."

To avoid charges of conflict of interest, Lyndon Johnson's name did not appear on the application to the FCC. Lady Bird was listed as the sole purchaser. She listed her qualifications as her experience running her husband's office and the management of her own inheritance. In a document on file with the FCC, Lady Bird was described as follows: "She is the wife of Lyndon B. Johnson, Congressman from Austin, Texas, and she has recently served approximately a year as the secretary for the congressman. She is widely and favorably acquainted with the business and civic interests of the Austin congressional district, and the area of the district is almost identical with the primary service area of KTBC."

On February 16, 1943, the FCC approved the sale in the first in a long series of favorable rulings that helped enrich the Johnsons. "Lyndon and I then talked about what to do next," Lady Bird recalled. "He told me I needed to get down there to Austin and learn all about the station—to familiarize myself with the staff, the market, and the accounts. I understood that we couldn't make a success of it and be running the station from Washington, so I went to work full-time."

For seven months, she commuted between Austin and Washington. During the week, she stayed with her mother-in-law in Austin and flew home to Washington for the weekends. As Lady Bird has often told the story over the years, the first thing she did was clean up the station—literally. "I got a bucket, a mop, and a pail and started to work on it," Lady Bird recalled.

This story and others were designed to depict Lady Bird as the "little woman at the radio station," part of the mythology that the Johnsons were creating that portrayed Lady Bird as a wife and homemaker who happened to have a lucky touch in business. The truth was that Lady Bird had rarely been without a maid in her life, and while she may have helped out with a few domestic chores around the station, her real contribution was financial and intellectual.

She knew how to read a balance sheet better than LBJ. Claud Pattillo and her father had both taught Lady Bird basic bookkeeping techniques. She started from the premise that, no matter what, she needed to keep her debt low—a lesson she imparted with authority to the nine employees who were working at the station when she bought it. Working with a female secretary, Lady Bird pored over the books and discovered the station was losing $600 a month. "The more I looked, the more I realized what a failure we were. There was nothing but red ink," Lady Bird said.

For instance, she found out that Kellogg Cereal Company, a firm to which she had a sentimental attachment from her days with Effie at the Battle Creek spa, had contracted for five advertisements per week but the station was running six and sometimes seven. The station had sent Kellogg invoices for the ads that ran, but the company had only paid for five, not six. Kellogg was listed as one of KTBC's bad debts, and Lady Bird kept her eye on every uncollected penny. "That kind of sloppiness was the routine," she recalled.

No one ever accused Lady Bird of being sloppy. Those who worked for her said she was extremely organized—"tough as nails" was the cliché used to describe her—and she had a reputation for being extraordinarily tight. The joke, according to one former employee, was that Lady Bird was so cheap that workers brought their own toilet paper and Kleenex from home to make sure they would have enough.

In those first few months, she put in long days at the station. The evenings at Rebekah's house were lonely and tense. Although the two women shared what Lady Bird called "excellent meals and pleasant conversations," their relationship continued to be distant. Her relationship with Johnson was also again being carried on long-distance by letters and telephone calls, and this time it was Lady Bird who seemed withdrawn. She was weighed down by her inability to have children, and found that work had given her a means of sublimating her feelings of failure.

In a letter written on May 7, 1943, LBJ asked Lady Bird to buy Rebekah a Mother's Day gift and complained that Lady Bird wasn't writing enough:

> I'm writing a letter to Mother for Mother's Day and I wish you would be a good girl and go down and buy her a suitable present. You know what she would like a lot better than I, so just use your judgment.
>
> If you don't start writing me more often I am going to have you drafted into the WAC. Then you have to write your next of kin at least twice a month.
>
> Had dinner with Bill Douglas [the future Supreme Court justice] last night and he was his usual entertaining self. He wished that you could have been there, but not half as much as
>
> Your Congressman,
> Lyndon B. Johnson.

At LBJ's suggestion and to relieve her own pressure at work, Lady Bird soon hired Harfield Weedin, an Austin radio and advertising executive, as KTBC's first station manager. Weedin served ten critical months in the job. Johnson made the initial telephone call to Weedin, who had helped him in his 1941 Senate campaign. Weedin had the impression that the station was a partnership. "He was just as interested as she [Lady Bird] and just as active as she," said Weedin. "The two of them did it together."

At first Weedin said no. The station was "very run-down" and operated out of two old studios, and Weedin insisted as a condition of his employment agreement that the station be moved to larger quarters in the Brown Building in downtown Austin, owned by Herman and George Brown. The move took place on May 17, 1943. Lady Bird wanted to clean house—she gave Weedin the authority to fire most of the original employees and hire new ones. She also bought new furniture.

Though LBJ worked behind the scenes as the dominating presence, Weedin said Lady Bird functioned as the day-to-day president of the company. "I gave her a report on everything," recalled Weedin. "She knew everything that went on. I recognized from the beginning that she was smart. She was not just a satellite of Lyndon. In her own mind, she was very strong."

With Weedin in Austin, Lady Bird stayed home in Washington and tackled the bureaucratic obstacles that crippled the station. In June 1943, Mrs. Johnson asked the FCC to double her station's power, increase its frequency, and grant unlimited broadcasting hours. The following month, the FCC approved her application, amid speculation that Johnson had arranged the prompt and favorable ruling. By August—six months after buying the station—Lady Bird showed her first monthly profit: $18.

The station was not the only purchase Lady Bird made in 1942. By then, she also owned a house in Washington, a two-story, brick colonial at 4129 Thirtieth Place, a few blocks off Connecticut Avenue in northwest Washington. The house had an attic, a basement, and a large porch in the backyard that overlooked an enormous garden, which Lady Bird eventually covered with zinnias and peonies. J. Edgar Hoover, the director of the FBI, lived directly across the street.

She had looked for a house for five years, but Johnson had always refused to allow her to buy one—even though she had her own money. Their ideas about creating the proper setting for a Texan in Washington were in conflict. Johnson believed buying a home in Washington would make him appear less of a Texan to his Austin constituents. During her eight years of marriage, Lady Bird had moved ten times. Politics, not business, was his real life, and one way or another, Lady Bird knew she needed to buy a permanent home in Washington.

One afternoon, she and her real estate agent confronted Johnson during a meeting with John Connally in the living room of the Johnsons' apartment on Kalorama Road about the house that Lady Bird wanted to buy. The owners of the house on Thirtieth Place were threatening to sell it to someone else. As Connally remembered the scene, Lady Bird was furious. She told Johnson that she was "sick of living out of a suitcase" and was in despair over her inability to have children. She told Johnson she had "nothing to look forward to but another election."

Johnson looked at her as though she were invisible. He simply turned and resumed his conversation with Connally. Lady Bird fled from the room in tears. Johnson was surprised by her outburst of emotion. "What do I do?" he asked Connally.

"Buy the damn house," Connally said.

The next day, Lady Bird made a down payment of $18,000, every penny of which belonged to her. Johnson insisted that their telephone number be listed in the telephone book, so that he would appear accessible to the general public. His number stayed listed in the Washington telephone directory until he was vice president.

Once he moved in, Johnson liked the house so much "you would have thought it was his idea from the beginning," Lady Bird said. Years later, he always advised young congressmen to buy a home in Washington as soon as possible. "He told them it was a good investment and would make their life in Washington so much happier," said Lady Bird. "Every time it happened, I had a good laugh."

The acquisition of the house on Thirtieth Place bought Lady Bird an increased sense of security. "I had desperately wanted a nest," she said. "Psychologically, I think it prepared me to have a family." The year before, in November 1941, Virginia Durr had taken Lady Bird to a gynecologist in Baltimore, who performed an operation to prevent future miscarriages.

As Durr remembered it, Lady Bird was extremely shy about the exact nature of her condition and offered no complaints on the drive to the hospital. "She was utterly stoic. She very much wanted to handle it by herself and asked me not to talk to anyone about the condition," Durr said. Although Lady Bird said LBJ was "tender and understanding" about her physical problems, she also recalled, "We never really talked about it."

The reason for Lady Bird's stoicism puzzled everyone, including her own husband. At times, Johnson wondered if his wife's failure to acknowledge pain was a reaction to Effie's hypochondria. Lady Bird appeared to be trying to avoid Effie's fate of dependency, so much so that she disregarded her own health problems. Johnson himself was most likely the reason for her reserve. She wanted to be independent, because that is what she thought Johnson wanted her to be. Her primary motivation was to please him. "He always wanted me to be lively and healthy and in good spirits and have my lipstick on," she said. "That's what I tried to be."

When she returned to Washington in August, she went to her doctor and discovered that she was pregnant. Throughout the pregnancy, she continued to make numerous trips to Austin to work at the radio station. For the most part, she worked from home and responded to Weedin's reports by mail.

Weedin pressed both Lady Bird and LBJ to seek a network affiliation with CBS. At the time, WOAI, a 50,000-watt radio station in San Antonio that boomed into Austin, had an affiliation with NBC. Without such affiliation, KTBC could not carry network news or programming nor would it have the ability to attract major advertisers. In September, LBJ went to New York and asked William Paley, president of CBS, for an affiliation with KTBC. Paley told him that CBS already had affiliates in Dallas and San Antonio, and he didn't think they needed one in Austin. Paley nonetheless referred Johnson to Frank Stanton, then manager of network affiliations, who signed a contract with KTBC for thirty-five hours per week of network programming.

With the CBS affiliation in place, KTBC's audience grew, as did its ability to sell local ads. Lady Bird issued orders to Weedin for each salesman to write her a daily report that included a list of all the sales calls he made that day, with a description of the pitch he had made and the response he had received. Weedin sent the daily reports in a large manila envelope from Austin to Washington.

It was Weedin who established the straightforward format of the station: music and news. He avoided country-and-western or "hillbilly" music and bought new records instead from wholesale distributors in Austin and Dallas. He and another announcer, John Hicks, both delivered the newscasts and also sold the ads. Lady Bird paid Weedin a salary of $265 a month, plus 10 percent of any profits he managed to generate. Hicks was paid $50 a month. "When I first took over the station I presumed she [Lady Bird] had a heck of a lot of money," said Weedin. "But I soon found out that I'd better make money or we were going to be in deep trouble."

Lady Bird stayed focused on the station's finances and personnel problems, all through a difficult pregnancy. On March 19, 1944, she went into labor. "I woke up on a Sunday morning and I told Lyndon I needed to go to the hospital," Lady Bird recalled. "He got on the telephone. I went on and got in the car, and still he didn't come. I was patting my foot and beginning to get mad. Finally, he came out of the house in a lope and we went to the hospital."

He took her to Garfield Hospital in Washington, then left and went riding around in his car for hours with a political friend. Twelve hours later, Lady Bird gave birth to their first daughter. "The Lord helped me through it," Lady Bird recalled. She was not angry with Johnson for leaving her alone at the hospital. She saw it as an example of the difference in their personalities. LBJ could not stand to be alone—he wanted people around all the time, especially in a crisis—while Lady Bird was the opposite. She preferred to manage her pain in solitude.

She knew that Johnson had wanted a boy and later recalled, "I wanted one, too." Johnson's mother, Rebekah, came to Washington, not to help with the baby but, as Lady Bird made clear, "strictly as a house guest." Lady Bird was not surprised when her mother-in-law suggested naming the baby Lynda. If the child had been a boy, his name would have been Lyndon. Rebekah also suggested that Lynda's middle name be Bird, a nickname that Lady Bird had been trying to avoid since she was thirteen years old. Johnson thought his mother's idea was brilliant and joked that all three members of the family—he, Lady Bird, and Lynda Bird—would be a "one suitcase family" because they would all share the same initials.

The following year, Lady Bird's station prospered, with the continued help of the FCC. In the fall of 1945, the agency increased KTBC's power to 5,000 kilowatts. In 1945, KTBC showed an after-tax profit of $40,000 and had an audience of 2.5 million. Lady Bird received at least one offer to buy the business, but she refused to sell. By then, she saw the station as her hedge against financial instability. No matter what happened to Johnson politically, she would always have KTBC.

In 1946, Johnson faced a reelection challenge from Hardy Hollers, an attorney and former Army colonel who had helped prepare the Nuremberg trials against Nazi war criminals. Hollers ran on an "honesty in government" campaign. He attacked Johnson for using his political influence at the FCC for building up his wife's radio station and keeping other competitors out of Austin.

Hollers also raised questions about another real estate investment that Lady Bird had made in 1943: the purchase of a large duplex at 1901 Dillman Street where they lived while in Austin. Lady Bird said she bought the duplex for $15,490 from W. S. Bellows, one of Brown & Root's partners, who had built it for a mistress who committed suicide. Hollers's point was that Lady Bird had spent a lot of money in a short period of time—to buy the station, the Thirtieth Place house in Washington, as well as the Dillman Street duplex—and the implication was that some of the money might have come from Brown & Root.

The Dillman Street house was, in Harfield Weedin's memory, "a big mansion, like a Hollywood house." Weedin was one of many people who worked for the Johnsons and lived for a while in a five-room apartment next door to where they lived. The house had a four-car garage, a central heating system, and a backyard that covered half an acre. "You could set your heat for six o'clock in the morning if you wanted to, and it would go on automatically," said Weedin. "Everything was just as plush as could be, with the best quality stuff that was all over."

Lady Bird was embarrassed by the accusations and afraid to defend herself in public. "At the opening rally of that campaign, I had to bring down a box of canceled checks that showed I had really paid for KTBC as well as the Dillman Street property," she recalled. "I sat there at that rally, with the box on a table beside me, hoping that I wouldn't have to make a speech. As it turned out, I didn't have to say a word. Lyndon did all the talking that day and answered all the charges."

Margaret Mayer, a reporter for the *Austin American-Statesman* who covered the Johnson-Hollers campaign, was present for that rally, which was held in Austin's Wooldridge Park. She said that Lady Bird was so obviously upset by the charges and afraid, that Mayer, a Johnson supporter, was "terrified for her." When Mayer asked her a question about the property, she recalled that "Lady Bird opened her mouth, worked it around, and looked for a word but couldn't come up with any. I suffered for her. The silence was just excruciating."

Whether she was afraid because she did not have the answers to the questions that Mayer and others were asking, or whether it was a case of stage fright is impossible to know. In the end, Johnson was able to convince the voters of the Tenth District that there was no chicanery in his or Lady Bird's business dealings. On July 27, he carried the ten counties in his district with a total of 42,672 votes to Hollers's 17,628, a margin of more than two to one.

Lady Bird continued to commute from Austin to Washington. At the start of every congressional session, she would pack up her dishes and household belongings and drive from Texas to Washington. She used to joke that her idea of being rich was having two sets of dishes and sheets—one for her house in Austin and the other for Thirtieth Place. Usually Johnson did not make the trip by car; more often than not, he flew back and forth in one of Brown & Root's private planes.

Sometimes Lady Bird flew with him, and when she did, friends and staff members drove their Lincoln and household belongings. At the end of December 1946, Margaret Mayer made the drive with Mary Rather, Johnson's secretary, and a Black woman named Patsy who worked for the Johnsons. At the time, every restaurant, gas station, and hotel was strictly segregated. Mayer remembered how difficult it was to find places for Patsy to eat, go to the rest room, and spend the night. "One night in Vicksburg, Mississippi, we had to sneak Patsy in our cabin and the hotel manager found out about it," said Mayer. "We had to get out of there fast, before he threw us out." They drove straight to Washington, without stopping, and arrived on Lady Bird's doorstep at Thirtieth Place at 2:00 A.M.

The reason Lady Bird had not made that particular trip was she was pregnant again. On July 2, 1947, Lady Bird gave birth to their second daughter, Lucy Baines. This pregnancy had been difficult as well. Moments after the birth, Lady Bird remembered that the doctor lifted the baby into his arms and said, "I never thought I'd see you."

When it came time to give the baby a name, Lady Bird did not consider her mother's name, Minnie, or her aunt Effie, or any of the other women in her family, even though she felt strongly influenced by them. For a second time, she went to the Johnson family well: Lucy was named for Lyndon's baby sister, Lucia, who was Lady Bird's favorite of his three female siblings, and Baines was his mother's maiden name. The joke about the "one suitcase family" still stood. (Lucy changed the spelling of her name to Luci when she was sixteen.)

Partly in an attempt to give Johnson a son, Lady Bird became pregnant in 1949 for the final time. At some point after the first trimester, she had another miscarriage—her fourth—this one due to a tubal pregnancy, the same condition suspected to have contributed to her mother's death. Johnson was not at home when the pain began, so Lady Bird telephoned an ambulance to take her to the hospital.

"I knew that I was in a life-threatening situation," she said of the miscarriage. "When they were putting me in the ambulance, I remember that I was glad that Lyndon and I were well off, that we had enough money, and wondered what it would be like to be that sick without any money at all."

At the hospital, when she was placed on the operating table, she felt as though she were falling through space and realized she might be dying. Before losing consciousness, her mind again returned to her financial security. She thought about a dress that she had just purchased for $90, a sum she considered extravagant. Again the thought came to her, "I'm glad I have enough."

Johnson was telephoned and came to the hospital. Horace Busby, who had begun work for him the year before as a speechwriter, was with him. The doctor who treated Lady Bird came out and said that she was losing a lot of blood and that he had given her a series of transfusions. The doctor explained that he could save Lady Bird or he could attempt to save the baby. The choice was up to Johnson. "That day his true colors came out: he was utterly devoted to Lady Bird," Busby recalled. "The idea of losing her filled him with panic. He told them to do whatever was necessary to save Bird."

When the girls were in grade school, they lived half the year in Washington and the other half in Austin with Willie Day Taylor, a former member of Johnson's staff who became their surrogate mother. As a child, Lucy called her Wil-Day, a nickname that stuck. By then, Lady Bird had a full-time cook named Zephyr Wright, a Black college student from Marshall whom she hired in 1942. Eight years later, she hired another Black couple, Eugene and Helen Williams, who organized the trips to and from Texas.

Motherhood did not come naturally to Lady Bird. After all, she had never had a mother and had no real model for the job. Apparently, Lynda accepted her mother's absences and the fact that Lady Bird put her husband first and her business second more easily than Lucy did. Every night after dinner Lady Bird pored over KTBC sales reports, or attended some kind of function for LBJ. Both daughters competed for their parents' attention. "I never saw a mother-daughter relationship like it," said Mayer. "In the early days, the girls were constant rivals, and Lady Bird let everyone know that, no matter what, Lyndon came first."

Lynda was bossy and tried to supervise her younger sister, which infuriated Lucy. "I felt deprived," Lucy admitted years later. "I wanted a normal life. I wanted a father who left the office and came home at a reasonable hour and a mother who made cookies. That wasn't what we had."

Instead, she learned to be on stage at all times. One of Lucy's earliest memories is of walking home from school in Washington one day, without her mother's permission. Lady Bird had sent a driver to pick her up by car, but Lucy had already left. The school was located nine blocks from her house. Along the way, she stopped at a shoe store to buy bubble gum and took her time getting home. When the driver came back to Thirtieth Place without Lucy, Lady Bird, who was hosting a luncheon for congressional wives, telephoned the police. "When I walked through the front door, I found all of these adult eyes—my mother, her guests, and the D.C. police—turned on me," she recalled. "I felt so guilty for having distressed my mother."

Her mother, in turn, felt guilty for not spending more time with her daughters. However, she let both daughters know that Johnson's career was a privilege, something for them to take advantage of and learn from, not to disparage. As she told Marie Smith, a reporter for the *Washington Post* and an early biographer, Lady Bird saw her role as a "balm, sustainer, and sometimes critic for my husband" and wanted to help her children "look at his job with all the reverence it is due." Lyndon Johnson was not the only member of the family that had power confused with love, since the message Lady Bird gave her daughters was not to expect much emotional support from their father, but to rather revere his job.

An early employee of KTBC remembered one particular incident at a Christmas party Lady Bird threw for her employees, which illustrated how she had trained her daughters to adapt to their father's whims. "Lady Bird arrived with both girls all dressed up in beautiful little Christmas dresses," said the employee. "But Lady Bird made the girls hold on to their coats for all the whole party." The employee overheard Lady Bird tell the girls to hold their coats "because when Daddy gets ready to leave, we all three better be ready to go real fast. We don't want to hold him up."

Despite her continued attitude of acquiescence, the marriage to Johnson had taken a lot of the shyness out of Lady Bird. Her own ambition made her even less reserved. In 1948, the year after she gave birth to Lucy and at a time when she was making preliminary plans to expand her business into television, Johnson decided to run for the U.S. Senate against former Texas governor Coke Stevenson. Jesse Kellam, a college classmate of LBJ's and close friend, took over as the general manager of the radio station, which freed Lady Bird to campaign with Johnson.

"I had regretted not doing more to help in 1941," said Lady Bird of Johnson's failed run for the U.S. Senate. "I was determined not to repeat the same mistake." Using two telephones set up in the backyard of her house on Dillman Street, Lady Bird organized a women's division of the campaign. She also participated in the strategy meetings with Wirtz, Connally, and others that were held on folding chairs in the backyard.

During those meetings, Johnson's mendacious side would surface, and, according to Jake Pickle, a future congressman and young Johnson protégé, during those "skull sessions" in 1948 Lady Bird developed a way to deal with the unpleasant side of politics. "If she heard something she didn't like or didn't want to know," recalled Pickle, "she would just stand up and walk out. She might be gone for twenty minutes, and Johnson would suddenly realize that she wasn't there, and then he would say, 'Where's Bird?' That's when he knew he'd crossed some kind of line. He'd go after her, or send one of us."

In the 1948 campaign, Lady Bird made her first substantial campaign speeches. Often she traveled with Mary Rather, who was Johnson's secretary. During one trip, Lady Bird and Rather left Houston and were planning to stop in a number of small towns before arriving back at headquarters in Austin. Lady Bird suggested to Mary that they buy only five gallons of gasoline at a time so that they would be forced to stop in more towns for gas. At each stop, Lady Bird walked up and down Main Street, shaking hands and asking people to vote for Johnson.

As usual, her greatest influence was felt behind the scenes. Johnson had decided to run on May 12 and opened his campaign at a Saturday night rally on May 22 in Wooldridge Park in downtown Austin. Shortly before the rally, he had told Lady Bird that he was in tremendous pain from a kidney stone, but he would not consider a postponement. Johnson had suffered from kidney stones before, and they had all passed without surgery. Lady Bird telephoned a physician, Dr. William Morton, who gave Lyndon a shot and some medication to ease the pain, and Johnson managed to make it through the rally.

Afterward, LBJ left Austin with Paul Bolton, a broadcaster who was working at KTBC, and Warren Woodward, a young campaign aide whose nickname was Woody, for a three-day swing through Amarillo, San Angelo, Abilene, and Lubbock. During the overnight train trip to Dallas, Johnson had severe chills, and Woodward piled blankets on top of him and crawled into bed next to Johnson to keep him warm. The next minute, the chills gave way to fever, and Johnson angrily threw off the blankets. He ordered Woodward to open the Pullman's window so that he could get some fresh cool air. "It was the longest night of my life," Woodward recalled.

The next morning, Woodward checked LBJ into the Medical Arts Hospital in Dallas. Johnson became enraged when he learned that Connally, his campaign manager, had issued a statement to the press revealing his illness. "Johnson was so damn mad at Connally," Woodward recalled. "He told me to call the press and tell them he was withdrawing from the race. If he couldn't run his own campaign, then he'd quit."

Woodward was at a loss about what to do, so he telephoned Lady Bird. Lady Bird told him she would take the next plane from Austin to Dallas. Woodward then issued instructions to the nurses not to let anyone into LBJ's room and to hold all of Johnson's telephone calls. He was afraid that Johnson might call the press and withdraw from the race while he went to pick up Lady Bird.

"When I met her at the airport, she calmly asked me to explain the situation and then she settled in her seat and told me to relax, that she'd take care of it," said Woodward. "I've never seen anyone so cool and steady in my life." At the hospital, Lady Bird asked Woodward to remain outside LBJ's room. She then went in and closed the door. A few moments later, she walked out and told Woodward that everything was okay. Johnson had agreed to stay in the race. She had told Johnson he couldn't quit now. He'd come too far; they'd both come too far.

On May 27, Johnson, Lady Bird, and Woodward flew to the Mayo Clinic in Rochester, Minnesota, where Johnson tried to convince the hospital staff not to remove his kidney stone surgically. He forced Woodward and Lady Bird to drive him over back roads near the clinic in a misguided effort to shake the stone loose. Then he ran up and down the back stairs of the hospital. "Everyone—the staff at the hospital and the campaign staff back at Texas—thought he was a royal pain in the ass," recalled Woodward. "Lady Bird, however, never lost her temper. She actually kept us all laughing about it." Finally, the doctors removed the stone in less than an hour using what was then a new procedure—a "basket extraction"—in which they inserted a tool through his urethra and took out the stone without having to make an incision.

When Johnson returned to Texas, he wanted a novel idea that would help him draw large crowds. He decided that since Texas was so large and his time for campaigning was so short, he would use a helicopter to cover the state. On June 15 he embarked upon a helicopter blitz through more than a hundred Texas towns.

Lady Bird went along and took photographs of some of his rallies on a handheld 16-millimeter camera that Johnson had given her as a gift. In those movies, she captured Johnson in perpetual motion. The helicopter flew low to the ground and Johnson had the doors of it removed so that he could hang from the side, with a microphone strapped to his neck. He shouted down to the people on the ground below, "Hello, down there. There is Lyndon Johnson, your candidate for the United States Senate." In the film, Johnson does look larger than life—a great force of a man—and it is easy to see why he was able to hold Lady Bird in such thrall.

Two days before the election, Lady Bird suffered a close call. She and Marietta Brooks, the volunteer in charge of the women's division, left Austin and were driving to San Marcos for a reception for a group of ladies at a friend's house when a truck ran their car off the road. With Lady Bird at the wheel, the car rolled over twice and came to rest in a ditch. Another driver stopped to help, and Lady Bird asked the driver to take Marietta to the hospital and then drop her off at the reception. She changed into a fresh dress and greeted the women at the reception. Afterward, she got someone else to drive her to San Antonio, where she met LBJ and made her first statewide radio broadcast during a campaign rally.

She arrived late. At the podium, Johnson asked, "What kept you?" She pointed to some scratches on her leg and whispered to him, "I'll tell you later."

The following day, the last one before the election, she reported for work at campaign headquarters in Austin. Rebekah Johnson and Lyndon's three sisters were also there. The five women divided up the Austin telephone book and took turns calling people, starting with the A's and working through to the Z's, urging them to vote. Lady Bird told her mother-in-law about the accident and said that her only thought as the car was rolling over into the ditch was that she should have voted by absentee ballot. By then, she was as driven to win as LBJ.

In early balloting, Stevenson thought he had won by 113 votes. But then a soon-to-be historic box of votes—number 13—arrived from South Texas, and Johnson pulled ahead with an 87-vote victory. Stevenson challenged the count before a series of judges, but in January 1949 at forty years of age, LBJ entered the U.S. Senate with a nickname that stuck: Landslide Lyndon.

The Christmas before he was sworn in, Lady Bird took home movies at the house on Thirtieth Place. It was filled with the people who had helped Johnson during the campaign—Warren Woodward, John and Nellie Connally, Mary Rather, Juanita Roberts, Glenn and Mildred Stegall, Jake Pickle, and others. Everyone seemed imbued with a sense of cohesion and victory. It was the heady aftermath of World War II, and Johnson—their leader—had finally made it to the U.S. Senate.

To entertain themselves, they put on funny plays in the Johnsons' living room, using homemade costumes and props. In one melodrama, entitled "Heaven Help the Working Girl," Lady Bird played a working girl who went off to the big city to seek her fortune. Mary Rather played her mother, who encouraged her to stay away from "wicked men," who would no doubt pursue her. In the film, Lady Bird, dressed in a straight skirt and crisp blouse, looks slim and is extremely animated. It was a clubby, close group of friends, and Lady Bird was at the center of it, radiant in her unlikely role as femme fatale.

"Believe it or not, heaven did protect that working girl," proclaimed Lady Bird during her narration of the home movies. "She got married." In the next shot, LBJ grabbed Lady Bird and kissed her beneath the chandelier, then pulled her close to his side. Under his arm, Lady Bird has the most exquisite look of satisfaction on her face, as though she had waited all her life to belong in this particular circle. Thirtieth Place was her house, this was her crowd, and Johnson, now a U.S. senator, was her husband and protector.

They continued to get rich. In 1947, the year before Johnson was elected to the U.S. Senate, Lady Bird's station listed assets of $213,140, including $82,191 in "undistributed profits." Until that point, Lady Bird had operated her business as a sole proprietor, but with the increase in profits, she decided the time had come to form a company, the Texas Broadcasting Corporation, and to distribute a few shares, first to her daughters and gradually to other trusted employees.

She expanded her business in Alabama as well. An elderly cousin named John Pattillo, who lived in Billingsley where her mother had grown up, managed her property in Autauga and Chilton counties. On his advice, Lady Bird seeded her land with pine trees, which were sold as pulp. With Pattillo acting as her trustee, she became one of the largest tree farmers in the state.

A short letter she received from Johnson during this period shows the kinds of conflicting demands she faced as a mother, a wife, and a businesswoman—a bind that Johnson did nothing to ease. The note, written on September 15, 1949, said:

Dear Bird:
   I think you should immediately write Uncle John and have him accept the timber offer, at once.
   I tried to get you last night, but, as usual, you did not leave word where you could be reached in case of an emergency. I am glad it was me, not Lucy nor Lynda. Love, Lyndon.

By 1951, KTBC had increased its value to $488,000, and the Texas Broadcasting Company had after-tax profits of $57,983. Lady Bird was investigating the possibility of what she called a "daring experiment"— the television business, a prospect that both terrified and excited her. Television was a completely new venture. In order to do it, she would have to become both a broadcaster and manufacturer of TV sets. She wasn't sure that ordinary Texans would spend the money to buy TV sets, and other companies that were trying to break into the business were losing money.

While she was thinking it over, Johnson distracted her with another major real estate transaction. In 1951, he took Lady Bird to the Texas Hill Country to a piece of property along the Pedernales River, located not far from where he was born, between the small communities of Hye and Stonewall. The title to the 243-acre ranch was held by Johnson's seventy-eight-year-old aunt, his father's sister—whom Johnson called "Aunt Frank"—as did the small two-story house made out of fieldstone and timber.

Aunt Frank was there that day, and she and Lyndon began talking about how wonderful it would be for him and Lady Bird to buy the house. They described the family reunions that they would have beneath the old trees along the edge of the river. Johnson told his wife that, as a little boy, he had made his first speeches in front of the hearth in the living room.

She was getting the Johnson treatment, and by now knew enough to resist. Lady Bird took one look at the house, which was in disrepair and had a colony of bats living in its chimney, and, according to her own memory, she screamed at Johnson, "How could you do this to me? How simply could you?" Lady Bird, the woman who had no house at the start of the 1940s, bought her third in 1951 for about $20,000.

While in Austin, Lady Bird began staying at the ranch, supervising the construction on the house, and driving into work at the radio station. In the fall, the Texas Hill Country suffered the worst flood in its history, and Lady Bird and her daughters were caught in the middle of it. It was raining fairly hard on Tuesday morning, September 16, 1952, when Lady Bird drove Lynda, then eight, across a small bridge on their ranch to catch a school bus. By the time she had made it back to the house, it was pouring, and she telephoned one of LBJ's cousins in Johnson City to pick Lynda up after school. She knew that the river would rise, and Lynda and she would be on opposite banks.

Johnson was not at the ranch. He was campaigning in South Texas for Illinois governor Adlai Stevenson, who was then running for President against Eisenhower. Lucy, then five, and Lady Bird were alone in the house and had nothing to do but watch the rain. "My mother heated up a can of tomato soup and spread peanut butter on saltine crackers," Lucy recalled. "It is the only time in my life I remember her cooking just for me. There was no one there—no staff, no other family—except the two of us. I thought it was great fun."

Soon Lady Bird began to worry that the two of them might be swept away. Twenty inches of rain fell in the next thirty-six hours. Every creek, draw, and river in Blanco County and nearby Gillespie County had become a raging torrent. Not a tree was left standing in Stonewall, where Johnson was born, and the Pedernales River, which flowed in front of Lady Bird's house, rose fifteen feet in those thirty-six hours, setting an all-time record. The electric clock in her house was stuck at 8:45 P.M. on Wednesday, September 17, the moment that the power lines had been swept away.

"Lucy and I sat in the house and watched topsoil from our neighbors' farm just float on by, right out to the Gulf of Mexico, and livestock—cattle and horses—were swept away, too," Lady Bird said. She had no lights or telephone. She lit a coal-oil lamp and read Lucy stories. There was nothing to do but wait.

It stopped raining after midnight on Wednesday. By daylight, there were clear patches in the sky. The roads were too muddy to use. Her ranch foreman, who lived in a separate house, rode to her house on a tractor and told her that Johnson was sending an airplane to get her and Lucy out of danger. By then, there were a number of rescue airplanes and helicopters flying over the area, trying to get injured people to hospitals. "There were squadrons of them," said Lady Bird. "It looked like war." The American Red Cross reported that it had helped 225 families in the area to safety during this particular flood, which had caused damage totaling $4 million in nine counties.

In the afternoon, Johnson managed to send an airplane to the ranch, but when the pilot tried to land, the ground was too soft and the airplane sank into the mud, which damaged a wing. Lady Bird and Lucy continued to wait. Later that day, a man from a nearby town arrived at their doorstep on horseback. He explained that LBJ had sent him to take one of the cars out of the garage and drive Lady Bird and Lucy to higher ground.

"He looked so funny standing there, dripping wet with the horse's reins in his hands. I felt like saying, 'Dr. Livingstone, I presume?' " Lady Bird recalled. She gathered up Lucy and they drove a mile or two north over a washed-out road, bound on both sides by uprooted trees, to safer ground.

During the flood, Lady Bird thought about how difficult life had been on the frontier for Texas women and how much of their life was controlled by forces outside of themselves—the weather and nature. The flood came as Lady Bird was preparing to expand into the new arena of television, and it motivated her to take advantage of the advancements of her age.

By that time, the FCC had begun the allocation of 1,945 new TV licenses. Lady Bird talked to Oveta Culp Hobby, owner of the *Houston Post,* who told her that she thought TV would be a lucrative investment. Still, Lady Bird worried about going into debt, so much so that Jesse Kellam suggested that perhaps the three radio stations in Austin—KVET, KTBC, and KNOW—should form a consortium and take the plunge. That idea never got off the ground.

Lady Bird invited Leonard Marks, a communications lawyer, to her house on Thirtieth Place in Washington for a meeting with Kellam, Johnson, and herself. "The meeting lasted all morning, all afternoon, and well into the evening," Marks recalled. After weighing all the pros and cons, Marks told Lady Bird that if she planned to stay in the communications business, she needed to go into television and specifically go after the one VHF (very high frequency) channel that would be allocated in Austin.

"I agree with you," said Lady Bird. "If we are going to go into it, let's get into it and do it right. It may take everything we have, but it is a gamble that I want to make." According to Marks, Johnson felt that a UHF (ultra-high frequency) channel offered better opportunities for a small city like Austin. Marks argued that VHF was not only superior, but it would avoid a competitive hearing. At the time, three local groups were preparing to file for three UHF channels.

Johnson grew irritated with Marks and said again he was opposed to the VHF application. At that point, Lady Bird looked directly at Johnson and told him that she agreed with Marks. "And," she said, "it is *my* money." Johnson got even angrier and left the room. Lady Bird told Marks to go ahead with the VHF application. On March 12, 1952, Lady Bird applied for the VHF channel in Austin, and her request was granted on July 11. Lady Bird's decision turned out to the correct one: UHF broadcasting was technologically inferior to VHF.

As soon as the request was granted, LBJ then moved quickly to tie up contracts with all three major networks—NBC, ABC, and CBS—for KTBC. When the station went on the air on Thanksgiving Day, 1952, to broadcast the annual University of Texas–Texas A&M football game, it boasted truthfully that KTBC had "the best of all three networks."

Although no traces of Johnson's direct influence show up on any FCC files, KTBC, Lady Bird's station, maintained a monopoly in the whole city of Austin largely because of its hold on the networks. Consequently, Lady Bird was able to charge higher rates for advertising than stations in most cities. For instance, in the early 1960s, KTBC's base hourly rate for ads was $575 an hour. Rochester, Minnesota, a city with roughly the same number of television sets but with competition from stations in nearby Minneapolis–St. Paul, charged only $325.

According to Jim Morriss, the first program director at the station, Lady Bird was a constant presence. Her reputation as a tightwad grew. "We were all paid a pittance—about $250 a month," Morriss said. "We didn't really care, because it was an exciting place to be." Also, there were other rewards for working for the Johnsons. For instance, Morriss ran his own cattle at the base of KTBC's transmitter tower. Lady Bird also invited employees out to the ranch to hunt deer and jackrabbits; their families came along for picnics.

For the first few years, KTBC had no movie cameras. They simply took photographs with Polaroids and put them on the air. The entire news operation was housed in one small room. Kellam communicated to the employees by leaving penciled notes, sometimes written on bank deposit slips to save paper costs, on spikes that sat on every employee's desk. KTBC only had one soundproofed cubicle in which to produce on-air shows. Morriss recalled that while one man read the news behind a desk, another hid on the floor beneath the desk and popped up during commercial breaks to read the advertising copy.

Despite the primitive working conditions, the station prospered, and Lady Bird's company, Texas Broadcasting, bought interests in radio and TV stations in Waco, Bryan, and the South Texas town of Weslaco. By spring 1959, the company had a stated value of $2,569,503.

She decided to sell a small amount of stock to Jesse Kellam and Paul Bolton, her news director, both of whom had helped build the company. According to a junior lawyer who drew up the stock options, the process was a long and tiring one. Lady Bird wanted to make sure all the details were spelled out. Finally, however, the day came for Lady Bird to sign over the stock. Bolton and Kellam arrived at the law firm of former state senator Alvin Wirtz, one of the Johnsons' closest friends, and took their places around a long table in a formal conference room.

When Lady Bird got there, she placed her purse on the conference table and straightened a batch of legal papers in front of her. One by one, she signed the papers without comment. When she was finished, Lady Bird looked Bolton and Kellam straight in the eye and told them, according to the memory of the lawyer who was present, "I want you both to understand one thing. I'm offering you this stock, not because I have to or because you've necessarily earned it. This stock is Lyndon's gift to you, and mine, too, for your loyalty to the both of us."

She then picked up her purse and walked out. The lawyer who was in the room was flabbergasted. Here were two men who had worked for her for years at long hours and little pay and were available to both LBJ and Lady Bird on a moment's notice, night or day. Lady Bird's implicit message was essentially, stay loyal or else.

At times, however, Lady Bird was a victim of her own standards of loyalty. The loyalty of these two men was ultimately to Johnson, not Lady Bird. Like Lady Bird, both Kellam and Bolton had a close view of the many sides of Johnson. According to Madeline Brown, a Dallas woman who claims to have had an affair with Johnson that began in 1948, both men encouraged LBJ's darker side.

"Jesse introduced me to him and arranged for many of our meetings," said Brown. "Sometimes Paul would pick me up at the airport in a KTBC car and take me to Lyndon's suite at the Driskill. They knew what the score was." Neither Kellam nor Bolton is alive to substantiate Brown's story.

The relationship, as described by Brown, was clichéd and sleazy. It started when she was twenty-three and working as an account executive for Glenn Advertising, a company that produced radio ads for KTBC. During a party in the summer of 1948 in Dallas, Johnson picked Brown, then five feet, eight inches tall and weighing 118 pounds, out of the crowd and instructed Kellam to bring her to Austin.

On October 29, 1948, Kellam sent Brown an airplane ticket on Trans Texas airlines for a flight to Austin. She attended a party at the Driskill Hotel sponsored by KTBC, and later that night became Johnson's lover.

"I threw away all my morals for him," Brown said. Her pet name for him was "Sandow" (for Eugene Sandow, an archetypal nineteenth-century strongman and bodybuilder), and, according to Brown, LBJ called her "Miss Pussy Galore." Brown reported that LBJ was such a robust lover that he threatened to "brand" her in bed like a cow.

According to Brown, Johnson told her that he regarded Lady Bird as his "official wife." He had married a woman of a higher social class who was helping him to achieve his desired goals in business and politics, but he felt free to pursue other women.

Brown gave birth to a son, named Steven, on December 27, 1951. She claimed that Steven was Johnson's illegitimate son and LBJ made regular monthly payments, through emissaries including Kellam, to both Brown and her son. The support stopped after LBJ's death in 1973. In 1987, the affair became public when Steven Brown filed a $10.5 million lawsuit in Dallas against Lady Bird, claiming that she and Jesse Kellam had denied him what he called his "legal heirship." Brown's description of the affair was carried in newspapers and on television.

The lawsuit was eventually dismissed when Steven Brown did not appear in court. In 1991, he died of lymphatic cancer. Publicly, Lady Bird refused to comment; privately, she discounted Brown's claims and told her staff she did not believe that the affair had ever happened. To her, Madeline Brown was a nuisance, nothing more.

Lady Bird knew she was Lyndon's wife, no matter what, and throughout the 1940s and early 1950s, she had good reason to believe that her marriage was reasonably safe. She had given him two daughters. He, in turn, had demonstrated his own feelings of loyalty for her after the tubal pregnancy and during the rescue mission in the 1952 flood. Even though Johnson was ultimately wedded to politics, Lady Bird had evidence to cling to that he, in fact, loved her. His acknowledgment of her as his wife was her lodestar.

She also felt confident because she held substantial control over their money. By the middle 1960s, the family fortune included a cable television company in Austin, a bank, three other ranches, and other real estate, and was estimated by *U.S. News & World Report* at $7 million. *Life* magazine put the value of Lady Bird's business, which was held in a family trust, at $9 million.

Other people, too, offered her reassurance. For instance, Russell

Morton Brown, an old friend and classmate of Johnson's in law school, recalled a party given by Lady Bird at Thirtieth Place at the end of the 1950s, well after her fortune had been made. During the course of the party, Brown and LBJ stood on the sidelines and had a conversation about what LBJ's old friend described as all the "self-seeking women" who threw themselves at LBJ. From the edge of the party, Brown complimented what he called Lady Bird's "poise" and "beauty" as well as her "business sense." He told Johnson how much she had grown as his wife, how outgoing, even glowing, she seemed that particular night. "The best day's work you ever did was the day you married her," Brown told him.

"Russ," Johnson told him, "believe me. I know that better every day."

CHAPTER NINE

✣

LBJ's Midlife Crisis

In the aftermath of Johnson's election as majority leader of the U.S. Senate in January 1955, a series of events forced him to wrestle with his own mortality. Six months after his election, he suffered a massive heart attack. Three years later, on September 12, 1958, close to LBJ's fiftieth birthday, his mother, Rebekah, died at seventy-eight of cancer. Johnson's reaction to these encounters with death was divided: one moment he was threatening to quit politics and the next racing toward the presidency.

In retrospect, George Reedy, a burly Chicago native and former United Press International reporter who first went to work for LBJ in 1951, believes that during this period Johnson was in the throes of a midlife crisis. "He used to tell me that he saw his life as a race in three parts: the first third he had to rush to position himself for future advancement, the second third he had to work like hell and accumulate power and money, and in the last third, he could relax," said Reedy. "It never occurred to him to enjoy himself a little every day. I think that was one of the differences between Johnson and Lady Bird. She knew how to be content in any circumstance. Johnson couldn't do that."

Instead, he continued to look to others as he had looked to Alice Glass and Madeline Brown—for diversion and release. "Sex to Johnson was part of the spoils of victory," said Reedy. "He once told me that women, booze, and sitting outside in the sun were the only three things in life worth living for. He collected women like some men collect exotic fish."

In Reedy's view, Johnson was a victim of his mother's Victorian view of sex. He believed, as his mother did, that men were basically depraved and could only be redeemed by the love of tender and compassionate women. "He thought all women were soft and morally superior to men and didn't want a thing in the world except to enhance the masculine role, preferably his own. As a result, strong women, like his mother, his wife, and certain women in the office, could get him to do almost anything," Reedy said.

When it came to feelings and emotions, Johnson believed women were superior. In order to feel anything, he needed the attention of women. If they laughed at his jokes, he felt joy. If they pitied the long hours he worked for the common good, he felt comforted. If they saw his idealism as heroic, he felt vindicated. He did not necessarily have to have physical sex with the women, according to Reedy, but he wanted them around for emotional security, and he wanted to dominate them. "It seemed to me it was a potency question for him—he wanted young women around to make him feel young."

His first private secretary was Mary Rather, who went to work for him in 1934. Rather became the prototype for the kind of slavish, single-minded devotion Johnson expected his secretaries to display. When Rather first met Johnson, she was a plump brunette who worked as a secretary for Wirtz, then a lawyer in Austin. Rather's first words after meeting LBJ were "He's like a tornado, that young man." She soon was swept up in his life.

As he did with others, Johnson set about remaking Rather according to his own ideas of what constituted the perfect female. He encouraged her to lose weight and bought her new clothes. He also expected her to work eighteen hours a day, to serve him drinks, to guard his door, and to befriend his wife. Rather did all of those things.

Twenty years later, as Johnson took over the leadership of the Senate, Rather's brother and his wife were killed in an automobile accident in Texas and Mary went home to take care of their three children. She was replaced in Johnson's office in January 1951 by another brunette, twenty-one-year-old Mary Margaret Wiley, who also had worked for Wirtz's law firm.

Johnson made a point of intimidating all new employees. For instance, Wiley started to work for him on a Monday, opening and sorting the mail, addressing letters, and other menial jobs. Five days later, she first met him. He stuck his head in the door of the mailroom, yelled out a few orders, and then was gone. Her first impression was similar to Rather's. "Blown away," she recalled, "and a little scared."

Soon Mary Margaret and another secretary, Ashton Gonella, ascended to the position of "top secretary"—as Johnson called it. Mary Margaret's desk was literally inside Johnson's office, not far from his own. She served as the physical gatekeeper between him and the outside world. All visitors, telephone calls, letters, and memos passed through her desk.

She was not the only woman in the office that Johnson called a "top secretary." According to Gonella, Johnson made it clear from the beginning that he saw her appearance as a reflection on him. "The first day I went to work for him, I wore my hair long and up in a chignon. He told me if I wanted the job, I needed to get two pounds of hair cut off," said Gonella, who was a twenty-seven-year-old divorced mother of two at the time. "He didn't want to look at me unless I looked the way he wanted. I cut my hair."

It wasn't only that Gonella needed the job. She said she was in awe of Johnson's personality. Often she found herself doing things—such as cutting her hair or getting rid of a dress he didn't like—and only later questioned why she did them. For instance, not long after she went to work for LBJ, he rang the buzzer at her desk and called out, "Coffee!" Johnson liked his coffee hot, and apparently the cup Gonella served him wasn't hot enough. "No wonder you don't have a husband," Johnson told her. "You can't make a simple cup of coffee."

Gonella did not consider the comment unusual, just as she never felt offended when he told her that her slip was showing or inquired about details of her private life. "That was just the way he was," she said. "All of us—Lady Bird included—knew it and accepted him." A lot of times the secretaries sat around and listened to him talk. At the end of the day, he would hold forth and rattle an empty glass until Gonella or Mary Margaret or any of the others magically appeared and filled his glass with Cutty Sark. He never asked for a drink; serving coffee, drinks, and snacks was part of the job description.

What would be considered sexual harassment today was part of the everyday atmosphere of LBJ's office. "He was absolutely terrifying," said Nadine Brammer, who worked for LBJ during the Senate years. "He was so large and his eyes seemed magnified behind those glasses. It was as though he was a great Tasmanian devil, darting in and out of offices, pouncing on you before you knew it." One day Johnson helped Brammer out of the back seat of a car. "As I leaned over to get out, he took the opportunity to feel me up," said Brammer. "It happened so fast I didn't even have a chance to complain."

Why did female staff members put up with such treatment? One reason, according to Brammer, was because it was the 1950s and jobs for women were limited. Johnson's office was an exciting place to be. He was in the middle of pulling the fractionalized Democratic members of the Senate into a cohesive whole, and his office was one of the few places on the Hill where conservatives such as Richard B. Russell of Georgia and liberals such as Stuart Symington of Missouri were equally at home.

One day, recalled Brammer, the telephone rang at her desk, and it was Johnson on the other line. "Honey," he told her, "come to my office quick. There's someone I want you to meet." When she walked into the office, Nadine, then twenty-five years old, found herself face-to-face with Eleanor Roosevelt. It was a small act, but it illustrates the way Johnson used his power to gratify the desires of those around him.

He rewarded female reporters in a similar manner, especially Nancy Dickerson, who became the first woman news correspondent of CBS in 1960. In her oral history, Dickerson recalled that when she first met him, she was "right out of college and, for the record, I had been elected a Badger Beauty at the University of Wisconsin." At the time, she was not a journalist but a staff member for the Senate Foreign Relations Committee. Johnson walked up to Dickerson's desk and made it clear, according to her, that he "liked beautiful women or pretty girls." He put his feet up on her desk and asked to use the telephone. "He was a powerful man, a forceful man—as everybody knows—and so of course he made an impression," she recalled.

He invited Dickerson and a few of her friends to lunch at his office with some of the most influential members of the Senate—Hubert Humphrey, John Kennedy, Stuart Symington—and placed himself at the head of the table. Dickerson recalled that she wore a green moiré dress—it was her first Dior—and that after lunch, Johnson telephoned Dickerson to find out where she bought her clothes and where she had her hair done. "He was still picking his wife's clothes very much then," recalled Dickerson, "and he wanted Lady Bird to have either that kind of makeup or that kind of dress."

Lady Bird reacted to Johnson's admiration for Dickerson's beauty by going out of her way to solicit the reporter's friendship. At one point, she borrowed four black suits from Dickerson, items that Johnson had admired. On February 20, 1960, when Dickerson was named a news correspondent, Lady Bird and Johnson threw a party on Capitol Hill. All of the members of the Senate were invited, and Frank Stanton, then the president of CBS and a friend of the Johnsons, also stopped by.

"Lyndon loved to play Pygmalion," said Lady Bird in reaction to Johnson's propensity to mold the physical appearances of the women around him. If Johnson was riding in the front seat of an automobile, he would often ask the driver to stop, and then he'd wheel around to the back seat and order every woman who happened to be in the car, whether it was Lady Bird, his daughters, or one of his secretaries, to apply fresh lipstick or comb their hair. If he thought Lady Bird's hair was teased too much, he'd tell her that she looked like a "tumbleweed" and ask her to comb her hair.

Sometimes he would telephone a department store and buy several dresses or bathing suits, and send them all to his wife and members of his staff. "The best-fitting bathing suit I ever had in my life was one he bought me," Gonella recalled.

Male staff members, including Nadine's husband, Billy Lee Brammer, were called "top assistants" as opposed to "top secretaries." The men were expected to dress in a certain way as well. Most kept extra pairs of clean shirts in their bottom drawers because Johnson liked to see them in freshly pressed shirts.

With men, he frequently exhibited the kind of depraved behavior his mother feared and condemned. "He could be unbelievably gross," said Reedy, "often a miserable human being." A favorite expression of his was to brag that he had a senator's "pecker in his pocket." He developed the habit of urinating in the sink of his office bathroom often in front of male staff members, or conducting business while sitting on the commode. Reedy believed these acts were misguided attempts to establish his authority over subordinates.

One day an old friend from Texas visited his Senate office, and they started gossiping about the sex lives of various politicians. In the course of the conversation, Johnson unzipped his pants, exposed himself to the friend, and asked, "Have you ever seen anything as big as this?" The friend thought it was not so much penis envy that Johnson wanted to provoke as power envy.

As majority leader, Johnson's day began about 6:30 A.M., when he ate breakfast at home while reading the *Congressional Record*. He left the house an hour later and arrived at his office at 8:00. Normally he met with Walter Jenkins, his chief of staff. Jenkins was the only person on the staff who worked as hard as LBJ. A high-strung, nervous man, Jenkins rarely left the office to eat meals and sometimes put in twenty-hour days. He lived in constant fear of not living up to Johnson's standards, of coming up short.

For instance, one afternoon Jenkins stretched out on a couch in the office to take a nap. Another staff member opened the door, and, mimicking LBJ's voice, shouted: "Walter!" Jenkins leaped off the couch, terrified. "Don't you ever do that to me again!" Jenkins said. It was Jenkins who divided up the mail and implemented Johnson's orders that every member of the staff answer at least fifty constituent letters a day.

Several times a week, Lady Bird came in the office. She gave tours of the Capitol to constituents and brought the staff Texas-shaped cookies and made sure the Senate dining room served Texas-shaped hamburgers to Johnson's guests for lunch. Lady Bird later said that Johnson's years in the Senate were the most stimulating for her intellectually. She often went to the gallery and listened to the debate. At home, she would listen as Sam Rayburn and Johnson talked for hours about how close votes could be swayed. Rayburn was a frequent guest at Lady Bird's house, and in time Lady Bird regarded him as a fatherly figure. She held an annual birthday party for him and sought out his advice.

One particular night when Rayburn was at dinner, Lady Bird served turkey hash as the entrée and Johnson criticized her choice. "Can't you serve the speaker of the house anything better than turkey hash?" he asked angrily. Rayburn immediately came to Lady Bird's defense and told her that turkey hash was one of his favorite things to eat and that he didn't get it often enough in Washington. After Rayburn left, Lady Bird, according to a family friend who was present, took Johnson into the living room and warned him in a firm voice never to criticize the menu again in front of a guest. He nodded his head, like an errant schoolboy.

Publicly, she took a more passive role. Hope Riddings Miller, the former society editor of the *Washington Post,* who covered Eleanor Roosevelt as First Lady, recalled that as the wife of the majority leader, "Lady Bird was the perfect politician's wife, because she always insisted on making the other person feel more important than herself. Her whole goal in life seemed to be to make other people feel big and herself small."

According to Miller, Rayburn once told her that he had cautioned Johnson about his sexual indiscretions. Specifically, Rayburn said the talk about his infidelity would hurt Johnson politically, and he felt protective of Lady Bird. "Bird knows everything about me, and all my lady friends are hers, too," Johnson told Rayburn, who repeated the remark to Miller, who wrote it down.

What Lady Bird seemed more concerned about was his physical health. By 1955, he was eating, drinking, and smoking cigarettes all to excess, and often behind Lady Bird's back. On January 18, 1955, he went to the Mayo Clinic in Rochester, Minnesota, for surgery to remove another kidney stone. After the operation, he and Lady Bird went to the ranch where Lady Bird supervised his care. "I had a lot of pain in childbirth," recalled Lady Bird. "But the pain that Lyndon had with that kidney stone was far worse. He was simply miserable."

Late one evening, Reedy saw Lady Bird and Lyndon walking down a road near the Pedernales River on the ranch. Lady Bird was holding his hand and had the most blissful look on her face. It was clear to Reedy how devoted Lady Bird was to him, despite his ill treatment. She seemed content to have him home, away from Washington. In February, however, LBJ returned to the capital, where he bragged about the size of the stone that had been removed and showed off his surgical corset.

All through the spring, as Congress debated immigration and tax bills, Johnson's complaints about his health steadily increased. At home, Lady Bird tried to control what he ate and drank, and Johnson complained about her constant nagging. He ate faster than anyone else at the table, and filled his plate many times. "Honey, please slow down," Lady Bird would say, in her most genteel voice. Despite her monitoring of his diet, his weight climbed to 225 pounds. Soon he began to suffer from chronic indigestion.

On July 2, he decided to visit George Brown's estate in Middleburg,

Virginia, which was located in the lush horse country about forty miles from Washington. It was Lucy's eighth birthday. She was sick with a fever so Lady Bird decided to stay in Washington to care for her. Lyndon left about 5:00 P.M. En route to Middleburg he felt nausea and pain in his midsection. He had eaten hot dogs and beans for lunch and thought at first it was indigestion, but by the time he arrived at Brown's house, the pain was so bad that Johnson went directly to a bedroom to lie down. Another weekend guest, Senator Clinton Anderson, who had earlier had a heart attack, took one look at Johnson and told him, "My God, man! You're having a heart attack."

Brown ordered Frank Oltorf, his Washington lobbyist, to call a local doctor. Since there was no ambulance, the doctor arrived in a hearse with the Middleburg undertaker, and they loaded Johnson into the back to transport him to Bethesda Naval Hospital. Oltorf climbed in as well and sat next to Johnson on the ride to the hospital. Johnson was in terrible pain and thought he was going to die. He leaned over and told Oltorf that if he died, his will was in Austin in a drawer at the KTBC office. "I've left everything to Lady Bird," Johnson told Oltorf. "She's been the most wonderful wife in the world."

What exactly did he mean by the cliché "wonderful wife"? Oltorf, who had intimate knowledge of Johnson's earlier affair with Alice Glass and was aware of the rumors about many other women, interpreted Johnson's remark as an expression of his ultimate loyalty to Lady Bird. "At bottom, I don't think he would have ever left Lady Bird. After all, he thought he was dying and in that moment at least he seemed to realize what he owed her. The feeling I had was that he felt incredibly guilty for the way he had treated her. I saw then how deeply he was tied to her," Oltorf recalled.

In the next breath, Johnson reverted to his ribald self. He turned to ask the doctor in the ambulance-hearse if he would ever be able to smoke again. "Frankly," the doctor replied, "no." Johnson was dejected at the idea of life without cigarettes. He sighed and said woefully, "I'd rather have my pecker cut off." Oltorf had telephoned Lady Bird from the Brown mansion. She was waiting for them at the hospital when Johnson arrived, along with Jenkins and Reedy. Johnson was carried into the hospital on a stretcher. Lady Bird bent down and told him she was relieved to see him alive. He nodded, then told Reedy not to downplay the incident with the press.

"Don't kid anybody," he told Reedy. "Don't say I'm in for a checkup. Say I had a heart attack—a real bellybuster." He begged the doctor for one last cigarette, smoked it slowly and sensuously, then turned to Lady Bird and told her that he'd been fitted for two new suits that morning, one brown and the other blue. "Tell 'em to go ahead with the blue," he told her, pitifully. "I'll need it whichever way it goes."

As he was wheeled into a large room on the seventeenth floor of the hospital, Johnson looked at Lady Bird in terror. "Stay with me, Bird," he told her. "I'd rather fight with you beside me." His face was steel-gray, the color of asphalt. Hurriedly, they put him in an oxygen tent, and he went into immediate shock. The doctors explained to Lady Bird that he had suffered a coronary occlusion. For the next forty-eight hours, he had a fifty-fifty chance of survival.

Lady Bird moved into a room next door to his and prepared for the long hospital siege. She called the office and made arrangements for important pieces of mail to be sent directly to her so that she could sign them. She answered phone calls and went back and forth from the hospital to the house.

By Wednesday, the fourth day after the heart attack, the crisis had passed. Johnson was able to sit up in bed and tried to adjust to what the doctors told him was a new way of life: one without smoking, strict adherence to a low-calorie diet, and a long recuperative vacation in Texas.

Lady Bird became the scapegoat. One of the doctors told key staff members that LBJ was so verbally abusive to Lady Bird that it was all he could do to stay on the case. Yet at the same time, Johnson did not want Lady Bird to leave his side—not even for a minute.

Day after day during his six-week stay in the hospital, the first words he spoke upon waking up were, "Where are you, Bird?" Inevitably, she would answer, "I'm here. I'm here." Not only was she present, but she also took extra care with the way she dressed. She wore long, colorful dressing gowns from Elizabeth Arden, and made sure her makeup and lipstick were fresh. She seemed to gain strength from the fact that he needed her more than anyone. Later Johnson told Liz Carpenter, Mrs. Johnson's press secretary, "During those long nights in the hospital, the first sound I heard every time I woke up was Lady Bird's foot hitting the floor, running to my side."

Why would a woman dress up in an extravagant gown, carefully paint her lips, and rush to the side of a man who was yelling at her one minute and whimpering for her the next? This was all part of the cost of being what LBJ called his "wonderful wife." It meant that she came whenever he called, and came with her makeup applied. "It was as though she was playing the part of some steely Southern heroine," said one of Lady Bird's closest friends. "She stood there in those regal gowns, not budging from his side, letting everyone know that she was the one he wanted by his side."

The weeks after the heart attack were, as Lady Bird called them, a true "battle of patience." To withstand his abuse, she convinced herself that LBJ wasn't quite himself, which was in fact true. As is common with many heart attack patients, Johnson quickly sank into a deep depression. Mary Margaret Wiley characterized this period a "Germanic low." Johnson would lie in bed, stare into space, unable to move. He was given medication for the depression, but it seemed to those around him—Jenkins, Lady Bird, Reedy, and others—that the medication was slow to take effect.

While physically inactive, he was manic about his cravings for food and cigarettes. "He would have a hellish tantrum when people told him he couldn't smoke," Reedy recalled. He kept a package of cigarettes by his bedside table and would sometimes take one out, roll it in his fingers, and threaten to light it up. Lady Bird begged him not to smoke. At mealtimes, she brought low-fat food that had been prepared by their longtime cook, Zephyr Wright, to spare him from hospital food. The wife had indeed become the mother: she fed him, she dressed him, she bathed him, she even tucked him in for sleep.

In reaction, he reverted to type and rebelled against Lady Bird's efforts to control him. For instance, on August 25 he flew by private plane from Washington to his ranch near Stonewall to rest. As his belongings were being loaded onto the plane, he called aside Mildred Stegall, one of his secretaries, and ordered her to sneak a couple of bottles of Cutty Sark on board. "Make sure Lady Bird doesn't know about the booze," he whispered.

Once at the ranch, he embarked upon an exercise program of swimming in the pool in front of his house and walking a mile to and from his cousin Oriole's house. Mary Rather was recruited to help Lady Bird manage the details of his life. Johnson's mother, Rebekah, came to the ranch as well, and attempted to persuade her son to rest and follow the doctor's orders.

The staff greeted Rebekah's arrival with dread. Essentially, she told Johnson that he didn't have a right to be ill, that he had too many important things to accomplish, and that he should get back to work. "She was so damn mean to him," said Reedy. "She just had all these impossible standards. I would rather face ten of Al Capone's gangsters in a back alley than have to spend one hour alone with that woman."

Johnson found no fault in his mother. Instead, he lashed out at Lady Bird. In front of a large group, Johnson once accused Lady Bird of "trying to kill me" by giving him extra slices of watermelon that he felt had too many calories. Lady Bird didn't respond directly, but privately she acknowledged that she was having a very bad time. "When Lyndon is out of danger," she confided in a friend, "I want to go off alone somewhere and cry."

Zephyr Wright, the Black cook, tried to take the pressure off Lady Bird. With each meal, she gave LBJ a sheet of paper, noting the grams of carbohydrates, protein, and fat in each plate of food. LBJ called the notes his "love letters." One day Wright got so irritated with Johnson's complaints that she told him it was up to him—not her—to lose the excess weight. She told him to eat what was put in front of him and not to complain. His response to Zephyr was to laugh at her notes, but he did what he was ordered.

By the fall, the care of Lady Bird and Zephyr paid off. His weight had dropped to 177 pounds. He was feeling so much better that he decided to have a news conference to show off his good health. One of the reporters who came to the ranch was Dan Rather, then a radio reporter for KTRH in Houston. Rather arrived at the ranch early in the morning and kept waiting for word from Johnson. None came. At noon, Rather decided he better telephone the station. He walked into the den and called his boss, letting him know that he supposed Johnson would emerge sometime in the afternoon—maybe there would be news then.

At that moment, Rather felt a huge figure behind him. Johnson grabbed the telephone from Rather and told his boss that the reporter was both rude and a liar. He ordered Rather off the ranch, and Rather left. A few minutes later, Lady Bird caught him by his car and told him to come back to the ranch and have a drink. "As you know," she told the young Rather, "that's just the way Lyndon sometimes is."

It was Mrs. Johnson in her role as mediator—part of her job was to patch up the wounds that Johnson inflicted, this time on Rather. She had no way of knowing that Dan Rather would become a TV news anchor, but her instinct was to repair the rift. In time, it became her life-time job.

Johnson returned to his duties as majority leader on January 3, 1956. He was determined to show his colleagues that he was the same "mira-cle man" (the phrase Reedy used with the press) that he'd been before the heart attack. However, in the wake of the heart attack, the darker aspects of his personality also surfaced. His brush with death had made him more aware of the high cost he was paying for his life as a politician. "He was absolutely tormented," said Reedy. "He believed that he'd missed out on something in his youth—I think he thought it was love—and he was determined to find it now."

When Eisenhower beat Stevenson, Johnson emerged as the Demo-cratic party's most powerful national leader. He started to steer a mid-dle course between liberals and conservatives in preparation for a presidential bid in 1960. At the same time, he was privately threatening to quit politics altogether and return home to Texas. Juanita Roberts, one of his secretaries, whom Johnson called "Miss Efficiency," recalled that shortly after the 1956 election he was at dinner at the ranch with a group of staff members and told Lady Bird to prepare for life outside of Washington.

"Now Bird, that was our last campaign," Johnson lectured Lady Bird, firmly. "I want you to do everything in Washington these next six years that you've ever wanted to do, because I'm not going to make another race." Lady Bird did not say anything in response; she knew his threats were idle.

Two years later, in 1958, his mother died from cancer. Lady Bird had never seen Johnson so morose as in the aftermath of his mother's death. He became lost in sentimentality and began to talk more about going home to the ranch to be near his "childhood memories." His threats to resign intensified, as did his drinking, and Lady Bird—for one—really believed he had decided against running for President in 1960. She thought that if he had been serious about the nomination, he would have actively pursued it before 1958. The combination of his heart attack, his mother's death, and his own erratic moods convinced Lady Bird that he would not run.

This time, she was wrong. Even though Johnson never made an all-out organized effort to win the presidency in 1960, by the start of that crucial year, the race between Kennedy and Johnson was unofficially in progress. By the time Kennedy announced on January 2, it was clear that the only candidates who would come to the Democratic convention with any real support were Kennedy and Johnson. On July 5, Johnson formally announced his candidacy, and the public battle between him and Kennedy commenced.

Johnson arrived in Los Angeles on July 8 and took a suite of rooms in the Biltmore Hotel. Reedy and others said Johnson was pessimistic and did not expect to win. On July 13, the night of the balloting, Johnson did not even go to the floor of the convention. He sent Mrs. Johnson and his daughters to the floor. A few staff members, including Mary Margaret Wiley, stayed with him. He sat in a chair, wearing a pajama top over his slacks and a pair of comfortable house shoes. According to notes Wiley made during the evening, Johnson was "composed and showed outward calm" as the first ballots were cast.

Once the balloting was over and Kennedy had won 806 votes to Johnson's 409, he walked into the living room of the suite, where a large group of reporters were gathered and joked with the press and then returned to his seat to watch the ballots.

"When it was certain that Senator Kennedy had won the nomination on the first ballot," Wiley wrote in her official notes, "Senator Johnson said this was the best thing that could have happened." He seemed relieved by the defeat. He suggested that the following day he and a few others might go to Disneyland, do something fun, and then go back to Texas. He considered the race over with. "I lost fair and square," he announced.

When his daughters and Mrs. Johnson returned to the suite, Lynda, fourteen, showed little emotion, but Lucy, then twelve, burst into tears and later vanished into a bedroom to change her clothes. A few minutes later, she walked back into the living room, wearing a black dress, black hose, and black shoes. Her mood was black as well. "My father has lost and I am in mourning and I want the whole world to know it," she announced.

Lady Bird was less melodramatic but equally disappointed. In the late hours of July 13, as Johnson prepared a congratulatory telegram to Kennedy, Lady Bird stared blankly at the television screen and cried. There was muddled, idle talk about the need to rally behind Kennedy and the Democratic party. The joke was that the initials LBJ now stood for "Let's Back Jack."

The following morning, Betty Carson Hickman, another of LBJ's secretaries, arrived at his suite at 6:30 A.M. and started answering the telephone and accepting telegrams that were coming in from all over the country. Lady Bird and Lyndon were both still asleep in twin beds in one of the bedrooms. At 7:30 the telephone rang and Jack Kennedy was on the line. He told Hickman that he wanted to speak to Johnson. "Just a moment," she replied and then tiptoed into the Johnsons' room, woke up Lady Bird and asked her if she thought they should wake up LBJ or ask the senator to call back later.

Lady Bird got out of her bed and spoke briefly to Senator Kennedy on the telephone. Then she knelt down beside her husband's bed. She touched Johnson's shoulders and told him that Jack Kennedy was on the line. "Do you want to talk to him?" she whispered.

Johnson bolted straight up in his bed. "Yes," he told Lady Bird. Then he turned to Hickman and ordered her to listen on another line and take down every word that was spoken in shorthand. By then, Kennedy was under pressure from Southern Democrats to offer LBJ the vice presidency, and his brother Bobby and other liberals were working hard to keep LBJ off the ticket. Johnson was suspicious, and he wanted a written record of exactly what Kennedy said.

"I want to come down and see you, Lyndon," Kennedy told him.

"No, I'll come up there, Jack," Johnson told him. "I was coming up there to congratulate you in person, so let me come up there."

Kennedy, however, insisted on coming to Johnson. "I'll see you in about an hour," Kennedy said.

"Well, fine," said Johnson.

Johnson jumped out of bed and told Lady Bird and Betty to get the living room cleaned up. Kennedy arrived at the suite at 10:58 A.M. He talked in vague terms about his need for a strong running mate but did not offer the vice presidency to Johnson. He seemed to want Johnson to volunteer for the job, but Johnson insisted he wasn't interested. Johnson suggested that either Hubert Humphrey or Stuart Symington would be a good running mate and advised Kennedy to "make up his own mind."

In the next few hours, Connally and Rayburn met twice with Bobby Kennedy, who told them that liberals, especially labor, were strongly opposed to Johnson. Bobby then offered LBJ the job of national chairman of the Democratic party. Rayburn was insulted and incensed.

Rayburn left the meeting and walked across the suite to Johnson's bedroom, where LBJ was meeting with Phil Graham, publisher of the *Washington Post* and a key broker between Johnson and Kennedy. Lady Bird was present for the meeting and got up to leave the room so the men could meet in private. Johnson stopped her. He wanted to hear what she thought. Rayburn told the three of them that Bobby Kennedy wanted to meet directly with LBJ. Johnson asked Lady Bird what she thought.

"I've never argued with Mr. Sam," she told him, "but I don't think you should see Bobby." None of them knew whether Bobby was acting on his own behalf to keep Johnson off the ticket, or if he was acting on behalf of his brother. Either way, Lady Bird believed that LBJ should deal directly with Jack, not Bobby.

Lady Bird's judgment proved to be decisive. Graham, Rayburn, and Johnson quickly agreed with her. Rayburn left to tell Bobby that Johnson wouldn't meet with him, and Graham telephoned Kennedy and told him that LBJ would only accept the vice presidency if Kennedy himself drafted him. During the conversation, Graham tried to portray LBJ as a reluctant candidate. Kennedy listened, then told Graham to call back in a few minutes.

At 2:45 P.M., Graham placed the second call, and Kennedy informed him that Johnson was his choice. No one in the Johnson suite was happy about LBJ being number two, and the feelings among the Texans about Jack Kennedy were already bitter. They believed that Johnson was by far the better qualified of the two, but blamed his failure to capture the nomination not on Johnson's lack of national organization but on Kennedy's money and the opposition of liberals. "They had it all," said Liz Carpenter, then a reporter. "The money, the headlines, they even had walkie-talkies on the floor of the convention."

Inside the crowded Johnson suite, the feeling was one of resignation. At around 4:00 P.M. someone opened the front door of the suite and Johnson faced a throng of TV lights and exploding flashbulbs. Lady Bird stood at the door of the hotel room. While he stood on a chair and read a statement saying that he was accepting the vice presidency, someone pushed Lady Bird up on a chair beside him. As Graham recalled in his notes, Lady Bird and Johnson both looked like survivors of an airplane crash. Carpenter said that Lady Bird looked tired and frightened.

Lady Bird's eyes were red from crying and she looked petrified in the glare of the TV lights. She recovered quickly. In the next instant, both LBJ and Lady Bird had regained their footing, and their public shields went back up. According to Graham, "their faces metamorphosed into enthusiasm and confidence."

Later that evening, Johnson waited in an underground tunnel near the podium while his name went before the convention as the vice presidential nominee. He listened as the balloting began and heard the roar of ayes and nays when the rules were suspended and the proposition was put to the delegates in the form of a voice vote. Eventually he made his way to the podium where he formally became the vice presidential nominee by acclamation, a victory that only deepened his midlife crisis. He was, by the unanimous vote of his party, Number Two.

CHAPTER TEN

The Trap of Her Father's House

Lady Bird relinquished the residue of her shyness in Los Angeles. At the close of the convention, Lady Bird, now forty-eight, emerged as a public matron who understood that her place in society, one that had been assigned to her by childhood and marriage, was significant. The dominance of the men around her—her father, the boss of Harrison County; her husband, the second most powerful Democrat in America; and the young would-be President, Jack Kennedy—was absolute.

At the same time, Lady Bird understood the possibilities of her own power. By now, after twenty-three years of marriage to LBJ, Lady Bird knew the full mixture of Johnson's private insecurities: his rage, his stunted ego, the deep valleys of his depressions, his hypersexuality, all of which threatened his future rise to power. In the aftermath of Los Angeles, Lady Bird no longer doubted that LBJ wanted to be President. She knew as well that she could cope with the recurrences of Johnson's inevitable emotional highs and lows. One aspect of marriage is coming to grips with the insidious wreckage of another human being's flaws. By then, Lady Bird had done that. "She knew him inside out and accepted him for what he was," said Reedy. "That acceptance probably gave him the strength to lead—without it, he would have crumbled." Ashton Gonella, another staff member, put it this way: "She always believed in him. I think the fact that she just always had a smile on her face, was always glad to see any friend that was his friend at any hour of the day or night—she was not a complaining-type female."

Johnson's political desire gave Lady Bird time to learn the more difficult lessons of love and marriage, how to discover her own peace within his storms. Johnson could not *afford* to leave her. It would be another twenty years before America would elect a divorced man, Ronald Reagan, as President. The hard reality was that Johnson needed to remain married to Lady Bird to be President. He would continue to "collect women"—as Reedy put it—but he would not leave her for any of them, and he would not quit politics.

Years later, in a televised interview with her daughter Lynda Johnson Robb, Lady Bird said she regarded LBJ as "my lover, my friend, my identity." From a chaise longue at the ranch, Lady Bird told her daughter, "The need for women to have their individual identity belongs to your generation, not mine." Even in hindsight, she could not acknowledge her need for a true identity. She was a married woman of the 1950s, a member of the "silent generation." To oppose her husband in the era of conformity would have been the equivalent of spitting at herself in the mirror.

For that reason, Lady Bird was as well suited for the pursuit of the presidency as LBJ. Then as now, the American presidency requires a husband and a wife to engage in a theatrical, courtly ritual. To be every inch the national king, the President must extol, even venerate, his First Lady. Unless a President gives the appearance of bowing to his wife, of demonstrating great affection, of paying her lavish public respect, he endangers his own power. The rules of the American court require that the more trouble the President gets into, the more respect he must pay his wife.

The Johnsons made comic use of this courtly ritual. At public dinners, he would sometimes pat Lady Bird on her bottom or give her a big public kiss. Once, a member of the press inquired about these displays of affection, and Lady Bird sent back word that not only did the pat on the fanny not embarrass her but that she wanted more of them. "I rather like it," she told the press.

Nonetheless, there is a reason that behind the ossified photo smiles and the adoring gazes so many First Ladies look like ghosts. Much of the time they have a vague, unfocused look because they have been required to sacrifice so much of who they are as individuals in service to an institution. Every act, opinion, comment, or sideways glance reflects not on themselves but on their husbands and the office of the presidency.

Even activist First Ladies such as Eleanor Roosevelt acquired their power by being an extra set of eyes and ears for their husbands, not by speaking on their own behalf. As a senator's wife, Mrs. Johnson ended almost every speech with the following phrase: "I'm going home and tell Lyndon tonight what a fine job you're doing." It was a line she had picked up from Mrs. Roosevelt, one that connected her at a superficial level to the public as an extension of her husband's power.

The first time the nation saw Lady Bird's ability to attach herself to a large national cause was in the opening days of the 1960 Kennedy-Johnson campaign. After leaving Los Angeles, she flew to the LBJ Ranch near Johnson City to sort out her newly expanded role. At first she assumed she would function the way she always had, as LBJ's primary caretaker, the eye in his perpetual storm.

While she was at the ranch, Jack Kennedy telephoned with an unusual request. He explained that Jackie, who was pregnant, was worried about a miscarriage and would not physically be strong enough to campaign.

"Would Lady Bird carry the load on the women's end of the campaign?" Kennedy asked Lyndon and Lady Bird, who were listening on separate telephones at the ranch. Even though the situation was filled with uncertainty, Lady Bird no longer reacted to it by withdrawing in shyness, as she had done since childhood. Her years as a political wife had hardened her, made her more confident of her abilities to handle the nuts and bolts of a campaign. "Certainly," she told Kennedy, without hesitation.

Though it was true that Jackie Kennedy was worried about her pregnancy, there were other factors that contributed to her lack of political enthusiasm. Kennedy's affair with Marilyn Monroe, which had started in 1959 in Palm Springs, California, was part of the subtext of her reluctance to campaign in 1960. Kennedy's aides lived constantly in fear of exposure. Marilyn, not Jackie, had accompanied Kennedy to the Democratic National Convention in Los Angeles. While Jackie watched her husband accept the nomination on TV in Hyannis Port, Marilyn was present in the convention hall on July 15 to hear Kennedy's speech in person.

The presence of Monroe and other "Kennedy girls" contributed to the feeling among LBJ's aides that Johnson's own extramarital affairs were politically manageable. "From what we were hearing, Kennedy was having sex with as many as six women a day," recalled Reedy. "We figured if Kennedy was getting away with six a day, Johnson had absolutely no problems. Lyndon Johnson was a choirboy compared to Jack Kennedy."

In the testosterone-addled world of presidential politics, Johnson and Kennedy had neutralized each other's liabilities. "Both Kennedy and Johnson had the same problem," recalled longtime aide Horace Busby. "They could have blackmailed each other."

For whatever reason—her pregnancy, her husband's affairs, her own private nature—the feeling among both Kennedy and Johnson camps at the start of the 1960 campaign was that Jackie was in a deep malaise and that her mood might negatively affect the campaign. "It seemed to me that she loathed politics," said Leslie Carpenter, a Texas reporter in Washington who was married to Liz and was close to the Johnsons.

Immediately after the convention, Jackie traveled to Washington from her home in Hyannis Port and hosted a luncheon for sixty newspaper reporters and editors, but after that she made an irrevocable retreat. Her main contribution to the campaign was a regular feature, offered to the press from the Democratic National Committee, called "Campaign Wife." She sent a copy of one column that she wrote on medical care for the elderly to Lady Bird, with a short note that said: "I knew you'd be interested." Jackie's health and her reluctance to meet the public forced Lady Bird into the fray.

After the convention, the Johnsons went to the Kennedy family compound in Hyannis Port, where Lady Bird had a one-on-one meeting with Jackie Kennedy that established the cautious, uneasy nature of their relationship. From Lady Bird's perspective, Jackie seemed nervous and frail, almost childlike. "She had a doll-like expression on her face and she spoke in a soft, airy voice," recalled Lady Bird. As the two women walked around the house, Lady Bird took refuge in well-mannered small talk. She admired several framed sketches of sailboats that were hanging on the wall of a den. Jackie told her that she had drawn them herself.

From out of nowhere, Jackie then blurted out that she felt "so totally inadequate, so totally at a loss" to help her husband.

To Jackie, Lady Bird seemed efficient and well organized, an integral part of Johnson's political life. In a 1974 interview, Mrs. Kennedy said that during the visit to Hyannis Port, Lady Bird carried a spiral pad "and when she'd hear a name mentioned she'd jot it down. . . . Or sometimes if Mr. Johnson wanted her, he'd say, 'Bird, do you know so-and-so's number,' and she'd always have it down. Yet she would sit talking with us, looking so calm. I was impressed with that."

The two wives talked in the strange, muted code of politics. Jackie had suffered a miscarriage in her first year of marriage and after the 1956 convention, and Lady Bird, who had several miscarriages as well, empathized with Jackie's concerns about her pregnancy. Her own miscarriages and inability to give Johnson a son, a male heir, were private regrets that Lady Bird carried with her all her life. Whether either woman attributed those early miscarriages to great tensions in their marriages—as others around them speculated—they did not say. While Jackie admired Lady Bird's efficiency, what Lady Bird remembered most was Jackie's vulnerability. "I don't know how to do anything," Jackie said, staring at Lady Bird with her large, round eyes.

Lady Bird was flabbergasted. Here was Jackie Kennedy, then thirty-one years old and the epitome of beauty and sophistication— everything Lady Bird felt she was not—confiding that she felt utterly useless. "If I were you," Lady Bird said after a long pause, "I'd find one or two reporters and have them in and talk about your home. You could do that much."

She was nudging Jackie to follow one of the unspoken rules of political wives. "No matter what," said Nellie Connally, "the political wives who survive learn to keep putting one foot forward and march. Politics is war. You learn to be a good foot soldier."

A few weeks later, Jackie Kennedy took Lady Bird's advice. She invited a group of reporters to Hyannis Port and talked about the sailboat sketches that Lady Bird had admired. It was one of the few concrete actions she took in the 1960 campaign.

During the visit to Hyannis Port, Jackie struck the other Texans on the trip not as vulnerable or frail, but rude. Betty Carson Hickman, one of Johnson's aides, had this to say about the visit: "Jack Kennedy could not have been more gracious. He came over three or four times. 'Betty, can I get you more coffee? What can I do?' But Jacqueline didn't even speak to Lady Bird. She hardly acknowledged that we were in the room. To me, that was not being a lady. That sort of thing really disturbed me, and I was afraid that the Johnsons wouldn't be treated with the respect they were due."

Such small differences in style and manners fueled enormous animosity between the Johnson and Kennedy camps. Just as their husbands represented different regions and generations, Lady Bird and Jackie, each part of her husband's image-making machine, were also mirror opposites. Jackie was a modern symbol; she hated the substantive work of politics, and she exuded style. Although her reserve struck Hickman and other Southern women as if she was peering down her nose at the average American housewife, those same women secretly admired Jackie's glamour. Lady Bird was a throwback—dutiful, thrifty, able to rub shoulders with ordinary Americans because she was so ordinary herself. "Lady Bird always reminded American women of their next-door neighbor," said Liz Carpenter. "Her down-to-earth style was her greatest asset."

Nowhere was the difference between Jackie and Lady Bird more apparent than when it came to clothes. Lady Bird dressed to please one person—Lyndon Johnson—while Jackie dressed to please herself. Stanley Marcus, president of Neiman-Marcus, who became Lady Bird's principal clothier in the 1940s and continued to help dress her throughout the White House years, said this in his oral history about Lady Bird's style: "In the early days, her taste was very, very conservative, reflecting her husband's taste. She had no daringness and she had not too much self-confidence in her taste. She was always concerned with whether she was going to look right and whether it was becoming."

In clothes and in life, LBJ was Lady Bird's authority figure. Johnson liked only straight skirts, so she wore only straight skirts. In 1960, LBJ advised her to wear a lot of black—as opposed to his earlier preference for bold colors—but this advice put her at odds with her public role. Political wives needed to wear colorful clothes so they stand out in a crowd, in photographs, or on TV.

During this period, Lady Bird looked drab and washed-out in most official photographs. One of the consistent remarks that other women made upon meeting Mrs. Johnson during this period was that she was so much prettier in person than in photographs. Part of the reason was how LBJ stage-managed her. Having grown up poor, Johnson had an obsession about clothes—his own as well as the clothes of those around him. As majority leader, he never paid less than $200 for a suit—a lot in the 1960s—and bought them five or six at a time. Lady Bird, who had grown up rich in the Depression, went to the opposite extreme and counted every penny. "It annoyed me," she admitted. "I just didn't want to spend that much time or money on clothes, but it was really important to Lyndon."

Stanley Marcus remembered that whenever Mrs. Johnson shopped at his store, she came in with a specific amount of money to spend for herself or Lynda and Lucy and she didn't go over it—not even as much as 10 cents. If a saleslady brought in a dress that was over Mrs. Johnson's budget, Lady Bird would look at it, admire it, but then say, "It's more than I can pay. Take it out of the room." The truth was there were few dresses that Mrs. Johnson could not afford to buy by 1960. The company she founded in 1942 had public assets of more than $3 million, and she controlled 52 percent of the stock. Her thriftiness was a quirk of her personality, a leftover from a childhood spent without a mother to dress her or counsel her about clothes and a father who pinched pennies.

On the other hand, she did not object to LBJ's excesses. He often did her shopping for her and did it to suit himself. "Rather than choosing her own clothes, he chose them for her," said Leslie Carpenter. "I remember once he came back from a trip to New York with about six hats for her. Now, imagine a man going in and buying a hat for his wife that she hasn't even tried on. But he did."

Whether she liked the hats and dresses or not, Lady Bird wore them and pretended to like them. "Mrs. Johnson would do anything, and she always acted like they were the prettiest things she ever saw, whether she thought so or not," recalled Leslie Carpenter in his oral history. "She was that kind of wife—completely loyal." This was part of the accepted presumption in 1960 about what it meant to be a "loyal wife"—feigning appreciation to your husband to serve his ideals.

During the 1960 campaign, the Johnsons' mutual ambition centered on the vice presidency. Lady Bird's first task was to stage a series of "ladies tea parties" with Kennedy's mother and two sisters in Texas. The idea of the tea parties was one that Joe Kennedy, Jack's father, had initiated in his son's early races for Congress in Massachusetts. In those first races, various female members of the Kennedy clan attended campaign tea parties and greeted female voters en masse. The parties worked particularly well in Boston, site of the famous tea party that had touched off the American Revolution. For the 1960 presidential race, Kennedy designated his mother, Rose Kennedy; his sister, Eunice

Shriver; and his sister-in-law (Bobby's wife), Ethel Kennedy, as his female campaign representatives.

After the meeting in Hyannis Port, Lady Bird flew back to the ranch and began making plans to host the Kennedy women in Texas. It was at that moment that she realized she needed to hire someone to help her with the campaign. She called Liz Carpenter, who co-owned a news bureau in Washington with her husband that represented a chain of Texas newspapers. "Lyndon and I've been talking about it," Lady Bird told Liz, "we've got a campaign ahead, and I'm going to need someone to be traveling with me and helping me. We wonder if you will share the great adventure of our lives."

The partnership between Carpenter and Lady Bird proved to be critical to the shaping of Lady Bird's public image. "In our first meeting together, she told me she wanted to be a doer, not a talker," recalled Carpenter. "She kept insisting on deeds, not words." The idea of being a "doer" was something she had picked up from Johnson, who described himself as a "can-do man" and who often asked staff members if they were willing to be "can-do workers." It was a phrase with which Carpenter was familiar and liked.

Carpenter, who was born in Salado, a small town just north of Austin, was by nature Lady Bird's opposite. While Lady Bird resisted flair and flamboyance, Carpenter thrived on it. She had a way of turning news events into gimmicks, deeds into dramas. In 1956, when Carpenter was writing a column called "Southern Accents" for a number of Texas newspapers in Washington and was president of the Women's National Press Club, she arranged for Lyndon Johnson and Sam Rayburn to present then President Eisenhower with a live calf at the annual National Women's Press Club dinner held at the Statler Hotel. The gimmick was that Carpenter would give Johnson and Rayburn, the two Texans in charge of Congress, the fatted calf, a symbol of political prosperity. The gimmick worked. The following day, a photograph of Johnson, Rayburn, Carpenter, then a chubby thirty-six-year-old, and the Angus calf wound up in newspapers all across the country. "It was the highlight of my life up to that point," Carpenter recalled.

By 1960, Carpenter was friendly with both of the Johnsons and had informally advised Lady Bird at the convention in Los Angeles about how to field questions from reporters. She provided Lady Bird with a list of questions that she was likely to be asked by the press and then helped rehearse the answers. Liz was not surprised when the call came later that summer to go to work full-time for Lady Bird.

The two had first met in June 1942 when Carpenter stopped by Room 504 of the Old Congressional Office Building to pay her respects to her hometown congressman. Carpenter had never met a congressman before and she was anxious to speak with Lyndon Johnson. LBJ, however, was not in Washington but was away at war in the South Pacific. Instead Carpenter met Lady Bird, who was running the office.

During the same trip to Washington, Carpenter landed a job as a secretary to Esther Van Wagoner Tufty, the owner of a small news bureau, who was one of the first aggressive female reporters to cover Capitol Hill. Tufty's insistence on being taken seriously earned her the nickname "The Duchess." In demeanor and ambition, Carpenter was similar to Tufty. Soon she was tackling real news stories, in addition to doing the routine secretarial work, and developed a reputation around the city for her bravado and spunk. It was this aspect of her personality that Carpenter now brought to the task of managing Lady Bird's public persona. Carpenter had covered Eleanor Roosevelt, Bess Truman, and Mamie Eisenhower and considered Mrs. Roosevelt a heroine. "Every newspaperwoman in town stood taller because Eleanor Roosevelt was news," she recalled. Carpenter liked the power and excitement of Washington. She loved being a reporter, striding through life—notebook in one hand, pen in the other—moving quickly from one exciting event to another. But there were limits on how fast and far female reporters were allowed to travel in the 1950s. Carpenter realized she needed to find access to a bigger world.

In 1960, when Mrs. Johnson called and offered her a job, it was Lady Bird's line about sharing a "great adventure" that Carpenter seized upon. Mrs. Johnson's use of the phrase meant that she would be open to reinventing herself—with Carpenter's help. As she later put it, Carpenter understood that Lady Bird wanted a role that would require more of her than just "standing up and saying 'howdy' at the barbecue."

Despite her bravado, Carpenter harbored a private fear of flying that kept her from accepting the job for five days. She knew that if she went on the campaign, she would have to fly in airplanes in all weather, good and bad, and land on all kinds of strips, paved and unpaved. The idea petrified her. She talked it over with her husband and two children, and it was her twelve-year-old-son, Scott, who changed her mind when he told her, "There never has been a bird that crash-landed, and you'll be flying with Lady Bird." It was the mystique of Lady Bird's nickname that sealed a critical partnership.

Carpenter called Lady Bird back and said yes, then hurried to the ranch for a round of meetings with members of the Kennedy campaign staff about how to organize the Texas tea parties. Kenny O'Donnell, who was Kennedy's top aide, took an immediate dislike to Carpenter and she to him. O'Donnell privately considered Carpenter "about as crude as they come," while Carpenter resented the attitude of O'Donnell and other Kennedy insiders that women had no real role to play in politics. O'Donnell wasn't interested in the tea parties and thought the best place for the Kennedy and Johnson women was at home. "The whole attitude of the Kennedy men who worked in this operation was to keep women barefooted and have them on their feet, preferably pregnant, on election day—nothing beyond that," Carpenter recalled. Carpenter felt for the first time, as she later put it, the "strong heel of the Irish Mafia" and was furious.

By contrast, Carpenter said that Lyndon Johnson understood and respected the political value of women. He knew they could get out his vote. "He wanted women involved in all aspects of the campaign—he used to tell me that men get distracted with one thing or another and don't follow through, but the women get the vote out. He believed women had more 'stickability,'" Carpenter recalled.

George Reedy, an early press secretary to Johnson, disputed this liberated view of Johnson's ideas of the political value of women. "Johnson really did identify with poor people and with blacks and Mexican-Americans. He knew what it was like not to be part of the economic mainstream," said Reedy. "But the idea of a really liberated woman was beyond him. He thought the way to liberate women was to get them married and to give their husbands good jobs. The rest of it—pretending to take women seriously—that was all just snake oil."

No matter what LBJ's motive, Carpenter and Lady Bird took their jobs seriously in 1960. Prior to the tea parties, Liz and Mrs. Johnson worked from an extensive card file that Lady Bird had kept for years on all of their friends and political acquaintances. "She simply got on the telephone to her friends," said Carpenter. Lady Bird called the women and LBJ called the men, and—according to Carpenter's memory—barked at them on the telephone to "get out a crowd for Bird and the Kennedy women."

In that straightforward manner, six Texas tea parties were planned. The parties would start in Houston and Dallas and then go to Wichita Falls, Odessa-Midland, El Paso, and finish at the LBJ Ranch near Stonewall. In early September 1960, while Kennedy and Johnson fought in vain in the Senate to pass a series of minimum wage, housing, and education bills, Eunice Shriver, Ethel Kennedy, and Lady Bird flew from Washington to Austin for the start of the ladies' tea parties. Carpenter had charted an airplane and dressed up some female volunteers in white pleated skirts, blue and red shirts, and Kennedy-Johnson hats and banners.

In Washington, she made the mistake of giving both Ethel and Eunice Texas cowboy hats and tried to stage a photo opportunity. Her idea was for them to put on those Texas hats and then toss them in the air for the waiting photographers. The Kennedy women balked. They thought it was corny and refused to do it. Carpenter tried to convince them, but they continued to say no. "I kept thinking," recalled a dispirited Carpenter, "if we had been up in Boston we would have been glad to put on a derby or a homburg. But they practically sat on those Texas hats."

The spurned cowboy hats were only one of many incidents that deepened the growing cultural chasm between the Kennedy and Johnson camps. Even the smallest, most minor personal habits of people on one side rubbed the people on the other the wrong way. For instance, Eunice and Ethel insisted on separate hotel suites during the tea party tour, a natural request for privacy that seemed hostile to those who were accustomed to LBJ's habit of living and working with all the members of his staff and family. To Carpenter and others on Johnson's staff, the Kennedy sisters were snobs, fussy Boston women who were unwilling to do the nitty-gritty work of politics. Of Jackie Kennedy, Leslie Carpenter said in his oral history: "She only wants to be with the beautiful people." In turn, Kennedy staff members called the Johnsons "hicks" and "rubes."

In 1960, geographical differences in America were still sharply defined. Texas was primarily a rural state, whose population depended on the land for its livelihood. The land, in turn, defined the people. The

word "hick" or "rube" referred to people who were geographically isolated, people who were reared on family farms and ranches, and who
were mistrustful of outsiders or, for that matter, anyone who was not a
blood relative. In other words, hicks were people like Lady Bird and
Lyndon.

Often Johnson would describe his ranch in overly emotional terms
that embarrassed his listeners. "Sometimes," he told a group of
reporters in the early 1960s, "I sit back and I can almost feel that rough,
unyielding, sticky clay soil between my toes, and it stirs memories." The
Kennedy camp made fun of the way Johnson and his staff members
spoke in thick Texas twangs. In turn, Johnson, a gifted mimic, often
imitated the Kennedys, especially Bobby. It was during this campaign
that various Kennedy insiders reportedly first started using the word
"cornpone" to describe both Johnsons, a description that would stick.
Soon word circled back to the Johnson camp that Mrs. Kennedy privately referred to the Johnsons as "Senator Cornpone and Mrs. Pork
Chop," which infuriated the Texans and solidified her reputation as a
snob.

Given the hostilities, Carpenter was anxious for the Kennedy women
to at least give the appearance of being pro-Texas. In Texas and the
South, the antagonism against Jack Kennedy was focused primarily on
his family's religion. "At that point, none of us was sure how a Bible Belt
state like Texas would receive Roman Catholics," recalled Carpenter.
"It hadn't been tested before."

As a political bloc, Protestant ministers moved to incite religious
passions. On September 9, the Reverend Norman Vincent Peale, a
best-selling author who coined the phrase "the power of positive thinking," issued a statement with 150 other Protestants predicting doom if
Kennedy were elected President. Peale announced that as a Roman
Catholic President, Kennedy would be "under extreme pressure by the
hierarchy of his church."

In Texas, the attack on Kennedy's religion grew even stronger.
Anonymous campaign literature, some of it posted on telephone poles
throughout the state, called the pope the "antichrist," an agent of the
devil, even the "whore of Rome." The insinuation was that as President, Kennedy would be bound by his religion to take orders directly
from the pope. In this manner, Kennedy was literally demonized in
Texas. "We don't want the Kremlin or the Vatican running the coun-

try," said one sign. In Johnson's Senate office, the mail indicated that Richard Nixon, the Republican nominee, was leading in Texas primarily because of opposition to Kennedy's religion.

Johnson went berserk over the mail. He could not bear the idea of Nixon carrying Texas. His private grudge against Nixon had been one of his strongest reasons for accepting the vice presidential nomination. In Los Angeles, when Rayburn finally came around to the idea that Johnson should run, one of his strongest arguments to Johnson was LBJ alone could help Kennedy defeat Richard Nixon.

Much of Johnson's animosity toward Nixon stemmed from Nixon's red-baiting activities, which predated U.S. Senator Joseph McCarthy's crusade against communism. In the summer of 1948, Nixon led the investigation into whether Alger Hiss, an American diplomat, had been a communist. Hiss was later indicted for perjury, amid a chorus of anti-communist rhetoric led by Nixon. Four months later, McCarthy launched his campaign against communism at home.

It worked, and in the congressional elections of 1950, the Republican-led charge against communism led to the defeat of twenty-eight Democrats in the House and five in the Senate. However, LBJ's grudge was also private and personal. He took one of the losses in the Senate particularly hard: Helen Gahagan Douglas, a former actress and New Deal liberal from California who had come to the House in 1944, lost her bid for the U.S. Senate to Nixon.

According to Horace Busby and others, Johnson and Douglas had been lovers. "It started not long after she came to the House in 1944, and continued on and off for years," said Busby. He first became aware of the relationship when Douglas and Johnson spent a lot of time together behind the closed doors of his Senate office and rumors flew in the office.

During the campaign, Nixon accused Douglas of being a "pink lady," a euphemism for communist. Rayburn was so incensed by Nixon's hard treatment of Douglas and others that from then on he refused to shake Nixon's hand. Johnson particularly was angered by the "pink lady" remark and held it against Nixon for the rest of his life.

To LBJ, Douglas was a connection to his liberal past. "He cared about people," Douglas recalled of LBJ's early days in the House in her oral history. "He was never callous, never indifferent to suffering. There was a warmth about the man."

Douglas saw Johnson through the rosy lens of New Deal idealism. She and Johnson had their experience in the National Youth Administration in common and considered themselves joint crusaders in the battle against Depression-era unemployment. Douglas had been on the state committee in California in 1940 after Johnson had served as the NYA director in Texas. As House members, their desks were situated near each other. "He didn't spend much time listening to others in the House," she remembered. "He usually voted and then left the chamber, loping off the floor with that great stride as though he was on some Texas plain."

Her personal hold on Johnson followed a familiar pattern. Douglas had attended Barnard College for two years before becoming an actress and was smart, like Alice Glass and Lady Bird. She was independent— early on, she bolted the Republican party despite her family's allegiance to it. Then there were her good looks. In some of her black-and-white publicity photos, Douglas's dark hair is swept up off her angular face in a turban, revealing a classic movie star's beauty.

Mercedes Eicholz, who was the second wife of Supreme Court Justice William O. Douglas (no relation), described Helen Douglas as a woman who had defied traditional stereotypes by having beauty, brains, and wealth. "She figured out how to get along in the world," said Eicholz. "She was the greatest brain-pumper in the world and always surrounded by smart men that she counted on for advice, including Lyndon." Eicholz knew the two were close but was unaware of a physical affair. "Helen seemed like a prude to me," recalled Eicholz. "I thought the relationship was all mental."

When Douglas ran for the Senate in 1950, her campaign was virtually run out of Johnson's office. According to Busby, LBJ took Douglas's loss for the Senate personally. "It was almost as though he had lost the race himself," Busby recalled. "He was just absolutely crushed by it." LBJ never forgot Nixon's ability to demonize Douglas. Now, ten years later, he saw the same pattern at work with the Nixon campaign's anti-Catholic crusade against Kennedy.

Johnson realized the religious issue had to be confronted. It fell to LBJ, a Disciples of Christ convert who didn't really feel identified with any particular religious denomination, and Lady Bird, a staunch Episcopalian, to defend Kennedy's right to run for President as a Roman Catholic. In response to the Peale announcement, LBJ attacked the ministers for advocating a religious test for the presidency and warned that if Kennedy, who had served in the House and the Senate, were prohibited from being President because of his religion, then Americans might as well tear up the Bill of Rights. Privately, he encouraged Kennedy to go to Texas to speak before the Greater Houston Ministerial Association to face directly the religious question himself. Three days after Peale's press conference, Johnson and Kennedy went to Houston for that meeting.

Mrs. Johnson and the two Kennedy women were already in Houston for a tea party when LBJ and JFK arrived. Early in the afternoon, prior to Kennedy's speech to the ministers at the Rice Hotel, Lady Bird, Eunice, and Ethel arrived at the hotel for the party. Lines and lines of women turned out to greet them. Many lingered to shake hands. At one point, Eunice and Ethel grew impatient and wanted to leave. Carpenter went over to Lady Bird and whispered, "They say you're taking too long with the line."

"But this is my state," Lady Bird told Liz. "I won't disappoint these women who have waited to see us."

Behind the smiling façade, Lady Bird stood her ground. By refusing to hurry, she forced the Kennedy women to shake every last outstretched hand, and forced Texas women, a few of whom had never laid eyes on a Roman Catholic, much less touched one, to greet politely Kennedy's relatives. It was a political triumph of manners.

Later that afternoon, when LBJ asked her how the tea party had gone, Lady Bird's tone was serious and businesslike. She told him that the counter at the door said 5,025 women were present. According to an attendee at Lady Bird's performance, she seemed to be a "human tape recorder, someone who was making long, mental lists."

By this time, Lady Bird was as shrewd as LBJ. She realized that elections are won and lost one vote at a time. In addition, she also knew how to count not only numbers but also blocs of voters. She told Johnson that she had seen longshoremen's wives standing next to banker's wives, which meant that the campaign was gaining support across economic levels. She realized that the Kennedy-Johnson ticket was finally taking hold.

For the seventy-one days of the campaign, she forced herself to work at LBJ's pace, often to the point of exhaustion. She made sixteen campaign appearances in eleven states, traveling 35,000 miles. With Johnson, she made another 150 campaign appearances. She refused to stop. During one of the tea parties, Lady Bird tripped and sprained her ankle. Yet she stayed at the party and stood in line until she had greeted every woman who had come for tea. These sorts of campaign affairs were generally mind-numbing. After a while, the faces all blurred together and her hands would be swollen from constantly greeting voters. But at the end of this particular day, it was her foot that was swollen—three times its normal size. After the party, she boarded an airplane for the next stop, took off her shoes, and propped up her sore foot to rest. Liz Carpenter, seated beside her, thought to herself that if her own foot were that swollen, she would be screaming in pain, but Mrs. Johnson never said a word. "Really, it was a terrific lesson in how to be a woman," Carpenter recalled.

In Houston, while Lady Bird was debriefing LBJ about the politics of tea, the telephone rang in her hotel suite. The call was from a physician at Memorial Hospital in Marshall, Texas. He informed her that her eighty-six-year-old father, T. J. Taylor, had developed blood poisoning in his leg. The following day, September 13, Taylor's leg would have to be amputated. As Carpenter, who was present in the hotel room, remembered the incident, Lady Bird's entire body flinched as her hand clutched the telephone. She looked up from the telephone and saw her husband hurrying to get dressed for Kennedy's speech. He was preoccupied with the details of the evening. Lady Bird, not wanting to distract him, kept silent about her father's condition.

"What time will they operate?" she quietly asked the doctor. The doctor told her. "I'll be there," she told him.

After she hung up the telephone, Lady Bird motioned Carpenter to her side and asked that she make the arrangements for her to travel to Marshall the following morning. Across the room Johnson was still getting dressed and called out for Lady Bird to find his speech. Once LBJ was dressed and she had handed him the speech he would use to introduce Kennedy, Lady Bird put her arm on her husband's shoulder and whispered that her father would be having surgery on the following day. She told him she needed to break away from the campaign for a few days. Johnson, thoroughly absorbed in what he was doing, nodded his agreement.

Lady Bird was torn between her conflicting duties as a daughter and a wife. As a Southern woman of her generation, she was raised to think of herself as a father's daughter. In Lady Bird's case, her reliance on her father was even stronger because she had no other parent. "I feel sure my ideas of what a man was were formed by my father," she said. "I adored him." Emotionally she had survived the death of her mother by identifying with her father and working hard to please him. She even acknowledged that she had married LBJ because "subconsciously I suppose I was looking for my father." Now both men needed her.

Standing in the hotel room the night of September 12, Lady Bird focused her attention on what had to be done in that moment. She told Johnson that she must go to see her father but assured him that she would resume her campaigning as soon as possible. Then both she and LBJ put on their game faces and went downstairs to meet John Kennedy. "She has that fantastic capacity," said Liz Carpenter. "That night, she just closed the door on it [her father's condition] and went on . . . through the handshaking and everything that was required."

The evening was a political triumph for Kennedy and a strategic victory for Johnson. Kennedy told the ministers that he did not speak for the church on public matters and the church did not speak for him. He was poised and direct, and he completely disarmed his critics. LBJ had been right. The issue had to be confronted, and he had helped Kennedy confront it on his home turf.

The following morning, Lady Bird left Houston early and arrived a few hours later in Marshall, where she confronted a larger problem than she had anticipated. Her father's third wife, Ruth, who was two years younger than Lady Bird, was suffering from an addiction to prescription drugs.

As Taylor lay dying, Ruth had checked herself in as a patient on the third floor of the Marshall hospital and was being fed morphine through her veins in a room directly across the hall from Taylor. By then, Ruth looked like a caricature of a Southern woman beset by hysteria. She was thin and her blond hair was wispy and fried from too much bleaching. "I guess you could call it a cross-addiction," said Susan Taylor, one of Taylor's granddaughters. "Granny Ruth was being given drugs in the hospital to help ease the side effects from the drugs she took at home."

In the hospital, many of the private wounds of Lady Bird's family were finally laid bare. Susan's father, Tommy, had died two years earlier of pancreatic cancer, and everyone, especially his father, felt his absence. Tommy had been T. J. Taylor's favorite of his three children.

Tommy had lived near Karnack in Jefferson and was the only one of the three Taylor children who had visited the Brick House often. Tony, the younger son, had never forgiven his father for sending him away to school as a young boy when his mother was ill. Tony kept his distance from his father's bedside and stayed in Santa Fe, New Mexico, where he ran a successful trading company that imported items from Mexico and Latin America. "My grandfather never believed my father would amount to anything," said Gerry Hopkins, one of Tony's daughters who settled in Santa Fe. "My father was proud of his business success."

Near the end, Tony had a chance to demonstrate that success to his father. Shortly before he died, Taylor found himself short of cash. He owned tens of thousands of acres of land, but much of it was unproductive. He needed $50,000, and Tony loaned him the money. Diana MacArthur, Tony's other daughter, recalled that the loan partially settled the score between Tony and Taylor. "A child tries to meet the standard of the parent. I think my father felt he had done that by becoming a financial success," MacArthur said.

Lady Bird felt the debt she owed her father could never be repaid. "I always had a car and as many pretty clothes as I had the sense to pick out," said Lady Bird. If Taylor treated her as a stranger and embarrassed her by marrying a third wife who was roughly her age, Lady Bird never acknowledged it. She idealized Taylor and carried the burden of her father's illness all through the campaign.

At the same time, she was shrewd enough to take practical steps to protect herself and her family's share of the estate. As Taylor lay dying, his daughter sent several lawyers to the hospital to determine what provisions he had made in his will for the children and grandchildren from his first marriage.

Lady Bird had first moved to change her father's will in 1955. By then, Ruth's problems with drugs had surfaced, and Lady Bird wanted her father's assets protected from tax penalties, as well as from Ruth and her family. She sent one of LBJ's lawyers, Donald Thomas, to Karnack on Christmas Eve to have a talk with Taylor. Thomas met Taylor at his general store and explained that because so much of Taylor's estate was tied up in land, not cash, the amount of estate taxes his heirs would be required to pay would be extraordinarily high, perhaps higher than the revenue Taylor was earning from the land. Thomas had prepared a document that established a living trust. He wanted Taylor to place the assets of his entire estate in an irrevocable trust to be divided by his heirs at the time of his death.

Taylor resisted signing. He told Thomas he wanted to discuss the document with Ruth, who was out of town and could not be reached. "She was away, and he was distressed," recalled Thomas. "So finally, fearing that my Christmas was going to be ruined, he [Taylor] finally said, 'Let me just sign that paper.' " Thomas, acting as Lady Bird's lawyer, pushed the trust papers in front of Taylor and he signed them.

When Ruth returned home, she was outraged. She felt her share of the estate was unfair and feared that any trustee would be more influenced by Lady Bird's wishes and those of her powerful husband than by her own. Ruth insisted that the trust be set aside. Taylor filed a lawsuit against Lady Bird and the other beneficiaries of the trust. In the course of the lawsuit, Thomas testified that he had not adequately explained to Taylor that the trust was irrevocable, and the trust was rescinded. The lawsuit was a rebuke of Lady Bird and set the stage for the legal wrangling between Ruth and Lady Bird that would last the rest of both women's lives.

On October 22, T. J. Taylor died. His funeral was held a few days later in the Methodist church in Karnack. The small church was filled with Taylor's former tenants and customers. Speakers were set up in a facility next to the church called Taylor Hall to accommodate the overflow crowd. LBJ flew in for the funeral in a helicopter, which landed on a grassy knoll near the church. He entered, and moved restlessly to his pew, shaking hands with as many voters as possible.

In the Bible Belt of East Texas, the Kennedy-Johnson ticket was not a popular one, and Johnson's preoccupation with his own candidacy alienated many people. "The funeral turned into a political event. Johnson even stood out in front of the church and handed out campaign literature. He lost a lot of votes that day," said Jerry Jones, who was Ruth's nephew and had been raised by Taylor. "People were disgusted."

The public face Lady Bird showed at her father's funeral was dry-eyed and stoic. When her mother died, she had first pretended that she had just gone away for a while and later imagined that she had seen her face in the clouds. Now she did not have the comfort of such illusions. She was forty-eight years old and no longer welcome in her father's house.

Taylor left the vast majority of his estate, valued at slightly more than $1 million, to Ruth. She got not only the Brick House, which he had first purchased for Lady Bird's mother, but the 175 acres of land that surrounded it; all of the household goods, including silver, china, jewelry, even the family photographs; and more than $500,000 in community property. In his will, Taylor left his son Tony a small amount of real estate in Cameron County and he left his only daughter, Claudia Taylor Johnson, only one piece of land—a small brick office building in Missouri.

Soon the legal wars over the estate began. The following year Ruth sued the Marshall National Bank, the executor of Taylor's will, claiming that portions of the property she and Taylor owned in common were being used to pay debts that should have been paid by Lady Bird and her heirs. That lawsuit and others were settled quietly out of court. Over the years, Lady Bird made Ruth several offers to buy the Brick House. From time to time in the late 1980s, she dispatched Thomas, and offered to both buy the Brick House and build a separate house for Ruth someplace else. At that point, Lady Bird had begun to think about founding a wildflower center and initially wanted it to be located near the Brick House. She offered to support Ruth for the rest of her life, if only she would give up the Brick House.

Ruth refused all offers. By the 1990s, relations between the two were so strained that Lady Bird was for all practical purposes barred from the Brick House and the property that surrounded it. When she asked to visit, she was told, usually by Jerry Jones, who by then carried Ruth's power of attorney, that her timing was inconvenient. At certain times when she visited Karnack, she took photographs from the road of the house that held so many burdens and ghosts.

By then, much of the house was in ruins. The floor in the main dining room had caved in, leaving the room exposed to the black dirt. Most of the bedrooms upstairs were boarded shut to keep the wind out. The house did not look haunted so much as ignored. The fate of the Brick House confirmed a lesson that Lady Bird had learned long ago as a child of the woods. In the end, nature absorbs everything.

Despite the loss of her mother's house and the battles over her father's will, in Lady Bird's mind her father remained an idealized figure. Five years after Taylor's death, Lady Bird received the following letter from Representative Wright Patman of Texas, then chairman of the

House Banking Committee. It read: "I well remember the Taylor Mercantile Company at Karnack, run by your great father, and I well remember that your father had a wonderful reputation among the Negroes and the poor white people, as he was their friend."

Lady Bird wrote Patman back and told him, "Next to hearing fond words about Lynda and Luci, the thing I love most is hearing thoughtful words about Daddy." It was not merely a polite response. Her need to think of her father as a great man who treated Negroes and poor whites as his friends was as strong as her need to think of her husband in precisely those terms.

"The key to understanding Lady Bird," said Horace Busby, LBJ's old friend and trusted aide, "is to understand that in her mind her father was the role model for how all men are and should be. It explains why she put up with LBJ's womanizing, and why she idealized him for being a public servant. She grew up with her father and assumed all men had a wife but also had girlfriends. She didn't attach much importance to it."

Even though her father was dead, she was still mentally trapped in his house, stuck with his way of life. By the 1960 campaign, most of the people on LBJ's staff understood that Lady Bird and Lyndon had an informal arrangement: he did whatever he liked, and in return for being his wife, Lady Bird pretended not to notice. All wives of unfaithful men are forced to find some ways to adapt. Her mother had fled to Chicago to the opera, briefly back to her childhood home, and then to mental flights of fantasy. Her stepmother had turned to prescription drugs. Lady Bird was stronger and saner than both of those women. She found a more productive way to cope—she hid behind her public duties.

There was another crucial difference. Johnson did not withdraw his affection for Lady Bird. On car rides through the ranch, Lady Bird and LBJ would often kiss and hug and flirt in ways that made passengers feel like voyeurs. Especially after his heart attack, Johnson bragged about their vigorous sex life to male aides, and except for the large blocks of time that they spent physically apart, they usually shared the same bedroom and the same bed until they lived in the White House. In fact, Lady Bird made a ceremony out of going to bed. Every night they spent together either she or a maid laid out LBJ's pajamas and her dressing gown, side by side, on the top of the bed. These small gestures announced in deeds—not words—that LBJ did, in fact, love her best.

At times the arrangement was a strain on everyone. At one point during this period of time, one aide remembers an afternoon when Johnson, Lady Bird, a female friend, and several male staff members went for a ride around the ranch. Two staff members were in the back seat of Johnson's Lincoln, while Johnson was at the wheel, the female friend was seated in the middle, and Lady Bird occupied the passenger seat. "Johnson made a point of placing one of his hands under the woman's skirt and was having a big time, right there in front of Lady Bird," recalled one of the aides. "A lot of women would have slapped his hands, but Lady Bird didn't say a word."

This incident is a window into the darkest corner of their marriage. Johnson apparently not only had a need for other women, but he also had a need to make a show of it. He could be the ultimate bad boy. In these moments, Lady Bird mentally disassociated herself from LBJ. She developed the habit of staying above it all; the more he misbehaved, the more prim and proper Mrs. Johnson appeared. "He would sometimes say cruel things to me," she later acknowledged. "I had more calmness and justice than he did at times." This was how she got even with LBJ. She took the moral high ground and always stayed calm, no matter how trying the circumstance. Yet the cost of being superior was high. It kept her locked in the primary condition of her childhood: isolation.

All through the campaign, LBJ used her as a foil, often in comical ways. At a campaign rally in Indiana, he told Lady Bird not to let him speak over fifteen minutes. At the ten-minute mark, Lady Bird slipped him a note: "You have two minutes." Johnson kept talking. Ten minutes later, she slipped him another note: "You're five minutes over." He continued to speak and Lady Bird slipped a third note.

This time he looked at the audience and said, "Lady Bird and my staff are trying to rush me out of here, they're trying to push me out of here." The audience began chanting, "No, don't leave." Johnson looked back at Lady Bird, pretending she was the ultimate traitor to his cause.

That day Johnson talked until he was hoarse. When he was told he had six more stops to make that particular day, he blamed Lady Bird for not keeping better track of his time. "The point is," recalled Bob Waldron, a travel aide who was on the campaign trip, "he would blow up at Mrs. Johnson the same way he did a campaign member, and this great lady would just let him get it out of his system."

In 1960, she campaigned as hard as Johnson did. Back in Washington, Jackie remained at home and sent Lady Bird an item of jewelry in early October—a small donkey pin, the symbol of the Democratic party, with sapphires for eyes and small diamond chips in his ears—for Lady Bird to wear on the road. In her thank-you note, Lady Bird told Jackie, "The adorable golden donkey, who seems to be traveling at a fast clip, is so much appreciated and I will be wearing it with great pride." Jackie wrote back promptly, telling Lady Bird that the campaign would be over soon, "so keep your chin up."

The tone of these exchanges is polite, but the letters reveal the distinct differences between Lady Bird Johnson and Jackie Kennedy. By this time, Lady Bird genuinely liked politics and did not slow her pace despite her father's illness and death. Jackie wanted no part of it; she was content to send jewelry but seemed in awe of Lady Bird's stamina. On October 26, Jackie wrote a short sympathy note about her father's death. "What can one say to a friend who has lost a father in the midst of a presidential campaign?" she wrote, woefully.

Lady Bird's stamina was indeed something to behold. Fourteen days after her father died, Lady Bird's ability to martyr herself, this time in public, became one of the defining moments in the 1960 campaign. On November 4, four days before the election, Lady Bird joined LBJ in Dallas, where the two were confronted by a blockade of right-wing, mostly female, supporters of Nixon. The confrontation took place as the Johnsons attempted to cross the intersection of Commerce and Akard in the heart of downtown Dallas.

Shortly before noon, a crowd of four hundred all-white, well-dressed Dallas women, the wives and daughters of the most prominent businessmen in town, filled the streets to block Lady Bird's passage. The women, quickly dubbed the "Mink Coat Mob" by Carpenter, were led by Dallas congressman Bruce Alger, the only Republican member of the House from Texas, and were there to protest LBJ's liberalism. Alger carried a placard that read "LBJ Sold Out to Yankee Socialists." It pictured a Texan wearing a ten-gallon hat and carrying a carpetbag. All rules of manners and decorum were off, as the mood of the women grew meaner. One female heckler hit Lady Bird over the head with a sign that read "Let's Ground Lady Bird," and then spit in her face.

Lady Bird raised her head from the crook of LBJ's shoulders and started to yell at the woman, but Johnson covered her mouth. "Hush," he told her, then motioned for her to walk slower. He realized the TV cameras were rolling and that the scene would play to his advantage. Lady Bird buried her anger in his chest. It took thirty minutes to make the fifty-yard walk across the street.

Outside on the sidewalk of the Adolphus Hotel, where two thousand Democrats were gathered for lunch, a policeman urged LBJ to slip in through a back door. The lobby of the hotel was filled with more angry women. Johnson refused. "I don't want to go through there like this was another Cuba or Berlin," Johnson told the policeman.

He scooped up Lady Bird under his arm and plunged them both into the lobby. "This is a free country," he told the women, who pressed close and jostled both him and Lady Bird. "Everybody has a right to their opinion. Please don't shove." In photographs taken that day, Lady Bird looks genuinely terrified of the mob. Something about the mood of the crowd presaged the horror and violence that would occur three years later when she and Johnson joined the Kennedys again in Dallas on the day of the assassination. The rage on the faces of the Mink Coat Mob was primal, and it was the first time she experienced the anger of a group directed at her.

Finally, she and LBJ made it to the rear of the ballroom. Johnson handed Lady Bird a comb and urged her to smooth her hair. Then he grabbed her by the hand and walked to the head table, going straight for the microphone. "If the time has come that I can't walk with my lady through the corridors of the hotels of Dallas, then I want to know about it," Johnson said, draping his large body over the podium. Johnson used an old Southern ploy: the Republicans had made the mistake of attacking his lady. His remark brought down the house.

It was one thing for Nixon and his supporters to attack Catholics and communists, but in 1960, hitting and spitting at the wife of a vice presidential candidate, especially one as well mannered as Lady Bird, was an act of extremism. LBJ sensed that some line of decency had been crossed and that he and Kennedy had Nixon on the run.

Now it was LBJ who had seized the moral high ground. It had been given to him by Lady Bird, a valuable currency that was hers to offer—or take away—throughout the marriage. He looked out over the ballroom and asked if the Democrats in the room wanted a man for President who would call leaders of the opposition party "liars and traitors" in order to win.

"No," roared the crowd. Then Johnson lowered his voice and

became almost reverential. He recalled the death of John Kennedy's brother, Joe Jr., during a secret bombing mission during World War II. Joe Jr. had long been the symbol of the Kennedy family's patriotism, and now Johnson used him as proof of their loyalty. "They didn't ask Joe Kennedy, Jr., what church he belonged to when he went on that mission," Johnson told the crowd. Two thousand people jumped to their feet.

The following day, every major newspaper carried some version of the remark, and the rightness of it, followed by the assault on Lady Bird, effectively putting an end to the political ban on Catholics running for national office.

For her part, Lady Bird sat through the speech wearing an impassive expression on her face. At that moment, she was the physical embodiment of the silent generation. Her father had recently died and she thought of him and how "bone-weary he often seemed at the end of a long day's work." That day Mrs. Johnson felt that kind of tired. She later told Carpenter that she felt so weary her whole body felt like "cooked spaghetti."

As was her habit, she tried to find something good in what had been a bad situation. She knew some of the women in the Mink Coat Mob. One or two had called Johnson's office when he was majority leader to ask for favors. One in particular had wanted to know her son's whereabouts in the Korean War. Now they had spit on her. As Johnson spoke, she looked over the crowd and her eyes fell on Stanley Marcus, the owner of Neiman-Marcus. "I'll always remember that Stanley Marcus walked by his best charge customers to be a Democrat in Dallas publicly and that it was not the popular thing to do," Lady Bird recalled.

Four days later, on November 8, Kennedy won the presidency by 112,881 votes out of 66,832,818 votes cast. Thanks to Johnson, he carried seven Southern states, including Texas by only 46,333 votes, partly because of the way Lady Bird had been treated by the Mink Coat Mob.

On election night, Lady Bird and Lyndon waited out the results in a suite in the Driskill Hotel in Austin, where they had had their first date, over breakfast. It was a long, tense evening. Finally at 7:00 A.M., the TV announcers called the election for Kennedy-Johnson. A few minutes later, Bobby Kennedy called. "Well," said Bobby, already an enemy of LBJ, "Lady Bird carried Texas for the President." Bobby was being polite of course, but what he said was true. Lady Bird had in fact carried Texas, carried it without speaking a single word, simply by doing the right wifely thing.

On November 10, Lady Bird wrote a formal letter to Mrs. Kennedy congratulating her on her husband's victory. Said Lady Bird:

> I do want to express my admiration for all the ways you found to help your husband in that great endeavor of his life. You looked perfectly lovely on television. . . . Since our visit to Hyannis Port, I have thought many times of your own concern that your condition prevented active participation in the campaign. But, my dear, I want you to know that for an "inactive" campaigner, you certainly made a great contribution. . . . It is going to be very nice to have you as First Lady.

Lady Bird's manners continued to be an important bridge between Mrs. Johnson and Mrs. Kennedy, a bridge on which the country would unknowingly rely as 1950s decorum gave way to 1960s chaos and confusion. The Mink Coat Mob marked the beginning of the 1960s for Lady Bird.

At the time of the election, the Johnsons were still living in the white-brick house on Thirtieth Place, which by now was too small for them and not adequate for their official duties. After the election, they moved into a four-bedroom apartment in the Sheraton Park Hotel, not far from the White House. They lived in the hotel six months; then, in April 1961, the Johnsons bought The Elms, a large French-style house that was built on a hilltop in the Spring Valley neighborhood, from Perle Mesta, one of Washington's best-known hostesses. The house had parquet floors in the library and Viennese murals in the dining room.

One of the first things Lady Bird did was to schedule three luncheons for Senate wives at The Elms. Instead of the luncheons being purely social, Lady Bird asked each wife to stand up and say something about her home state. The high school graduate who was too afraid to make a speech was now initiating opportunities for herself—and other women—to express themselves.

The vice presidential years were sheer misery for Johnson, who missed the action of Capitol Hill and resented being Number Two. George Reedy said Johnson's use of alcohol increased, and he spent entire days in bed at home staring at the ceiling. "He just couldn't accept anything short of being President. It was like a demon in him," Reedy recalled.

Nancy Dickerson, the NBC correspondent, interviewed Johnson from his bedroom on the night that Kennedy won. In her oral history, Dickerson said that Johnson's mood was despondent and angry. "I am like a wild animal," Johnson told Dickerson. "I keep myself on a very tight leash. My instinct is always to go for the jugular. Somehow I have an uncanny way in life to be able to hit the jugular of most men, but I keep myself on a tight leash."

Johnson's attitude about his new job affected every detail of Lady Bird's life. The first thing she did was to adjust to the new demands on her time, while coping with LBJ's depression. She hired Bess Abell, who later became her social secretary, to help answer her sudden onslaught of mail. For a while, Bess worked at a small desk located in Lady Bird's closet.

It wasn't satisfactory for either of them. In the morning, Bess would sometimes find Lady Bird's stockings from the night before draped over her typewriter, and in the evening, Lady Bird would have to pick through paper clips and stamps to get to her makeup. Lady Bird didn't yet see her role as important enough to merit a full office or staff. Even as the wife of the vice president, she was operating out of her closet.

It wasn't long before the calls started coming in from Letitia Baldrige, Jackie Kennedy's social secretary. Whatever Mrs. Kennedy did not want to do—meetings with Girl Scout troops, photos with the muscular dystrophy child, luncheons with the American Red Cross—she told Baldrige, "Give them to Lady Bird." In Washington, society columnists took to referring to Lady Bird in print as "the best pinch-hitter in town."

Jackie was younger, more aloof, and busy with two small children. Lady Bird was happy to take the load off Jackie, even though she realized that some members of the Kennedy staff were making fun of the Johnsons and she was hurt by it. "She knew what was going on. She knew they expected all Texans to walk around with ten-gallon hats, boots, and spurs," Bess Abell said. "Yet she had this terrific ability to focus on what was important. She would tell us all to focus on deeds, not words."

In the first year of Kennedy's presidency, Lady Bird substituted at more than fifty official functions. By that time, Lady Bird was a well-seasoned political wife: Johnson had served a total of twenty-four years in the House and Senate. Jackie Kennedy had been a senator's wife only seven years before she moved into the White House. However, because of the backbiting between the Kennedy and Johnson camps, the press and staff members looked for proof that the Johnsons were being slighted. Kennedy issued orders that the Johnsons were to be invited to all White House dinners, orders that were sometimes ignored. When Baldrige would send guest lists over to the President's office, the Johnsons' name would inevitably be left off. The list would often come back with the Johnsons' name added in Kennedy's own hand. Johnson used to complain to Lady Bird in front of staff members, including Bess Abell. "I've got one friend at the White House—the President," Johnson would say repeatedly.

Given the suspicions of the staff, both of the Johnsons went out of their way to win over the Kennedys. As usual, LBJ went overboard in his efforts to woo. In 1961, he gave Jackie two prized Hereford heifers and a pony named Tex. Two years later, Jackie wrote him that she no longer had a place to keep the cows, and so Johnson bought them back and had them shipped to the LBJ Ranch, where they were sold. With the money from the sale, he purchased President Lincoln's first record book of appointments, a forty-two-page document that was kept from March 5 to March 27, 1861, and donated it to the White House.

In response to a thank-you note from Jackie, Johnson drafted the following letter on June 13, 1963: "Never before has Texas beef found a market of such quality in winding up on Mrs. Kennedy's bookshelves between the covers of Mr. Lincoln's records. Too bad it couldn't be on Mr. Lincoln's bookshelves between the . . . well, never mind." The tantalizing ellipsis were LBJ's. The letter never made it to Mrs. Kennedy: the draft was sent to Liz Carpenter, who noted on the margin "too flip." His attempt to flatter and then flirt with Mrs. Kennedy was just one example of Johnson's impulsive nature.

There were others. For instance, immediately after Kennedy was sworn in, he asked Johnson and Lady Bird to fly to Paris for a NATO meeting. It was a goodwill trip, and Johnson did not want to go. A creature of legislative action, he couldn't believe that such a trip could have any real value. However, he accepted the assignment and made a speech at the opening session. Still, he was in a volatile mood, and Busby and others who accompanied him were braced for trouble.

It came the second night of the trip. Johnson went with a large entourage, including Lady Bird, to Maxim's for dinner. Lady Bird was seated at one end of the table and Lyndon was at the other. As the evening wore on, Johnson started paying noticeable and inappropriate attention to the wife of a State Department official. "After a few drinks, the woman moved down and sat on LBJ's lap. The two of them started horsing around, groping each other. It was pretty obvious and everyone was embarrassed," Busby recalled.

After a while, Lady Bird leaned over to Busby and indicated someone should take charge of the situation. Busby realized Lady Bird meant him.

He walked over to Johnson and told him firmly, "Mr. Vice President, we have to leave. The Secret Service will have the cars out front in five minutes." Johnson nodded. Busby returned to the other end of the table, and took Mrs. Johnson by the arm and escorted her out of the restaurant.

Johnson stood up and followed a few minutes later, leaving the State Department wife behind to regain her composure. In the car, the Johnsons rode back to the hotel in complete silence.

There was no need to speak. By then, the pattern was predictable: Johnson had misbehaved and Lady Bird had retreated behind her wall. Everyone else followed her lead. This was also part of her power as his wife. If she ignored his misdeed, everyone else was expected to do the same. Her silence had the effort of magic; it made LBJ's indiscretions seem to disappear.

Sometimes her silence was interpreted as acquiescence. LBJ's relationships with certain women lasted a long time. For instance, he corresponded with Alice Glass and Helen Gahagan Douglas for as long as he lived, even though both Glass and Douglas became opponents of his policies in Vietnam.

Certain staff members came to believe that Lady Bird not only knew about his affairs but condoned them. For instance, Busby recalled that one weekend while LBJ was vice president, Johnson invited Douglas to spend the weekend with him. Mrs. Johnson left The Elms the morning Douglas was scheduled to arrive and went shopping in New York for the weekend.

At one point during the weekend, Johnson telephoned Busby and asked him to come over. Busby found Douglas and Johnson in the backyard alone, lounging by the swimming pool. They held hands throughout the conversation, and it was obvious to Busby that their feelings for each other were genuine. "He was capable of having real and deep feelings for more than one woman at a time," said Busby.

For whatever reason, Lady Bird remained loyal to Douglas. A few years later, when Lady Bird was First Lady, Douglas hosted a gathering of liberal Democratic women in New York. It was a hostile crowd. Most of the women didn't like Lady Bird simply because of the Southern way she spoke and carried herself—and because she was not Jackie Kennedy.

"I would say that more than half of them were prejudiced against her before she rose to speak," Douglas said in an oral history. One of the women at Douglas's table voiced the prevailing sentiment. "I just can't bear now to hear that Southern accent," the woman told Douglas. Douglas asked the women to ignore Lady Bird's accent and listen to what she had to say.

The speech was a strong, intelligent defense of her husband's civil rights policies. "Those at my table were captivated," said Douglas. "I knew we could rely on Bird's decency and common sense." This decency that Douglas and others relied upon cut two ways. Decency and common sense were Lady Bird's tickets to power, as well as her private trap.

CHAPTER ELEVEN

Lady Bird's Thin Line

"If you don't do anything else for me, please be sure that I get the President and Mrs. Kennedy into the living room door at the ranch and not the kitchen door," Lady Bird told her assistant, Bess Abell, on the morning of Friday, November 22, 1963. Lady Bird was already in Dallas with the Kennedys on their campaign swing through Texas.

Abell was at the LBJ Ranch near Johnson City preparing for the group's arrival later that night. The schedule called for the President and Jackie to spend Friday night at the ranch and stay over the following day for a barbecue and mini–Wild West show. The question of which door—the front or the back one—the Kennedys would use for their entrance was only one detail that preoccupied Abell that morning.

She also was rehearsing a sheep-and-dog act on the banks of the Pedernales in front of the ranch house. Someone had the idea that perhaps after eating a plate of barbecue, Mrs. Kennedy would enjoy an afternoon of watching Texas dogs round up sheep, a regular practice on ranches but not one likely to appeal to Jackie's tastes. Lady Bird had good reason to be worried.

Three nights before, Mrs. Kennedy had made her first official White House appearance since the death of her third child, Patrick Bouvier Kennedy, who was born prematurely on the morning of August 7, 1963, and who died two days later. The Johnsons were among the many people who sent sympathy notes. Theirs, written by Lady Bird and signed by both of them, said: "You give so much happiness—you deserve more.

We think of you and grieve with you. Would say more but you would have to read it—and I fear want to answer it—don't." Now Jackie, still shaken from the loss of her child, was on her way to Texas for a campaign trip she was in no mood to make.

Kennedy had pushed her to come. A split in the state Democratic party between U.S. Senator Ralph Yarborough, a liberal, and Governor John Connally, a conservative, threatened to damage the ability of the Kennedy-Johnson reelection ticket to raise substantial contributions in Texas, where politics is a high-stakes business.

Connally thought Jackie's presence would soften the President's visit, make it appear less acquisitive of campaign dollars. He also knew Jackie would help draw both large crowds and big money. Texas women, like women everywhere, gravitated to her sense of style; they would gladly pay $100 each to have dinner with her, if only to get a firsthand look at her clothes. Connally's insistence infuriated Jackie. Later she would complain to William Manchester in his book *The Death of a President* that she "hated" Connally, whom she described as having had a "petulant, self-indulgent mouth" and "ruinous" good looks.

Given Jackie's state of mind, there was probably nothing Lady Bird could have done to please her, even if tragedy had not intervened. Still, in those final hours of preparation, Lady Bird walked her usual thin line. On one hand, she wanted to entertain Mrs. Kennedy in her own unpretentious way, out of doors with cut flowers from her yard casually placed on red-checkered tablecloths. Yet she was also eager to avoid playing the part of the rube.

That's why she issued last-minute orders to bring Mrs. Kennedy through her front door. Most visitors to the ranch drive up a narrow road, park near the back of the house, and enter through the kitchen door, where the first thing they see is a washing machine and dryer. To the right is the door to a large, airy yellow kitchen with 1950s-style tile floors and a bulletin board over a telephone where the day's menu is posted alongside telephone numbers for the ranch foreman and veterinarians, as well as the hardware store in Johnson City. The ranch is a working operation, and the kitchen is its center.

On this particular day, Mrs. Johnson's kitchen was filled with twenty pecan pies and eighteen loaves of homemade bread, plus several large pots of red sauce that were simmering on the stove for the next day's barbecue. The image of Jackie Kennedy, immaculately dressed in her pink suit, white gloves, and pillbox hat, being herded through the busy ranch kitchen seemed like a waking nightmare to Lady Bird.

"Bring her through the front door," Lady Bird reminded Bess.

She also made sure the staff had been instructed how to pour champagne on the rocks for Mrs. Kennedy. A private telephone had been installed in one of the six upstairs bedrooms—the one with flowered wallpaper—where Mrs. Kennedy would be staying. She placed fresh fruit in her room and a book on Texas folklore. She also wanted to know if the President's mattress and bedboard had arrived, the special one he slept on to alleviate back pain.

By this time, Mrs. Johnson was the wife of the vice president and an accomplished entertainer. Yet she viewed the Kennedys' visit through the lens of a traditional Southern hostess. If the food was good enough, the surroundings relaxed and comfortable, the flowers fresh, and the entertainment pleasant, then maybe she would survive the ordeal unscathed. Beneath her determined graciousness was Lady Bird's lingering insecurity. "The two of us lived in different worlds," recalled Lady Bird, speaking of Jackie and herself.

Lady Bird's measured courtesy did shield her from the animosity that Bobby Kennedy and other members of the family felt for LBJ. Though Jackie later complained of Johnson's mannerisms—she once called him a "cowboy oaf"—Lady Bird was careful never to give Jackie a reason not to like her. It fell to Lady Bird to fill the chasm, both generational and geographical, between the two families. She did this by putting Jackie Kennedy first and herself second. She knew that Jackie did not like the mundane business of politics and tried to save Mrs. Kennedy steps.

Her strongest impulse for Mrs. Kennedy was empathy. In the transcript of Lady Bird's diary about the events of November 22, 1963, it's clear from the emotion pouring through her voice that Lady Bird, like most of the rest of the country, was in awe of Jackie. For instance, at a critical moment in Dallas, Lady Bird fixed her gaze on Jackie's gloves. "She always wore gloves like she was used to them," Lady Bird said, speaking in a shaky, fragile voice. "I never could." Privately, Lady Bird did not like being compared to Jackie, yet she herself couldn't resist making her own private negative comparisons. "We belonged in different social frames," she recalled.

On the afternoon of November 22, 1963, in Dallas, the three political wives—Jackie, Lady Bird, and Nellie Connally—all shared a common goal. They were expected to raise money in a state that loved wealth yet despised aristocrats. Their target, as a class, was the "cowboy oafs."

The power of Texas oil money was distinctive and not to be underestimated. Virginia Durr, Lady Bird's friend from Alabama, recalled a lavish party for the Johnsons that she attended during this period. The women at the party, all wives of rich Texans, wore mink coats as casually as raincoats. One woman also wore an elaborate diamond-studded tiara that spelled out the word "Texas," precariously situated in a sprayed and teased nest in her big hair. The woman had a bulb hidden beneath her sleeve. When she squeezed the bulb—as she did repeatedly during the evening—the diamonds in "Texas" blinked, lighting her face in a halo of new money. To Durr, the glimmering tiara became a symbol of the terrific power of Texas wealth.

George Reedy, Johnson's press secretary, believed these kinds of displays cost LBJ. "What really hurt Johnson with the public is that he was a Texan," recalled Reedy. "The blatant vulgarity of the oil-rich Texas millionaires aroused strong antipathies." Reedy, like others around Johnson, resented the fact that no one called attention to how much money the Kennedys were spending on their house, or the thousands of dollars a month they threw away on clothes and art, yet the Johnsons were constantly cast in the role of vulgar, uncouth Texans.

At any rate, the issue of Texas money cut both ways. On that trip, Mrs. Kennedy, Mrs. Johnson, and Mrs. Connally were charged with raising as much of it as they could (Kennedy's personal goal was $1 million), vulgar or not. Specifically, their job was to act as buffers, to be nice to the people who were at odds with their husbands. It was the kind of job that Jackie Kennedy loathed; this time, Lady Bird could not spare her.

On that morning in Dallas, the breach between the liberals and conservatives in Texas widened over a minor issue—which politician would ride in which car. The lead story that day in Texas newspapers was that the day before, Yarborough had threatened not to ride in the same automobile with Lyndon Johnson. The headline in the *Houston Chronicle* read: "Yarborough Choosey About His Partners, Skips Ride With LBJ."

"The President told Yarborough that he could ride in the car with

Johnson or he could walk," Nellie Connally recalled. That edict, though final, did not ease Mrs. Connally's anxiety. Like Lady Bird, Nellie felt personally responsible for smoothing over the state's opposition to Kennedy, as well as Texas's growing identification with the Republican party, large forces over which she had no control. "That day I felt like a nervous mother," Nellie Connally recalled. "I just wanted everyone in Texas to get along and behave well."

At the last minute, standing in front of the Texas Hotel in Fort Worth, where the Kennedys and Johnsons had spent the night, Yarborough agreed to ride in Johnson's car. Lady Bird climbed in the back seat with the senator, leaving the front seat vacant for Lyndon. Thanks to Lady Bird, the two biggest archenemies in Texas could ride in the same car without visibly sharing the same seat or speaking to each other. She had saved face for both men.

A few hours later at 11:55 A.M., when the motorcade left Love Field in Dallas, Lady Bird could see the President, Jackie, and John and Nellie Connally in the black 1961 presidential limousine. She noticed the bouquet of long-stemmed red roses that Jackie had placed on the back seat and looked up at the sun high in the sky, grateful that the early morning drizzle had burned off. It felt good to be outdoors in the open car.

For thirty minutes more, the motorcade headed toward downtown on streets lined with people, as Lady Bird noted, "lots and lots of people, the children all smiling, placards, confetti, people waving from windows."

At 12:29 P.M., the motorcade turned at the corner of Elm and Houston streets in downtown Dallas, and Lady Bird heard what she thought were firecrackers coming from the crowd but were in fact gunshots from the sixth-floor window of the Texas School Book Depository.

The next sounds Lady Bird heard were those of someone screaming over the car radio, "Let's get out of here!" Rufus Youngblood, the Secret Service agent assigned to Johnson, jumped over the front seat, threw Johnson to the floor, and covered him with his own body. She heard Johnson groan as his shoulder hit the floorboard. Then Youngblood shouted, "Get down!" In the back seat, Yarborough and Lady Bird dived for the floorboard as well. Lady Bird covered her head.

Nellie, seated next to her husband in front of the President, heard the first shot, the one that hit the President in the back of the neck and exited his throat, and watched—as if in slow motion—the President's hand fly up to his neck in pain.

Nellie then saw Kennedy slump into the seat without speaking a word. Her husband automatically turned to face the President, and it was at that moment that she heard the second shot, the one that hit Connally in the back.

"My only thought was to get John out of the line of fire," she recalled. She pulled him onto her lap and bent over him. His signature white Stetson hat fell off his head, and she used it to cover his wound. Then she pressed Connally close to her and heard a sucking noise coming from near his lung, the sound of blood gurgling. She felt sure he was dying. She pressed harder, slowing the flow of blood.

Nellie saw—and as a home movie made by Abraham Zapruder, a Dallas businessman, showed—that Jackie did not move for several seconds after the first shot. The First Lady sat, blood spattered on her suit, frozen in her seat. Later, some would wonder if Jackie could have spared her husband from the third shot if she had reacted quickly and pulled him to her lap.

In the car, Nellie kept repeating the same mantra over and over, to herself, to John, and to Jackie, "Be still, be still. It'll be all right. Be still." From his place on her lap, Connally was in and out of consciousness. At one point, he said, "My God, they are going to kill us all."

Then Nellie heard the final shot, the one that struck the President in the head. She looked up and saw pieces of his brain flying all over the car. She heard Mrs. Kennedy scream, "My God, what are they doing? I've got his brains in my lap. My God, they've killed my husband . . . Jack, Jack."

Out of the corner of her eye, Nellie then saw Jackie climb out of the car onto the trunk of the speeding limo. Even in the midst of the crisis, Nellie thought to herself what a ridiculous spectacle the two women must have made: one sitting absolutely still in the blood-soaked car, cradling her husband's head, and the other scrambling out of the car, legs flying and arms reaching precariously for a handgrip far on the end of the trunk.

To this day, no one knows for sure exactly what Jackie Kennedy was trying to do. She told the Warren Commission she had no memory of climbing onto the trunk, and she told Theodore White of *Life* magazine that she was trying to crawl out of the car to get help for her husband.

From the street, a Secret Service man, Clint Hill, jumped onto the back of the moving car and pushed her back into the seat. Nellie believed Jackie's instinct was a normal one: she was trying to save her own life. "No one knows what they will do in a moment like that one," said Nellie. "I suppose she was in shock. She was getting out of it."

Meanwhile, in the car behind them, Lady Bird moved along the streets in a blur, her head against the floorboard. "The car accelerated terrifically fast, faster and faster," recalled Lady Bird in her diary. "Suddenly they put on the brake so hard I wondered if we were going to make it as they wheeled left and around the corner." When the car stopped, she looked up and saw a sign that said, "Hospital."

It was Yarborough who voiced the question. "Have they shot the President?" he asked, over and over. No one volunteered an answer.

At Parkland Hospital, Lady Bird was led by Secret Service agents into a small trauma room lined with white sheets. She still didn't know for sure what had happened to Kennedy or to Connally, but she kept looking at Ken O'Donnell, Kennedy's close friend and assistant, trying to read from O'Donnell's facial expression what had happened. She asked no questions.

In the small room, people kept coming in and going out. Lady Bird tried to sit absolutely still, tried to be calm, and was surprised how remarkably subdued Lyndon seemed. Years before Mary Rather had told Lady Bird and others that Johnson was easily irritated over minor things—Rather's line was "if a door squeaks, he'll scream out to get the oil can"—but in a crisis Johnson's habit was to keep quiet and still.

He was quiet now. Secret Service agents, friends, two Texas members of Congress kept coming into the room and leaving, and Johnson talked to them all in a whisper. There was confused speculation on whether Johnson himself was at risk and where he and Lady Bird should go next. She heard muted discussions about the whereabouts of the infamous "black bag," the one that contained codes for the President in case of nuclear attack. It did not register to her in that moment that her husband, not Kennedy, now bore the burden of the bag's inescapable power.

She heard Johnson tell the Secret Service to place agents on his daughters: Luci, who was sixteen and a junior at National Cathedral School for Girls in Washington, D.C., and Lynda, nineteen, a sophomore at the University of Texas at Austin. Luci was in a Spanish class when a student ran in the room and announced that Kennedy had been shot in Dallas. At first, no one said anything about her father, and Luci wondered if he, too, had been shot. In Texas, Lynda was in her room at Kinsolving Dormitory on the UT campus when she heard the news. Soon, two Secret Service officers arrived and told her what had happened. She asked to be taken to the governor's mansion to see the Connallys' children.

Lady Bird was gratified that Johnson was worried about their daughters. Even though both of his daughters idealized Johnson, he often ignored them. For instance, in her whole life, Luci never remembers a single incident in which she was alone with her father. Members of the press and close staff helped Lynda Bird with her homework and offered advice about boyfriends. "They were an unfortunate combination of spoiled and neglected children," said one family friend. Later that night, Johnson confided to Horace Busby that he knew he had not been the kind of father he should have been and had often neglected his daughters. On this day, however, he admired their levelheadedness and desire to help. Johnson told Busby, "I was proud of the way they reacted today."

In the small hospital room in Dallas, Johnson suggested to Lady Bird that she better go and see Jackie and Nellie. In her diary, Lady Bird noted that she felt a surge of affection for her husband, calling him "a good man to have in a tight spot." In moments of crisis, Presidents and their families grow closer. Public duty requires a sense of togetherness— psychologically, they have to pull together and call on the very sense of unity that is often missing from their private lives.

Lady Bird busied herself in a flurry of activity that presented her and Johnson as a united front. At 12:45 P.M., she stood up and told a Secret Service officer, "I want to find Mrs. Kennedy." She walked down a hall and found Jackie seated in a chair outside Trauma Room 1, where John Kennedy already lay dead. Equipment was being rushed past the two of them through the trauma room doors. "You always think of someone like her as being insulated, protected," Mrs. Johnson dictated into her diary. Later, she said that Jackie looked like a "helpless heap of pink."

Lady Bird was only minutes away from being exactly "like her," a First Lady, an individual subsumed in a gargantuan role. What struck Lady Bird in that instant was the vulnerability and loneliness of the job. "I never saw anyone so alone in my whole life," Lady Bird recalled.

The exchange between them was brief and awkward. Clumsily, Lady Bird threw her arms around Jackie, who did not move, and then Lady Bird gasped, "God help us all." An elderly Catholic priest, Father Oscar Huber, was already on his way to speak to Mrs. Kennedy and to pray for her husband.

Across the narrow hallway in front of Trauma Room 2, directly in front of Mrs. Kennedy, Nellie Connally was seated in another straight-backed chair. They had not spoken since their joint arrival at the hospital; both stood watch over their husbands in silence. Lady Bird crossed the hall, hugged Nellie tight, and both women cried for the first time since the shots were fired.

Nellie and Lady Bird had shared a long history dating back to the early political days in 1938. Over the years, they had vacationed together at San Jose Island near Galveston and had built sand castles with their children on the edge of the surf as their husbands relaxed on the porch, talking politics. As Nellie put it, "Politics is a tough taskmaster. It wants all your time, all your loyalty."

They stayed friends even though their husbands were competitors as well as allies, and sometimes at odds with each other. In fact, prior to the trip to Dallas, Johnson and Connally were once again estranged. Bob Strauss, a friend of both men who later became chairman of the Democratic National Committee, said that Johnson had not been advised that Connally had earlier met with Kennedy about plans for the Texas trip. Johnson felt snubbed.

Each of the wives had long ago put their husbands first, leaving their children in the care of relatives and housekeepers, and had learned to live with their own private guilt. Luci's primary caretaker, Willie Day Taylor, once said when Luci complained that she felt cast aside by both of her parents, "Every politician ought to be born a foundling and remain a bachelor." Luci made no secret that she felt orphaned to politics and resented it. "I never understood why my mother had to leave and travel with my father," said Luci. "I remember one time I clung to her skirts and tried to keep her from leaving. I screamed at her, 'You're not a real mother! A mother stays home!'"

Lynda Bird, three years older than her sister, was less dramatic but also occasionally felt orphaned. As a child, when her mother would be gone, Lynda would feel so lonely that she would go into her mother's room and smell her perfume to get what she called a feel of "her presence." Lady

Bird, who had been lonely herself as a child, had unconsciously passed along this emotional inheritance to both of her daughters.

Instead of screaming like Luci, Lynda retreated into books and, to some extent, into her father's world of politics. Even as a teenager, she would come home from school and immediately go to her room, where she found the day's newspapers waiting for her in neat stacks on her bed. She read all of them, carefully tracking the progress of bills, and then telephoned her father's office and inquired about specifics. Once her father used one of her ideas in a speech and later LBJ called her "my best speechwriter." Lynda was thrilled. When she was in college, John Kennedy had been so surprised by Lynda Bird's knowledge of politics that one day, standing in the hall of the White House, he teased her about one day becoming President herself.

Lynda, whom Lady Bird often called "that obliging girl," believed her father's career was the most important thing in the world and that it should come first. The Connallys' daughter, Kathleen, was more like Luci. She took refuge not in books, as Lynda had done, but in Elvis and boys. In 1958, Kathleen, then sixteen, became pregnant by a boy in her Fort Worth high school. The two eloped and were married. A few months later, on April 28, 1958, Kathleen threatened suicide, and in a scuffle with her young husband over a loaded shotgun in their small apartment in Tallahassee, Florida, Kathleen was killed.

The memory of Kathleen's death must have come back to Lady Bird as she held Nellie outside the operating room at Parkland. "I'm so sorry, Nellie," she told her, and she was indeed deeply sorry—not only for the President and John but for Kathleen and for the Kennedys' own two small children—sorry to the core.

"John's going to be all right, Nellie," Lady Bird told her.

"Yes, he'll be all right," she replied.

The enormity first hit Lady Bird in the car, on the way back to Love Field to board *Air Force One* for the first time. Out the window she saw a flag flying at half-mast and knew that Kennedy was dead and that her own life was never going to be the same. She would have to sell her house in Washington, The Elms, and sell her business in Texas. She would have to convince Lynda to leave the University of Texas and move to Washington and help Luci, prone to melodrama, to manage her life on an enlarged public stage. It would not be easy for the girls. Ever since they were small, they had been at each other's throats, fighting each other for the limited pieces of their parents' attention. The sibling rivalry was well known to the staff and to the whole family. Luci as a teenager once publicly characterized her relationship with her sister by saying, "I love her. I just don't like her very much." Now both teenagers would be living under the same—very public—roof.

Air Force One was all but dark when Lady Bird stepped on board. All the window shades had been lowered. The plane was crowded with people, standing in the aisles, sitting in seats, all of them crying. A television set was turned on. Lady Bird heard the commentator say somberly, "Lyndon B. Johnson, now President of the United States." She took a seat, waited for Mrs. Kennedy to arrive with her husband's bronze coffin, and tried to save her strength.

When Lady Bird was a little girl, her mother had read the Greek myths to her. She knew her tragedies well, and in her diary and later interviews, she carefully reconstructed the events of Kennedy's assassination according to the plot of a Greek tragedy. Kennedy was the fallen hero, Jackie was his grieving widow, Johnson was the reluctant successor, and she cast herself in the role of comforter.

If Lady Bird was aware of the bitter behind-the-scene arguments that went on about whether Johnson should be sworn in on board *Air Force One* in Dallas or wait until they returned to Washington—as Bobby Kennedy was advising—she never acknowledged it. What she remembered was Johnson's fears that Kennedy's assassination might be part of a larger conspiracy and the need to get away from Love Field in a hurry.

She followed Johnson to the presidential cabin and sat near him as he reached for the telephone and called the attorney general, Bobby Kennedy. She took out a page from a notebook and started making notes in shorthand. While her husband talked on the telephone, Lady Bird scribbled notes so that Johnson could remember what he had said. Her job was to stay calm, take notes, and pour on the empathy.

At about 2:25 P.M., Judge Sarah T. Hughes, a liberal whom Kennedy had appointed to the federal bench in Dallas, arrived in a polka-dot dress to administer the presidential oath. Judge Hughes carried a Bible with her. Lady Bird took her place to Johnson's right in the tight office quarters of *Air Force One*. Jackie stood to Johnson's left. In the famous photos, twenty-seven people are crowded around Hughes, whose hands shook and voice cracked during the brief ceremony. A loose strand of hair covered Jackie's impassive face.

Lady Bird wore a simple, light-colored A-line dress with a boat collar and a triple strand of pearls, and kept her eyebrows arched high and her eyes focused downward on the Bible, making her look as though she was stretched tightly in opposite directions. "I, Lyndon Baines Johnson, do solemnly swear that I will . . ." Hughes said and Johnson repeated. Lady Bird focused on the last four words of the presidential oath. "So help me, God," Johnson said.

After repeating those words, Johnson looked at Lady Bird, leaned down and kissed her on the forehead, then he turned and kissed Mrs. Kennedy on the cheek before Jackie hurriedly disappeared to the back of the airplane.

Every word Lady Bird spoke en route to Washington that afternoon seemed scripted as tragedy. In secretly taped conversations aboard *Air Force One*, the empathy in her voice is so raw it sounds almost stagy. From the air, LBJ called Rose Kennedy, the dead President's mother, and Lady Bird got on the line and delivered a eulogy. "We're glad the nation had your son as long as it did," Lady Bird told her.

"Well, thank you for that, thank you," said Rose Kennedy, before breaking into sobs and hanging up the telephone.

Next Lady Bird called Nellie at Parkland and learned that Connally had survived his surgery. Shouting over the crackling *Air Force One* radio, Lady Bird called this news "reassuring" before losing contact altogether.

Then she made her way to the back of the airplane for another uncomfortable visit to Jackie and found her seated in a small room near her husband's casket. The hose on one of Jackie's legs was ripped and caked with blood. The sight of it made Lady Bird flinch. Lady Bird asked if Jackie wanted her to find someone to help her change clothes. Jackie told Lady Bird what she angrily told others, "No, I want them to see what they have done to Jack."

She was displaying to Lady Bird and the nation a tangible reminder of Kennedy's murder, disregarding all protocol and control in order to let his death become visible. Her refusal to change into something clean, something sanitized, was a radical act, one that made Lady Bird uncomfortable.

Jackie then broke into tears. "I'm so glad I was with him," she told Lady Bird. "Oh . . . what if I hadn't been there. What if I hadn't come?"

Lady Bird then vented as well, repeating how sorry she was that this had happened, sorrier still that it happened in Texas. Already, she knew that the Kennedys and the rest of the country would hold Texas responsible for the President's murder, would blame Texas and by extension the Johnsons, for murdering the young President with the smooth and silky voice.

"Oh, Mrs. Kennedy," she said finally, "you know we never even wanted to be vice president, and now, dear God, it's come to this."

What are we to make of this exchange? At this point in their lives, neither Jackie nor Lady Bird had many genuine female friends. Each had lived inside the tight circle of official Washington, an official world in which the demands of power outweigh the bonds of friendship. Even Nellie and Lady Bird measured their words to each other carefully, never knowing for sure when their husbands might next be on unfriendly terms. Yet here were Lady Bird and Jackie, with all their history of incompatibility, suddenly thrown together in the back of an airplane, holding on to each other. In such a moment, even the most powerful seek out one another to whisper their weakness in the face of death. Lady Bird and Jackie were linked by the assassination. Though there continued to be external strains on the relationship, their bond was indelible, and in time, it eased the transition of power.

On Lady Bird's way back to her seat, Johnson asked where she wanted to go when they returned to Washington. "I want to go home and begin organizing my thoughts," she told him, meaning home to The Elms, not the White House. Lady Bird went back to her seat and spent the rest of the trip to Washington in silence. When they landed at 5:59 P.M. (Washington time), Johnson issued a perfunctory, four-sentence statement to the reporters gathered at the airport, then got into a helicopter and was airlifted to the White House. Lady Bird simply said, "I have no statement. The way I feel, it has all been a dreadful nightmare and somehow we must find strength to go on."

Lady Bird and Liz Carpenter got into a car and drove straight to The Elms, where Luci was waiting at the front door. Willie Day had picked up Luci at school and was also at the house, as were Horace Busby, one of the members of Johnson's staff, and his wife, Mary. It was Mary Busby who asked if Luci realized her father was now President. "Don't tell me that," Luci screamed.

Lady Bird took her daughter and led her to the terrace room of The Elms for a private talk. She called her Lulu, a pet name. "Your daddy's all right," Lady Bird told her younger daughter. "He'll be home soon. All this will change our lives, of course. You must give it real thought. But it needn't—it doesn't—change you, or the rest of us." The two of them telephoned Lynda in Austin. Lady Bird delivered the same message: everything has changed, but the four of us must stay together.

At 9:47 P.M., Johnson arrived back at The Elms, and Lady Bird met him at the front door, and this time she took him to the terrace room, served him an orange soda, and Johnson looked at a color photograph of former Speaker of the House Sam Rayburn, who had died two years before. "Mr. Speaker," he said, lifting his glass. "I wish you were here tonight."

Horace and Mary Busby sat with Johnson as he watched TV, which continually showed images of the assassination. The shots of Kennedy shaking hands and speaking earlier that day, with only hours more to live, particularly bothered Johnson. "I can't watch those anymore," he told Horace Busby. "Turn it off." He then asked Mary to move her chair close to his and hold his hand so that he could rest. She held his hand quietly until the new President of the United States was sufficiently calm to go to bed.

At about 3:00 A.M., Johnson decided to go upstairs to bed. Even then he did not want to be alone and asked Horace Busby to come with him. In the master bedroom, Lady Bird was still awake. She was seated at a dressing table in front of a mirror, cleaning her face. As Johnson put on his pajamas, he and Busby talked about his future campaigns for President, the one in 1964 and the one after that, in 1968.

Lady Bird didn't want to hear it. She picked up some earplugs from her dressing table and placed a black mask over her eyes, sat in her bed, and pulled the covers around her. On her fingers, she started counting the months until the next presidential campaign would start in earnest, a time she placed in August. "If I count from the end of November until the end of August, it's only nine months," she said. "That's it, nine months, right?"

Busby shook his head, and told her that Johnson expected not only to serve out this term—which would take him to January 20, 1965— but run for President himself in 1964 and probably in 1968 as well. "It's more like nine years," he told her.

Lady Bird glared at Busby and said, "Don't you say that!" She placed the mask over her eyes and went to sleep.

The following morning, Bess Abell, who had flown back to Washington from the ranch in the middle of the night, was one of the first to arrive at 8:30 A.M., ready to work. Lady Bird greeted her with, "Oh, poor Bess, what you've been through!" Abell shrugged, and thought to herself that she had been through nothing compared to Mrs. Kennedy and Lady Bird.

Abell helped her get ready to go to the White House, where Lady Bird stood next to Johnson as the two met the entire Kennedy family in the Green Room. Then they walked slowly into the East Room, where Kennedy's casket was in the center of the room, draped in an American flag.

It was her first visit to the White House as First Lady, and the house was filled with uneasy spirits. Her external surroundings had changed since her mother died, but internally Claudia Taylor Johnson was remarkably the same. Everyone knew her as Bird and she stood in yet another large and troubled house. She looked up and saw that the chandeliers in the East Room were swathed in black net. "Everywhere I looked, the house was draped in black," Lady Bird recalled.

Death and disillusionment were everywhere: on the streets, in the newspapers, in American homes, where families stayed glued to their television on which all three networks broadcast live events nonstop throughout the weekend.

On Sunday, November 24, as Lady Bird was waiting in the White House to drive up to the Capitol where Kennedy lay in state, Eunice Shriver turned to her in line and said, "I hear Oswald has been killed." This was the first news she had heard that Lee Harvey Oswald had been shot in Dallas.

The next day, Johnson walked with Mrs. Kennedy and a procession of international leaders behind Kennedy's coffin to the funeral at St. Matthew's Cathedral. Lady Bird made a strange comment in her diary. She said that Jackie's composure and dignity that day earned her something that Jackie had never achieved in her time at the White House—"a state of love, a state of rapport between herself and the people of this country." For all her glamour and good looks, Lady Bird felt that Jackie had not been loved as First Lady. It was that prize—the love of the American people—that Lady Bird set out to win for herself.

After the funeral, Lady Bird returned to The Elms. Virginia Durr was one of the people who greeted her. "As she walked in her house, she began pulling off her hat and gloves to see if there was enough fried chicken to go around." Durr thought the scene typified Lady Bird's Southern stoicism. Her emphasis was on doing what was necessary "so the survivors could be fed."

On November 26, Lady Bird went to the White House and met with J. B. West, the head usher, for a brief tour of the 132-room house and to talk about how to approach the delicate task of moving the Johnsons in and the Kennedys out. She explained that she would be selling The Elms and planned to move only three rooms of furniture from there— the items from her bedroom, and her daughters'—into the White House. Everything else that belonged to her in The Elms would be sent to the ranch or to storage.

At 3:00 P.M., she met with Jackie in the family quarters, who told her repeatedly, "Don't be frightened of this house. Some of the happiest years of my marriage have been spent here. You'll be happy here."

Jackie asked the Johnsons if Caroline Kennedy's kindergarten class, which met at the White House, could finish the fall term. Lady Bird told her to take as much time as she needed. After Lady Bird left, Jackie went to see Johnson in the Oval Office and asked him to rename the Space Center in Florida after Kennedy. Johnson changed the name immediately. In an oral history done in January 1974, Jackie said she regretted making the request. "Now that I think back on it, that was so wrong, and if I'd known [Cape Canaveral] was the name from the time of Columbus, it would be the last thing that Jack would have wanted," she said. She also asked Johnson to continue the work she had started both to renovate the White House and to renew several blighted blocks in downtown Washington.

Johnson assured her the work would go on. In fact, he told her that Lady Bird herself would make the beautification of Washington a primary goal, a remark Johnson made idly and without thinking. Yet it shaped much of Mrs. Johnson's future as First Lady.

Late that night, in a fit of grief that Liz Carpenter later described as "ghoulish," Jackie sat down at the White House to write by hand a stream-of-consciousness letter to the new President that reveals the complicated nature of the relationship between her and the Johnsons.

She began the letter with "thank you for walking yesterday—behind Jack. You did not have to do that—I am sure many people forbid you to take such a risk—but you did it anyway." It was a reference to Johnson's decision to follow Jackie during a procession of international dignitaries to St. Matthew's Church for President Kennedy's funeral.

She also thanked Johnson for letters he had written to both of the Kennedy children on November 22, 1963. "You can always be proud of him," Johnson told John Jr. Johnson continued his correspondence with the Kennedy children. For instance, three years later, on November 23, 1966—two days before John's birthday—one of Johnson's staff wrote a clever birthday letter for John Jr. that LBJ signed. It said: "When I was six, I wanted to be sixteen. But today I wish I were six again, like you."

In her letter written after Kennedy's funeral, Jackie described the relationship between her and Kennedy and the Johnsons in terms that now seem overly friendly. She called Johnson "Jack's right arm" and said that although the relationships between presidential and vice presidential families were often strained throughout history, the Kennedys and Johnsons were "friends." She also indicated that even before the nomination in 1960, she thought Lady Bird should be First Lady, not her. "But I don't need to tell you here what I think of her qualities—her extraordinary grace of character—her willingness to assume every burden—she assumed so many for me and I love her very much," wrote Mrs. Kennedy.

She described how the night before she had wandered through the White House and saw two items that Johnson had given to the White House—a chandelier in the East Room that he had asked be moved from the Capitol and the Lincoln Record Book—and she came upon a man who was moving her husband's personal items from the Oval Office. "I thought you would want to put things from Texas in it—I pictured some gleaming longhorns—I hope you put them somewhere," Mrs. Kennedy suggested.

On December 1, Johnson responded, congratulating her on the way she had handled herself during the funeral. "Jackie," he said, "you have been magnificent and won a warm place in the heart of history. I only wish things could be different—that I didn't have to be here. But the Almighty has willed differently and Lady Bird and I need your help."

At 2:42 P.M. on December 2, he telephoned Jackie. During the conversation, which was held in the Oval Office and taped by one of Johnson's secretaries, Johnson continued to woo Jackie.

"I just wanted you to know you are loved by so many and so much," Johnson told her. "I'm one of them."

Jackie responded with equal affection. "I got my letter that was waiting for me last night," she said, in an airy and breathless voice. "I didn't dare bother you again."

"Listen, sweetie," said Johnson. "One thing you gotta learn is that you don't bother me. You give me strength. You just come over and put your arm around me. That's all you do. When you haven't anything else to do, let's take a walk around the backyard."

But Jackie did not want to come back to the White House. Though the Johnsons repeatedly invited her (she was issued an automatic invitation to every state dinner), Jackie always declined, explaining that it was just too difficult for her to return. In a tired, sad voice, she steered the conversation back to LBJ's letter.

"Do you know what I wanted to say to you about that letter?" she asked. "I know how rare it is to have a letter in a President's handwriting. Do you know I have more letters in your handwriting than I do in Jack's now?"

Her voice broke and the sound on the tape is of Jackie Kennedy's quiet sobs. "Well, now," he told her, clearly flustered.

"I told my mama a long time ago . . . when everybody else gave up about my election in '48, my mother, my wife, my sisters didn't . . . you females got a lot of courage we men don't have," said Johnson awkwardly, and then he all but threw himself at her feet.

"You got something to do. You've got this President relying on you," he begged her. "And this is not the first one you had."

On the other end of the line, Jackie did not offer her help, but she did not refuse him, either. Instead, she laughed. "She ran around with two Presidents," said Mrs. Kennedy, sounding mesmerized. "That's what they will say about me."

Johnson laughed, too, before ending the conversation with "Kisses."

Meanwhile, Lady Bird struggled to figure out when and how she should move into the White House. Hundreds of members of the press requested interviews with Lady Bird, and all of them wanted to know when she was moving in. At The Elms, Carpenter, by this time Lady Bird's staff director as well as press secretary, pressed Lady Bird for an answer. She grew angry and refused to be pushed. "I would to God I could serve Mrs. Kennedy's comfort," she snapped at Liz. "I can at least serve her convenience."

Liz wrote the remark down verbatim and distributed it to the press.

Lady Bird had managed to sound both firm and polite at the same time, and it went a long way toward sealing her image as a steel magnolia, a force to be feared as well as admired. Historically, she found herself in the same position Bess Truman had been in when she moved into the White House. She, like Mrs. Truman, who followed Eleanor Roosevelt, found herself in the shadow of a presidential widow, struggling to be gracious while at the same time forging her own way.

She and Johnson quarreled on the morning of Saturday, December 7, about when exactly to make the move into the White House. Jackie and the children had left that morning, and Johnson wanted to move in that afternoon. According to Luci, it was the only time she ever heard her parents argue. "My mother always did what my father wanted. She just wouldn't argue," said Luci. "This time she did."

Lady Bird's objection was that December 7 is the anniversary of the bombing of Pearl Harbor, and Lady Bird, who vividly remembered the bombing, did not want the two events connected in either her memory or the country's. Already her eye was on history. She asked Johnson to wait a few days.

Johnson would not hear of it. On his orders, Luci picked up the family dogs, two beagles named Him and Her, and put them in the back seat of her convertible and drove off to the White House. Lady Bird, Liz, and Bess followed in a government car. At the last minute, when she was about to leave, Lady Bird picked up the framed photograph of Speaker Sam Rayburn, the one that Johnson had toasted the night of the assassination, from its place of honor in her terrace room, and clung to it during the drive to the White House.

Like Lady Bird, Rayburn had not wanted Johnson to run for vice president. In fact, over the years, Lady Bird and Rayburn had agreed about every detail of LBJ's career. When LBJ would not listen to her advice, she funneled it through Rayburn, whom he dared not ignore. Rayburn was the person she most trusted, and she wanted him with her—in spirit—as she faced the prospect of life in the White House. "I always thought if Lady Bird had been a man, she would have wound up like Sam Rayburn," said George Reedy. "Neither one were ideologues, like Lyndon, and both were absolutely practical in everything they did. What they both wanted was to unite people in order to get things done."

When Lady Bird arrived at the White House, she went upstairs to her bedroom and found a small bouquet of flowers from Mrs. Kennedy with a note that said: "I wish you a happy arrival in your new house, Lady Bird—Remember—you will be happy here. Love, Jackie."

On December 7, Johnson held his first press conference as President, and later that afternoon, at 5:20 P.M., he again placed a telephone call to Jackie Kennedy. During the conversation, Jackie sounded strained to the point of exhaustion, but she is surprisingly affectionate.

"Oh listen," she said at the start of the conversation. "I'm just collapsed. I haven't gotten out of bed." Then she asked Johnson if he and Lady Bird and Luci were going to spend the night in the White House.

"I guess so. I'm afraid to," Johnson replied.

"You all three sleep in the same room. It's the worst thing the first night. The rooms are all so big. You will all get lost," said Jackie, trying to be helpful.

"Darlin'," said Johnson, "I'd give anything in the world if I wasn't here today." Again, he pressed her to come back to the White House, and again she put him off. "Someday I will," she told him, then advised him to take a sleeping pill so that he would get a good night's sleep.

Johnson then asked about her children, and laying it on, said, "Tell 'em I'd like to be their daddy."

This was Johnson at his most awkward. For a man reputed to be so persuasive and such a political genius, in public and in private he could be amazingly clumsy, even oblivious. The highest compliment he could pay anyone was to make them part of his family—even if they didn't want to be. The image that one sometimes gets of LBJ is of a person who was simply too large to fit into any conceivable frame. His offer to serve as a surrogate father to Jackie's children less than a month after Kennedy was murdered was an example of this tendency to overreach. Nonetheless, Jackie Kennedy's response continued to be warm. If she was offended, she did not express it. "You're awfully nice," she told him.

Lady Bird wrote a letter to Janet Auchincloss, Jackie's mother, telling her that "if Lyndon could, he would take the stars out of the sky and make her a necklace."

Meanwhile, Johnson's relationship with Lady Bird cooled after they moved into the White House. In her diary, Lady Bird described that she felt as a "gulf" between her and Johnson. She was not specific about what caused the gap, but part of it was the sheer physical toll of the job. Johnson, always a hard worker, now worked eighteen-hour days, and

when he came home to the family quarters, he always brought work
with him.

Lady Bird's own workload increased as well. In the first few weeks
after the assassination, she received about ten thousand letters a week.
On one particular day, she received forty-four thousand communications, all expressions of grief for Kennedy and prayers and good wishes
for the Johnsons. Both of them felt consumed by the presidency.

As taped conversations from the Oval Office show, their relationship
often sounded businesslike. They often double-teamed people on the
telephone. At one point in 1964, Johnson telephoned former President
Harry Truman to ask him to accompany Lady Bird to King Paul's
funeral in Greece. To entice him and his wife, Bess, to make the trip,
Johnson told Truman that he would send a maid along to help Bess and
then said, "Lady Bird will fix her a good old-fashioned—bourbon and
water—whatever she wants."

He was wisecracking, of course, playing the familiar part of the Texas
good old boy. It was Lady Bird who broke in to clinch the deal. "It would
be so much more of a meaningful trip if you went along," she told Truman, as she trilled her vowels and pressed down hard on "meaningful."

The tapes show that Johnson repeatedly used her as his consort, his
adviser, his personal prop, even at times an accessory to his extramarital
escapades. For instance, on January 1, 1964, Johnson called Helen
Gahagan Douglas and asked her to travel to Liberia as his representative for a celebration of the one hundredth anniversary of the relations
between the two countries. Lady Bird was in the Oval Office at the time
of the call. She overheard him tell Douglas that he had given her a full
four-day notice for the trip, which, Johnson said, was "four days more
notice than I usually give you." The remark begged: notice for what?

Douglas laughed and told LBJ she'd have to check with her husband,
Melvyn Douglas, the actor, and then reminded LBJ that Melvyn "never
knew you the way I did."

Near the end of the conversation, Johnson handed the telephone to
Lady Bird, who, in her most saccharine voice, crooned: "Ah, Hell-en, so
nice to hear you, and honey, let me—"

Douglas cut her off in mid-sentence to say that Johnson was getting
high praise from everyone in her home state of California, even the
Republicans.

Lady Bird interrupted Douglas and said that she knew things were going well in California. She had recently been there and met some of Douglas's closest friends, who seemed really to like Johnson. Then Lady Bird said something close to the truth. "I guess I'm used to it 'cause I like for women to like him, and I like him to like them."

A few months later, Douglas spent the night in the White House. Johnson had seen her at an event in Washington and invited her home on the spur of the moment. Since she had no bedclothes, he furnished Douglas with one of Lady Bird's nightgowns and robes for the evening. Lady Bird did not realize Douglas was a guest in her house until the next morning, when she found Douglas walking around on the third floor in her nightgown. She did not get angry or snub her. Instead, she behaved as if everything was fine and invited Douglas to breakfast. Over coffee, the two women watched through a window as Johnson left the South Lawn by helicopter.

It would be impossible not to feel rejected and resentful in such a situation. Occasionally, she did complain about the loneliness of the job and the fact that she and Johnson spent less and less time together. She often tried to set up "dates" with Johnson, but most of the time, he begged off. He was either too busy or did not want to spend time alone with her. For instance, on December 17, 1963, she called the Oval Office at 7:30 P.M., exhausted after the past few weeks.

"I'm lonesome over here and I wish you'd come home," she told Johnson, sounding genuinely forlorn. Johnson, surrounded by a few aides, told her he was about to go swimming in the White House pool. "Why don't you go swimming with us?" he asked.

"I just can't go swimming," said Lady Bird. "I don't have enough calories left." He didn't respond to her exhaustion or misery but rushed her off the telephone, telling her he'd be home in a little while.

"I hope you come soon," she said, sounding like a lost soul.

Five days later, on Lady Bird's fifty-first birthday, and one month after the assassination, Johnson issued orders that the black net be removed from all the chandeliers in the White House. That night, the Johnson family put up Christmas decorations. "I walked the well-lit hall for the first time with a sense that life was going to go on, that we as a country were going to begin again," Lady Bird recalled.

The following day, Johnson took time out from running the country to telephone his favorite hairdresser, Eddie Senz, in New York to ask him to come to the White House to fix not only his wife's hair but that of both daughters and his entire secretarial staff. What's more, he wanted Senz to work cheap—all he was willing to pay was $100 in cash. "I don't make much money, but I got a wife and a couple of daughters, and four or five people that run around with me, and I like the way you make them look," Johnson, a multimillionaire, told Senz.

He then asked Senz to fly down to Washington that afternoon and do Mrs. Johnson's hair "and not give her too much of his makeup, but give her enough to do it." Still pretending to be poor, he made an appeal to the hairdresser's patriotism. "This is your country and I want to see what you want to do about it," Johnson told him. Senz was flabbergasted, assured him he would be flattered to do all he could in service to the First Lady's hair, and said he would catch the first flight from New York.

Later that afternoon, Senz arrived at the White House and spent the entire afternoon doing hair and makeup. At 7:35 P.M., Lady Bird telephoned Johnson from under a bubble-hooded hairdryer. The conversation took place over the dryer's dull roar.

"Are they working on your hair?" LBJ asked impatiently. "Yes," said Lady Bird. "I was under the dryer." Then he asked if Senz had done Luci's hair and wanted to know the hair status of two of his secretaries, Marie Fehmer and Yolanda Boozer.

"I don't know what we can do about Yolanda," said Lady Bird, with a sigh. Apparently, Boozer's hair was unruly and long. "Tell him to go on and do Yolanda," barked Johnson. "She's got to have a bale cut off if I'm going to look at her through Christmas."

"All right, honey," Lady Bird said, who did not laugh or even seem to notice that her husband had just compared his secretary's hair to hay. Instead, she asked Johnson when he would be home for dinner and how many people he was bringing. Johnson dodged both questions, so Lady Bird, sounding like an efficient secretary, inquired, "Dinner for three on trays at an indefinite hour?" He said yes, then hung up the telephone.

During Christmas, Johnson continued his efforts to identify himself with Jackie Kennedy. He sent Christmas gifts to her and to John and Caroline, and on December 27, he telephoned Ken O'Donnell and asked if he could talk to Mrs. Kennedy about a "personal matter." He wanted to make her ambassador to Mexico. O'Donnell wasn't sure it was such a good idea, but Johnson was insistent. "I believe President Kennedy would do my wife that same way," he told O'Donnell. To sell

O'Donnell on the idea, he told him that the embassy in Mexico was fully staffed and that Mrs. Kennedy would be free to come and go whenever she liked.

"I think it would be a ten-strike if she would consider it," said Johnson. "It might keep her from worrying herself to death."

O'Donnell told Johnson that he thought Mrs. Kennedy would refuse such an offer.

"Hell," Johnson replied. "I'd make her pope if I could."

He seemed to believe if he could win Mrs. Kennedy's loyalty that he could somehow free himself from the spell of the Kennedy family. However, beyond the considerations of politics, he seemed really to want her approval. It went back to Johnson's peculiar view of women—he saw Jackie as the embodiment of what was left of the Kennedy mystique and wanted to capture her, like a prize.

A few days later, on January 9, the day after Johnson delivered the State of the Union address, he telephoned Mrs. Kennedy and again asked her to come for a visit. Flexing his political muscle, this time Johnson threatened to come to Georgetown and bring her to the White House.

Finally, Mrs. Kennedy was firm. "I just can't," she told him flatly. "Don't make me come down there." The tone of her voice was tired, frightened, and defensive, but she was clear that she would not return to the White House. "I don't want to start crying again," she told Johnson.

The compulsion to charm was as strong in Jackie as it was in LBJ. With unsparing clarity, Jackie continued to cling to the illusion that the political bond between JFK and LBJ had not been severed by Kennedy's murder. As the tapes reveal, Jackie was as solicitous of LBJ as he was of her.

"Will you please start taking a nap in the afternoon?" she asked him on January 9 and then went on to say that taking regular naps as President had "changed Jack's whole life." She reminded Johnson that Churchill had taken naps to save his strength as well. "You just can't tear around," she told Johnson, sounding almost like his wife.

Throughout the winter, Lady Bird also continued to manage Johnson's personal habits and to help soothe frayed relationships. For instance, Bob Strauss recalled a trip to New York that he and his wife, Helen, took with John and Nellie Connally shortly after Connally was released from the hospital. On the way back home to Texas, they stopped in Washington. Lady Bird found out they were in town and made sure that the Connallys and the Strausses were invited to the White House for dinner and to spend the night. "It was the first time the President and Connally had seen each other since the assassination," recalled Strauss. "There were still some leftover bad feelings about what had happened before the assassination. As usual, it was Lady Bird who knew just how to break the ice."

She was doing all the usual things she had done for years—begging Johnson to rest, monitoring his diet, encouraging his staff—but behind the scenes she also increasingly played the part of counselor and adviser. For instance, after a press conference on March 7, nearly four months after her husband had assumed the presidency, she telephoned Johnson to offer him her opinion, which included tough questions about whether he was withholding information about the buildup in Vietnam, about his troubled relationship with Bobby Kennedy, and whether he would travel to France to meet with French president Charles de Gaulle.

"You want to listen for about one minute to my critique, or would you rather wait until tonight?" Lady Bird asked, following the press conference.

"Yes, ma'am. I'm willing now," Johnson replied, bracing himself for his wife's assessment.

"I thought you looked strong, firm, and like a reliable guy. Your looks were splendid. The close-ups were much better than the distance ones," Lady Bird said. Johnson reacted defensively, explaining in an irritated voice that he couldn't force the national TV crews to do close-ups.

Lady Bird hurried on to her more negative comments about his opening statement. "You were a little breathless and there was too much looking down and I think it was a little too fast," she told him. "Not enough change of pace. Dropping voice at the end of sentence. There was considerable pickup in drama and interest when the questioning began." For someone shy about public speaking, Lady Bird had no trouble distinguishing good speaking technique from bad.

"Every now and then," she continued unrelentingly, "you need a good crisp answer for a change of pace and therefore I was glad when you answered one man, 'The answer is NO to both your questions.'"

Johnson then complained that the press criticized him for taking too much time on his opening statements, and about the pressure he felt from them. "If you don't give them news, you catch hell," he complained.

"Um-hmm," said Lady Bird, refusing to coddle him. "I believe if I'd had that choice I would have used thirteen minutes or fourteen for the statement." She was not always subservient; in private, she could also be imperious, as generous with her criticism as with her praise, a co-sovereign as well as a consort. Few people in Johnson's inner circle had the nerve to issue Lyndon Johnson a grade. Lady Bird was one who did.

"In general," she said of his press conference, "I'd say it was a good B plus."

LBJ took his grade, but he was too proud to allow his wife's critique to go unchallenged. "I thought it was much better than last week," he said, still agonizing over his performance.

At that moment, the anxiety in his voice was audible. It was clear that Johnson meant what he had told Jackie Kennedy three months earlier about how lost he felt and how much he needed the support of women. Beneath his bellow, LBJ was a fragile and bewildered man who relied on the strength and sympathy of everyone around him, especially his wife. It's difficult to imagine how he would have kept himself emotionally together without her.

Lady Bird knew he depended on her not to let him give up, and this, too, was part of their bargain. On this particular day, she ended the conversation by telling Johnson she would see him at a "reasonable hour" for dinner, and then she said before hanging up the line, "And I love you very much."

CHAPTER TWELVE

❧

Whistling in the Dark

Nineteen sixty-four was a watershed year for Lady Bird. While she held Johnson together as he pushed the Civil Rights Act through Congress and waged his own race for the presidency, she also discovered her own political voice.

During a four-day, 1,628-mile campaign train trip through eight Southern states in the fall, Lady Bird played a role straight out of the Gothic era of Southern politics. In defense of her husband's support of the Civil Rights Act, she traveled to cities and towns that were in such racial turmoil it was not considered safe for Johnson to go. Her message was that the Civil War should at long last come to an end, which could only happen if the South shed its racist past and moved into the modern world.

As a Southerner, she was divided about how the region should go about its transformation. She wanted to keep the old customs—as she put it, "keeping up with your kinfolks, of long Sunday dinners after church, of a special brand of courtesy"—but throw out the system of inequality. "I knew the Civil Rights Act was right and I didn't mind saying so, but I also loved the South and didn't want it used as the whipping boy of the Democratic party," Lady Bird said as she prepared for her trip.

She resented the prejudice that she had felt as a white Southerner living in Washington. "There are plenty of people who make snide jokes about the cornpone and redneck," she said. "What I want to say to those people is that I love the South. I'm proud of the South. For me this is going to be a journey of the heart." It was her way of answering the Kennedys. Johnson also wanted her to go. He knew that Southern Democrats felt abandoned and thought Lady Bird could lay out a welcome mat, better than he could, given his own unpopularity.

She viewed the whistlestop trip as a test of her loyalty to her Southern roots. There was an awful lot of mythology in Lady Bird's view of the South, and in turn, of the South's view of her. Through Johnson and her own support of the New Deal, she identified with the downtrodden, family farmers and small business owners who had agrarian roots and felt alienated from an increasingly urban world. However, her earliest, deepest identity was that of a white woman of privilege: by 1964, Lady Bird was the nation's most visible Southern belle, a powerful symbol of her region.

For generations, white Southerners had sworn to defend the virtue and honor of women exactly like Lady Bird Johnson, women who worked hard to be soft, loyal, and, above all—"gracious"—the adjective most often used to describe Mrs. Johnson. Even as late as the 1960s, rural Blacks in the South dared not look too long or admiringly at women of Lady Bird's class and color for fear of being lynched.

Lady Bird realized that Southern Democrats held her on a pedestal, and during her whistlestop tour in the fall of 1964, she used that pedestal as a moving political platform. For those four days, the most courageous of her public life, Lady Bird was able to briefly transcend the limitations of her region's view of both women and Blacks.

The South did not make it easy for her. This particular period in Southern history, the mid-1960s, is remembered by modern-day Southerners only when necessary and with shame. The summer before Lady Bird's trip, three civil rights workers who were attempting to register Blacks to vote had been murdered in Neshoba County, Mississippi. The threat of the strengthened Black vote in the South to segregationists was real. In the four years since 1960, the Negro vote in the region had doubled.

Newspapers all over the South were filled with accounts of Blacks who had been abducted, flogged, arbitrarily arrested, and forced to close their businesses—all efforts to discourage them from registering to vote. In a single town—McComb, Mississippi—ten Black churches and sixteen Black homes were firebombed in the summer of 1964.

Mrs. Ora Bryant, one of the Black women from McComb whose

home was bombed, traveled to Washington and met with Johnson in his office to tell him about her terror-filled summer. During the meeting in the Oval Office, Bryant told Johnson that when she allowed civil rights workers, both Black and white, to eat at her small cafe, her white landlord encouraged her to close it down.

"Why don't you just close up for a couple of months?" the landlord suggested to the woman.

"I can't afford to," she replied.

"Take a vacation," the landlord threatened.

Mrs. Bryant then told Johnson, "I stayed open and they bombed my house." She also lost her lease on the cafe. She had lost her home and business, and had gone three times to her local courthouse to try to register to vote, each time without success. "The white man ain't gonna let us vote," she told the President. Johnson's only advice was for the woman to keep trying.

Mrs. Bryant's despair was in reaction to the violence touched off by the passage of the Civil Rights Act, which LBJ signed on July 2, 1964, only eight months after assuming the presidency. During the signing ceremony in the East Room of the White House, Lady Bird noticed Attorney General Bobby Kennedy situated prominently in the front row. She knew that Bobby was considering challenging LBJ at the upcoming Democratic National Convention and had little hope that passage of the act, a version that was stronger than the one President Kennedy had sent to Congress the year before, would buy peace.

By putting an end to Jim Crow laws in the South, the Civil Rights Act rearranged the political and social landscape of the country. It guaranteed Blacks access to all public accommodations—the use of bathrooms, buses, water fountains, restaurants, public parks, and places of business, and guaranteed equal access to employment. Lady Bird knew that when she left the East Room that day, she had seen the beginning of something new in the country, an era that would bring, as she later said, "untold good and much pain and trouble."

Unlike LBJ and the liberal wing of the Democratic party, Lady Bird did not assume that the problems between the races would be easily solved. The passage of the Civil Rights Act was like walking into the living room of an antebellum mansion, throwing out all the antiques, ripping up the rugs, tearing down the drapes, and then walking out of the room, expecting new furniture, rugs, and shimmering curtains to magically spring into place, at no cost.

LBJ understood the politics of the equation well. He knew that the passage of the Civil Rights Act would deliver the South to the Republican party, and, to his credit, he fought for it anyway. Like Mrs. Bryant, Lady Bird understood the high personal sacrifices that would have to be paid by Blacks and whites alike.

Like Mrs. Bryant, Lady Bird came from the segregated South. She understood how separately Blacks and whites lived even though they shared the same land and customs. Unlike LBJ, she had grown up buttressed, both physically and economically, by the Black underclass. Black maids had named her, raised her, fed her, and clothed her. Her playmates were, for the most part, their children. Their husbands worked her father's land, brought in his crops, and spent their yearly wages in his store.

In an old photograph taken of Lady Bird as a toddler, sometime around 1913, she and her brother Tony are pictured with six Black servants, all dressed in floppy hats and long aprons. On the back of the disintegrating photo years later, Mrs. Johnson noted the names of as many of the servants as she could identify—Alice Tittle, the nurse who named her, "Prince," and "Sonny." On the back of the photograph, she wrote: "We always had six or more staff in those days!"

The barely freed slaves that Mrs. Johnson grew up with were not the people who launched the Black protest movement. That was led by middle-class Blacks—students, preachers, intellectuals—not the class Lady Bird Johnson had known in East Texas or during her summers in Alabama. She had heard the men in her town speak of Blacks as "niggers," but until the mid-1960s when Malcolm X and others publicly called all whites "devils," Lady Bird had not directly experienced Black rage. The first sit-ins in the country came in 1960, when four Black college students were denied service at a lunch counter in a Woolworth's in Greensboro, North Carolina. In the spring of the following year, the Congress of Racial Equality (CORE), made up largely of students, sponsored the first "freedom rides" into the South to call attention to segregated waiting rooms.

As the freedom riders moved deeper into the South, white Southerners publicly and vehemently revealed their opposition. John and

Bobby Kennedy had been slow to embrace the movement in 1961, and Johnson's own strong support came only after Kennedy's assassination. Neither Kennedy nor Johnson controlled the civil rights movement nor could claim credit for it; they merely reacted to it, each in his own way.

Lady Bird's reaction was that of an Old South aristocrat. On Friday, June 19, 1964, called the "Teenth" in the South, the Civil Rights Act passed in the Senate, and Lady Bird noted the irony in her diary. "I wonder if anybody but me will remember that June Teenth was always celebrated by all the Negroes in Texas. Nobody's maid worked on June Teenth because it was the day the Emancipation Proclamation went into effect in Texas a hundred or so years ago."

This was the point of view from which she started. In memory at least, she inhabited a world in which ladies had maids, and maids, like field workers, took the day off to attend barbecues, church services, and gospel singings on June Teenth. The Civil Rights Act changed that world, and Lady Bird's role in the transformation revealed the dilemmas that haunted white Southern populists throughout the century. In order to change herself and her region, she had to go nose-to-nose with segregationists who were openly calling Johnson a "nigger-lover," and find a way to placate them, to ask for their vote, without pandering to their racism.

First, she had to manage Johnson's own bifurcated emotions. In the summer of 1964, Johnson had doubts about whether he should even run for the presidency, even though his victory was never really in doubt. His doubts were centered on his obsessive fear that the country really wanted Bobby Kennedy—or any Kennedy for that matter—as President, not him. In August, at the Democratic convention in Atlantic City, he voiced those doubts in telephone conversations with trusted staff members.

"I don't think a white Southerner is the man to unite this nation in this hour," Johnson told Walter Jenkins, his chief of staff, on August 26. "I don't know who is, and I don't even want that responsibility. . . . I've had doubts about whether a man born where I was born, raised like I was raised, could ever satisfy the Northern Jews, Catholics, and union people."

Johnson was so distraught he worried that he might lose his mind. He told Jenkins, "I do not believe, Walter, that I can physically and mentally. . . . Goldwater's had a couple of nervous breakdowns, and I don't want to be in this place . . . and I don't, I do not believe I can phys-ically and mentally carry the responsibilities of the bomb, and the world, and the Nigras and the South, and so on and so forth."

Jenkins, a quiet, nervous man with a bloodred face and high blood pressure, continued to serve as Johnson's most trusted staff member. As a student at the University of Texas, Jenkins, a devoted New Dealer and true Johnson believer, took a job as a clerk-accountant in Johnson's congressional office. He left Johnson's employment briefly during World War II when he served in the Quartermaster Corps in Africa and Italy.

Lady Bird admired Jenkins's loyalty as well as his frugality. One night over dinner, after Jenkins had returned from the war, he told her that he had put every penny he had made in government bonds. Lady Bird had been buying government bonds since she was a bride. She admired Jenkins's business sense and urged Johnson to expand Jenkins's duties to clerk-accountant. Soon he was involved in all aspects of Johnson's political and business life. In the office, he was known as "Mister Fixit."

Like Lady Bird, Jenkins functioned as an emotional bulwark, as was clear from the conversation with LBJ on August 26 from Atlantic City. "I don't see any reason I ought to seek the right to endure the anguish of being here," said Johnson, meaning the anguish of the presidency. "They think I want great power. What I want is great solace and a little love, that's all I want."

The vague emptiness and distended neediness that Johnson expressed in that conversation came at a time when he was at the peak of his power. In his transition year as President, Johnson had success-fully seized control of the government and had far surpassed his liberal opponents in the passage of the Civil Rights Act, a victory that seemed only to make the liberals hate him more and further alienated him from Southern Democrats. His despair was genuine. He sensed he was des-tined to become a victim of the political antagonisms of the era.

Jenkins, like Lady Bird, tried to convince Johnson that love and power were not mutually exclusive goals, and that he, in fact, had plenty of both in his life. In response to LBJ's plea for solace and love, Jenkins, who had a soothing melodic voice, like a Southern radio announcer, whispered softly, "You have a lot of that, Mr. President."

Lady Bird offered the same kind of unflinching assurance in a letter she marked "personal" that she wrote shortly before Johnson's conversation with Jenkins, a letter that encouraged Johnson to accept the Democratic nomination, despite his fear of critics, including *Time* magazine, which was then researching a story about the family finances. The letter, written to "The President" on White House stationery, reads as follows:

Personal

Beloved—

You are as brave a man as Harry Truman—or FDR—or Lincoln. You can go on to find some peace, some achievement amidst all the pain. You have been strong, patient, determined beyond any words of mine to express.

I honor you for it. So does most of the country. To step out now would be wrong for our country, and I can see nothing but a lonely wasteland for your future. Your friends would be frozen in embarrassed silence and your enemies jeering.

I am not afraid of *Time* or lies or losing money or defeat.

In the final analysis I can't carry any of the burdens you talked of—so I know it's only your choice. But I know you are as brave as any of the thirty-five.

I love you always—

Bird.

Lady Bird was living at the height of her powers as well, offering her "beloved" the passion of her own political courage in his dark hour of doubt. No longer a shy wallflower, Lady Bird sat hunched over her White House desk, pen pressed to page, furiously writing her own and Johnson's future into reality.

Not only did she declare her own willingness to bear defeat and disgrace on behalf of the presidency, she issued a veiled challenge to Johnson's manhood. Be a man, she told him, don't humiliate yourself in front of your enemies. Don't embarrass yourself, your friends, or your family. There were only two people that Lyndon Johnson allowed to speak to him in that particular voice: his mother, who'd been dead six years, and Lady Bird. She was deploying the full power of her status as his wife.

During the Democratic National Convention in Atlantic City, Lady Bird briefly saw Jackie Kennedy. The two women stood together to greet the delegates at a reception honoring Mrs. Kennedy. The reception was the only public appearance Jackie made during the 1964 convention.

By then, the relations between the families were strained by the battle lines drawn between LBJ and Bobby Kennedy. During an emotional speech to the convention, Bobby had described his brother in poetic terms as a "star" that outshone a "garish sun," a supposed reference to Johnson. Johnson was livid. In the end, LBJ was renominated, but his relationship with Bobby had been permanently damaged. The only peace between the Kennedys and the Johnsons at the convention was what Lady Bird and Jackie had managed politely to extend to each other.

During the convention, Lady Bird instructed Liz Carpenter to come up with a way for her to campaign in the South and mentioned a train trip as one possible scenario. Truman had earlier sold LBJ on the idea of whistlestop campaigns. "You know," Truman had once told Johnson, "there are a lot of people in this country who don't know where the airport is, but they know where the depot it. Go find them."

After meeting with a group of Democratic Southern governors, Carpenter suggested that each host a reception for Lady Bird in the South's statehouses. There was a lukewarm reaction. The governors feared that Lady Bird's trip might provoke support for the Republicans, who were gaining strength in the South because of opposition to Johnson's support of civil rights. Their advice was, stay away and let local candidates carry the ticket.

The Democratic governors did not want to be responsible for Lady Bird's safety, either. In the post-assassination period, paranoia ran high. On September 27, the Warren Commission issued its "no conspiracy" report on Kennedy's assassination, but the atmosphere in the country remained suspicious. Even Johnson privately thought there had been a conspiracy. A few days later, on October 1, James Reston, a *New York Times* columnist, criticized Johnson for being "rash and careless" by leaving his car to shake hands with voters.

Lady Bird was not afraid for her life. "I don't think assassination is part of my destiny," she later told reporters. But she did fear criticism from the press and did not leave herself open to charges of being careless. Prior to the trip, the Secret Service assessed the possibility of attacks by assassins in every possible campaign venue and thought that

Lady Bird would be particularly at risk from a sniper's bullet during receptions. These receptions would be held in the marbled rotundas of Southern statehouses, closed and circular in design, the kind of buildings that were difficult for the Secret Service to cover. Lady Bird told Carpenter to scratch the idea of receptions.

Carpenter then returned to the idea of the whistlestop and made her argument to the Secret Service that a train tour would be safer because they could place agents on board and at every stop. Lady Bird wanted to do it because the trip would make history. It would be the first time that any First Lady had made her own whistlestop tour—without her husband.

Ken O'Donnell, by then a special assistant to President Johnson, was opposed to the idea. The trip would be largely run by Lady Bird's staff and the wives of Southern senators. O'Donnell didn't think the women could do it. "He didn't want Mrs. Johnson to do anything," recalled Bess Abell. "He just didn't think she could make a contribution. He'd never met anyone as organized or strong as Mrs. Johnson."

Carpenter went over O'Donnell's head and took the proposition straight to Johnson. In late August, following the convention, Carpenter and Abell met with LBJ and O'Donnell on the second floor of the White House. By then, Carpenter had a map of the possible train routes through the South, as well as a proposed itinerary, and laid both out on a conference table along with her proposal for what she now officially called "The Lady Bird Special."

The plan was for Lady Bird to go to Southern states that had benefited from NASA and the Kennedy-Johnson space program and emphasize her own Southern background. She would be combining two powerful traditions within Southern politics—pork and personal campaign appearances. Johnson turned to O'Donnell and said, "Let's do it."

However, Johnson seemed less enthusiastic about the idea the following March 10, when at 11:55 A.M., Lady Bird telephoned him at the Oval Office to tell him that Senator John Stennis of Mississippi had warned against visiting a NASA installation in that state. Stennis thought it was politically hopeless for Lady Bird to campaign there; the opposition to the Civil Rights Act was too strong.

During the conversation, Johnson seemed preoccupied, but Lady Bird pressed the issue. After explaining that Stennis objected to the trip,

Lady Bird told Johnson, "I'll give you all the reasons if you want but I've knocked it out so no need to tick 'em unless you want to hear them."

"Yeah," replied Johnson. "I'd like to hear one or two."

In a brisk, efficient voice, Lady Bird then explained that Stennis told her that the NASA installation near St. Bay Louis, Mississippi, was not yet finished. "It's just a bunch of turned-up dirt and bulldozers," Lady Bird said, speaking fast. Then she explained that the eight hundred people in the town had lost their land in condemnation proceedings, which had provoked statewide controversy. In the background, Johnson said, "Yes . . . uh huh." From the tone of the conversation, they could have been professional political analysts, weighing the pros and cons.

"That's good, that's enough," said LBJ, not wanting to hear bad news. He was dismissing her, but Lady Bird was not easily turned aside.

Next she tried to describe a proposed visit to Huntsville, Alabama, not far from where her parents grew up. "Huntsville would be an interesting and good place to go . . . it seems to be really tying the South to the future," said Lady Bird. Then her voice trailed off. Lady Bird had lost her husband's ear.

"Shall I call John Sparkman [the Democratic senator from Alabama] . . . and just discuss it with him?" she asked.

"Yeah, yeah," replied Johnson, churlishly.

She would get no real help from Johnson. This trip was hers. Acting on her own behalf, Lady Bird planned and executed every detail of the whistlestop tour. First, she assembled a phalanx of zealous staff members and friends to help her plan every detail of the trip. Abell purchased large volumes of old-fashioned souvenirs that Lady Bird would distribute during her trip: 30,000 plastic train whistles, 24,000 paper engineer hats, 160 cases of saltwater taffy with wrappers imprinted with the words "Choose LYNDON," 6,000 ladies' straw hats with "LBJ" in red, white, and blue stitched into the rim, and 100,000 postcards that said "sent from the Lady Bird Special."

Lindy Boggs, the wife of U.S. Representative Hale Boggs of Louisiana, scribbled a few prosaic lyrics for the whistlestop theme song. The first line of the campaign ditty was "From the north, to the south, from the east to the west, we're on our way to a whistlestop." It was played by local high school bands across the South, when the bands were not playing "Hello, Lyndon!" a variation of "Hello, Dolly!" made famous by Carol Channing, or "Happy Days Are Here Again." Later Boggs said that Mrs. Johnson enjoyed the trip so much that it was then that she realized "without politics, Lady Bird would have half a life."

The 19-car train was outfitted to carry 150 members of the media; 15 official hostesses; wives of senators and congressmen; and Johnson staff members, plus a revolving cast of staff members and advance teams. Three cars of the train—4, 5, and 5A—were working press rooms, equipped with typewriters and a Western Union filing desk. Three others housed the staff and hostesses. Carpenter and Abell traveled in the third car. Lady Bird and her secretary, Mary Rather, were in car No. 2. The first car—nicknamed the "Queen Mary"—functioned as a receiving room, where Mrs. Johnson met local politicians for photo opportunities.

There were two dining cars. To feed everyone, Mrs. Johnson chose the menus for the trip herself, selecting specialties of each state. In Louisiana, for instance, they ate shrimp creole, rice, tomatoes, and okra. In Texas, they were served deermeat sausage and steak. In Kentucky, the menu was biscuits and burgoo, a beef stew cooked traditionally on Derby Day.

In Georgia, where opposition to integration seemed impenetrable, she served Betty Talmadge's special recipe for ham (prepared with a basting mixture of ginger ale, apple juice, and orange juice and cooked in two inches of water or Coca-Cola) and distributed printed copies of the recipe to the press and public. At the same time that Talmadge's husband, Herman, a senator from Georgia, walled himself off from any kind of contact with LBJ because of civil rights, Lady Bird cunningly and effortlessly leaped across the lines of color and politics with menus that appealed to all Southerners. She used Southern cuisine as a means to political ends. On the trip, copies of Mrs. Johnson's own recipe for pecan pie were distributed like campaign flyers.

Along the way, others picked up the connection between Southern food and Southern politics. At stop after stop, Congressman Hale Boggs of New Orleans introduced Mrs. Johnson with the line, "How many of you-all know what red-eye gravy is? Well, so do I, and so does Lyndon Johnson."

As Carpenter put it, "The Johnsons were hearing from their Southern friends, 'You've forgotten about us. We aren't important. Our votes don't count.' Her role was to get on a train and travel to eight states in four days, give forty-six speeches, and say, 'This President and his wife respect you and you are loved. We stand on the civil rights program. This is the New South.' We were out to blow kisses off the back of the train, to woo with real courthouse politics on that train."

Two days before they formally announced the trip, Lady Bird called Carpenter and told her, "Before we put this out in the newspapers, let's make the courtesy calls." By then, Lady Bird was a pro, having learned at the hand of her husband, the master politician. She understood that politics is a parlor game and that she needed to show all the players the cards in her hand—before they read about her trip in the newspapers— and do it a personal enough way to persuade them to join her game.

On September 9, she worked the telephone for eleven straight hours, calling every governor, senator, and congressman in eight Southern states. Hour after hour, her message to each person that she reached was similar. "I'm thinking about coming down and campaigning in your state and I'd love your advice," she told them disarmingly.

Of course, the trip was already planned down to the last detail. Yet she pretended to solicit their opinions. This was Lady Bird's own version of the Johnson treatment, a variation on the one that Southern women had used for generations to manipulate supposedly stout-hearted men.

The Scarlett O'Hara routine did not work on everyone. Senator Willis Robertson of Virginia listened but told Lady Bird he couldn't help her on the train trip. On the day she was scheduled to be in Virginia, Robertson, an opponent of the civil rights bill, planned to go antelope hunting in Montana.

"Have a nice time," Lady Bird told Robertson sweetly. South Carolina's Strom Thurmond also told her no. In North Carolina, the nominee for governor, Dan Moore, did not return her calls. In Georgia, Dick Russell, one of LBJ's oldest friends who nonetheless opposed him on civil rights, told Lady Bird he couldn't bring himself to ride the train with her, but Russell did not have it in him to totally reject Mrs. Johnson. He said he would lend her a couple of advance men from his staff to help her in Georgia and gave her advice on where to go.

She didn't even bother to place a call to Alabama's governor George Wallace, who in 1963 issued the segregationist's battle cry, "Segregation then. Segregation now. Segregation forever." "I don't even think it would be good manners to place the call," she noted of Wallace. However, she did call Louisiana governor John McKeithen, another segregationist, who also refused to ride her train.

Where was this persistence coming from? By defining herself in opposition to her husband's political opponents, Lady Bird was able to summon her own potential, asserting herself like a feminist at a time when feminism had not yet emerged as a force within American society. Only the year before, in 1963, Congress had passed the Equal Pay Act, which prohibited pay discrimination on the basis of gender. Women were only beginning to move into the mainstream workforce in numbers that counted. As Lady Bird prepared to make her working tour across the South, only 30 percent of married women had jobs. The number of women working outside the home who had children was even smaller—only 20 percent. Lady Bird had always been a working mother, but publicly she was considered an extension of her husband— a stereotype that had more to do with cultural expectations of political wives than with her.

Even before leaving, the trip was beset by obstacles. The Secret Service received reports from the FBI that hate groups might try to blow up the train. As a security precaution, a separate engine preceded Lady Bird's train fifteen minutes down the track to clear potential bombs from her path.

Even the weather seemed to work against her. In the early morning of Sunday, October 4, two days before she embarked on the vote-seeking tour, a mammoth, fifth hurricane of the season, called Hilda, crossed the Mississippi panhandle and passed into Alabama. The previous day, the hurricane, carrying 130-mile-per-hour winds, hit Franklin, Louisiana, killing 25 people and injuring 200 others. As his wife prepared to head south, Johnson declared the entire state of Louisiana, the final state on her tour, a federal disaster area.

Miraculously, two days later, at 7:08 A.M., when Lady Bird boarded the freshly painted red, white, and blue train at Union Station in Washington, the air was chilly but there was not a cloud in the sky. At fifty-one years old, Lady Bird was physically and mentally in her prime. She stood five feet, four inches tall and weighed only 114 pounds. She wore her hair in an updated version of a 1950s bob: it was rolled, teased, waved at the front and sprayed into place. She had a sensible, unwavering look; she could have walked into a garden club meeting anywhere south of the Mason-Dixon line, sat down, and had lunch.

Her twenty-year-old daughter, Lynda, was by her side. LBJ came on board for the fifteen-minute ride to Alexandria, Virginia, the first of forty short stops—the most stops of any during the four-day trip. According to the *Washington Post*, ten thousand people, many of whom had arrived at sunrise, waited along the track in Alexandria for Lady Bird to arrive.

"Sunshine and lots of friends—what could be a better way to start a whistlestop?" Lady Bird told the crowd, standing beneath a striped awning on an open platform at the rear of the train. "For me this trip has been a source of anxiety and anticipation—anxiety because I am not used to whistlestopping without my husband; anticipation because I am returning to familiar territory and heading into a region that I call home."

Lady Bird had given many public speeches before, but until now, she always looked stiff and nervous. From the moment she got on the back of the train headed south, however, she spoke in a lower, more natural voice. The train trip was a throwback, of course, an anachronism even in 1964, but nostalgia came easily to Lady Bird. She could look down on the blur of smiles and the wave of hands and did not feel shy or fearful. She was, as she said, headed home. In that moment, all of the lessons she learned in 1955 about voice control and platform appearance during a public speaking class called the Capital Speakers Course clicked.

The key was to give the audience what her teacher, Mrs. Hester Belle Provenson, called "reaction time"—time to hear a thought and take it in. Lady Bird simply needed to speak slowly, like a Southerner. "Finally," said Carpenter, "she got to speak in a drawl."

During that first speech, Lady Bird defended Johnson on civil rights by taking the Constitutional high ground. "I never expected for a moment that my husband would do other than all American Presidents have done—and this is to make it clear that the Constitution means the same for all the people in all sections and all States," she told the crowd, adding, "Lyndon has offered to unify this country, to put behind us things of the past."

She also attempted to paint Barry Goldwater, LBJ's Republican challenger who had voted against the act, as an extremist, reminding the crowd that three fourths of the Republicans in Congress had voted for the Civil Rights Act and two thirds of the Democrats also opposed its passage.

Johnson took the microphone and played the part of the grateful husband. "Alexandria has been chosen as the first stop for one of the greatest campaigners in America," LBJ told the crowd. "I'm proud to announce that I am her husband."

When he disembarked from the train, Johnson threw himself into the middle of the cheering spectators, shaking hands with as many people as he could reach. He worked the crowd for several minutes, then took a helicopter back to the White House. Lady Bird was on her own.

An hour later, when the train stopped in Fredericksburg, Virginia, and Lady Bird once again made her way to the rear platform, she saw a Goldwater supporter in the crowd carrying a sign that read: "Lyndon, We Will Barry You." Another sign said: "Brinksmanship Is Better Than Chickenship."

Lady Bird nodded politely at the picketers and gave the same speech she had given a few minutes earlier in Alexandria, this time emphasizing her purpose. "This is a campaign trip, and I would like to ask you for your vote for both Johnsons," she told the crowd. The placards lowered slightly. She was making it personal—vote for both of us—and the signs suddenly seemed discourteous.

"Those first stops set the tone," recalled Carpenter. "She made it very difficult for people not to like her. It was a domino effect: one by one, the signs would come down and the crowd would get friendlier. The momentum started to build."

At every stop, there was a frenzy of behind-the-scenes work. The train had no modern air-conditioning units and was kept comfortable by a continual supply of fresh ice shoveled into large, noisy steel coolers. When the train stopped, advance men were dispatched to buy more ice. Meanwhile, on board, Carpenter and her staff wrote press releases with local angles for all the newspapers. "We blanketed the press in every town for days before and afterwards," Carpenter recalled. "Sometimes Mrs. Johnson made thirteen speeches in a day, and each one of the newspapers in those towns got a press release."

The wooing process was ritualized. Each time the train stopped, the press jumped off the car and ran to the back of the train to hear Mrs. Johnson's speech. Afterward, they fanned out to interview the crowd. Meanwhile, fifteen hostesses, dressed in blue shirtwaist dresses with "LBJ" embroidered on the pocket and wide-brimmed hats, escorted local politicians and Johnson supporters onto the train and into the living room car for a brief meeting and a photo opportunity with Mrs.

Johnson. Usually the visitors brought gifts—flowers, bags of peanuts, homemade cookies, pie, or jelly—which Lady Bird turned over to two secretaries, Mary Rather or Ashton Gonella, who made plans to deliver the gifts to hospitals and orphanages in towns down the line.

The secretaries wrote notes, all signed by Mrs. Johnson, which had the same message: "I was given these lovely flowers on my train trip through the South and I hope that you will enjoy them." At future stops, advance men made the deliveries. At one point, Rather joked to Mrs. Carpenter that she had delivered so many flowers that she finally felt like a bride.

By mid-morning on the first day, Lady Bird rolled into Richmond, Virginia, and made a twenty-minute stop at Broad Street Station, where five thousand people were gathered. Lady Bird had been warned that Richmond was Goldwater country. Senator Strom Thurmond, a Republican, was campaigning heavily for Goldwater on the civil rights issue. From the platform, Lady Bird faced a huge white banner with red letters that read: "Fly Away Lady Bird. Here in Richmond, Barry Is the Cat's Meow."

The *Washington Post* noted that even the Goldwater supporters "listened respectfully" to Mrs. Johnson. After the speech, one woman carrying a Goldwater placard told Maxine Cheshire of the *Post*, "Well, she is certainly prettier than I expected. But she can't make me believe like her husband believes, even if she does talk real well."

At the end of the first day, during a happy hour in the club car crowded with more than a hundred reporters, Carpenter gathered around a television set and watched whistlestop coverage on all three networks—NBC, ABC, and CBS. The Huntley-Brinkley show on NBC had given Lady Bird a full five minutes, emphasizing the fact that Virginia's Democratic senator, Harry Byrd, had refused Mrs. Johnson's invitation to ride the train and had snubbed her by not coming to the station to see her off.

That segment established the script that TV anchors read from throughout the whistlestop. Night after night, commentators compared her to Eleanor Roosevelt and depicted her as out in the country building support for her husband, one train stop at a time. She was finally cast in the light in which she wanted to be seen—an activist First Lady.

The whistlestop was a natural stage for Lady Bird because it kept her in a predominantly rural landscape. Prior to her trip, she had announced that she wanted to go "to the land where the pavement runs out and city people don't often go." At some level, she seemed to want to flee the modern world altogether. Every chance she got, she added small towns to the itinerary. One was Ahoskie, North Carolina, a town of five thousand, after she had received a telegram that said, "Nobody important has been through here since Buffalo Bill came through in 1916. Please have your train stop here."

When it did, there were ten thousand people, twice the population of the town, to greet Lady Bird. The crowds translated into support for Johnson. In her report for the *Washington Post*, Maxine Cheshire wrote, "Her crowds have been so big and boisterous that no local politicians in her path could fail to notice the Johnsons' popularity with the populace."

In the rural areas, she sometimes left the train to shake hands with voters, but there was not the usual intimacy between the people and a political candidate. Lady Bird was surrounded by Secret Service agents. Most of the people she met were poor and white, although Blacks came to see her as well. One white Southern woman told her, "I got up this morning at three o'clock in the morning and milked twenty cows so I could be here." She felt the woman's affection and experienced what long ago had ensnared her husband—the intoxicating mix of admiration and power.

In the evening, she watched the news on a small remote-control TV in her own private car, but even then she continued to work, putting in the same long hours as LBJ. Her car, a combination office and dining room, had an electric typewriter, a radio, a thermofax machine, and a television set. The area was just outside a small bedroom, which, noted the *Washington Post,* had a "phone, a shower, a wall clock, a mahogany dresser with lockable drawers, and a real bed."

The reporters slept in berth bunks, shared bathrooms, and balanced typewriters on their knees in the club car, where they wrote stories for the morning newspapers during the 4:00 to 5:00 P.M. cocktail hour. The railroad companies paid for drinks and snacks. Carpenter fed them press releases and kept them laughing. She posted a Dixie Dictionary bulletin board in the press car "for folks from the Nawth covering the South." "Kissin' kin," for instance, was defined as "anyone who will come to the depot." "Beri-beri" (pronounced Barry-Barry) was posted as a "disease wiped out in the South."

Despite the gimmicks, Lady Bird's efforts to charm her audiences paid off in substantial ways. She picked up support in each new town. In Wilson, North Carolina, a local politician introduced Lady Bird "as much a part of the South as tobacco, peanuts, and red-eye gravy." In Raleigh, Lady Bird invited the wife of Democratic gubernatorial nominee Dan Moore to ride with her and, according to the *Washington Post*, "Mrs. Moore got so excited that she started telling North Carolinans to vote for LBJ."

Behind the scenes, Johnson had earlier encouraged Moore to support Lady Bird's trip. On September 24, he had Connally place a telephone call to Moore in which Connally acknowledged Johnson's unpopularity in North Carolina but asked for Moore's help anyway. "God," groaned Connally on the telephone, "we can't let a state like North Carolina just sit on the vine." Moore assured Connally that "Lady Bird will be greeted warmly" in North Carolina but remained neutral. He warned Connally that the last twelve months in his state had been "bitter" because of infighting among the Democrats over civil rights. As the nominee, he didn't want to take a chance on supporting Johnson. Connally said he understood and confided in Moore that he was personally advising Johnson not to meet Lady Bird in Raleigh for a rally, as was planned, in order not to arouse further party tension.

LBJ ignored Connally's advice. He joined Lady Bird in Raleigh, and Moore was by his side on the podium at a rally in front of a large audience. Mrs. Moore hugged Johnson and publicly endorsed the Johnson-Humphrey ticket to the audience. Moore stood silent, but his presence was interpreted as a signal to his supporters that he did, in fact, stand with Johnson.

Lady Bird encountered the first real trouble on the trip on Wednesday, October 7, when she arrived in Columbia, South Carolina. The train pulled into the station to boos at 4:10 P.M. When Lady Bird emerged, several in the crowd started chanting, "We Want Barry!" In the *Washington Post*, Cheshire again cast Lady Bird as the heroine. "A mere scattering of Republican placard-bearers attempted in vain to disrupt her speech at a railway station welcoming ceremony here with a noisy, taunting cacophony of catcalls that could not be quieted."

South Carolina governor Donald Russell was the first to try and quiet the crowd. Russell appealed to "the good manners and hospitality" of the Southerners and said, "I know of no one who is more undeserving of a boo" than Mrs. Johnson.

Nonetheless, when she tried to speak, she had to shout over the crowd. "I am here on behalf of the Democratic party—the party of your ancestors and mine," said Lady Bird, who was described by Cheshire as having "a tight-jawed fervor that dared anyone to stop her." This was the image of Southern womanhood that Lady Bird carried. Dressed formally in a light green coat over a darker green dress, she stood on her heritage and demanded to be heard.

First, she tried to talk about the threat of nuclear war and the need for a test-ban treaty. The hecklers interrupted her and she stopped in mid-sentence, holding up a single, white-gloved hand high into the air to silence them. Finally, she was angry. "This is a country of many viewpoints," she said firmly. "I respect your right to express your own. Now it is my turn to express mine. Thank you." To everyone's surprise, the crowd was silent.

The voices grew louder six hours later when Lady Bird's train arrived in Charleston, South Carolina, which had voted for Republican candidates in the last three elections. According to Carpenter, Lady Bird knew the kind of opposition she would face in Charleston and in Savannah. "She wanted to go where other Democrats weren't going. In 1964, anybody could go to Atlanta and speak out for civil rights and still get out with their hides on. She told us to give her the tough towns. And so we took Charleston."

The advance team that had helped organize the Charleston stop had warned Lady Bird that there might be trouble. Mrs. Cecil Burney, one of Lady Bird's friends from Corpus Christi who was a member of the team, wrote in a history for her family that when she arrived in Charleston, she confronted fears that Lady Bird's scheduled rally at a shopping center might turn into a "Negro riot."

The rumor, according to Mrs. Burney, was that Lady Bird planned to bring to the rally a Negro band with a "hot beat" and that the music might incite the Negroes to violence. Twenty-four of the merchants in the shopping center threatened to seek an injunction to keep Mrs. Johnson from holding the rally, but the owner of the shopping center, a Democrat, insisted that it go on. He threatened to sue the shopkeepers if they didn't stay open. Tensions ran so high in Charleston that on the day before Lady Bird arrived, the local newspaper had pleaded with residents to show "courtesy towards the First Lady."

Lady Bird arrived at the shopping center at around dusk. In one corner of the crowd of ten thousand people were a group of Goldwater supporters, who greeted her with boos. Cheshire identified the group as members of the John Birch Society. She wrote in the *Washington Post*: "They had painted signs which they distributed among their own children, the oldest of whom proved to be a pretty blonde fifteen-year-old high school girl. . . . One of the signs carried by the school girl said 'Barry for Prayer.' " Other signs were more ominous. One said: "Black Bird. Go Home." Isabelle Shelton of the *Washington Star* reported that she saw signs that said: "Johnson Is a Communist. Johnson Is a Nigger-Lover."

Shelton interviewed one man who said he intended to vote for Johnson, in spite of the President's support of civil rights. "I'd rather stand beside a Negro in a factory than stand behind a white man in the soup line," Shelton quoted the unidentified voter as saying. It was exactly the message Lady Bird had come to spread: to survive economically and move into the modern world, segregation in the South must end.

As Mrs. Johnson began to speak, the dissenters again tried to drown her out. She raised her hand to stop them. This time they did not cease. She talked over them, emphasizing the need for a federal and state partnership that, she said, "means jobs and a better community" and "prosperity for Charleston." She firmly reminded the residents that their shipyard, their military installations, and the Polaris missile base were all products of that partnership. At no time did the booing stop.

Louisiana congressman Hale Boggs, who had introduced Mrs. Johnson, was frightened and angry. "This is reminiscent of Hitler," he told the crowd. "This is a Democratic gathering, not a Nazi gathering." At the same time Lady Bird met the demonstrators in Charleston, Johnson was campaigning to warm and affectionate crowds in Indiana. LBJ was routinely briefed about Lady Bird's whistlestop progress and was concerned about the treatment she was receiving. He also worried that he would be criticized for subjecting his wife to dangerous taunts.

At 9:40 P.M., LBJ placed a telephone call to Lady Bird and his daughter Lynda aboard the train from Chicago, where he was campaigning. Both Lady Bird and Lynda told him about the hecklers.

Over the roar of the train, Lynda told her father that she thought the opposition would work to their advantage. "A lot of these people are lackadaisical," she shouted into the line, speaking of Johnson's supporters. She told him that the small group of demonstrators invigorated their own troops. "I think if we just don't say anything, we'll be doing real well," Lynda advised, sounding like her father.

Johnson then teased Lynda about a newspaper article in which the writer criticized Lynda for singing "Hello, Lyndon!" in an "off-key girlish soprano voice."

"Well so what, Daddy?" shot back Lynda, defensively. "That will just get me the sympathy vote for all the people who can't sing on-key. Besides, I don't think I sing off-key, but if you'd been singin' for as many hours as I had, you'd sing off-key, too." Lynda not only had political sensibilities, but she had a sense of humor as well, one that she kept concealed from the press. Much later, Lady Bird described Lynda as a "very private person," whose feelings about the press were not unlike Mrs. Kennedy's. Carpenter jokingly accused her of having a bit of a "Greta Garbo complex." Said Lady Bird of Lynda, "It wasn't so much that she was haughty as she was shy."

On this day, Johnson laughed, and pressed his daughter further. "Why don't you learn to sing on-key?" he asked her jocularly. Then he explained that the writer also criticized Lady Bird for having so many armed policemen and security guards at the Charleston rally. "They say it proves I'm unpopular in the South," he said.

"Ohhh . . . she's just talkin', Daddy," Lynda said of the reporter, clearly irritated now. "If we didn't have people looking after us, she'd say we were beggin' to get hurt."

"Okay, I love you," Johnson tells his daughter. "Don't run out with the Marines too much. You tell 'em to get you in by 2:30 or 3:30 or 4:00 A.M."

"I love you, too, Daddy," replied Lynda, ignoring his teasing about her private life. "You take care."

"Let me talk to your mama," he told her.

Lady Bird came on the line, and Johnson told her, "I just wanted to tell you I love you and I'll see you Friday."

This particular private conversation, one of many Johnson secretly taped in 1964, reveals a more affectionate and tender side of Johnson. In it, he sounds like any ordinary father and husband, calling to check on a daughter who was devoted to him and a wife that he both missed and loved. He was past middle age by now and had absorbed some of life's harder lessons, including a realization of his reliance on his family.

According to Carpenter, LBJ made such telephone calls every night during the whistlestop. "When he would call, it was just like someone had waved a magic wand over Lady Bird," recalled Carpenter. "It just kept her going and made her want to work harder."

Johnson need not have worried about press criticism. The following day, the *Atlanta Constitution* ran an editorial praising both Lady Bird and—by extension—Johnson for not avoiding the South. The editorial said that Lady Bird's whistlestop reminded Southerners that LBJ is "the son of a Southern tenant farmer and that he asks for the vote of this state not as a distant theorist but as a native Southerner who understands his kin." The newspaper asked the question that it said Lady Bird's train trip had posed. "Can Georgia turn away . . . from the first Southern President in a century? That question goes deep, and so did Mrs. Johnson's visit."

Lady Bird had crossed into Georgia at mid-morning on Thursday, October 8, where she hit five cities with mixed results. She faced hecklers from Goldwaterites again in Savannah, but this time it was her seventeen-year-old daughter who shouted down the chants of "We Want Barry!" Shortly after moving into the White House, Lucy had changed the spelling of her name to Luci. "It was a small way to establish my independence," recalled Luci years later. "I didn't have a name like Elizabeth that I could shorten, so I just changed the spelling." Unlike her sister, who avoided the spotlight, Luci did things, including changing her name, that purposefully made news.

With her dark hair combed in a shoulder-length flip and pulled off her forehead with a headband, Luci turned to the group and said, "It's easy to make a lot of noise when you're not going to solve the problem."

The crowd, momentarily quiet, then received a lecture from Luci. "What we do now, what we do in this campaign is important because soon—probably even before you're ready to handle it—my generation and yours is going to be responsible for what happens in this country," she told them. The next day, Luci was praised in an editorial in the *Atlanta Constitution* for her good citizenship. On the front page, the headline on the whistlestop story read, "It's a Bandwagon Now, Cheers for Lady Bird."

Later that night, as the whistlestop crossed into northern Florida, the Secret Service received an anonymous report that the train might be bombed. In addition to the extra engine, a team of FBI agents and other law enforcement personnel swept a seven-mile bridge that the *Lady Bird Special* was scheduled to cross. A security helicopter and several boats were dispatched to escort the train across the bridge. According to Abell, it was the longest, edgiest seven miles of the journey.

At noon on October 9, the last day of the trip, the train crossed into Alabama and picked up six of Lady Bird's cousins from Autauga County. Nobody expected Governor Wallace or his wife to board the train; their opposition to LBJ was well known. The night before the train arrived, Mrs. Wallace had joked during a dinner party in Montgomery that she would not be able to board the train because she was "going fishing." However, in Flomaton, Alabama, the wife of the lieutenant governor, Mrs. James Allen, brought Lady Bird a bouquet of roses that she said were from Wallace and his wife.

"I was bringing roses anyway, even if I had to grow them myself," Mrs. Allen said during the rally. By this time, Lady Bird's train had picked up so much momentum that not even George Wallace could ignore her.

In Mobile, Lady Bird saw evidence of Hurricane Hilda's damage. The windows of storefronts were still boarded up for protection against high winds, and she toured areas where the roofs of houses had been ripped away. At a rally in downtown Mobile, she again encountered a group of young people carrying Goldwater placards. This time Lady Bird didn't have to defend herself. Mary Grice, one of her supporters who was a retired civics teacher, approached the protesters and told them, "Don't you know the Goldwater people have themselves asked you all to be courteous to Mrs. Johnson?" Courtesy to Lady Bird had become a political imperative.

At 8:16 that evening, Lady Bird and Luci arrived at the train station in New Orleans, where Johnson, who had traveled from Louisville, Kentucky, met them on the rear of the platform. Johnson hugged both his wife and daughter, and Lady Bird, exhausted from her four days of travel, burst into tears. Inside the depot were thousands of cheering Black people. Inside the plaza, within hearing distance of Mrs. Johnson, stood an even larger crowd of whites. "You have brought to the depot the one person I wanted to see, for he can take over the speaking," Lady Bird said of Lyndon. By then, she had traveled through eight states, more than 1,600 miles, and made 47 formal speeches to an estimated 500,000 people.

At the end of the line, despite her stand against segregation, she found Blacks and whites standing in New Orleans separating themselves into two distinct groups. Segregation would not disappear in four days. From the platform, Lady Bird appealed for Southern unity. "I am aware that there are those who would exploit the South's past troubles to their own advantage," she told them, "but I do not believe that the majority of the South wants any part of the old bitterness."

Katharine Graham, by then publisher of the *Washington Post,* was present for the rally in New Orleans. She recalls: "I was on the station platform when they arrived. It was a tremendously dramatic moment. It was a hot and steamy night, and we all watched the President greet Lady Bird with a big hug and kiss. Then Lady Bird talked in such a moving way about how the South had to turn away from hatred, how wounding the hatred was for everyone. She talked with such authority because she belonged there. It was very clear to me what a team they were. He couldn't have been Lyndon Johnson without Lady Bird."

Later that night, in an after-dinner speech at a downtown hotel, LBJ made what columnist Mary McGrory called "the most moving speech of his campaign and the toughest speech of his career on civil rights." Johnson quoted Huey Long, Jack Kennedy, and Robert E. Lee, all in the same speech, and told the crowd, "If we are to heal our history and make this nation whole, prosperity must know no Mason-Dixon line and opportunity must know no color line."

Throwing away his prepared speech, Johnson then told the crowd that he was sick of the politics of race baiting and said that other principled Southern politicians were as weary of it as he was. He talked about one unnamed senator from the South who confided to Johnson at the end of his career, "I wish I felt a little better. I would like to go back home and make 'em one more Democratic speech. I feel like I have just one more in me. The poor old state! They haven't heard a Democratic speech in thirty years. All they ever hear at election time is nigger, nigger, nigger."

At first the audience was stunned and silent. Then the Blacks started standing up and applauding and cheering. Soon everyone in the crowd, Black and white alike, was on their feet. The South's problem wasn't race or economics, Johnson told them, but indecision about whether—as a people and a region—the South wanted to live or die.

The following day, Max Freedman, another nationally syndicated columnist, wrote that Mrs. Johnson had not only helped Johnson in the South but may have redefined the First Lady's role in national campaigns. "Perhaps this marks the emergence of women as central figures in a national contest instead of being on the edges of a campaign," Freedman said of the *Lady Bird Special*.

In 1964, Freedman was not willing to commit to whether presidential wives should play such a central role. That was considered too risky a proposition. "How many husbands would want their wives and daughters to be active political campaigners?" Freedman asked. Bess Truman, Mamie Eisenhower, and Jackie Kennedy, all had resisted campaigning. However, Lady Bird, wrote Freedman, was "no passive partner" in her marriage.

Four days later, on October 14, 1964, she again played a pivotal role in the 1964 campaign. That morning Lady Bird was at the White House and Lyndon Johnson was in New York at a campaign appearance. At about 10:30 A.M., Carpenter, who was also at the White House, received a telephone call from Charlie Seib, a reporter at the *Washington Star*, who told her that he had received a tip that, the week before, Walter Jenkins had been arrested for disorderly conduct. He had allegedly been caught in a homosexual act with a sixty-two-year-old man in the rest room of the downtown YMCA.

Carpenter, devastated, immediately telephoned Jenkins at home. She told him what she had heard, and Jenkins told her, "I'll call you right back," then hung up the telephone.

He didn't call back. At 9:36 that night, Johnson received a telephone call in New York from Abe Fortas, a partner in Arnold, Fortas and Porter, a powerful law firm in Washington, and a friend of both Johnson and Jenkins. By then, Fortas had met with Jenkins and had convinced him to submit his resignation as a special assistant to the President.

Jenkins's wife, Marjorie, had heard about the arrest over the radio. Fortas told Johnson that she was "hysterical." Marjorie Jenkins didn't believe that the incident had happened, and—above all—she did not want her husband to resign. She expected Johnson to support her husband. "She thinks it's a put-up job and a lie. We've got to help that woman," Fortas insisted to Johnson.

Johnson told Fortas that he was worried that the FBI would soon be at the White House to sweep Jenkins's office and find what he called "certain confidential material." Johnson told Fortas to get to the White House right away and remove the material. Exactly what material he wanted removed is unclear. It could have been anything. Jenkins not only had top security clearance, but he had access to all of the Johnson family's financial records, information that LBJ carefully guarded.

At 1:31 A.M., Fortas telephoned Johnson back and whispered, "I have that material in boxes at my home."

Only then did Johnson ask how Jenkins was doing. In a grave voice, Fortas told him, "Mr. President, he was pretty well off his rocker this morning." Johnson wanted to know if the man he was arrested with could have "gotten any secrets off him." Fortas assured him that was impossible.

Jenkins's companion was a former sergeant in the U.S. Army who was living in the Old Soldier's Home, a retirement facility for military personnel. He had four prior felony convictions, three of them sexual. "He's just sort of a bum," Fortas told Johnson. It seemed unlikely that he would be a spy, which was Johnson's concern.

Fortas then told Johnson that Jenkins had not denied that the incident had taken place. All Jenkins had volunteered was that he had left a cocktail party at *Newsweek* and stopped in the rest room because he was feeling nauseated. He was fuzzy about what happened in the rest room.

Fortas then explained to Johnson that Jenkins had been arrested in 1959 in the same rest room of the YMCA for "loitering." In light of the other arrest, Fortas thought that Johnson had no choice but to seek Jenkins's resignation and distance himself from him as much as possible.

Clark Clifford, another Johnson adviser, agreed. "There is no use defending something you're going to lose," Clifford told Johnson. A statement was drafted saying that Jenkins had submitted his resignation and that Bill D. Moyers would succeed him. Johnson himself edited the statement so that Jenkins was not identified by his true title—"special assistant to the President"—thereby obfuscating his close relationship with Jenkins. The statement simply said that Walter Jenkins had submitted his resignation, without any identification relating him to Johnson.

In New York, Reedy made the case that Johnson needed Jenkins— he was too close a friend and too valuable a member of the staff—and that Johnson should defend him, but Johnson would not hear of it. By telephone in Washington, Ed Weisl, another lawyer, also suggested that Johnson not use the word "resignation." Weisl urged him to try and ride out the controversy. Johnson said no. He worried that Jenkins's arrest might cost him the election.

"This could be the whole ball game," he told John Connally later by telephone. Connally, who was also a close friend of Jenkins's, told LBJ he found the whole thing "damn hard to believe" but advised Johnson to get Jenkins out of the White House as soon as possible. "You have no choice," Connally told Johnson. "They'll be digging up the communists and homos that have infiltrated the government . . . it can't be helped."

Then Connally and Johnson had an extraordinary exchange about whether either of them suspected that Jenkins was a homosexual.

"Did you suspect anything?" Johnson whispered.

"I would have to say not," said Connally. However, after a brief pause, Connally reconsidered. In hindsight, Connally told Johnson, he might have known. "There have been times, fleeting times, when I detected some gestures and mannerisms that might have indicated it, but nothing ever to give a second thought to," Connally said.

In retrospect, Connally and Johnson appear to have overreacted to the entire situation, but this was 1964. Both men saw themselves as cattlemen, gentlemen, powerful politicians—the very personification of Texas heroes. Connally was routinely referred to in the press as the "Marlboro man." Each man believed his own press, and the idea that someone close to both of them might have been a homosexual was extremely threatening.

Connally advised Johnson to move "swiftly and decisively" to distance himself from Jenkins and paint a picture of himself as a moral, upstanding American. He told Johnson to cancel all campaign appearances on Sundays—traditionally the day that people go to church—and to not go anywhere else without Lady Bird or his daughters for the rest of the campaign. Apparently he did not want anyone to get the idea that Johnson and Jenkins might have been involved. "You've got two weeks left," said Connally. "The image you need to project is . . . you're consolidated . . . you're an American family."

The next morning, Carpenter arrived at 7:30 at the White House and went to Lady Bird's bedroom. Lady Bird had ordered coffee but had not slept much the night before and looked "very worn, shaken, and worried," according to Carpenter.

By then, Lady Bird had spoken by telephone with Marjorie Jenkins, and Mrs. Jenkins had told her how angry she was at both Lady Bird and Lyndon for putting so much pressure on her husband. Mrs. Jenkins expected them to stand by him now.

At noon, Lady Bird talked to LBJ by telephone from New York. Johnson had also been up all night, talking on the telephone, and his voice was hoarse. In the conversation, Lady Bird argued that the Johnsons simply had to take care of Jenkins and put friendship ahead of politics.

"I would like to offer him the number two job at KTBC," she told Johnson at the start of the conversation.

"I wouldn't do anything along that line now," Johnson said.

Then Lady Bird told him that she intended to tell the press that she fully supported Jenkins. "I'm going to say this is incredible for a man I've known all these years, a devout Catholic, the father of six children, a happily married husband. It can only be a small period of nervous breakdown," she said.

Again, Johnson warned her to keep silent. "This is not something for you to get involved with. We've got the best minds in the country working on this," he said, trying to soothe her into staying quiet.

But Lady Bird would not be soothed. She told him that Marjorie blamed both of them for Jenkins's trouble. "She feels that her life is ruined, that their life is ruined, and it's all been laid on the altar for working for us," said Lady Bird, clearly tormented.

To get Johnson's attention, she hinted that Marjorie might make trouble for both of them publicly by talking to the press, and she told Johnson that if both of them did not express support for the Jenkins family, "we will lose the entire love and devotion of all the people who have been with us."

Her argument was clear. No one had been as loyal to the Johnsons as Walter Jenkins. If they didn't stand by him now, they could lose the support of everyone close to them.

Johnson refused to listen. "Don't create any more problems than I've got," he snapped. He then lectured her about the politics of the situation, explaining that the "average farmer" would not understand a

President that would condone homosexuality. Finally, he warned her that if she gave Jenkins the job at KTBC-TV "you won't have your license five minutes." He hoped to appeal to Lady Bird's pocketbook.

Lady Bird was unmoved by all of those arguments. "I'd just rather offer it to them and let the license go down the drain," she told him angrily. If forced to choose between her business and friendship or friendship and politics, there was no doubt about her choice. In this moment, she had more courage than her husband. Loyalty was the bedrock of her character.

Johnson appealed to her pragmatism. "That doesn't do anybody any good, does it?" he asked. He told her he would be willing to give Jenkins "anything we have," but he wanted it done privately, not publicly. He told her to offer him the job of running his ranch at exactly the same salary but to do it quietly. "I don't think you realize the First Lady shouldn't be doing it," he told her.

This reminder of her public duty forced Lady Bird to back off. She realized that she had pushed her husband as far as she could. "My poor darlin'," she told him. "My heart breaks for you, too."

"I know it, honey," he replied, and then he confided, "I feel this worse than you."

"My love, my love," she said. "I pray for you, along with Walter."

Johnson said he had to get off the telephone. He told her he had three speeches to make that day and the airplane was waiting for him. Lady Bird said she'd see him at the White House later that night, said goodbye, and hung up the telephone. Then she turned back to her desk and got to work.

Carpenter wrote out a three-sentence statement for Mrs. Johnson that was distributed to the press. It said: "My heart is aching today for someone who has reached the point of exhaustion in dedicated service to his country. Walter Jenkins has been carrying incredible hours and burdens since President Kennedy's assassination. He is now receiving the medical attention he needs."

It was an elegant, dignified statement, one that called attention to Jenkins's medical problems, not his sexual orientation. Jenkins had many friends in the press, and Lady Bird had given them a way out. Within three days, the entire incident simply disappeared from the pages of the newspapers.

The following month, Lady Bird and Lyndon flew home to Austin to await the results of the election. LBJ finally got his landslide, carrying every state in the North, the West, the Southwest, and most important for Lady Bird, six Southern states that Goldwater had considered his own. That victory was as much Lady Bird's as it was Lyndon's.

The Johnsons did not get one vote that they both eagerly sought. Jacqueline Kennedy, who moved to New York in the summer of 1964, cast no vote on election day. National newspapers reported that she had not voted for LBJ, which embarrassed both of the Johnsons.

Ten years later, Mrs. Kennedy explained in her oral history that she had not meant to hurt Johnson and would have voted for him if she had voted for anybody. "I'd never voted until I was married to Jack," explained Mrs. Kennedy. "This vote would have been—he would have been alive for that vote. And I thought, 'I'm not going to vote for any [other person] because this vote would have been his' . . . it was some emotional thing."

On November 17, Lady Bird celebrated her thirtieth wedding anniversary in the White House. Instead of feeling jubilant, she wrote in her diary that she felt "a curious pall of sadness and inertia, a feeling of having come to a standstill and being bound up in gloom." Earlier that day, she had visited Walter and Marjorie Jenkins, who were packing up their house and moving home to Texas. Lady Bird had not been successful in arranging a job for Jenkins. Jenkins was headed back to Austin to open his own business. She told them both goodbye and felt sad.

Later that night, at a dinner in the White House, Johnson gave her a pair of gold and diamond earrings, and she tried her best to shake her sense of despondency. A person in a state of melancholy feels, among other things, captured. The campaign was over, and while they had won the election on their own, they had lost a pivotal partner in Walter Jenkins. To some degree, they would never escape the shadow of the Kennedys. In 1965, when George Gallup released his poll of the most admired women in the country, Jackie Kennedy was number one on the list, Lady Bird was number two. The following year, 1966, the standings remained the same: Jackie first, Lady Bird second.

During her anniversary dinner in 1964, Lady Bird had good reason to feel melancholic. However, she stoically told herself she should have the good sense to "cherish the moment." A thirty-pound wedding cake was served for dessert, and there were warm and sentimental toasts all around. With a glass of champagne lifted high in the air, Johnson turned to her and offered one of those toasts. "To happiness," he told her, and then he added, "and to courage." It was the beginning of four more years.

CHAPTER THIRTEEN

Paradise Lost

As First Lady, it fell to Lady Bird to fight for beauty in a fractured land. If loneliness was the dominant theme of her youth and early adulthood, then chaos and crisis, the leitmotiv of the 1960s, were the primary impulses that defined her life in the White House. It was Johnson who encouraged Lady Bird to embrace what he called "beautification," a term that even Lady Bird despised. She said it sounded "so prissy, so slight," and she asked her East Wing staff to use the word as little as possible.

"Don't fritter your time away," Johnson instructed Lady Bird on her role as First Lady. "Spend it on Head Start and beauty."

"Beauty" was the frame in which Johnson automatically placed women. He felt Lady Bird could best help him by managing her own appearance, and by extension, the rest of the country's. She, too, desired beauty because she equated it with order. For instance, at one point in the spring of 1966, when Johnson was beset by dissenters at home and abroad, Lady Bird lamented the fact that there wasn't much concrete she could do to help her husband. "The only thing I can think of is to learn how to do my hair, keep my lipstick perfect, and be devoid of problems," she wrote in her diary. She viewed her life through his lens.

By the middle 1960s, Lady Bird could see that much of what she valued—her own pre–World War II values of coherence, order, discipline, unity—was unraveling. The times were changing, and Lady Bird feared her role as a public leader. "I have a kind of schizophrenic feeling I am cast in a role that I was never meant for," she told Carpenter and various members of the press. She had good reason to feel divided. Part of her resisted following the traditional public path required of First Ladies—the displaying of clothes, the choosing of White House china, and other decorative features. Still, she saw herself as Johnson's full partner.

For instance, when Johnson took the inaugural oath on January 20, 1965, it was Lady Bird, wearing a wool hat pushed back high on her head and tied off her face with a sealskin string, who began what is now a tradition among First Ladies. She did not keep her seat in the reviewing stand, but stood glued by Johnson's side and held the Bible with her black silk-lined gloves while he repeated the oath. She didn't just use any Bible, but the one Johnson's mother had given them for Christmas in 1952 after they purchased the ranch. If Rebekah Johnson had been the source of ambition in LBJ's childhood, then clearly that mantle now had passed to Lady Bird Johnson.

In time, as both she and Johnson became more caught up in the ideal of the presidency, much of their intimate connection was lost. Eventually they had separate bedrooms at the White House. Johnson continued his flagrant pursuit of other women—from 1965 on, the daily White House logs are full of notations of forty-five-minute and one-hour private sessions in the Oval Office between LBJ and a half-dozen women that he bragged to others about having sex with.

Nonetheless, he and Lady Bird continued to keep their bargain: LBJ made her feel worthwhile, and she gave him the loyalty he required. For instance, on January 14, 1964, she welcomed Johnson's old lover, Alice Glass, to the East Room of the White House to hear Robert Merrill of the Metropolitan Opera sing Rossini's *Barber of Seville.* The pattern of befriending competitors continued. "It was very odd," said one long-time staff member. "Johnson would add someone new to what he called his 'harem' and the next thing we knew Lady Bird was inviting them to dinner, taking them to the ranch, and treating that woman like her best friend."

The façade was a way to defend herself against not only Johnson's infidelities but the pressures of life in the White House. One of her early dreams was of wandering around the house, going from room to room, feeling lost. In time, this dream would become her reality. Life in the White House sometimes felt like a nightmare. Over the next four years, Lady Bird watched her two daughters bicker over boyfriends, religion, and the Vietnam War; saw her husband lose his ability to lead; and waged her own war over—of all things—America's beauty.

Her reaction to the divisions—inside and outside the White House—was to try and hold on to the life she knew. While Johnson tried to buy peace in his administration by surrounding himself with members of Kennedy's cabinet and staff, Lady Bird knew instinctively that to the Kennedy crowd she would always be, as her elder daughter, Lynda, once put it, "a little brown wren." The comparisons in the press between Lady Bird and Jackie were swift and cruel. Lady Bird was seen as older, frumpier, and Texas crass; Jackie was young and effortlessly beautiful. Mrs. Bernice Singer, a history teacher at South Portland High School in Maine, one of many interviewed for the *New York Times* after LBJ's inaugural, got it right: "What she [Lady Bird] suffers from is having had to follow a goddess."

Jackie's shadow was everywhere. In the bedroom that Lyndon Johnson slept in, there was a plaque that Jackie had placed that read, "In this room lived John Fitzgerald Kennedy during the two years, ten months, and two days he was President of the United States." Lady Bird continued to try and reach out to Jackie. She continued to issue her an automatic invitation to every state dinner, but Mrs. Kennedy always refused. "I just couldn't go back to that place," she said in an oral history. "Even driving around Washington, I'd try to drive a way where I wouldn't see the White House."

Instead of trying to win over Jackie's friends or deny their differences, Lady Bird moved quickly to establish her own turf. She hired her own staff and set up not one but two offices in the East Wing: one for the press, and one to coordinate her official activities. At state dinners, Pablo Casals and other classical artists were suddenly out; Carol Channing and wholesome American musicals were in. René Verdon, Mrs. Kennedy's hypersensitive French chef, was asked to leave. He was replaced by Zephyr Wright, the Johnson family's cook for twenty-one years, who tried without success to keep Johnson on a diet of 1,100 calories a day.

Extravagance in any form was out; thriftiness was in. To the press, Lynda described her mother as a wealthy woman with a "Puritan guilt complex against spending a lot in nonproductive, frivolous activity." Both of the Johnsons walked around the White House switching off lights that weren't being used in order to save electricity and encouraged the country to follow their lead. Lady Bird felt self-conscious about paying high prices for clothes and often dashed into Garfinckel's, Washington's staid old department store, to buy a black patent purse, shoes, or dresses off the sales racks, sometimes only hours before official events. When the Smithsonian Institution asked Lady Bird for one of her dresses for the First Ladies Hall, Lady Bird sent back the following message: "I'd better wait a while unless I can work out an arrangement to borrow the dress back after the museum's closing hour."

In clothes and in style, Lady Bird made no attempt to compete with Jackie Kennedy. While Mrs. Kennedy concentrated on a lavish and expensive restoration of the White House and the promotion of the arts, Lady Bird's own ideas were much more earthbound. She continued Mrs. Kennedy's White House restoration committee—as LBJ had promised—but her own legacy was "flowers for the masses." Jackie Kennedy privately advised Lady Bird not to employ an American company to manufacture her china. "The results always looked more like hotel china," Jackie told her in one letter. In this matter, Lady Bird ignored Mrs. Kennedy's advice. She chose a pattern with native wildflower designs—her own signature—and insisted it be made by an American firm.

Mrs. Kennedy was the most photographed First Lady in history, but she never held a press conference and shrank from interviews. Lady Bird was the reverse. White House photographers found it all but impossible to get a good photograph of her, but just two days after LBJ's first State of the Union address in 1964, Lady Bird invited sixty-five newspaperwomen to tour the family quarters.

That day Lady Bird let the press know that Eleanor Roosevelt was her admired role model. She finished up the tour in the Treaty Room, where Mrs. Roosevelt had once held her press conferences. About twelve of the sixty-four newspaperwomen had covered Mrs. Roosevelt. As Johnson tried to mold his presidency after FDR, refashioning the New Deal into his own Great Society, Lady Bird tried to follow his lead and pattern herself after Mrs. Roosevelt.

"I want to be a useful First Lady," Lady Bird told the women reporters, who understood that "useful" was code for Eleanor Roosevelt, not decorative in the style of Jackie Kennedy. The next day, January 11, 1964, she invited the reporters to travel with her to Wilkes-Barre, Pennsylvania, to visit poverty-stricken and out-of-work coal miners. During the trip, Lady Bird talked with some of them who were training for new careers as painters, woodworkers, and paper-hangers. She also visited a textile mill that employed mostly women, and she bemoaned the fact that the women were forced to be the major breadwinners for their families. If women were forced to work full-time in the mills, Lady Bird wondered, who would hold their families together? It was a pre-feminist question, and Lady Bird, a woman who came of age in the 1930s and 1940s, did not have the answer.

Nonetheless, the trip got her the results she wanted. The next day, several newspaper reporters predicted that Lady Bird was likely to be the most political First Lady since Eleanor Roosevelt. "We were all thrilled to have the access that she gave us," said Helen Thomas, who covered the White House for United Press International during the Johnson years. "We were often left out in the cold by Jackie—she didn't want anything to do with the press—and here came Lady Bird and Liz [Carpenter] and they just practically threw open the doors to us. Very soon, they had us climbing mountains, swimming rivers, and planting flowers all over Washington."

Despite the warm reaction, there were important differences between Eleanor Roosevelt and Lady Bird. Here is how Liz Carpenter described the two: "Mrs. Roosevelt was in instigator, an innovator, willing to air a cause without her husband's endorsement. Mrs. Johnson was an imple-menter and translator of her husband and his purpose. . . . She was, first and foremost, a wife."

In February 1965, Lady Bird summoned Secretary of the Interior Stewart Udall, a holdover from the Kennedy administration, and several key female staff members, to a private meeting in the Queen's Sitting Room in the upstairs of the White House to discuss what would become her own true legacy—her crusade on behalf of the environment.

On this particular day, the landscape outside her window was bleak and cold. A heavy snow was falling. Beyond the White House fence there was a large group of civil rights marchers kneeling in the snow, praying and singing a hymn that had become synonymous with the civil rights movement, "We Shall Overcome." The song of protest was clearly audible when Mrs. Johnson, whose Secret Service code name was Victoria, regally entered the room, wearing a bright red dress, and shook hands with her guests.

"What are they doing?" Mrs. Johnson asked, speaking of the demonstrators. Sharon Francis, an aide to Udall who had graduated from Mount Holyoke College and had come to work full-time for Mrs. Johnson as what Carpenter called the "East Wing egghead," pulled back the curtain and replied, "They're singing . . . and they're kneeling in the snow."

Mrs. Johnson's reaction was to sink into a chair and weep. The other people in the room—Udall and his wife, Francis; Carpenter; and Elizabeth Rowe, the chairman of the National Capital Planning Commissions in Washington and the wife of James Rowe, a New Deal lawyer who was part of Johnson's early brain trust—sat silently and uncomfortably as the voices penetrated the walls of White House. "We all stood there," recalled Francis, "and let the moment sink in."

The siege mentality had set in early. Her response to the protestors was to try harder. The small sign on her desk in the East Wing read: *Can Do*. That day, Lady Bird told the group that she had two main goals for her conservation effort. First, she wanted to mobilize individuals—particularly women—to improve the physical landscape of their own cities and towns in specific ways, and second, she wanted to use her own city—Washington, D.C.—as a laboratory. The planned improvements included planting flowers, burying power transmission lines, promoting better freeway design, and encouraging ordinary citizens to simply pick up after themselves in public spaces.

She tried to adapt the spirit of activism of the 1960s to her own purposes. For instance, in Columbus, Ohio, in 1965 a group of teenagers that called themselves CRUD (Campaign to Remove Unsightly Debris) picketed at city hall carrying signs that said: "Stash That Trash!" and "Don't Be a Grub, Pick It Up, Bub!" Other such groups formed around the country.

By nature and habit, Lady Bird was one of those fastidious people who picked up loose trash on roadways and parks and placed it in nearby trash cans. Edith Royal, the wife of the University of Texas football coach Darrell Royal, said that once while on a vacation with Lady Bird in Mexico she dropped a tissue paper on the ground. Lady Bird said nothing to Mrs. Royal, but reached down and picked up the tissue paper and put it in her own bag. "That was the last time I ever purposefully littered," Mrs. Royal recalled.

As First Lady, Lady Bird set out to make that same kind of change in the nation's habits. She raised money from private corporations to launch a national anti-litter campaign. Her attention to detail became notorious. For instance, during one anti-litter meeting, a group of Pepsi executives showed Lady Bird a litter bag that they planned to distribute. She studied the bag, congratulated them on their efforts, but pointed out that it was too small to hold a six-pack. She was polite, grateful, but made it clear that she was interested in substance, not just show.

The word she favored for her cause was "conservation," which implies saving something that is in danger of being lost. Lady Bird's belief in the power of the land to shape the lives of individuals and communities was as sweeping as Johnson's vision of the Great Society, which he described in his State of the Union address in 1964 as a "civilization where leisure is a time to reflect."

Both pursued parallel versions of political utopia. Lyndon's saw paradise as an end to poverty, illiteracy, and racial disorder. Lady Bird viewed it as a struggle to live harmoniously in nature. Her pitch was that if Americans could drive on better-designed highways, reduce the number of junkyards, build more playgrounds and parks, and keep the streets swept clean, then those physical changes would produce better living conditions. Behind her commitment was the assumption that such improvements would bring about a reduction in the need for antagonism and protest, like the one that took place outside the Queen's Sitting Room. By the time they left that day, the Committee for a More Beautiful Capital had been established.

From the beginning, its efforts were pulled in two competing directions. One part of the committee, represented by wealthy New York philanthropists such as Mary Lasker, Laurence Rockefeller, and Brooke Astor, advocated the "garden club solution" of planting trees, shrubs, and flowers in the public areas of Washington, while the other group, headed by Walter Washington, a moderate Black who was then head of the National Capital Housing Authority and later became mayor of Washington, pressed for public projects that would benefit poorer neighborhoods.

There were also conflicts within the two camps. In the flower camp, the philanthropists watched one another to see who was donating what, and then looked for other ways to contribute. Each wanted to make his or her own individual mark, outdo the others, and be given credit for it. As an example, one night at the White House, Lady Bird hosted a birthday party for Mary Lasker. Brooke Astor, who was also present, looked around the room, admired the French wallpaper, and then turned to Mrs. Johnson and asked, "Bird, is this the wallpaper I gave?" "Yes," noted Lady Bird, giving Mrs. Astor her due. "I believe it is."

Lasker's clear turf was flowers. In the spring of 1965, she donated 9,300 azalea bushes and dogwoods that were planted along Pennsylvania Avenue. In time, she gave $70,000 for the planting of cherry trees on Hains Point, and donated 100,000 daffodil bulbs for planting on Rock Creek Parkway, as well as 175 dogwoods in the area near Key Bridge.

Lasker's money for flowers translated into clout on Lady Bird's committee, influence that Lasker did not hesitate to use. In 1965, when the Democratic National Committee gave $40,000 to use on a project of Lady Bird's choice, it was Mary Lasker who insisted that the money go to plant 200 dogwoods, 60 evergreens, and many daffodils on Columbia Island, a 121-acre tract of land on the Virginia side of the Potomac that was renamed Lady Bird Johnson Park in 1968.

Carol Fortas, the wife of Abe, whom Johnson later nominated for the U.S. Supreme Court, was "absolutely furious," according to Francis. Fortas, who was aligned with the Walter Washington camp, felt that the money should be used in the needier Black neighborhoods. Lasker put her foot down, and the $40,000 went to trees and flowers. "There were a very few instances when the society finally threw a bone to the Blacks," recalled Sharon Francis, "but not many."

The beauty effort continued to be concentrated primarily in public areas. Laurence Rockefeller gave $25,000 to clean the city's most prominent statues. Liz Carpenter recalled that Lady Bird was chagrined to learn that the statue of General Sherman, the Civil War general who led Union forces in the march on Atlanta, was the first to be cleaned. Private money was used to plant flowers in Washington's circles and triangles. She encouraged the Park Service to plant shrubs near National Airport. Everywhere, she planted daffodils, like the ones she had seen as a child in East Texas and privately named "queen." The service kept a running tab of the number of daffodil bulbs that were planted at Lady Bird's direction: in four years, the number reached two million, the largest planting in history.

In May 1965, following a White House conference on natural beauty, Johnson asked Bill Moyers, then a special assistant to the President, to draft what LBJ called "Lady Bird's bill on highway beautification." The bill that Moyers produced was written primarily by members of the outdoor billboard lobby. It gave states the power to regulate billboards and junkyards along interstate and major highways and said that the secretary of commerce could withhold 20 percent of federal highway funds from states that failed to implement stricter controls. Conservationists considered the bill too weak because it provided no funds for the removal of existing junkyards and billboards.

Even so, the bill faced strong opposition from small businessmen who depended on large highway signs for advertising, much of it aimed directly at Lady Bird. In Montana, the following message went up on one billboard: "Impeach Lady Bird." U.S. Senator Bob Dole of Kansas was one of the few members of Congress, however, who singled out Lady Bird for personal criticism. On the Senate floor, Dole questioned the propriety of Lady Bird's activism. He suggested that every time "secretary of commerce" appeared in the bill, it should be changed to "Lady Bird." The implication was that the President was giving his wife too much power, an irony given the fact that in time Dole's own wife, Elizabeth, became secretary of labor under President Ronald Reagan and secretary of transportation under President George Bush and a presidential contender in her own right.

The highway bill passed in the Senate but stalled in the House. Proponents of Lady Bird's bill agreed to reduce the penalty for failing to comply from 20 to 10 percent. By then, Johnson felt that his political manhood was on the line. He sent word to the Hill that he considered a vote against highway beautification "a matter of personal honor" to his wife.

The bill came up for a vote on October 7 in the House. On that night, Lady Bird hosted a previously scheduled congressional White House dinner. Johnson sent word over to the Hill that no members would be welcomed at the White House event until they had passed Lady Bird's bill.

The bill passed, but Lady Bird shrank from the controversy it had generated. She instructed her staff to think of ways to improve highways without having to go to Congress, and shifted her focus to public appeals for more landscaping and better-designed highways. "She just wasn't comfortable with the arm-twisting," Carpenter recalled.

By then, Johnson's decision to escalate the war in Vietnam cast a pall over his entire administration. At the time he became President, the military situation in Vietnam was rapidly deteriorating. During his first year as President, Johnson had launched an air war and sent 25,000 troops into Vietnam. In 1966, U.S. troops numbered 184,000; three years later, the number stood at over 500,000. As the number of troops increased, so did the number of casualties: in 1965, there were officially 2,500 Americans killed, wounded, hospitalized, or missing in Vietnam; by 1968, the official tally was 138,000.

In Vietnam, as in every other crisis of Johnson's life, Lady Bird's role was to create a strange, even suffocating atmosphere of support around LBJ in which he could be assured that no matter how unreasonable his decision or petulant his behavior, his family and staff would stay forever loyal and submissive. She helped create a matrix of constant fidelity, which had the effect of restricting real debate about Vietnam or anything else. Her own power lay in soothing him, and she took great pains to keep him calmed, even when he was on the verge of a mistake. "It got to the point," said Reedy, one of his press secretaries, "that it was a com-pletely closed court and no one could express a doubt about anything, not in the office or in the family quarters. No one could tell Lyndon Johnson to go soak his head. Lady Bird helped perpetuate this. She did not like for Johnson to hear bad news."

But it became increasingly impossible to shield him from such news. In June 1965 the poet Robert Lowell wrote a public letter to LBJ in protest of the war in Vietnam. The letter was covered prominently by the *New York Times* and the *Washington Post,* and more letters followed from other writers and artists. Bess Abell, Mrs. Johnson's social secre-tary, used to start her day by clipping out the letters and advertisements that appeared in the *New York Times* signed by poets, actors, musicians, and writers that said, "Dear Mr. President: You have killed so many North and South Vietnamese. How can you sleep at night?" These dis-senters were not invited to the White House. "It became chic to march on the White House and march on the Pentagon," Abell recalled. The feeling in the East Wing was that some writers and artists were trying to boost their careers by protesting the war.

One such writer, John Hersey, did appear at the White House at the Festival of the Arts in June 1965 and read portions of *Hiroshima,* his book about the dropping of the atomic bomb over Japan. Lady Bird had not wanted Hersey to read from his book. In fact, she had asked Eric Goldman, who planned the festival, to cancel Hersey's appearance. In icy tones, she told Goldman, "The President and I do not want this man to come here and read this."

Goldman convinced Lady Bird that canceling Hersey would create a larger furor than letting him read. Over her objections, Hersey did, in fact, read at the White House. When he finished, an aggrieved Lady Bird, her face tense and brittle, sat perfectly still and refused to applaud.

Try as she might, Lady Bird could not ignore the growing opposition to Vietnam. Those inside the White House who had doubts about Vietnam—including Sharon Francis and some of the other members of Lady Bird's own staff—told themselves that their job was to concentrate on Lady Bird's programs and tried not to ask questions about Vietnam.

As for Lady Bird, she told friends and family it did not occur to her to raise questions that she could not answer. "I couldn't handle the war in Vietnam," she later told her staff. "I wasn't big enough." Liz Carpenter also lectured the staff in what became known as periodic "pep talks." Her speech went like this: "We don't all have to expect to be able to solve the Vietnam War, because none of us really can just by sitting and brooding about it."

Carpenter told Abell and Francis that one reason Mrs. Johnson wanted to go on the so-called beautification trips—she made forty of them to places like Big Bend National Park in Texas and the Snake River in Idaho—was that in the wild the "only pickets would be the crickets." As always, nature was her refuge from the problems of the world.

Lady Bird's diary reflects the growing sense of despair and isolation inside LBJ's court, even in the queen's chamber. For instance, on March 3, 1965, she wrote: "Life is lived these days against the air strikes by our planes in Vietnam, attacks on our Embassies—this week it's another in Moscow involving stones and ink bottles hurled by mobs of students and other dissenters—and rising murmur of the press here in Washington about secretiveness or not enough press conferences. It's like shooting the rapids, every moment is a new struggle, every moment a new direction—trying to keep the craft level and away from the rocks, and no still water in sight."

Four days later, Dr. Martin Luther King, Jr., led his famous march from Selma, Alabama, to Montgomery to initiate support for legislation that would remove legal barriers that prevented Negroes from voting. Alabama governor George Wallace responded by sending in state police, who—in the full glare of TV lights—beat unarmed Black marchers with billy clubs. Within hours, picketers had surrounded the White House. Johnson sent in the National Guard two days later to protect the protestors, a move that Lady Bird—and most of the rest of the country—regarded as brilliant. "This was sanity," she wrote in her diary. "A temporary lid on the volcano to grant time for the good sense of the nation to take hold, and we have a strong Voting Rights Bill in Congress to save us from catastrophe."

In the early morning, when Johnson was too troubled to sleep, he would sometimes walk into her adjoining room and bemoan his decline in public support and agonize over the Vietnam War. These early morning hours were among the few they shared together alone in the White House. "We can't get out," he said of Vietnam, "and we can't finish it." At 7:30 they had breakfast in his bedroom with military advisers and cabinet members gathered around his bed. Lady Bird would sit quietly in her dressing gown, often with her hair in rollers, drinking her coffee and listening to every word.

Johnson once explained to Nan Robertson, for a story in the *Saturday Evening Post*, why he wanted Lady Bird near him when he faced major decisions. "I never saw her slice a corner on anything. She is the first to tell me about my mistakes, whether they are financial extravagancies or a political boner, and to me that is the test of real character."

Increasingly, she heard LBJ talk about not running again. He had threatened to quit politics at least three times before. He had done it in 1948 when he ran for the U.S. Senate, and he issued the same sort of threats in 1960 before he agreed to become Kennedy's running mate. In 1964, he drafted a statement that said he would not run for President. In crucial moments, it was Lady Bird who encouraged him to continue his drive.

This time, however, Lady Bird realized there was no going back. Increasingly, his health was failing him. As early as the spring of 1964, she had decided Johnson probably should not run again for two reasons: she didn't think he would live through a second term, and she had become convinced he couldn't unite the country. She was particularly bitter about the increasing level of unrest over civil rights. In her mind, Johnson, a Southerner, had done more to help Negroes by fighting for the passage of the Civil Rights Act in 1964 than any President since Lincoln. The level of Black anger in the country mystified and disappointed her. She made up her mind that the best thing she could do was to figure out a way to, as she put it, ease LBJ out of the presidency and "off the mountain."

She could feel the futility in her bones. On Sunday, March 7, 1965, as Blacks demonstrated in front of the White House, she wrote, "For some time I have been swimming upstream against a feeling of depression and relative inertia. I flinch from activity and involvement, and yet I rust without them. Lyndon lives in a cloud of troubles, with few rays of light." Four days later, twelve protestors walked into the White House with a group of tourists, sat down on the floor, and refused to budge. The White House switchboard reported angry messages and death threats every single day. The Secret Service constantly reminded her that she was in danger and not to take chances. "What a house," she wrote. "What a life."

On that day, she predicted what would happen three years later on March 31, 1968. "I am counting the months until March 1968 when, like Truman, it will be possible to say, 'I don't want this office, this responsibility, any longer, even if you want me. Find the strongest and most able man and God bless you. Good-bye.'"

Historians have long debated why exactly Johnson withdrew from politics when he did. One factor was his wife's refusal to talk him out of it. The most important subtext of Lady Bird's role as First Lady was how she maneuvered his retreat. She noted in her diary the month and year he would announce his retirement, three years before he actually did it, and, by all accounts, before Johnson knew he would do it.

On April 16, 1965, Good Friday, she and Johnson went to the LBJ Ranch for a three-day weekend with a large entourage. Johnson's weight had climbed to 226, more than he weighed at the time of his heart attack ten years before. "I don't know whether to lash out in anger or sarcasm," Lady Bird wrote. Instead, she issued new orders about LBJ's diet: he was to be served one helping of oatmeal in the morning, one helping of chili at lunch, one jigger of Cutty Sark with his nightly meal.

One night Johnson got up long after everyone else in the White House had gone to bed, quietly walked down the hall to the family kitchen, and pulled a bowl of tapioca—his favorite dessert—from the refrigerator and started eating it. Lady Bird heard him, got out of bed herself, and followed the sound of the metal spoon scraping against the side of the bowl until she found him. She took the tapioca away from him. The next morning, Johnson told his staff the story and ordered an assistant press secretary to buy him a wooden spoon.

Meanwhile, Lady Bird set her goals on finishing the term and not running again. "Lyndon keeps talking more and more about retiring," she wrote. "For the first time, I am convinced that he could. I have always believed that he had to stay lashed to the mast until the last gasp of breath, but I think that is changing." Her instincts told her the truth—that Johnson, who could not stand to be alone, would never really be happy out of public office. However, she wanted to believe such rest was possible for both of them. "I see him yearning towards the days of peace and retirement," she wrote. Johnson did, in fact, yearn for peace—peace at home and peace abroad—but it was Lady Bird who yearned for retirement.

There was no such peace in the White House, not even in her family. By then, the differences in style and personality between her two daughters, Lynda and Luci, were obvious to everyone. "The rivalry between the two of them had always been well known," recalled Reedy, "but when they all got to the White House, it just exploded. Luci was very self-willed and dramatic, and Lynda was very smart and anxious to please her father."

Lynda, whose Secret Service code name was "Velvet," was a born introvert and resistant to public life. At five feet, ten inches tall, Lynda entered the White House shy, gawky, and slightly overweight. When her father became President, Lynda did not want to leave the University of Texas at Austin, where she was a sophomore, a history major, and a member of Zeta Tau Alpha sorority, but Lady Bird insisted that Lynda transfer to George Washington University in Washington.

Lady Bird needed her. In temperament, Lynda was frugal and practical, like her mother, and less prone to dramatics than her younger sister, who was known as "Venus" to the Secret Service. Luci, the blue-eyed child whose father called her "the pretty one," made the kind of news that did not please her mother. She called the White House the "Great White Zoo"; was photographed dancing the Watusi and driving around in her convertible; and she complained that her father would not allow her to go to Union Station for the arrival of the Beatles.

Both girls viewed their mother as remote and unemotional. However, Lynda saw this quality as positive. Lynda described her mother as "calm" and "always on an even keel" and once compared her to Melanie in *Gone With the Wind*. Luci saw these qualities as negative. She lashed out at her mother for being "unduly controlled and unemotional" and often asked her caretaker, Willie Day Taylor, who had a master's degree in psychology from the University of Texas, whether or not Taylor believed her mother loved her.

"I was angry and struck out at my mother a lot," Luci recalled as an adult. "Even when I was a kid, Mother used to have a little pillow that she hung on her door that said 'I want to be alone.' Once or twice, I threw that pillow on the ground, but I did not dare knock on that door. She just put up a wall."

The reason for the wall was that so much of Lady Bird's energy was going into soothing and caring for their father. Whenever possible, she encouraged her daughters to care for him as well, to stay by his side at White House functions, and cautioned both of them not to do anything that would embarrass him. Each daughter found different ways to cope with this fundamental fact of their lives, even as both of them vied for their father's attention. Luci struck out at pillows and transferred some of her affection to Willie Day. Lady Bird described Luci as "uncomfortably intuitive" and seemed to resent her constant probing. "One thing about Luci, she is very sure of her verdicts," Lady Bird wrote on October 6, 1966.

Lynda patterned herself more after her mother. She made good grades, guarded her privacy, learned to play bridge, graduated from charm school, and kept the rules.

During Luci's final year in high school at the National Cathedral School, she announced that she wanted to convert to the Roman Catholic faith. It was not a sudden decision: she had been attending Catholic services since she was thirteen. As Liz Carpenter once put it, "Luci was born with a rosary in her hand." Johnson was still a member of the Christian Church in Johnson City, and Lady Bird and Lynda were both Episcopalians. All three opposed Luci's decision and made their opposition plain. But Luci was insistent. She took instruction for nine months and chose to be baptized into the church on July 2, 1965, her eighteenth birthday and the tenth anniversary of Johnson's major heart attack. "I cannot be happy about it," wrote Lady Bird in her diary, and added, "Maybe her earnest search is at an end, because it always had been a search."

The baptism was scheduled for 2:00 P.M. at St. Matthew's Cathedral in Washington, where President Kennedy's funeral service had been held, a coincidence that made Lady Bird uneasy. Around noon, Lady Bird had lunch in her bedroom with Lynda before going to the church, and as they munched on sandwiches, Lady Bird wrote out a simple statement to the press, announcing Luci's upcoming baptism. In her dairy, Lady Bird noted that Lynda was even more distraught about Luci becoming a Catholic than she was. After lunch, Luci swept into the bedroom wearing a white lace dress that made her look, as Lady Bird put it, "as inconspicuous as Brigitte Bardot." Johnson arrived soon afterward, and they all four went to church together.

Father James Montgomery, who had given Luci her instruction, officiated. After the service, Lyndon shook hands with Father Montgomery. Lady Bird stood by his side as she watched Luci disappear into a confessional and Lynda head in the opposite direction—out of the church in tears. Lady Bird felt an overpowering sense of loss. "I could not help but think we went in four and came out three," she wrote.

That evening, Willie Day Taylor presided over Luci's eighteenth birthday party in the Solarium upstairs in the White House, while Lady Bird boarded a flight to New York with Johnson for a speech, then on to Austin that same night for a few days at the ranch. As she left, she wrote that she cast a "forlorn look over her shoulder at this fragmented life of mine," leaving her daughter in the care of Mother Church and Willie Day Taylor.

Luci's search for an independent life was not over. By the time she converted to Catholicism, she had already met Pat Nugent, of Waukegan, Illinois, and at midnight on Christmas Eve 1965, the engagement was announced from the LBJ Ranch in Texas. Both Lady Bird and Johnson thought Luci was too young to marry and tried to talk her out of it. Looking back on it as a grown woman, Luci believed that one reason she married Nugent at nineteen years old was to "get out of the fishbowl that was the White House." If so, her wedding had the opposite effect—with twelve bridesmaids and seven hundred guests, it was one of the showiest weddings of the 1960s.

The fact that Luci, who was younger than Lynda, married first exacerbated the tensions between the two sisters. It was during this period that Lynda started dating George Hamilton, the tan, dark-haired movie star that LBJ reportedly called "Charlie" behind his back as a joke. Though staff members say LBJ didn't much like Hamilton—he worried that the actor was using Lynda for publicity—the glamour of Hollywood agreed with Lynda, and Lady Bird liked him. "He was extremely good for her—he really brought her out as a woman," Lady Bird said in 1997.

The first public notice of the romance came in the *New York Times* on January 2, 1966, when a sleeker, more sophisticated Lynda emerged on Hamilton's arm in New Orleans at the Sugar Bowl game. The following month, Lynda flew to New Orleans again to meet Hamilton, and news of the trip again made headlines. Lady Bird was divided in her feelings about Hamilton. She could see that Hamilton was "showing her there was more to being a woman than books," but she worried about public criticism. In her diary, Lady Bird wrote that she hovered between wanting her then twenty-one-year-old daughter to have independence, and knowing that everything she did reflected on her father, the President.

Two days later, the battle among the sisters intensified when *Women's Wear Daily* carried a story that said all three Johnson women were among the worst dressed women in America. Luci blamed Lynda for her habit of wearing bobby socks, loafers, and owlish glasses. Lynda blamed the press but launched a rigorous self-improvement campaign. Hamilton introduced her to Hollywood hairdresser George Masters, who gave her a new, more relaxed hairstyle—freeing her from the Texas style of teasing to produce bigger, puffier hair—and changed her makeup, starting with thinning out her bushy eyebrows. She lost more weight, eventually getting to a sleek size eight. Soon her metamorphosis became news. After one party, the *Washington Post* described her as "resplendent in a white dress with dark hair down over her shoulders. . . . Lynda looked absolutely lovely with her hair pulled back and cascading down her back."

But the two daughters continued to be played against each other in the press. Johnson himself contributed to the rivalry. At one point he boasted to the Associated Press that he wasn't worried about either of his girls. "Lynda is so smart that she'll be able to make a living for herself, and Luci Baines is so appealing and feminine that there will always be some man around waiting to make a living for her." It was Lynda who was most upset about the remark. "He makes it sound like no man will have me," Lynda told her friends. Her romance with Hamilton may have been a public attempt to prove her father wrong.

The month before Luci's wedding, newspapers carried prominent sketches of the pink bridesmaid dresses, and on the same day the following headline appeared about Lynda's return to Washington from a trip: "Eludes Press at Airport." *Women's Wear Daily* continued to savage Lynda. They ran one story that said she still needed better shoes, and interviewed four hairdressers who suggested that her long hair was passé and that she should cut it. Every decision that each girl made— the color of a dress, the cut of her hair—had to be weighed against public reaction. Johnson complained to his aides that Lady Bird wanted out of the goldfish bowl as much as Luci and Lynda. Lady Bird noted in her diary, sadly, "And now in a way it's daughter against daughter."

Luci's wedding was held on a sweltering Saturday—August 6, 1966—at the National Shrine of the Immaculate Conception, which was not air-conditioned. An offer from National Airlines to provide portable blowers to cool down the church was rejected at the last minute because the airline was involved in a tense labor dispute. Johnson himself telephoned Liz Carpenter and told her he would rather "sit in church and sweat" than be criticized for provoking an airline strike.

Sit and sweat they did. The service lasted longer than an hour. Lady Bird described it as "interminable." Guests fanned themselves to stir a breeze. When the priest got to page nineteen of the missal, Lynda physically wilted. She put down her head on her prayer rail, and then slumped to a seated position as if she were about to faint. From her seat, Lady Bird sat quietly, longed for smelling salts, and prayed that the service would be soon over.

Later that month, LBJ and Lady Bird had an unusual exchange of gifts. On August 25, after a day of shopping in New York, Lady Bird returned to the White House about 9:30 P.M. to find Johnson at work. On his desk was a small package. At first, she thought the package was for him—after all the next day was his fifty-eighth birthday—but Johnson looked up, pointed at the box, and said, "There is something you will want to open." Inside was a large and expensive diamond ring.

Lady Bird, whose original wedding band cost $2.50, was overwhelmed and didn't know what to think. "All these years I've taken a rather condescending view of women who wanted or needed diamonds, saying something like this: 'A diamond is just a shiny rock that advertises that a successful man cherishes you. And I already know that, so I don't need it.' Now I find myself, at 53, proud to have that shiny rock, delighted to be told that I am cherished."

The following day, she gave him a very different kind of gift for his birthday: a wooden seaman's chest, made in the 1840s, an antique once owned by a German family that had immigrated to the United States. It was a soulful gift, crudely built, but emblematic of the American experience. Johnson's response was to ridicule it. "If I live long enough I guess Lady Bird will get enough of these chests!" he announced to the thirty-two guests who had gathered at the ranch for his birthday dinner of barbecued beef and homemade peach ice cream. The implication was she had bought the chest to please herself.

Johnson's diamond—as Lady Bird recognized—was flashy proof that she was married to a rich and powerful man. Lady Bird had reached the point where she was content with the bargain she had made. Lady Bird's gift, on the other hand, was a different kind of symbol. She offered an old chest—a container to pack up their treasured belongings and move back to the German Hill Country of Texas—but Johnson had rejected it, and Lady Bird felt ashamed. "I am chagrined with myself," Lady Bird wrote, late on the eve of her husband's birthday.

By then, she realized that Johnson was going back and forth in his mind about whether to seek another term. On January 5, 1967, she felt that she had entered what she called "the valley of the black pig." The artist Peter Hurd, who had painted an official portrait of Johnson two years before that LBJ had rejected, had publicly complained to the press about his treatment. Johnson, insulated in the White House, had little patience for opinions other than his own. Those who did not agree with him on the policy of escalating the war in Vietnam began to drift away: first McGeorge Bundy, his special assistant for National Security Affairs, left, then George Ball, undersecretary of state, then Bill Moyers, one of Lady Bird's favorites.

Five days later, during Johnson's State of the Union message, he called for the nation to stand firm in Vietnam even as it continued to fight the war on poverty at home, a divided expensive path that would cost him his presidency. From her place in the gallery, Lady Bird watched and pronounced the audience "cold" and was particularly worried about the lack of response from the Democrats. She noticed then Senator J. William Fulbright, chairman of the Foreign Relations Committee, who had been holding hearings on Vietnam that drew the nation's attention to the futility of the war, "sat silent, above it all, the whole evening," and that Bobby Kennedy, by then also an outspoken opponent of Johnson's policies in Vietnam, was "stony-faced." That night, Lady Bird recognized that opposition to the war had ceased to seem disloyal, even among Johnson's staff and on the Democratic side of the aisle.

Two months later, after Johnson had stepped up the bombing in Vietnam, Lady Bird joined him in the East Room for a televised press conference. It was the first time he was asked directly if he would run for reelection in 1968. Johnson brushed aside the question, but Lady Bird, dressed in a green silk suit, felt herself freeze as she sat in a straight-backed chair to Johnson's right. "It was like a play," she recalled. "The climax and the audience was very quiet. Lyndon rose to it like a good actor." Beneath the drama was the reality; the national consensus on Vietnam was unraveling, day by day.

Everywhere she went, she saw picketing. The irony of her beautification efforts became clear even to Lady Bird. As she planted daffodils around the city, the forests in Vietnam were being destroyed by defoliants. By May she was so miserable that she faced the prospect of another campaign as if it would be an "open-ended stay in a concentration camp."

She talked over her private feelings with Abe Fortas in the Queen's Sitting Room on May 13, 1967. Fortas insisted that Johnson should not make a decision about a second term right away because he felt it would cripple his ability to lead. Lady Bird felt otherwise—he needed to find a way out of not just Vietnam but the White House—and continued to press for a decision.

In late summer, Johnson summoned George Christian, his press secretary, to his bedroom, as he did every weekday morning. Johnson, with Lady Bird present, explained to Christian that he had decided not to seek another term. He cited his health as the major factor and asked Christian to research how former President Truman had announced his own decision not to run again in 1952. During that first conversation, Johnson explained that every time he looked at President Woodrow Wilson's portrait in the White House, he was determined to get out of office before he became physically or politically incapacitated. As he spoke, Lady Bird nodded her head in agreement. Wilson had a stroke in

1919, and for two years, his cabinet—and his wife—ran the country.

"Johnson expected to die young, and he was even more worried about being disabled than dying," said Christian. "The feeling I had that morning was that he was living under a sword. He knew his days were numbered and that he didn't have four more years in him." During the meeting, Lady Bird gently persuaded him to make the retirement announcement in March. "Her style was to listen to him and then to tell him that she agreed with him," recalled Christian. "She did not make any speeches, but I do recall that she said it was important to leave at the right time and to do it in the right way." Christian knew that Johnson had threatened not to run in 1964 and thought the odds were good that Johnson would change his mind again. Johnson swore him to secrecy, saying, "Nobody knows this but you, me, and Bird." Christian left the bedroom without giving it too much more thought.

Shortly after that, on June 21, 1967, Lady Bird was in Austin when Luci gave birth to her first child, Patrick Lyndon. Johnson was asleep at the White House when she called to wake him up. "A boy?" he said. "That's fine." Lynda was in New York at a party with George Hamilton, but they had already decided not to marry. In July, Lynda went to London without him, and soon after that she began dating Charles Robb, who was from Virginia. Robb, a Marine Corps officer, led the White House Color Guard.

Less than a month later, on August 10, Lynda woke up both of her parents in the White House to tell them that she wanted to marry Robb. Lady Bird did not seem concerned about the suddenness of the decision. She thought Robb looked like an all-American boy—a poster boy for the Marine Corps—and her first impressions were favorable. Robb had graduated in 1961 from the University of Wisconsin, and two years later from law school at the University of Virginia. He was first in his class in Quantico, Virginia, in training as a Marine Corps officer.

At the time, Lady Bird was so preoccupied with Johnson and his problems that she didn't have much time to think about another White House wedding. Later that same day, she flew to Texas to supervise an addition to their bedroom at the ranch. "Sometime during the evening Lyndon called and I could sense the loneliness in his voice and the desire just to talk to me," she wrote. "I try to keep that loneliness at bay and I felt torn between doing what I was doing, which must be done, and being with him."

His neediness and her willingness to fill it was why friends and staff members concluded that in this marriage, Johnson was far more dependent on Lady Bird than she on him. "No matter what happened, Mrs. Johnson went about her business. She was a self-contained woman," said Christian. "He wanted and needed her to cater to him, to be around at all times. It was harder on all of us when she wasn't there."

On September 8, 1967, Johnson held a critical eight-hour meeting with two of his oldest friends—Governor John Connally and U.S. Representative Jake Pickle—to talk about his retirement. He intended to announce his withdrawal in December and wanted to hear his friends' ideas about what he should say. In the morning, the three men rode around the ranch, analyzing whether Johnson should run for another term or quit. "He was blowing hot and cold on his decision," recalled Pickle, who, for one, did not really believe that Johnson would not run again. He knew that Bobby Kennedy was probably going to run, and Pickle simply didn't believe that Johnson could stand for Bobby to succeed him. Connally on the other hand could not visualize another term—by now there were so many peace demonstrations it was hard for Johnson physically to leave the White House. His argument was that Johnson should announce the decision during the State of the Union message in 1968.

Around 7:00 P.M., Johnson sent for Lady Bird, who was having her hair done in her bathroom at the ranch. She quickly got out from under the dryer, and with her hair in small rollers—"sausage rollers," as she put it—she joined the three men in their discussions. When asked, she let everyone know that she did not want the pressure anymore. She told them that she didn't want to face another campaign. Her argument was that even though Johnson still had strength and leadership, she feared that if he took office at sixty years of age, his health might fail and that it would be "unbearably painful for him to recognize and for me to watch." She reminded him that his father had died at sixty. Johnson nodded his acknowledgment. "If we ever get sick," she told him, speaking of him as part of her. "I want to be sick on our time."

That line made all three men laugh, and Johnson promised Lady Bird that he would indeed resign. According to Pickle, Lady Bird told him, "Get me a yellow pad and a No. 2 pencil. I want you to write it down and sign it." They ordered dinner on TV trays, and all four, Lady Bird in her curlers, sat and ate. Johnson did not write his promise down and sign it, and that night Lady Bird went to bed feeling that nothing had been firmly decided.

The following month, one of his doctors, Willis Hurst, called Lady Bird back to the White House at midnight from a visit at the ranch. Hurst confided that he was worried about Johnson's health. Lady Bird asked him point-blank if Johnson were well enough to seek another term. Hurst did not answer, but suggested two things: she should limit her own travel schedule so that she could stay close to Johnson and have a physical herself to guard her own health. She agreed to do both things.

In effect, Lady Bird became his duty nurse. That night she went upstairs for another long talk with Johnson. They covered the same topics—when he would quit, how he would make the announcement. "Our mood was bleak and dispirited and no answers came."

Despite her promise to Dr. Hurst, Lady Bird was determined not to become a prisoner of the White House. "I want to know what's going on—even if to know is to suffer," she wrote on October 8, after a difficult trip to Williams College in Massachusetts and to Yale University in Connecticut. On both campuses she came face-to-face with the strength of the student anti-war movement.

As she walked into Chapin Hall at Williams, with the president of the college beside her, she saw a small group of picketers, and read one sign that said: "Confront the War Makers in Washington, October 21." Inside, the students all wore black robes, and she noticed that some wore white armbands, a symbol of mourning for those killed in Vietnam. When she was introduced, thirty-five members of the graduating class stood up and walked out of the service to protest her husband's policies. Lady Bird was angry. She felt she had been used as bait for the protestors—"their creature for the day"—but she was determined not to lose control. Her compelling desire was to maintain her dignity, so she went on and gave her speech.

The ordeal was not over. On her way out the door, she encountered a larger group of demonstrators. They chanted at her: "Shame! Shame!" In the buzz of protests, she sensed something "weird and animal about mass psychology" and privately wondered what would happen if she broke into a run. She didn't run, of course, but kept walking and smiling, until the procession ended beneath a grove of elm trees. Only then did she rest.

The next day at Yale was even uglier. She was met by a crowd of more than a hundred protestors, who jeered at her as they ran along the side of her car. Dr. Kingman Brewster, the president of Yale, greeted her and was polite, but she could sense that her presence was really not welcome. When he introduced Lady Bird, he compared her to Eleanor Roosevelt, but also said that when he was a college student he had been opposed to Roosevelt's policies during World War II, a clear signal that he was in sympathy with the student and faculty protesters at Yale. When Lady Bird rose to speak, she heard the boos and hisses from eight hundred protestors who were camped outside the hall. Throughout her speech, they screamed "Peace now" and "Hell no, we won't go."

Carpenter, who was present with Lady Bird, could only stand on the sidelines as Lady Bird plowed through her speech and wish that she had protected her from this moment. "We should have junked the speech," she said later. Johnson called after it was all over, and he, too, was angry that Lady Bird had suffered the boos and hisses that were meant for him. "I just hate for you to have to take that sort of thing," he told her.

The following month, on November 12, it was Lady Bird's turn to feel angry on his behalf. That day, a Sunday, Lady Bird suggested that she and Lyndon go to church at Burton Parish Episcopal Church in Williamsburg, Virginia. That day, the Reverend Cotesworth Pinckney Lewis, who had been forewarned that the President would be in attendance, said from the pulpit that there is "something wrong in Vietnam." From her pew, Lady Bird sat rigid as a stone while inside she boiled in anger. She felt as if she had been slapped in the face. When the service ended, both she and Johnson walked outside to face a crowd of demonstrators. The Reverend Lewis stood with his hand extended. Lady Bird, ever the Southern lady, shook it firmly and said icily, "The choir was beautiful."

Inside the White House, the reality of the war came closer. Luci's husband, Patrick, a member of the National Guard, was making plans to leave for Vietnam in April 1967; Lynda's fiancé, Chuck Robb, who had been a Marine for six years, had put in his request to go to Vietnam and planned to leave in February or March. Chuck and Lynda set their wedding date—December 9—around Robb's scheduled departure.

Robb was extremely gung ho about his tour of duty. Before he left, he went to see Liz Carpenter, and gave her a written statement that was only to be released to the press in the event that he was captured or killed. "I believe in what we're doing in Vietnam," Robb told Carpenter. "If the enemy should try to broadcast some phony statement or claim, you and the Pentagon know my views and can release them." Carpenter took the statement and scribbled on the envelope: "To be opened only in the event of death or capture."

Lynda had a military wedding in the East Room of the White House. On the day of the wedding, Johnson teased Lady Bird about her own small and hurried ceremony in San Antonio thirty-three years before. He compared Lynda's wedding dress, a long-sleeved, high-collared, white silk and satin dress designed by Geoffrey Beene, with the simple lavender shift she had worn at St. Mark's Episcopal Church in San Antonio. "You sure have made progress since that purple dress," Johnson told her while dancing at Lynda's wedding.

Just a few days before Christmas, Johnson and a large entourage left Washington and went to Melbourne, Australia, for a memorial service for Prime Minister Harold Holt, who had died at sea while taking a swim. After the service, Johnson also traveled to Thailand, Vietnam, Pakistan, and the Vatican, a total of 27,300 miles in five days. Busby, who was no longer working on Johnson's staff, was with him on the trip.

After leaving Karachi, Johnson sat down next to Busby and asked what he should do in 1968. Busby did not hesitate. "Not run," he said. Johnson, according to Busby, looked a little surprised. The two men stared at each other a long time, and then Johnson got up from his seat and went back to the presidential cabin. One by one, Johnson's oldest advisers were telling him not to run.

On January 1, 1968, Johnson and Lady Bird started the year with a swim in the pool in front of the main house at the ranch. Connally arrived later in the day and again urged LBJ to make his surprise announcement during his State of the Union message on January 17. Connally argued that Johnson would never have more listeners and that it would work to his advantage to deliver such an important speech before a live audience in a familiar setting.

The next week Johnson called Busby to the White House and asked him to write the closing for his speech. Busby struck the major theme—that Johnson had done his best and it was now time to step aside and let someone else lead the country—and the next day Connally and Christian put final touches on the speech that was to end, "I have prayerfully concluded that I will not be a candidate for reelection."

On the afternoon of January 17, only hours before the speech, Johnson called Busby and Christian into his bedroom at the White House and read aloud the draft of the announcement. Lady Bird listened quietly, and then she added the following line in her own handwriting: "I will not seek—nor will I accept—the nomination of my party." Johnson told her he felt that her line strengthened the speech. It also made his decision irrevocable. Busby and Christian left the bedroom and returned to the West Wing to have her additions to the draft retyped on cards.

Around 6:30 P.M., Lady Bird took the closing pages over to Johnson, who was already at the Capitol, and placed them in his pocket. He asked her again what he should do. Lady Bird gave him the results of the family poll: Luci wanted him to announce that he would not run. Lynda voted for another term. "Me," Lady Bird shrugged. "I don't know."

She took her place in the gallery without knowing for sure what he was going to say. She could see Johnson standing in the back of the House chamber, with Christian at his side. Immediately before walking in, Johnson turned to Christian, and said, "Boy, am I going to shock these birds." He spoke for forty-nine minutes. As he neared the end, Lady Bird was on the edge of her seat. She was listening for the key phrase that would signal the end: "And now I want to speak to you about a personal matter."

He did not say it. The suspense, at least, was over. "I just couldn't quit," LBJ told Christian afterward. "I couldn't lay out a big program and then say . . . so long." Later, he claimed that Lady Bird had the cue cards with his intended withdrawal in her purse and that he'd forgotten to get them from her. Busby and Christian thought he must have been joking—the speech was in his hand.

The following day, January 18, Lady Bird, still exhausted from the cliffhanger of the night before, arrived in the Family Dining Room around noon for the first Women Doers luncheon of the new year. She had started the luncheon series in 1964. Each Doers lunch was organized around a specific topic—such as health, education, or the economy—and small groups of women who had worked in those areas were invited to the White House as luncheon speakers. This day the subject was crime, and one of the fifty guests seated at the five tables was Eartha Kitt, a Black actress and dancer who had begun her career at the age of sixteen. By 1968, Kitt had appeared on Broadway in *Shinbone Alley* and other productions. She had also starred in several movies, including the title role in *Anna Lucasta,* and was a well-known nightclub performer.

Kitt was invited to the Women Doers luncheon because she worked

as a volunteer with a group of Black teenagers in a high-crime neighborhood in Washington. The group was called Rebels With a Cause,
and it provided recreational activities for young people who had either
been arrested for crimes or were on probation. The FBI did a routine
background check on all the guests including Eartha Kitt, and she was
cleared to attend.

After Lady Bird introduced the topic of the lunch—"What Citizens
Can Do to Help Insure Safe Streets"—Johnson made a surprise appearance. He spoke briefly, and as he turned to leave, Kitt, seated in front of
the podium, rose and asked him angrily, "What do you do about delinquent parents—those who have to work and are too busy to look after
their children?" Johnson seemed taken aback, but he replied that the
Social Security bill that had recently passed through Congress contained funding for day-care centers where such mothers could leave
their children. He then turned and walked out of the room.

Lady Bird introduced the scheduled speakers, then braced herself for
questions. Kitt's hand was among the first raised. Lady Bird nodded at
her. Kitt rose and told the women they had all missed the point on why
juvenile crime existed. "I have lived in the gutters," said Kitt. "The
youth of America today are angry. They are angry because their parents
are angry." The members of Mrs. Johnson staff—including Carpenter and
Francis—were alarmed. Kitt took a step toward Lady Bird, and, for a split
second, Francis thought she might in some way harm the First Lady.

Instead, Kitt just kept talking. "I am sorry, Mrs. Johnson, if I am going
to offend the President or you, but I am here to say what is in my heart.
Boys I know across the nation feel it doesn't pay to be a good guy. They
figure with a record they don't have to go off to Vietnam."

Kitt stared at Lady Bird, and Lady Bird returned her stare. "No wonder the kids rebel and take pot," continued Kitt. "They will smoke a
joint and get themselves high to avoid getting shot at. And, Mrs. Johnson, in case you don't understand the lingo, that's marijuana."

Kitt was speaking in the voice of the counterculture, the same voice
that was thundering all over the country, and she was doing it in the
State Dining Room of the White House. No First Lady had ever faced
down such an explosion of personal rage. Lady Bird was flabbergasted,
and asked herself the question silently, "Is this a nightmare?"

Finally, she found her own voice and answered Kitt: "Because there
is a war on—and I pray that there will be a just and honorable peace—

that still does not give us a free ticket not to try and work at bettering the things in this country that we can better. I am sorry I cannot understand as much as I should because I have not lived the background as you have. Nor can I speak as passionately or as well as you can. But I think we must keep our eyes and our hearts fixed on constructive aims. Violence will not help it."

Kitt had not advocated violence—she had voiced her fury and frustration—but Lady Bird had seized her power as First Lady, the power to elevate herself, to rise to a high public plane. The reaction was swift and overwhelmingly in Lady Bird's favor. When Carpenter returned to her office, the first telephone call she received was from the actress Jane Wyman, who introduced herself as "Ronald Reagan's first wife" and registered her fury at Kitt and support for Lady Bird. Betty Ford called as well, and told Lady Bird she had "proved herself the perfect First Lady." The actor Gregory Peck sent Lady Bird a wire that said "none of my children are smoking anything because the United States has problems at home and abroad."

The aftermath quickly revealed the nation's racial divisions. The Reverend George R. Davis, pastor of the National City Christian Church, sent a telegram to the White House that said that "all Americans are in a sense a family" and apologized "for any member of the family including Negroes who are ill-mannered, stupid and arrogant." The remark triggered its own reaction. The following Sunday, demonstrators ringed his church, some of whom carried signs that said: "Eartha Kitt Speaks for the Women of America." Dr. Martin Luther King, Jr., came to Kitt's defense. He told the press that Kitt's comments were a "very proper gesture."

LBJ demanded an explanation of the Kitt affair, and it fell to Carpenter to provide it in a scathing memo that she wrote late at night on January 18. In the memo, Carpenter wrote that Kitt had no "previous peacenik record" and told Lyndon Johnson that she had married a white man and "was not well thought of by a lot of people." Carpenter suggested that the confrontation was a publicity stunt. "To keep a career going and to be in demand, a performer must stay constantly in the public eye or be forgotten," Carpenter wrote in the memo.

Kitt continued to defend her actions, but she paid a price for confronting Lady Bird. A radio station in Oklahoma—KHEN—immediately announced that it would no longer play her songs, and a nightclub in Los Angeles canceled a scheduled appearance. For years, she had a difficult time securing acting roles and lived and worked for a while in Paris. In 1975, Kitt revealed to the *New York Times* that an extensive dossier— including information from the FBI, the Secret Service, the National Security Agency, and the CIA—was forwarded to the Johnson White House one week after the luncheon. Without directly involving herself, and beneath the First Lady's gracious exterior, Lady Bird had extracted her revenge.

The last week of January, the controversy over Kitt quickly receded. The North Vietnamese launched the attack known as the Tet Offensive, in which they hit more than 150 cities and towns. On January 30, 1968, twenty Vietcong soldiers blasted the wall of the American embassy in Saigon. Americans were deeply shocked at the sight of diplomats trapped inside the embassy. On February 1, 1968, South Vietnamese National Police Chief Brigadier General Nguuyen Ngoc Loan executed a Vietcong officer in the streets of Saigon. The murder was caught on film by Associated Press photographer Eddie Adams, and later the photograph was broadcast on the evening news. That photograph came to symbolize what Lady Bird had earlier called the valley of the black pig: Vietnam had become her husband's nadir.

Johnson told Lady Bird and his aides that he was relieved he had not yet made the announcement to withdraw. He felt that if he had, the United States would appear even weaker in the face of Tet. In February, as he was trying to decide whether to send more troops to Vietnam, LBJ went to Austin for a dinner honoring Connally's fifty-first birthday and faced a crowd of University of Texas protestors. One threw a soft drink bottle at his car. More and more, Lady Bird faced signs that said: "Let's Build a Beautiful World . . . End War Now."

After the New Hampshire primary, which Johnson almost lost to Senator Eugene McCarthy, Bobby Kennedy jumped in the race. On March 30, Johnson telephoned Busby and asked what he should do. Busby told him he had to make up his mind: the Wisconsin primary was scheduled for the following Tuesday.

Johnson continued to agonize over what to do. Politically, he knew that if he ran, he very well might lose. If he didn't lose, the prospect for a second full term was more riots, a continuation of the war, and more campus unrest. Harry McPherson, a White House lawyer, had put his dilemma clearly in a memo earlier in the month. "When you say stick with Vietnam, you're saying stick with a rough situation that shows signs of getting worse," wrote McPherson. "When you say persevere at home, you're saying keep the new programs proliferating, although the Negroes for whom we adopted these programs rioted last summer and will probably riot again."

For Lady Bird and her family, the crisis came at 7:00 A.M. on March 31 when Lynda returned to the White House from California after dropping off her husband at Camp Pendleton, where he was to leave for Vietnam for a thirteen-month tour of duty. Lynda was pregnant and due to give birth to her first child in the fall.

Both Johnsons were at the entrance to the Diplomatic Reception Room to greet her when she arrived, and both were stunned by Lynda's appearance. She'd taken a sedative on the airplane and looked, as Mrs. Johnson recalled, "like a wraith from another world." Lynda looked at her father and asked directly, "Why do we have to go to Vietnam?"

Johnson stared at her, and Lady Bird thought she had not seen that much pain in his eyes since his mother died. At 10:00 A.M., Johnson went to Mass at St. Dominic's Catholic Church, and when he arrived back at the White House he again called for Busby to help him with the speech he was scheduled to make later that night.

At 2:06 P.M., according to the White House log: "The President was sitting in the Treaty Room at a small oval marble-topped table, reading a handwritten draft [Busby's first draft of the ending for tonight's speech]. Horace Busby was the only other person in the room. The President read the draft aloud, making changes, patting his foot a good bit, showing the words to m.f. [Marie Fehmer, one of his secretaries], clarifying Busby's handwriting, and doing some editing of his own. President then told m.f. to type the draft quickly, count the words and show it to no one and return it to him with several copies." Marie made the copies, and handed it to him in an envelope marked "L. B. Johnson."

Johnson called Lady Bird, Luci, and Pat, and two longtime friends, Mathilde and Arthur Krim, the president of United Artists, and read the speech, which included his decision not to seek another term. Luci burst into tears, and Lady Bird started scribbling notes on a 5 x 7 inch White House pad.

Busby worried that Johnson would change his mind, because everyone in the family seemed so emotional. He and Christian continued to work on the speech all afternoon. At 6:55 P.M., two hours before his remarks to the nation, Busby realized that he had made a mistake in the final draft. He had written that Johnson had served sixty-four months as President, but it was actually fifty-two. The change was made. The final pages were put into the President's speech book at 8:55 P.M., five minutes before the live broadcast.

Lady Bird was his final coach. She stepped over the TV cables all over the floor of the Oval Office and walked to Johnson's desk seconds before he started speaking and told him, "Remember—pacing and drama." She stood in the room for the entire speech, never really knowing for sure what he would say. During the speech, he announced the curtailment of American bombing in North Vietnam, "except in the area of the demilitarized zone," as a bid for peace talks. He explained that this meant bombing would be stopped in areas inhabited by "almost 90 percent" of the population of North Vietnam, and called upon Ho Chi Minh to respond to "this new step of peace."

As the final passage of the speech rolled up on the TelePrompTer Johnson paused and looked directly at Lady Bird before he went on. She returned his gaze, holding the tension, and then LBJ read the words that rolled in front of him. "This country's strength lies in the unity of its people. There is division in the American house tonight. . . . I do not believe that I should devote an hour or a day of my time to any personal partisan causes or to any duties other than the awesome duties of this office—the presidency of your country. . . . Accordingly, I shall not seek—and I will not accept—the nomination of my party for another term as your President."

When the TV lights were turned off, Lady Bird went to a small sitting room just off the Oval Office and picked up the telephone. Carpenter was on the other line, stunned by the announcement. Lady Bird had not warned her, and now she spoke in a voice that was quiet and calm. By then, Lady Bird felt nothing but relief.

She dictated a statement that Carpenter immediately released to reporters: "We have done a lot; there's a lot left to do in the remaining months; maybe this is the only way to get it done." Lady Bird went to sleep that night and slept well, thinking that the nightmare might be over.

CHAPTER FOURTEEN

Home to Texas

Four days later, on April 4, 1968, Lady Bird realized the violence was just beginning. She was having her hair done at the White House when Lynda burst into the room and told her that Dr. Martin Luther King, Jr., had been shot on a motel balcony in Memphis. A few moments later, she learned he was dead. "I thought, and maybe everybody else did, that we had been pummeled by such an avalanche of emotions that we couldn't feel anymore, and here we are, poised on the edge of another abyss, the bottom of which we could in no way see."

Lady Bird was scheduled to leave the following morning on a five-day trip through Texas with forty-four editors from European magazines and newspapers. By then, Johnson had canceled his planned trip to Hawaii for a Democratic fund-raiser. However, he believed Lady Bird should keep her commitment and go to Texas. Neither one attended King's funeral in Atlanta.

For the next five days, as riots broke out in every major city in the United States, Lady Bird took a surreal journey back through time to her home state. In Fredericksburg, a small town located about twenty miles from the LBJ Ranch, she piled the journalists in orchard wagons, pulled by tractors, and led them through the main streets of the quaint, historic town. She showed them blooming fields of wildflowers, trying in her words to show the writers that "there are places in this country that are not aflame with hatred and riots." Her goal was to disassociate herself—and the writers—from the painful and destructive realities of 1968.

When she telephoned Lynda at the White House later that night, she learned that there had been riots and fires as close as four blocks from the White House. Lynda told her seven people had so far been killed and three hundred wounded in the District of Columbia alone.

That same night, Sharon Francis, of her staff, drove to Fourteenth Street into one of the neighborhoods that had been decimated by riots. She saw storefronts that had been smashed and whole blocks barricaded by police. One of the few stores that received no damage was a Giant grocery store that had been targeted for one of Lady Bird's beautification efforts. The parking lot had been landscaped and lined with well-tended flower beds. A bus stop had been built near the parking lot with a bench. The bus stop was still standing, and there were still fresh flowers in the ground.

Lady Bird greeted the news from Washington with ambivalence. "Though I was right in the middle of it, because of my husband's job and the presence in Washington of all my family, I, myself, seemed removed and encased in a different world," she wrote. From that moment on, Lady Bird looked at Washington as an alien place. She thought of life there as though it were the dark side of the moon.

In April, Luci's husband, Pat Nugent, went to Vietnam, and soon letters and tapes from both Lynda's husband, Chuck Robb, and Nugent began arriving at the White House. Johnson took them and often read them aloud to cabinet members and close members of his staff. In May, Robb came under direct fire while leading a company of about 210 Marines on a sweep of Vietcong-controlled areas south of Da Nang. Neither Robb nor any of his company were injured, but his letters describing the five-hour battle were graphic and made clear the horror of the war. Johnson was both enthralled and disturbed by the letters. By then, the peace talks were at a stalemate, and Johnson knew that events in Vietnam were out of his control.

So were events at home. On June 5, when Robert Kennedy was shot in Los Angeles while celebrating his victory in the California primary, Johnson woke up Lady Bird at 4:20 A.M. to tell her the news. At first, Lady Bird thought that this could not happen in America, King murdered two months ago, and now Kennedy. A persistent pattern in her life reemerged: she went to her desk and wrote telegrams of condolences to the Kennedy women, first to Rose, then to Ethel, and finally to Jackie.

At the funeral three days later in New York at St. Patrick's Cathedral, she saw all three Kennedy women face-to-face. Ethel thanked her for her kindness, and then Lady Bird found herself in front of Jackie, who, she recalled, "looked at me from a great distance, as though I were an apparition." It was the way the two First Ladies had always seen each other—politely but from the distance of geography and political competitiveness—but now Lady Bird saw the distance more clearly. As always, manners ruled. A few days later, Lady Bird received from Jackie a reply to her wire. Jackie said, in part, "Sometimes there are no words to say things—only this—I am deeply grateful."

Lady Bird used the events of 1968 as an excuse to encourage Johnson to spend more time at the ranch. Slowly she was preparing him for retirement. A check of White House daily logs shows that in 1968, Johnson and Lady Bird spent more time on the ranch together than at any other time in his presidency. Only once, in October 1968, did LBJ make a trip to the ranch and stay there without Lady Bird. On that occasion, Luci went in her place. In August, LBJ and Lady Bird went for a scheduled monthlong vacation on the ranch.

It was then that Lady Bird watched the Democratic convention in Chicago. Johnson had hoped to be invited to the convention, but no invitation came. As Lady Bird watched on TV the bitter floor fight over the Vietnam plank and the violent protests outside the convention hall, she was horrified at what she called the "seething cauldron of emotions . . . hippies and yippies" and was happy to be at the ranch, away from the turmoil. Four years before, Johnson had won in a true landslide, and now public opinion had shifted dramatically in the other direction. Sometimes Lady Bird asked herself and her daughters, "How did all this happen to us?"

Finally, January 20, 1969, her last day at the White House, arrived and Lady Bird realized, as she put it, that "the golden coin is spent." On her way out of the White House, Lady Bird leaned over and told Johnson that she had no regrets. She was happy to be going home and wanted, she said, twenty more years of peace with him on the ranch.

However, on *Air Force One* en route to Texas, LBJ gave Luci and his grandson, Lyn, a vivid indication that there would be no such peace.

The moment Johnson boarded the airplane, he lit up a cigarette and drew several deep breaths into his lungs. Luci begged him to put out the cigarette. His doctors had issued orders that he could not smoke, drink, or eat to excess if he hoped to extend his life. "How could you smoke now?" Luci asked her father. Her son, Lyn, then only eighteen months old, must have been alarmed by his mother's reaction, because Lyn pointed to his grandfather's cigarette and motioned for him to put it out.

"Luci," snapped LBJ, "take that child out of here."

For a moment, Luci sat motionless, staring at her father. "Look," exploded Johnson, "for fourteen years I've wanted to smoke when I wanted to smoke and for fourteen years I had a country to serve, children to raise, and a job to do. Now, the job is done, and the children are raised. It's my turn." Luci took her son to the back of the airplane. Already LBJ was preoccupied with death.

They arrived at the ranch at dusk. Lady Bird had readied the house for his arrival. There was a fire burning in the living room, and there were three TVs on because Johnson liked to watch all three networks at once, a worn lounge chair that was big enough for him, Bentwood rockers on the front porch facing the river, and the needlepoint pillows that said, "This is my ranch and I can do as I damn please." The cliché became his way of life.

Lady Bird urged the steady stream of friends that visited him at the ranch not to talk to him about the Vietnam War or Nixon's attacks on the Great Society. She tried to keep the conversation steered to life at the ranch. The boundaries of their marriage—what was acceptable, what was not—had been laid down years before. "There was a definite line between them," said Jim Hardin, one of their Secret Service agents. "She was the only person around the ranch he didn't cross."

For instance, one day Hardin drove LBJ and Lady Bird to Austin. He was sitting in the back seat, and she was in the front. As the journey began, Johnson started issuing directions from the back about how Hardin should drive and which route he should take. With every passing mile, LBJ issued more and more orders. It was as though he were running a cabinet meeting from the back seat of a car on a country road. At first, Lady Bird said softly, "Lyndon, please." Another fifteen minutes passed, with Johnson firing nonstop orders. Finally, Lady Bird raised her voice. "Lyndon!" she said. She merely shouted his name. "He quieted right down," Hardin recalled.

By then, his dependence on her was complete. Another day they flew into San Antonio by helicopter to hear a speech given by Jesse Kellam, their old friend and business partner. Jewel Malechek, the pretty wife of LBJ's foreman, was riding in the back of the helicopter with LBJ. Lady Bird was up front with the pilot. Jewel's in-flight job was to comb

LBJ's hair, which was by then almost shoulder-length and white. During the forty-five-minute helicopter ride, Jewel combed and sprayed Johnson's hair repeatedly. No matter how hard she worked, strands of it kept popping out in all directions. The harder she tried to fix his hair, the more impatient Johnson became. Finally, he broke down in tears, the former master of the Senate and leader of the free world hovering over San Antonio in his helicopter, weeping over his hair.

Lady Bird had been silent throughout the entire ordeal, but finally she turned to Johnson and said calmly, "Lyndon, that's enough. We'll fix your hair when we land."

They had come full circle. In the beginning of the relationship—on August 1, 1934—it was Johnson who issued orders, gave ultimatums, and took control. That was what drew Lady Bird to him. In all the years that followed, as Johnson ascended to the heights of power, Lady Bird followed along, agreeing when she could and keeping her silence when she could not. She belonged to him more than she belonged to herself. The roots of a marriage are seldom found in logic or reason. Lady Bird's marriage was an exercise in endurance and identification. She endured his bad treatment of her and identified with his suffering, even as she denied her own. All through the years—no matter what he did or did not do—Lady Bird busied herself in the daily details of marriage: clipping his nails, tending his homes, raising his children, sharing in his power and his glory.

Never once had she stooped to play the part of the wronged wife. Over the years, she somehow found her own balance in Johnson's precarious world. Whatever mistakes he made—in politics, business, or in his personal life—she accepted them without admitting that he was right or blaming him for being wrong. This was part of her marriage vow. She accepted his faults and loved him for who he was, not for what he aspired or pretended to be. Still, she had not given in to him either. She had constructed a parallel life for herself in his world. Now, in retirement, it was he who most needed her.

She was so clearly in charge of the day-to-day management of his life that some former staff members got to the point that they did not want to be alone with Johnson unless Lady Bird was with him. "Without her, he was impossible: depressed one minute, raging the next," said one longtime member of his staff. Outside her presence, he would relive the Vietnam War, vent his poisonous feelings about Bobby Kennedy and

East Coast liberals, gulp Cutty Sark (he carried a portable bar in his car and golf cart), smoke cigarettes, eat too much, and sometimes cry himself to sleep. He couldn't stand to be left alone. "There was immense pressure on him after he left office," said George Christian, his former press secretary. "I don't know what he would have done without her. She held him together. She held all of us together."

On a few occasions the pressure got too intense even for Lady Bird. Once she called a close family friend and told him that LBJ had become a "holy terror." Women that Johnson had been rumored to be involved with over the years regularly visited at the ranch. Often he would go on long walks with other women, and tell them in Lady Bird's presence that they reminded him of his mother. He had often told her that, of course, and according to sources close to her, the comparisons were difficult to hear. Besides, he was no longer making any effort to conceal his sexual gamesmanship. One day Lady Bird opened a box that was delivered to the front door of her own home. It was from a lingerie store. She opened the lid, separated the sheets of tissue paper, and slowly held up a lavender bikini. "I don't think this is for me," she told Johnson, who was in the room. "It must be for one of your lady friends." The story made the rounds of the staff and friends.

Still, he wanted her physically close to him every single day. If she went to Austin, he wanted to know when she would be back. Often she would come back from shopping trips and model for him the new clothes she had bought. More than ever, he insisted on managing her appearance; since there wasn't much left for him to manage, Lady Bird gave him the ultimate authority to dress her completely as he liked. "Take that one back," he'd bark, if he didn't like a dress. "It makes you look short and fat." If he liked one, however, he'd tell her to keep it and warn her that she would soon be the "prettiest and richest widow in Texas."

Sometimes he would telephone the department stores himself, and rack after rack of clothes would suddenly be brought to the ranch and wheeled into the den, the room with the big fireplace. Johnson would go through the clothes, picking out what suited him for Lady Bird, his daughters, and all of his secretaries. It was shopping by force. The President of the United States had become president of the ranch.

Yet if Lady Bird grew tired of it and walked out of the room, he'd call out, "Bird, come here. Where are you?" Said Luci: "My father knew that my mother loved him, warts and all, and he knew that she would never leave him. That became very important to him during the last four years of his life when he desperately did not want to be alone."

In her efforts to shield him from events in Washington, Lady Bird reached out to one couple in particular: Darrell Royal, the football coach at the University of Texas, and his wife, Edith. The Royals were part of a small group of friends who went on vacation to Acapulco with the Johnsons during the last two years of his life. "He didn't know much about football, and I was consumed by it, and I didn't know or care anything about politics. We were a good match," Darrell Royal recalled. During the vacations in Mexico, Lady Bird would slip off to bed early and leave her guests to stay up all night talking with Johnson. "She would just quietly disappear," said Edith Royal. "I had the feeling she was saving her strength. By that time, she was managing so many of the details of his life—what he ate, what he wore, his general health—that she took her rest when she could get it."

According to Mrs. Royal, Lady Bird seemed content with this role. During her vacations, she admired the flowers in Mexico, took historic tours, studied her Bible in the evening, and read spiritual meditation books in the morning. "I think she made a happy life for herself out of those activities," Mrs. Royal said. "I would describe her as a gentle woman with a backbone of steel." Her spiritual studies gave her a place of inner retreat, a place where she could avoid the conflicts that continued to haunt LBJ.

In the summer of 1972, Darrell Royal arranged for Johnson to play golf with the former president of Mexico, Gustavo Díaz Ordaz, at a seaside course in Acapulco. Johnson was a notoriously bad golfer. Former U.S. Representative Jake Pickle, who occasionally played golf with LBJ, used to complain that it was frustrating to play with Johnson because he hit as many shots as he wanted and wrote down the score that suited him.

On this particular day, the two Presidents played a foursome with Royal and San Antonio banker Tom Frost, Jr. As the game wore on, the competition between LBJ and former President Díaz sharpened. The atmosphere was cordial and good-hearted, but the two former Presidents played golf with all the intensity with which they had once wielded power in their countries. Both wanted to win. "It got down to a real battle between the two of them," Frost recalled.

Royal and Frost dropped out of the game and let the two Presidents continue to go after each other, stroke for stroke. The lead changed many times during the last nine holes, but the outcome of the game came down to LBJ's final approach shot, which landed in a sand trap on the last green. Johnson angrily stalked over to his ball, raked the area around it, and putted out of the trap directly onto the green. He sank the ball in the cup on his next put and won the game.

Later Royal told LBJ that—technically—he violated two rules of golf: he raked the sand and grounded his club in the sand. "Nobody ever told me those rules," Johnson complained. "Why didn't you tell me?"

"Because, Mr. President," said Royal, laughing, "I was pulling for you." It was LBJ's last golf game, one that symbolized his approach to politics and to life. He had played it to the hilt and won by his own rules.

Shortly thereafter, in June 1972, Johnson suffered a severe heart attack while visiting his daughter Lynda at her home in Charlottesville, Virginia. Even though he recovered, the angina attacks grew more severe and more painful. He began to rely on a portable oxygen unit, which was kept near his bed, to help him breathe. Dr. Hurst had explained to Lady Bird that Johnson's arteries were so blocked that when his death came, it would come quickly. LBJ talked about death often with Lady Bird, warning her it was coming. "That would make me mad, but I knew it was true," she said.

She continued her own public life. In 1970, Texas governor Preston Smith had appointed her to the board of regents at the University of Texas and she agreed. Three years later, when Nixon announced a cease-fire in Vietnam, it was Lady Bird Johnson, not Lyndon, who met with student demonstrators at the University of Texas and listened to their protracted opposition to the war. She was saddened anew that Johnson had not been able to bring the war to an end.

On the morning of January 22, 1973, Lady Bird left the ranch to attend a regents' meeting in Austin. Johnson rose early and went for a ride in a car around the ranch at around 11:00 A.M. with Jewel Malechek. Mike Howard, a Secret Service agent, followed them in a second car. They all drove to the top of the hill, and Johnson had a long look at his ranch.

After lunch, Johnson poured himself a glass of milk and went to his bedroom for a nap. At 3:50 P.M., Howard had just finished feeding and watering one of the horses on the ranch—a black Tennessee walking horse named Lady B—when he heard Johnson's voice crackle over the ranch radio. "One to Mike! Get me Mike," Johnson said. Howard and three other agents went quickly to the bedroom in the main house. By the time they reached him, Johnson was lying unconscious on the floor, with the telephone beside him. According to Howard, Johnson was alone.

They quickly put Johnson on a stretcher and airlifted him to San Antonio, where he was pronounced dead at 4:35 P.M. Lady Bird was notified about his heart attack during the regents' meeting and immediately flew to San Antonio. Her helicopter landed fifty feet from the ranch plane at the San Antonio Airport. Howard walked toward her on the tarmac and took off his cowboy hat as a sign of respect. "We lost him, Mrs. Johnson," he told her quietly.

"Well," she said, stoic at the end, "we expected it, didn't we?"

They took his body first to Brooke Army Medical Center in San Antonio. On the car ride over, Lady Bird asked Howard to telephone most of Johnson's staff. She telephoned Lynda Bird and Luci herself. Much later that evening, Lady Bird went back to the ranch house. When both daughters arrived, the three went into her bedroom, the room where LBJ had died, closed the door, and it was at that moment that Lady Bird broke down and cried.

In the family room, a small group of men planned Johnson's formal funeral arrangements. Around midnight, Lady Bird emerged dry-eyed from the bedroom and asked them to make sure that Johnson's body was taken to the LBJ Library, where it would lie in state the next day. She had already telephoned several of his oldest friends and organized an all-night honor guard. "I do not want him to be alone," she told each one of them. "Stand with him." The following morning, starting at 9:00 A.M., thirty-two thousand people filed into the library to pay their respects. The visitors came all day and all night.

Two days later, during a light snowstorm, Johnson was buried at his family's cemetery on the LBJ Ranch, near the Pedernales River. A number of people made speeches, but John Connally had the last spoken word: "He first saw light here. He last felt life here. May he find peace here." However, it was Lady Bird, dressed in a fur hat and boots, who had the final say, not in words, but in deeds. Soon she had seeded pasture after pasture of their ranch with wildflowers, making it her own.

EPILOGUE

❧

Our Lady of Flowers

"I seek to celebrate my glad release, the Tents of Silence and
the Camp of Peace."
                              —India's Love Lyrics

Those were the lines of poetry that drifted through Lady Bird
Johnson's mind during the final, sleepless night that she spent in
the White House on January 20, 1969. However, it was not until
Johnson's death four years and two days later, on January 22, 1973, that
she sought to put them into practice in her own life.

During the first few years of widowhood, Lady Bird continued to live
through her husband by becoming the chief steward of his memory. She
presided over public events at the LBJ Library in Austin, interpreted his
legacy for historians and the press, and continued to run the radio and
TV business. When reporters asked her how she was handling life without LBJ, Lady Bird replied in a falsely cheerful way that her primary
antidote to grief was "Work. Work. Work." It was the same formula she
had employed to manage LBJ's melancholy.

To friends and to family, however, she also acknowledged the depth
of her loneliness. The nights she spent by herself at the ranch were
indeed "tents of silence," but she found them long and difficult. In the
beginning, she found no "glad release" from the public pressures of her
long and public marriage. The presence of LBJ was everywhere. She
often found herself absentmindedly turning down pages of books and
underlining passages that she wanted to talk to Johnson about. In conversations with old friends, she would often say, "Oh, wouldn't Lyndon
have loved this? . . . Can't you just hear him saying that?" Busby remem-

bers that not long after Johnson died, he visited Lady Bird at the ranch and they spent a few hours reliving old times. "You know what I miss most?" Lady Bird told him. "He was so funny, so very funny, and I miss the way he made us all laugh."

During those initial years after Johnson's death, Lady Bird also moved in decisive ways to claim her own legacy as First Lady, a legacy that gave her a level of personal popularity that continues to elude her husband. In speeches, she let it be known that during the Johnson years—1963 to 1968—150 laws were passed that benefited the environment, including the Clean Air Act, the National Park Boundaries Act, and the Highway Beautification Act, all laws that she had actively supported. "The environment—clean air, clean rivers, wilderness spaces, and wild seashores—we put it on the national agenda," Lady Bird said proudly in speeches.

There were tense encounters, too, not only with the press and Johnson's many critics, but also with other First Ladies. In September 1976, Rosalynn Carter toured the LBJ Library shortly after her husband, Jimmy Carter, the Democratic nominee, made a critical remark about Johnson in an infamous interview with *Playboy* magazine. In addition to acknowledging that he had, from time to time, "lusted in his own heart," Carter said in the same interview: "I don't think I would ever take on the same frame of mind that Nixon or Johnson did—lying, cheating, and distorting the truth."

Bob Strauss, then the chairman of the Democratic National Committee, who accompanied Mrs. Carter to Austin, recalled a conversation he had with the future First Lady only moments before she was scheduled to meet Lady Bird. "What on earth am I going to say to her?" Mrs. Carter asked Strauss. Strauss assured her that Mrs. Johnson had often felt the sting of her husband's words and would probably sympathize with Mrs. Carter's predicament. Strauss was right. When Mrs. Carter emerged from her tour of the LBJ Library, she looked relieved and told the press, "We didn't say *Playboy* one time." It was another triumph of manners.

In Lady Bird's hometown of Austin, she spent five years raising money to rebuild a very popular twelve-mile hike and bike trail along the Colorado River in downtown Austin. In celebration of her seventieth birthday, she opened the Wildflower Research Center near Austin, where botanical data is collected for the future propagation of wildflowers. She wanted wildflowers or native plants along the right-of-way in highways and roadways in every state—not just for the beauty of it, but to save the public the cost of mowing weeds. Ever alert to economy, Lady Bird calculated that Texas alone could manage $24 million in such savings if wildflowers were planted instead of grass along all highways. "Besides that, I want Texas to look like Texas and Vermont to look like Vermont and every state to look like itself," she said. "I just hate to see the land homogenized."

In 1983, the same year she opened the wildflower center, Lady Bird gave a series of interviews in which she announced her public retirement. By then, President Reagan had all but dismantled LBJ's Great Society, and Johnson's failure in Vietnam had been thoroughly examined in a number of books. Instead of defending him, she retreated behind a new wall: retirement. "I'm just going to put down a certain amount of my burdens and say no more," she told the *Dallas Times Herald.*

In the next few years, she took each of her seven grandchildren on individual trips. Her only grandson, Lyndon Nugent, said that when he was thirteen years old, Lady Bird took him on a white-water river raft trip in West Virginia. "I think that my grandmother could have become completely engrossed in my grandfather's death," said Nugent, who is now a lawyer in San Antonio. "She has worked hard to move on."

To some degree, both daughters lived out their mother's pattern. Each attempted to find her primary identity in marriage; each with ambivalent results. Luci was divorced from Patrick Nugent in 1979. She remarried in 1983 to Ian Turpin, an investment banker from Great Britain. In 1996, when Lady Bird retired as chairman of the board of the LBJ Holding Co., Luci bought out her older sister, Lynda, reportedly for $80 million. Lynda, the shy White House bride who thought she was marrying a career military officer, wound up being the wife of a politician and a continued target of unwanted media scrutiny. Today, Lynda remains married to Senator Chuck Robb of Virginia, who in 1987 was forced to publicly deny an alleged affair with a former beauty queen. Both daughters have defined themselves in firm opposition to their father's expectations: Luci, the pretty one, runs the family business, and Lynda, the smart one, is primarily a mother and political wife.

Lady Bird has stayed faithful to the pattern as well. Often, in the process of writing this book, I wondered, Why didn't she ever leave him? I asked the question at the difficult crossroads in Lady Bird's life:

his affairs with Alice Glass and others; her repeated miscarriages; when she faced down her fears of public speaking; and later when she was spit on and screamed at by demonstrators. This question led to others. When would have been a good time to leave? Perhaps she could have left when he was a young congressman, before her daughters were born. Or maybe she could have struck out on her own during his midlife crisis, right before he accepted the vice presidency. Surely, after that, there would have been no way out. By then, duty alone and fear of public rebuke would have kept her in the marriage, if not the money and the glory. At some point, however, I realized that those were questions Lady Bird, by all accounts, never asked herself.

"He was the catalyst. I was the amalgam," she said, over and over. In other words, Johnson was the mold and she poured herself into it. In some ways, Lady Bird has stayed an eternal girl, a motherless child who never had a sense of constancy in her life until the moment she met Lyndon Johnson, who became her primary object of identification. From the beginning, her relationship with him was symbiotic.

The last time I saw her at the LBJ Ranch on July 2, 1997, Lady Bird was eighty-five years old. She had silver hair, her face was creased with deep lines, and her body was old and round. She wore a baggy cotton dress and an enormous pair of white-rimmed sunglasses. Her visual handicap—macular degeneration—had grown worse.

That summer was a good one for wildflowers. Cobalt-colored bluebonnets were growing all over her ranch, as well as Indian paintbrushes, and fat-faced sunflowers with inky, black eyes. Lady Bird's near-blindness only increased her longing for the sight of beauty. Her desire for it has, if anything, increased with age. From her rocking chair on the porch of the ranch house, she said that she had recently been out in one of the pastures, armed with a magnifying glass, and had spent an entire afternoon examining the five-star Texas phlox that surrounded her.

"To think," she said, then paused for a long while to do just that. "I've owned this land since 1951—forty-six years—and I saw things growing out in the pasture that I've never seen before. As I sat in the middle of the pasture, I wondered how many seeds can grow in a cubic foot of soil. Then I thought about how many of those seeds lay dormant for years and years, waiting in the dark—only for this specific year—to bloom."

She continued to talk about flowers in a way that became no longer graspable: it was vague, elusive, mystical. It was clear that, at eighty-five, Lady Bird had returned to what had sustained her as a child in East Texas. Her relationship with nature was every bit as symbiotic as her relationship with Lyndon Johnson, and the ties to Mother Nature have endured after him.

Finally, her thoughts about flowers were interrupted by the noisy sound of a bus roaring up her driveway. Years before, Lady Bird had donated the ranch to the National Park Service, and busloads of tourists routinely drive in front of her house as a regular part of the tour. When she heard the bus come to a stop, Lady Bird's demeanor changed completely. Suddenly, she was no longer a dreamy-eyed mystic but an alert and savvy political wife, back on the campaign trail. Bolting up from her chair, she waved at the tourists and shouted, "How are ya'll? Are you having a nice day?" From the window of the bus came the flash of twenty or so camera bulbs. Momentarily, she was back on the public stage, an aging character actress.

When asked if she minded the intrusion, Mrs. Johnson settled back in her rocker and replied, "No, not in the least. I've had a long, satisfying love affair with G.P.—general public. Lyndon gave me that."

Author Interview List

Bess Abell
Gordon Abney
Benjamin Baldwin
Ben Barnes
Margaret Berry
Calvin Bishop
Sylvia Bishop
Winston Bode
Nadine Brammer
Anita Brewer
George Bristol
Madeline Brown
Horace Busby
Liz Carpenter
George Christian
Nellie Connally
Virginia Durr
Mercedes Eicholz
Tom Frost, Jr.
John Gardner
Joe Golden
Arthur E. "Tex" Goldschmidt
Ashton Gonella
Charles Grace
Katharine Graham
Nell Fenner Grover
Bob Hardesty
Jim Hardin
Jack Hayner
Betty Hickman
Gerry Hopkins
Mike Howard
Morris Jaffe
Dolores Jansu
B. K. Johnson
Claudia Taylor Johnson
Luci Baines Johnson
Dorsey Jones
Franklin Jones, Jr.

Jerry Jones
Dan Love
Diana MacArthur
Cecille Harrison Marshall
Maury Maverick, Jr.
Margaret Mayer
Victor McRea, Jr.
Hope Riddings Miller
Marta Miller
Jim Morriss
Bailey Mosley
Robert Wilkinson Notti
Lyndon Nugent
Frank Oltorf
Jake Pickle
Peggy Pickle
Jid Porter
Dorris Powell
George Reedy
Darrell and Edith Royal
Earl Simons
Mildred Stegall
Marshall and Patsy Steves
Robert Strauss
Diane Taylor
Susan Grey Taylor
Helen Thomas
Lucille Pattillo Thomas
Betty Tilson
Mary Margaret Wiley Valenti
O. J. Weber
Nancy Brown Wellen
Bob Wheeler
Nellie White
Isabel Brown Wilson
Warren Woodward
Nellie Pattillo Woodyard
Sander Vanocer

Oral Histories

Bess Abell
Edie Adams
Ivan Allen, Jr.
J. Lindsay Almond, Jr.
Harry Ashmore
John E. Babcock
Malcolm G. Baldwell
Ben F. Barnes
Lindley Beckworth
Mrs. Lloyd Bentsen, Jr.
W. Sherman Birdwell, Jr.
James Blundell
Charles Boatner
Paul Bolton
Russell Morton Brown
Gordon Bunshaft
Dr. James C. Cain
Elizabeth Carpenter
Leslie Carpenter
Mrs. Ellen Taylor Cooper and
   Mrs. Elaine Fischesser
Willard Deason
Nancy Dickerson
Helen Gahagan Douglas
Clifford and Virginia Durr
Virginia Durr
Virginia Wilke English
Frank Erwin interview about
   Mrs. Johnson
Truman and Wilma Green
   Fawcett
Sam Fore, Oliver Bruck, and
   Dan Quill
Mrs. Sam Fore, Jr.
Abe Fortas interview about
   Mrs. Johnson
Sharon Francis
Elizabeth Wickenden
   Goldschmidt
Mrs. Ashton Gonella
Katharine Graham
D. B. Hardeman

Betty Carson Hickman
Henry Hirshberg
Welly K. Hopkins
Walter Jenkins
Luther E. Jones
Jesse Kellam
Mrs. John F. Kennedy
Eugenia Boehringer Lasseter
Gene Latimer
Robert E. Lucey
Stanley Marcus
Leonard Marks
Cecille Harrison Marshall
Cameron and Lucille McElroy
Mr. and Mrs. Dale Miller
Dr. R. H. Montgomery
Frank "Posh" Oltorf
Thomas O. Paine
Mollie Parnis
James Cato Pattillo and
   Nettie Pattillo Woodyard
Carl L. Phinney
J. J. "Jake" Pickle
Dorris Powell
Daniel J. Quill
Dan Rather
Mary Rather
George Reedy
Ray Roberts
Barefoot Sanders
Emily Crow Selden
Antonio J. Taylor
Donald S. Thomas
Emma Boehringer Tooley
Jack Valenti
Bob Waldron
Terrell Maverick Webb
Harfield Weedin
Eugene and Helen Williams
Mrs. Alvin J. Wirtz
Zephyr Wright

Selected Bibliography

Anthony, Carl Sferrazza. *First Ladies: Volume II, The Saga of the Presidents' Wives and their Power, 1961–1970*. New York: William Morrow, 1991.

Baker, Bobby, with Larry L. King. *Wheeling and Dealing: Confessions of a Capitol Hill Operator*. New York: W. W. Norton, 1978.

Beschloss, Michael R. *Taking Charge: The Johnson White House Tapes, 1963–1964*. New York: Simon & Schuster, 1997.

Campbell, Randolph B. *A Southern Community in Crisis: Harrison County, Texas, 1950–1980*. Austin, Tex.: Texas State Historical Association, 1983.

Caro, Robert. *The Path to Power: The Years of Lyndon Johnson*. New York: Vintage Books, 1983.

———. *Means of Ascent: The Years of Lyndon Johnson*. New York: Knopf, 1990.

Carpenter, Liz. *Ruffles and Flourishes*. New York: Pocket Books, 1971.

———. *Getting Better All the Time*. New York: Simon & Schuster, 1983.

Chandler, David Leon. *The Natural Superiority of Southern Politicians*. Garden City, N.Y.: Doubleday, 1977.

Conaway, James. *The Texans*. New York: Knopf, 1976.

Connally, John, with Mickey Hershkowitz. *In History's Shadow: An American Odyssey*. New York: Hyperion, 1993.

Cormier, Frank. *LBJ: The Way He Was*. Garden City, N.Y.: Doubleday, 1977.

Dallek, Robert. *Lone Star Rising: Lyndon Johnson and His Times, 1908–1960*. New York: Oxford University Press, 1991.

Dugger, Ronnie. *Our Invaded Universities: Form, Reform, and New Starts*. New York: W. W. Norton, 1972.

———. *The Politician: The Life and Times of Lyndon Johnson*. New York: W. W. Norton, 1982.

Flynn, Jean. *Lady: The Story of Claudia Alta Johnson*. Austin, Tex.: Eakin Press, 1992.

Gould, Lewis L. *Lady Bird Johnson and the Environment*. Lawrence, Kans.: University Press of Kansas, 1988.

Graham, Katharine. *Personal History*. New York: Knopf, 1997.

Haley, J. Evetts. *A Texan Looks at Lyndon: A Study in Illegitimate Power*. Canyon, Tex.: Palo Duro Press, 1964.

Hardeman, D. B., and Donald C. Bacon. *Rayburn: A Biography*. Austin, Tex.: Madison Books, 1987.

Heymann, David C. *A Woman Named Jackie*. New York: A Lyle Stuart Book, Carol Communications, 1989.

Johnson, Lyndon Baines. *The Vantage Point: Perspectives of the Presidency, 1963–1969*. New York: Holt, Rinehart and Winston, 1971.

Johnson, Mrs. Lyndon Baines. *A White House Diary*. New York: Holt, Rinehart and Winston, 1970.

Johnson, Rebekah Baines, *A Family Album*. New York: McGraw-Hill, 1965.

Johnson, Sam Houston. *My Brother Lyndon*. New York: Cowles, 1969, 1970.

Kearns, Doris. *Lyndon Johnson and the American Dream*. New York: Harper & Row, 1976.

Manchester, William. *The Death of a President, November 20–November 25, 1963*. New York: Harper & Row, 1967.

Middleton, Harry. *Lady Bird Johnson: A Life Well Lived*. Austin, Tex.:Lyndon Baines Johnson Foundation, 1992.

Montgomery, Ruth. *Mrs. LBJ*. New York: Holt, Rinehart and Winston, 1964.

Reedy, George. *The Twilight of the Presidency*. New York and Cleveland: World, 1970.

———. *Lyndon B. Johnson: A Memoir*. New York: Andrews and MC Meel, Inc., 1982.

Salinger, Pierre. *With Kennedy*. Garden City, N.Y.: Doubleday, 1966.

Smith, Marie D. *The President's Lady: An Intimate Biography of Mrs. Lyndon B. Johnson*. New York: Random House, 1964.

Thomas, Helen. *Dateline: White House*. New York: Macmillan, 1975.

Webb, Walter Prescott and H. Bailey Carroll, eds. *The Handbook of Texas*. Austin, Tex.: Texas State Historical Association, 1952.

Notes

Abbreviations used in notes:
CTJ: Claudia Taylor Johnson (Lady Bird)
LBJ: Lyndon Baines Johnson

INTRODUCTION: LADY BIRD'S RED SHOES

11. "Do you take your coffee?": Interview with CTJ for *Texas Monthly,* November 1994.
13. "Your conclusion about me": Letter from CTJ, December 5, 1997.

CHAPTER 1: MARRIAGE, THE ULTIMATUM

15. "Let's get married": This letter is in "A National Tribute to Lady Bird Johnson: On the Occasion of Her Sixty-fifth Birthday," December 11, 1977.
15. "Well, his ears are a little too long": Emily Crow Selden, oral history, second interview, page 7.
15. Later that night: Emily Crow Selden, oral history, second interview, page 9.
16. Emily was flabbergasted: Ibid., page 8.
16. Her aunt Effie Pattillo: Ibid., first interview, page 7.
16. Description of Effie Pattillo's health: Dorris Powell, oral history, page 5.
17. Description of the Brick House: Harrison County Historical Record.
17. Though Lady Bird kept it a secret: Civil Case No. 8834, in the district court of Harrison County, Texas, September 1934 term, divorce decree, Miss Beulah Taylor, plaintiff, T. J. Taylor, defendant.
17. "Miss Beulah was one fine-lookin' woman": Interview with Dorsey Jones, December 12, 1995, Karnack, Texas.
17. Beulah worked for Taylor: Interviews with CTJ and Sylvia Bishop.
17. "I threw $5,000": Interview with Jerry Jones.
18. "I guess what settled it": Interview with CTJ.
18. Somewhere on the edge of East Texas: Dan Quill, oral history, page 4.
18. Lady Bird didn't want to offend her many friends: Interview with CTJ.
18. "Fix everything up!" and problems with getting the license and arranging for the wedding: Dan Quill, oral history, pages 4–5.
19. "I'm getting married at 8:00 P.M.": Cecille Harrison Marshall, oral history, page 14.
19. Lady Bird seemed serene and absolutely sure: Interview with Cecille Harrison Marshall.
20. On the eve of her eighty-second birthday: Interview with CTJ for *Texas Monthly,* November 1994.
21. Description of view from Lady Bird's upstairs bedroom: Author tour of the Brick House, February 1996.
21. For Southern women born in the early 1900s: Interview with Virginia Durr, March 1996.
22. When news of FDR's affair with Lucy Mercer: Carl Sferrazza Anthony, *First Ladies, Vol. 2, The Saga of the Presidents' Wives and Their Power, 1961–1990,* page 148.
22. "a fly on the wedding cake": Ibid., page 148.
22. "Everyone felt sorry for her": Interview with Virginia Durr, March 1996.
22. "She handled the affair": John Connally with Mickey Herskowitz, *In History's Shadow,* page 71.
22. "I am": Interview with CTJ.
23. "Amid the most": Doris Kearns Goodwin, *Lyndon Johnson and the American Dream,* page 87.
23. "Are you with me?": Interview with Jake Pickle.
23. "Lyndon and I committed matrimony": Eugenia Boehringer Lasseter, oral history, second interview, page 10.
24. The dress she wore: Interview with CTJ.
24. "Did you get the ring?" Dan Quill, oral history, page 10.

24. "I doubt this marriage will ever last": Dick Halter archives, St. Mark's Episcopal Church, San Antonio, Texas.
25. "Have you read these vows?": Interview with CTJ for *Texas Monthly*, November 1994.
25. After the wedding: Henry Hirshberg, oral history, page 8.
25. It was a cool, clear night: Interview with Cecille Harrison Marshall.

CHAPTER 2: GONE TO TEXAS

26. Description of the Brick House: Harrison County Historical Record.
26. C. C. Baker, a postmaster: CTJ interview, Texas Collection, Baylor University.
26. "You could": Interview with CTJ.
26. Description of Karnack from Port Caddo: *Dallas Morning News*, 1964.
26. It was here, however, that Lady Bird's father: *Marshall News Messenger*, June 10, 1951.
27. Description of Taylor's business: Harrison County Historical Association, document written by Mr. H. S. Calloway, county tax assessor.
27. He loved the feel of money: Interview with Jack Hayner.
27. "My father was a very strong character": CTJ interview, Texas Collection, Baylor University.
27. "I worked for him sunup to sunset": Interview with Dorsey Jones.
27. "He was the law around here": Interview with Diane Taylor.
27. As a young girl growing up: Interview with CTJ.
27. Description of Lady Bird's room: Dorris Powell, oral history, page 19, and author tour of the Brick House.
27. Miss Eunice ghost story: *Dallas Morning News*, feature story by Frank Tolbert, December 12, 1965. Confirmed with CTJ.
28. Lady Bird never saw the girl ghost herself: *Dallas Morning News*, October 31, 1983.
28. "I felt quite likely": Interview with CTJ.
28. Pattern of depression in the family: Interviews with Diana MacArthur, Susan Grey Taylor, Jerry Jones, and other family members.
29. Description of Autauga County, Alabama: Author tour, March 1996.
29. J. B. West, former chief usher: Carl Sferrazza Anthony, *First Ladies, Vol. 2*, page 111.
29. "He describes a South": CTJ interview with Lee Kelly in *Austin American-Statesman*, April 9, 1995.
29. "My parents came from different worlds": Interview with CTJ.
30. Pattillo family history: J. C. Pattillo, *The Family of Littlebury Pattillo and the Connected Families by Marriage*.
30. Passages from the textbook of the Reverend Henry Pattillo: Ibid.
31. Date of Minnie Pattillo's birth: Ibid.
31. "She was a quiet little thing": Ellen Taylor Cooper, oral history, page 8.
31. The Taylors were poor tenant farmers: Interview with Calvin Bishop, half-nephew of T. J. Taylor, and Taylor family records.
32. The only thing Luke owned and description of Luke Pattillo's business: James Cato Pattillo, oral history, page 5.
32. "My grandfather used to do something": Interview with CTJ.
32. "Do you know who I am?": James Cato Pattillo, oral history, page 6.
33. Description of collection of nickel for pill: Ibid., page 7.
33. Luke's lack of affection: Interviews with Lucille Pattillo Thomas and Nettie Pattillo Woodyard, March 1996.
33. Luther Pattillo's will: Probate court, Autauga County, Alabama.
34. Effie, who studied piano: Interviews with Lucille Pattillo Thomas and Nettie Pattillo Woodyard, March 1996.
34. "Uncle Claud took care of his emotions by himself": Interview with Lucille Pattillo Thomas.
34. Description of Taylor family history: From copies of Taylor family genealogical records compiled by Geni Cory, provided by Calvin Bishop, March 1996.
34. Death of T. J. Taylor's older brother Preston: *Prattville Progress*, February 1885.

35. wanted to escape his farm: Interview with Jerry Jones, Taylor's nephew by marriage, March 1996.
35. "He told me that one day": Interview with Susan Grey Taylor.
35. Minnie used to sit outside: Interviews with Nettie Pattillo Woodyard and Susan Grey Taylor.
35. Description of Minnie as "handsome" and other characteristics: Interviews with Dorris Powell and Dorsey Jones; oral histories, Cameron McElroy and various Alabama relatives.
36. "Oh please!": Interview with Susan Grey Taylor.
36. Description of Minnie's intellect: Interviews with Nettie Pattillo Woodyard, Dorris Powell, and Susan Grey Taylor.
36. Description of Taylor as a rebel: Ibid.
36. Taylor described as "white trash" by Minnie's father, and Taylor's reaction: Interview with Susan Grey Taylor.
36. Account of why Taylor left Alabama: *Marshall News Messenger,* 1951, on file at Harrison County Historical Association.
37. Rumors of Taylor's possible involvement in train robbery: Multiple family sources.
37. "Give me": Interview with Jerry Jones.
37. Taylor's first investment of $500 in land, and $5 a week for room and board: *Marshall News Messenger,* June 10, 1951.
38. The port was a vital transportation link: Randolph B. Campbell, *A Southern Community in Crisis, Harrison County, Texas, 1850–1880.*
38. In 1860, Robert W. Lougherty: Ibid.
38. "Real estate is advancing": *Marshall Evening News,* on file at Harrison County Historical Association.
38. Description of Minnie Pattillo's wedding: *Prattville Progress,* December 14, 1900.
39. T.J. called her "dearie": Interview with Dorris Powell.

CHAPTER 3: MOTHERLESS CHILD

40. Description of Minnie's first house in Texas: Dorris Powell, oral history, page 4.
40. Minnie's Hudson Super Six, and her chauffeur: Ibid., pages 11–12.
40. "My father was a very busy man": Antonio J. Taylor, oral history, page 3.
41. Minnie Taylor's love of books: Interview with Diana MacArthur, her granddaughter.
41. "My mother had an enormous supply of books": Interview with CTJ.
41. Religious views of Minnie P. Taylor: Interviews with Dorris Powell and CTJ.
42. "A lot": Cameron McElroy, oral history, page 3.
42. "My grandmother": Interview with Diana MacArthur.
42. "I remember that she wore this large hat": Lucille McElroy, oral history, page 2.
42. "Miss Minnie's skullcaps": Interviews with Dorsey Jones and Jid Porter.
42. "I wish I knew more about her": Interview with CTJ.
42. "No one dared": Ibid.
43. "I was one of five children": LBJ interview with Ruth Montgomery, 1963.
43. "My memory of her": Interview with CTJ.
43. "I remember how she looked": Dorris Powell, oral history, page 7.
44. "Almost every person": CTJ, *Austin American-Statesman,* April 9, 1995.
44. Minnie built a birdbath: Dorris Powell, oral history, page 8.
44. Minnie's involvement with politics: Interviews with Dorris Powell and Susan Grey Taylor.
45. "I know she must have been": Interview with CTJ.
45. The birth of Minnie's two sons: Antonio J. Taylor, oral history.
45. The subsequent sapping of her strength: Interview with Diana MacArthur.
45. "Our mother was in bad health": Antonio J. Taylor, oral history, page 3.
45. The separation lasted several years: Interviews with Nettie Pattillo Woodyard and Lucille Pattillo Thomas, J. C. Pattillo, oral history, page 2.
45. For help, he turned to Dr. John Kellogg: Ibid.
45. The sanitarium, founded in 1866: Richard W. Schwarz, *John Harvey Kellogg, M.D.* page 59.

46. List of important visitors to the sanitarium: Ibid., page 76.
46. the Pattillos ordered granola: Interviews with Nettie Pattillo Woodyard, Lucille Pattillo Thomas, and Susan Grey Taylor.
46. Kellogg's remedies had a lasting impact: Interview with Diana MacArthur.
46. One of Lady Bird's early memories: Interview with CTJ.
47. Kellogg placed a beefsteak under one microscope: Richard W. Schwarz, *John Harvey Kellogg, M.D.*, page 40.
47. Kellogg treated seven thousand patients: Ibid., page 77.
47. Treatment for "neurasthenia": Ibid., page 50.
47. "There was sort of an old bull": Interview with CTJ.
47. Three or four times a day: Interview with Jerry Jones.
48. "He took farmhands in": Interview with Jack Hayner.
48. When men who worked for Taylor were arrested: Interview with Jerry Jones.
48. "I pay. You pray": Ibid.
48. "This is the way": Interview with Dorsey Jones.
48. "Communism ain't nothing new": Interview with Franklin Jones, Jr.
48. The court records of the Harrison County courthouse: *T. J. Taylor v. Ollie Haggerty, et al.*, March 1931 term, and interview with Bailey Mosley, Marshall attorney.
49. He was rich and wanted everyone to know it: Interview with Jack Hayner.
49. Taylor made no secret of the fact that he was a ladies' man: Interviews with Jack Hayner, Jerry Jones, Dorsey Jones, Jid Porter, and others.
50. "Perhaps he wanted to anchor her": Interview with CTJ.
50. Description of the Brick House at Christmastime: Interview with Dorris Powell.
50. "He would": Interview with Jerry Jones.
50. Despite Kellogg's remedies: Interview with Benjamin Baldwin, Philip Baldwin's grandson, December 20, 1995.
51. Description of Claudia Taylor's birth: CTJ narration in her biological film at the LBJ Library.
51. Letter from Taylor to Effie, dated January 8, 1913: Dictated to author by Betty Tilson, Mrs. Johnson's secretary, August 1996.
51. "Lady Bird, Lady Bird": James Cato Pattillo, oral history, footnote no. 3.
51. Shortly thereafter, both boys were sent away: Interview with Diana MacArthur, and Antonio J. Taylor, oral history, page 5.
51. When Lady Bird was still an infant: Interview with CTJ.
52. Description of Lady Bird's first memory of Christmas: Ibid.
52. "I remember once when I was a little girl": *Lady Bird Johnson: A Life Well-Lived.*
52. In the summer of 1918: Dorris Powell, oral history, page 7, and Eugenia Boehringer Lasseter, oral history, page 2.
53. Minnie was fifty years old and pregnant again: Interviews with several family members.
53. "She looked over at me and said": Interview with CTJ.
53. Taylor did not notify either of his sons: Interview with Diana MacArthur.
53. "There was a vacant place": Interview with CTJ.
54. Some time later, it was Tommy who wrote her epitaph: Ellen Taylor Cooper, oral history, page 21.
54. Wording of epitaph: Author tour of cemetery.
54. "I had never seen my father lose his temper": Interview with CTJ.
54. "What are those long boxes?": CTJ interview, Texas Collection, Baylor University, and in the narration of her biographical film at the LBJ Library.
55. "I was incensed that people thought": Interview with CTJ.
55. A few months after her mother died: Mrs. Elaine Fischesser, oral history, page 5.
55. "I knew the conductors": Interview with CTJ.
55. "We were told not to mention it": Interview with Nettie Pattillo Woodyard.
55. Antonio Taylor's letter written to his father on September 16, 1919: Provided to the author by CTJ, July 1996.
56. Taylor continued to nurse his own private wounds: Interview with Susan Grey Taylor.

CHAPTER 4: FIRST FLIGHT

57. In July 1923: Interview with CTJ.
57. "Those strange Yankee people": Ibid.
57. Descriptions of what Lady Bird saw at Battle Creek: Ibid.
58. "I remember": Ibid.
58. The painting is of a slim woman: Author visit to Billingsley, Alabama.
58. "I saw": Interview with CTJ.
59. The epitaph on Effie's tombstone: Ibid.
59. "Somehow, instead of Aunt Effie": Interview with Dorris Powell.
59. "The list came first": Dorris Powell, oral history, page 15.
59. "I was her reason for being": Interview with CTJ.
60. Description of first flight: Ibid.
60. She started elementary school: Interview with CTJ, Texas Collection, Baylor University.
60. The teacher, Nancy Lawrence: Dorris Powell, oral history, page 10.
60. The highlight of Lady Bird's regular week: Interview with CTJ.
61. "Well, I don't want to work but I must": Dorris Powell, oral history, page 15.
61. "Everybody": Interview with Jerry Jones.
61. On Sundays, she sometimes attended services: Interview with CTJ.
61. Dorris Powell took her to the weeklong revival meetings: Dorris Powell, oral history, page 16.
62. Lady Bird listened to the hellfire: Interview with CTJ.
62. Everyday life at the Brick House: Interview with Sylvia Bishop and CTJ.
62. "Effie and I were the ones who belonged": Interview with CTJ.
62. Lady Bird found a flesh-and-blood female role model: Photos of Beulah Wisdom, Harrison County Historical Association.
63. "Yes, in a coarse": Interview with CTJ.
63. "Daddy didn't tell Beulah": Ibid.
64. "In the end, Beulah had to seek solace somewhere": Ibid.
64. In 1933: Divorce records, case No. 8600, Harrison County courthouse.
64. Letter from Antonio to Lyndon and Lady Bird, written on May 15, 1935: Copy provided to author, July 1996.
64. History of Jefferson: Randolph B. Campbell, *A Southern Community in Crisis*, and author tour.
65. Effie and Lady Bird moved into the house of Miss Bernice Emmett: Interview with CTJ.
65. "He was funny and good-looking": Ibid.
65. "This woman had suffered a lot": Ibid.
66. "one of the most determined": Flora Rheta Schreiber, "Lady Bird Johnson's First Years of Marriage," *Women's Day*, December 1967.
66. Another early boyfriend: Robert Caro, *The Path to Power*, page 197.
66. "Even when we went on a picnic": Ibid.
66. "I was Cap'n Taylor's daughter": Interview with CTJ.
66. Description of trip to Billingsley with her cousin Nettie: Mrs. Nettie Pattillo Woodyard, oral history, pages 9–10, and interview with CTJ.
67. Her summers in Alabama: Ibid.
67. Driving to school in a pickup truck: Interview with CTJ.
67. "I had two heavy crosses to bear": Jean Flynn, *Lady, The Story of Claudia (Lady Bird) Johnson*, page 12.
68. Copy of 1928 *Parrot*: Harrison County Historical Association.
68. "I have come to realize": Copy of letter from Emma to Claudia, in the Harrison County Historical Association files.
68. Portion of her 1928 notebooks: Ibid.
69. Marshall High School grades: Ibid.
69. Class rankings: *Marshall News Messenger*, May 1928.
69. "I had enough pride": Interview with CTJ.

69. Class prophecies: "Lady Bird Johnson's Montage of Memories," in *Marshall News Messenger,* 1978.
70. Helen Bird, her high school friend: Interview with CTJ.
70. "I'm not in favor of this": Ibid.
70. Letter from C. A. Pattillo to Lady Bird dated May 5, 1927: Harrison County Historical Association.
71. Her Bible teacher at St. Mary's: Interview with CTJ.
71. Description of her life at St. Mary's: Ibid.
71. She was in two plays: Emily Crow Selden, oral history, page 5.
71. She considered the University of Alabama: Eugenia Boehringer Lasseter, oral history, page 4, and interview with CTJ.
71. Description of flight to Austin: Interview with CTJ.
72. "It was though the gates": Ibid.

CHAPTER 5: THE MOTH FINDS THE FLAME

73. "Bo never would amount to anything.": Emily Crow Selden, oral history, page 11.
73. "Most girls are in full bloom": Interview with CTJ.
73. The face she caught sight of: Photos of CTJ in 1928, Taylor family collection, LBJ Library.
73. She was a slim and stylish secretary: Eugenia Boehringer Lasseter, oral history, page 6.
74. Through Terrell, Gene got to know: Ibid., page 7.
74. "She was one of those tremendously outgoing people": Interview with CTJ.
74. By then, Gene had lived for four years: Eugenia Boehringer Lasseter, oral history, page 5.
75. During a trip home to Karnack: Ibid.
75. The University of Texas was founded: Ronnie Dugger, *Our Invaded Universities,* page 5.
75. By the time Lady Bird arrived: Interview with Margaret Berry, a UT historian.
76. "I liked the thought of the six girls": Interview with CTJ.
76. Before she left the Brick House to go to St. Mary's: Interview with Dorris Powell.
76. "I was determined to let go": Interview with CTJ.
76. The first person Lady Bird met: Cecille Harrison Marshall, oral history, page 1, and interview with Mrs. Marshall.
77. "You're not going to need that bedding": Cecille Harrison Marshall, oral history, page 2.
77. "She took what she learned from Battle Creek": Interview with Cecille Harrison Marshall.
77. There were other differences: Cecille Harrison Marshall, oral history, page 6.
77. "She was very conscientious": Emily Crow Selden, oral history.
78. "She was quiet about it": Interview with Cecille Harrison Marshall.
78. One anonymous publication: Ronnie Dugger, *Our Invaded Universities,* page 28.
78. "She was a little dowdy": Interview with Gordon Abney.
79. "If you don't clean up this car": Eugenia Boehringer Lasseter, oral history, page 6.
79. "She had more money": Interview with Cecille Harrison Marshall.
79. In the fall of her freshman year: Emily Crow Selden, oral history, page 29.
79. "I don't think I behaved very well": Interview with CTJ.
80. "Bird was crazy about bluebonnets": Emily Crow Selden, oral history.
80. "Navajo parties": Interviews with Margaret Berry and Cecille Harrison Marshall.
80. On at least one occasion: Interview with Cecille Harrison Marshall.
81. Henry VIII's six wives: Ibid.
81. "I fell in love every April": Interview with CTJ.
81. She attended a heavily chaperoned formal dance: Cecille Harrison Marshall, oral history, page 6.
81. Description of Victor McRea, Jack Mayfield, and Wayne Livergood: Interview with CTJ.
81. Description of trip to Mexico: Emily Crow Selden, oral history, pages 23–25.
82. Among the influential men that Gene introduced her to: Emily Crow Selden, oral history, page 26, and interview with Cecille Harrison Marshall.
82. Gene also introduced her to Jack Aldridge: Emily Crow Selden, oral history, page 27.

82. "We didn't think of him": Interview with Cecille Harrison Marshall.
83. What drew her to Aldridge: Interview with CTJ.
83. Romance with Dawson Duncan: Ibid., and interview with Margaret Mayer.
83. "I saw journalism as an outlet": Interview with CTJ.
83. Association with DeWitt Reddick, and feature writing: Ibid.
84. On January 18, 1933, her byline appeared: Morgue of *Daily Texan*, student newspaper, University of Texas.
84. One weekend she and Emily went home: Emily Crow Selden, oral history, second interview, page 16.
84. They did discover oil: T. J. Taylor's will, Harrison County courthouse.
85. "I literally saw oil and gas flare": Interview with CTJ.
85. The same day her story on Keats: *Daily Texan*, January 18, 1933.
85. Historical information on Ma and Pa Ferguson: *Texas Almanac.*
86. "the best farmers make the best bootleggers": Interview with Jerry Jones.
86. Repeal of prohibition: Interview with Cecille Harrison Marshall.
86. Politically, Lady Bird and her friends: Eugenia Boehringer Lasseter, oral history, page 7.
86. Description of visit to Longhorn Caverns and encounter with prison inmates: Emily Crow Selden, oral history, pages 33–34.
87. Taylor later said he had caught the two of them in bed: Interview with Jack Hayner.
87. Transcript of her grades: University of Texas admissions office.
87. Description of Brick House: Emily Crow Selden, oral history, first interview, page 16.
87. The fact that Taylor would send Jack Moore to paint: Eugenia Boehringer Lasseter, oral history page 8.
88. "Oh wonderful": CTJ interview, Texas Collection, Baylor University.
88. But Lady Bird had no intention: Interview with CTJ.
88. Victor McRea's background: Interview with Victor McRea, Jr.
88. At the port of Galveston: Interview with Cecille Harrison Marshall.
89. Trip to New York and trip to Washington: Interview with CTJ.
90. Description of first meeting with Johnson: CTJ interview, Texas Collection, Baylor University.
90. "I had a sort of queer moth-in-the-flame feeling": Ibid.

CHAPTER 6: A TEN-WEEK AFFAIR

91. At 8:00 the following morning: CTJ interview, Texas Collection, Baylor University.
91. "He always used to lecture me": Interview with CTJ.
92. "He was so dynamic": Ibid.
92. Thirty years later: LBJ interview with Ruth Montgomery, 1963.
92. Before she answered any of the questions: CTJ interview, Texas Collection, Baylor University.
93. Description of Roosevelt's inauguration and impact on Johnson: Robert Dallek, *Lone Star Rising*, page 107.
93. After breakfast, he invited her: Interview with Cecille Harrison Marshall.
93. "He talked a great deal": Interview with CTJ.
94. LBJ's romance with Kitty Clyde: Robert Caro, *The Path to Power*, pages 113–14.
94. Condition of his father's finances: Ronnie Dugger, *The Politician*, page 89; Robert Dallek, *Lone Star Rising*, page 55.
94. LBJ's romance with Carol Davis: Robert Caro, *Path to Power*, pages 161–63; Doris Kearns Goodwin, *Lyndon Johnson*, page 56; Robert Dallek, *Lone Star Rising*, page 81; Ronnie Dugger, *The Politician*, page 124.
95. "My feeling was": Interview with CTJ.
95. "She won't admit pain": LBJ interview with Ruth Montgomery, 1963.
96. "I was one of five children": Ibid.
96. "My mother was everything": Ronnie Dugger, *The Politician*, page 61.
96. "We welcomed you": *Letters from the Hill Country: The Correspondence Between Rebekah and Lyndon Baines Johnson.*

96. Description of Rebekah's memories: Family correspondence, RBJ, LBJ Library.
97.   The Reverend George W. Baines and details of Johnson's family history: Robert Dallek, *Lone Star Rising,* pages 26–61; Ronnie Dugger, *The Politician;* Doris Kearns Goodwin, *Lyndon Johnson,* pages 21–49.
98.   "Normally": Rebekah Baines Johnson, *A Family Album,* a collection of her early autobiographical writings.
98.   "It was daybreak": Ibid.
99.   In letters to her mother: Family correspondence, RBJ, LBJ Library.
99.   Johnson's earliest memory: Robert Dallek, *Lone Star Rising,* page 36.
100. "He [Sam] doesn't want to get any": Family correspondence, RBJ, LBJ Library.
100. "That really hurt his mother": Wilma Green Fawcett, oral history.
100. Description of dream about an old hag: Doris Kearns Goodwin, *Lyndon Johnson,* page 43.
101. "So often in my life": Correspondence, LBJ, letters to RBJ.
101. "All my life": Ibid.
102. "My first impression of her" and description of initial meeting: Interview with CTJ, and CTJ interview, Texas Collection, Baylor University.
103. "It is bad to fall in love": Courtship letters, LBJ Library.
103. Description of trip to King Ranch: Interview with CTJ.
103. "He seemed quite proud of that": Cecille Harrison Marshall, oral history, page 13.
104. "Listen. Don't lose that girl": Interview with B. K. Johnson, and confirmed with CTJ.
104. Trip back from the King Ranch: Interview with CTJ.
104. In San Antonio, they picked up: Malcolm Baldwell, oral history.
105. "Hmmmm, you've been bringing home": CTJ interview, Texas Collection, Baylor University.
105. Three years later, on February 7, 1937: Marriage records, Harrison County courthouse.
105. "I'm going to marry this girl.": Malcolm Baldwell, oral history, page 11.
105. *Nazism: An Assault on Civilization*: Courtship letters, LBJ Library.
106. She chose a classic: CTJ through her secretary, Betty Tilson.
106. "To my knowledge": Ibid.
106. Courtship letters: LBJ Library.
110. Visit to see Aunt Effie: CTJ interview, Texas Collection, Baylor University.
110. Visit to Ellen Cooper: Ellen Taylor Cooper, oral history, page 5.
111. Courtship letters: LBJ Library.

CHAPTER 7: A LIFE BEHIND WALLS

113. The morning after their wedding, and details of the honeymoon trip: Interview with CTJ.
114. "Those places by the side of the road": Ibid.
114. Honeymoon photo: Photo collection, LBJ Library.
115. "If he concentrated on a girl": Willard Deason, oral history, page 11.
115. Nothing about marriage: Interview with CTJ.
115. "Right away I learned": Ibid.
116. In January, she convinced him: CTJ interview, Texas Collection, Baylor University.
116. "Heavens no": Interview with CTJ.
116. Handling the family finances: CTJ interview, Texas Collection, Baylor University.
116. "He spoke of himself": Interview with CTJ.
117. The original of this letter is framed and on exhibit in Johnson's boyhood home in Johnson City.
118. "I felt it was important": Interview with CTJ.
118. "I would get angry": Ibid.
118. One night Johnson himself came home drunk: Sam Houston Johnson, *My Brother Lyndon,* pages 64–65.
119. Incident when LBJ slapped the hind flank of Lady Bird's horse: Interview with CTJ.
119. "I thought if we went to a party": Ibid.

120. "You probably don't remember me" Dale Miller, oral history, page 4.

120. As Scooter Miller put it: Mrs. Dale Miller, oral history.

120. Arthur E. "Tex" Goldschmidt: Interview with Arthur E. Goldschmidt.

120. In Mamie Kleberg: Interview with B. K. Johnson.

120. Description of Kleberg's extramarital problems: Robert Dallek, *Lone Star Rising*, page 103.

120. "It was an impossible situation": Interview with CTJ.

121. Looking for advice and a role model: Terrell Maverick Webb, oral history.

121. The first people she invited to dinner: CTJ interview, Texas Collection, Baylor University.

121. "I didn't want to be separated": Ibid.

122. "He thought I was good-looking": Interview with CTJ.

123. "Bird was a sweet-looking": Virginia Durr, oral history, page 8.

124. One evening in the late 1930s: Interview with CTJ.

124. Lyndon's relationship with Kleberg: Terrell Maverick Webb, oral history, and Robert Dallek, *Lone Star Rising*, pages 122–23.

124. "How would you like to live in Austin?": Interview with CTJ.

125. Living arrangements on San Gabriel Street: Willard Deason, oral history.

125. Montgomery knew Johnson well: Robert Montgomery, oral history.

126. "Man had found job": CTJ interview, Texas Collection, Baylor University.

127. Letter to Welly Hopkins from LBJ on NYA stationery, April 6, 1936: LBJ Library.

127. Johnson's relationship with Alice Glass: Robert Caro, *The Path to Power*, Chapter 25; John Connally, *In History's Shadow*, page 70; Ronnie Dugger, *The Politician*, pages 253–54; Robert Dallek, *Lone Star Rising*, pages 189–91.

128. "Alice had a great presence": Interview with Frank Oltorf.

130. "I liked Senator Wirtz": Interview with CTJ, and Mary Rather, oral history.

130. Taylor still balked: Interview with CTJ, and CTJ interview, Texas Collection, Baylor University.

131. "Lyndon was never so young": CTJ interview, Texas Collection, Baylor University.

131. Letter from Arthur "Tex" Goldschmidt: Copy given to author.

131. In his congressional office: Interview with O. J. Weber.

133. "He was depressed": Robert Caro, *The Path to Power*, page 704.

133. "He did get out": Ibid.

133. "very jolly and putting": CTJ interview, the Texas collection, Baylor University.

134. "steady diet": Ibid.

134. Her reaction was to work harder: Home movies, LBJ Library and interviews with Margaret Mayer, O. J. Weber, and Frank Oltorf.

134. She also worked hard at learning the rules of social protocol: Marie Smith, *The President's Lady*, pages 84–85.

134. "One afternoon I was at her house for dinner": Interview with Margaret Mayer.

135. The office staff as of December 7: Interview with O. J. Weber.

135. To save money, she moved into Nellie Connally's one-bedroom: Interview with Nellie Connally.

136. Letter to Ernest Pearcy, March 2, 1942: LBJ subject file, LBJ Library.

136. "If it was chicken": Interview with Nellie Connally.

136. "When I think of Lyndon's being captured": Emily Crow Selden, oral history.

137. Johnson's only close call: Ronnie Dugger, *The Politician*, pages 244–47.

137. World War II diary: LBJ subject file, LBJ Library.

138. Oltorf, who was Alice Glass's friend, believes that Johnson: Interview with Frank Oltorf.

138. "Charles believes": LBJ subject file, container number 74, LBJ Library.

138. "a little frayed": Interview with Diana MacArthur.

138. She became a lost soul: Audiotape conversation between LBJ and unidentified aide, February 26, 1964, LBJ Library.

138. "I just travel as much as I can" and the other letters: Alice Glass folder, LBJ Library, also listed under Mrs. R. J. Kirkpatrick.

140. "How did Alice spend her last days?": Interview with Frank Oltorf.

CHAPTER 8: GETTING RICH

141. "I had a degree in journalism and planned to practice it": Interview with CTJ.

141. In September of that year: Ronnie Dugger, *The Politician*, pages 273–87; Robert Caro, *The Path to Power*, page 743; Robert Dallek, *Lone Star Rising*, page 252.

142. Taylor's fortunes had increased dramatically: Real estate records, Harrison County courthouse, and history of Longhorn Ordnance in *Marshall News Messenger*.

142. Cameron McElroy said: Cameron McElroy, oral history, page 16.

142. "they both wanted the same things": Interview with Nellie Connally.

142. "I felt a peculiar sense of failure": Interview with CTJ.

142. "I learned while Lyndon was away": Ibid.

143. From 1937 to 1942: Financial details drawn from the account of the Johnson family business that was reported and written by Louis Kohlmeier, Ray Shaw, and Ed Cony. The series ran in the *Wall Street Journal*, March 23, 1964, page 7. The series won a Pulitzer Prize and has been the basis for much of what has been written about the Johnsons' finances to date by all of Johnson's biographers. Other articles used in this chapter include: "The Story of the Johnson Family Fortune," *U.S. News & World Report*, May 4, 1964; a two-part series in *Life*, Keith Wheeler and William Lambert, "The Man Who Is the President," August 14, 1964; "LBJ's Wealth Grows and an Issue," *Business Week*, August 22, 1964.

143. "We were a team": Interview with CTJ.

143. "His life became": Ibid.

144. Evetts Haley: J. Evetts Haley, *A Texan Looks at Lyndon*.

144. "Newspapers were what I knew": Interview with CTJ.

144. KTBC, a small radio station in Austin: Ibid.

144. The battle for the license: Ronnie Dugger, *The Politician*, pages 266–73.

145. The application was submitted to the FCC: *Wall Street Journal* series.

145. Clifford Durr, her friend from Alabama: Virginia Durr, oral history.

146. "Lyndon and I then talked about what to do next": Interview with CTJ.

146. "I got a bucket": Ibid.

146. Details about the Kellogg account: Ibid.

147. "excellent meals": Interview with CTJ.

147. Letter of May 7, 1943: Liz Carpenter, *Ruffles and Flourishes*, page 58.

148. "He was just as interested as she": Harfield Weedin, oral history, page 15.

148. "I gave her a report on everything": Ibid., page 22.

148. The story of how she bought Thirtieth Place: Interview with CTJ and John Connally, *In History's Shadow*, page 71.

149. "You would have thought": Interview with CTJ.

149. "He told them it was a good investment": Ibid.

149. The year before, in November 1941: Interview with Virginia Durr.

150. "We never": Interview with CTJ.

150. The reason for Lady Bird's stoicism: Ibid. and interviews with other family members.

150. Weedin pressed both Lady Bird and LBJ: Harfield Weedin, oral history, page 20.

151. It was Weedin who established: Ibid., p. 27.

151. Lynda's birth: Interview with CTJ and account of Lynda's birth in the *Johnson City Record-Courier*.

151. The following year, Lady Bird's station prospered: Multiple magazine and newspaper accounts.

152. Hollers also raised questions: Interview with CTJ and multiple Johnson biographers.

152. Description of Dillman Street house: Harfield Weedin, oral history.

152. "At the opening rally": Interview with CTJ.

152. Mayer's memory of rally: Interview with Margaret Mayer.

153. Lady Bird continued to commute: Interview with Isabel Brown Wilson.

153. Trip across the South: Interview with Margaret Mayer.

153. "I never thought I'd see you": Interview with CTJ.

154. "I knew that I was in a life-threatening situation": Ibid.

154. LBJ's reaction: Interview with Horace Busby.
154. House staff situation: Helen Williams, oral history.
155. "I never saw": Interview with Margaret Mayer.
155. Lucy's memories: Interview with Luci Baines Johnson.
155. As she told Marie Smith: Marie Smith, *The President's Lady.*
156. "I had regretted not doing more to help in 1941": Interview with CTJ.
156. "If she heard": Interview with Jake Pickle.
156. In the 1948 campaign, Lady Bird made her first substantial campaign speeches: Newspaper accounts and Marie Smith, *The President's Lady*, page 139.
157. Account of kidney stone: Interview with Warren Woodward.
158. When Johnson returned to Texas: Lady Bird's home movies, Audiovisual Department, LBJ Library.
158. Two days before the election: Marie Smith, *The President's Lady*, page 140.
159. To entertain themselves: Lady Bird's home movies, Audiovisual Department, fall 1941, LBJ Library.
160. Description of family finances as of 1947: Multiple newspaper and magazine sources.
160. Letter of September 15, 1949: LBJ family financial records, LBJ Library.
161. Buying the ranch: Ronnie Dugger, *The Politician*, page 357.
161. "How could you do this to me?": Interview with CTJ.
161. Account of the 1952 flood: Interviews with CTJ and Luci Baines Johnson, and *Johnson City Record-Courier*, September 19, 1952.
163. Lady Bird invited Leonard Marks: Leonard Marks, oral history, and Leonard Marks, "The Birth of KTBC-TV," LBJ Library.
164. "We were all paid a pittance": Interview with Jim Morriss.
165. "Jesse introduced me to him": Interview with Madeline Brown, and copy of a manuscript written by her, "Texas in the Morning."
167. From the edge of the party: Russell Morton Brown, oral history, page 72.

CHAPTER 9: LBJ'S MIDLIFE CRISIS

168. "He used to tell me": Interview with George Reedy.
169. In Reedy's view: Ibid. and George Reedy, *Lyndon B. Johnson: A Memoir.*
169. His first private secretary: Mary Rather, oral history.
170. "Blown away": Interview with Mary Margaret Wiley Valenti.
170. "The first day I went to work for him": Interview with Ashton Gonella.
170. "He was absolutely terrifying": Interview with Nadine Brammer.
171. He rewarded female reporters in a similar manner: Nancy Dickerson, oral history.
172. "Lyndon loved to play Pygmalion": Interview with CTJ.
172. "He could be": Interview with George Reedy.
173. As majority leader: Interview with Mildred Stegall.
173. Several times a week, Lady Bird came in the office: Interviews with Ashton Gonella, Mildred Stegall, and Betty Hickman.
174. According to Miller, Rayburn once told her: Interview with Hope Rillings Miller.
174. "I had": Interview with CTJ.
175. Description of Johnson's heart attack: All of Johnson's biographers; interviews with Warran Woodward, Frank Oltorf, CTJ, George Reedy, Mildred Stegall, and others.
178. The staff greeted Rebekah's arrival with dread: Interview with George Reedy.
178. With each meal, she gave LBJ: Zephyr Wright, oral history.
178. Description of LBJ ordering Rather off ranch: Dan Rather, oral history.
179. Johnson returned to his duties as majority leader: Interview with George Reedy.
179. "Now Bird": Juanita Roberts, oral history.
180. According to notes Wiley made: The notes were made July 13, 1960, and can be found in the U.S. Senate file, LBJ Library.

180. Lady Bird was less melodramatic: Interview with Robert Wilkinson Notti, Betty Hickman, and others who were present.

181. The following morning: Betty Hickman, oral history, and interview with Betty Hickman.

182. Description of what happened in the hotel suite: "Notes on the 1960 Democratic Convention" made by Phil Graham, LBJ Library.

182. "They had it all": Interview with Liz Carpenter.

CHAPTER 10: THE TRAP OF HER FATHER'S HOUSE

184. "She always believed in him": Ashton Gonella, oral history, page 32.

185. "The need for women": Interview with Lynda Johnson Robb, Audiovisual Department, LBJ Library.

185. "I rather like it": Interview with Liz Carpenter.

186. "I'm going home and tell Lyndon": Press clippings from 1948 and throughout the Senate years.

186. "Would Lady Bird carry the load": Liz Carpenter, oral history, and interview with Liz Carpenter.

186. Kennedy's affair with Marilyn Monroe: C. David Heymann, A *Woman Named Jackie,* pages 233–36.

186. Reaction of Johnson's staff: Interviews with George Reedy, Horace Busby, and others.

187. "It seemed to me": Leslie Carpenter, oral history.

187. "I knew you'd be interested": From a selection of letters by Mrs.Kennedy to the Johnson family on file at the LBJ Library.

187. "She had a doll-like expression": Interview with CTJ.

187. In a 1974 interview: Mrs. Kennedy, oral history.

188. "I don't know how to do anything": Liz Carpenter, oral history, first interview, page 31.

188. "No matter what": Interview with Nellie Connally.

188. "Jack Kennedy could not have been more gracious": Betty Cason Hickman, oral history, page 49.

189. "Lady Bird always reminded American women": Interview with Liz Carpenter.

189. Lady Bird dressed to please one person: Stanley Marcus, oral history, pages 6–12.

190. "It annoyed me": Interview with CTJ.

190. "Rather than choosing her own clothes": Leslie Carpenter, oral history, page 9.

190. Description of the tea parties: Liz Carpenter, oral history, first interview, pages 23–28.

191. Carpenter's background and first meeting with Mrs. Johnson: Liz Carpenter, oral history, pages 1–7.

193. "about as crude as they come": Kenny O'Donnell, oral history.

193. "Johnson really did identify": Interview with George Reedy.

194. "She only wants to be": Leslie Carpenter, oral history.

195. "Sometimes, I sit back": Frank Cormier, *LBJ, The Way He Was,* Chapter 2.

195. "At that point, none of us was sure": Interview with Liz Carpenter.

195. As a political bloc, Protestant ministers: Robert Dallek, *Lone Star Rising,* page 585.

196. Much of Johnson's animosity toward Nixon: Various Johnson biographers and interviews with George Reedy and Horace Busby.

196. "It started not long after she came": Interview with Horace Busby.

196. "He cared about people": Helen Gahagan Douglas, oral history.

197. "She figured out how to get along in the world": Interview with Mercedes Eicholz.

197. "It was almost": Interview with Horace Busby.

198. Mrs. Johnson and the two Kennedy women: Liz Carpenter, oral history, page 27.

198. "human tape recorder": J. Evetts Haley, *A Texan Looks at Lyndon.*

199. After the party, she boarded an airplane: Liz Carpenter, oral history, page 25.

200. "I feel sure my ideas of what a man was": Various interviews with CTJ by multiple sources, including a televised interview with Lynda Johnson Robb, LBJ Library.

200. "She has that fantastic": Liz Carpenter, oral history.

200. Description of what happened as Taylor lay dying: Interviews with Jerry Jones, Susan Grey Taylor, Diana MacArthur, and Gerry Hopkins.

201. Lady Bird had first moved to change her father's will: Donald Thomas, oral history, second interview, page 7.
202. "The funeral turned into a political event" and description of Lady Bird at her father's funeral: Interview with Jerry Jones.
203. Taylor left: Last will and testament of T. J. Taylor, Harrison County courthouse, Vol. 82, page 630.
203. By the 1990s, relations between the two: *Bank One, Texas, U.S.A. v. Ruth Scoggins Taylor et al.*, probate court, Dallas, Texas.
203. Letter from U.S. Rep. Wright Patman and Lady Bird's response: Provided by CTJ.
204. "the key to understanding Lady Bird": Interview with Horace Busby.
204. At times the arrangement was a strain: Ibid.
205. At a campaign rally in Indiana: Bob Waldron, oral history, and press clippings.
206. "The adorable golden donkey": Lady Bird Johnson to Jacqueline Kennedy, Box 5, White House Famous Names Collection, LBJ Library.
206. "What can one say?": Jacqueline Kennedy to Lady Bird Johnson, Box 5, White House Famous Names Collection, LBJ Library.
206. Account of "Mink Coat Mob" and Dallas speech: Oral histories of Charles Boatner, Liz Carpenter, Barefoot Sanders, Stanley Marcus, Carl L. Phinney, and accounts in Dallas and Houston newspapers.
208. "I'll always remember": Lady Bird Johnson to Liz Carpenter, in Carpenter's oral history.
208. "Well, Lady Bird carried Texas": Interview with Liz Carpenter.
209. Lady Bird's November 10, 1966, letter to Mrs. Kennedy: File of letters between Mrs. Johnson and Mrs. Kennedy, LBJ Library, Box 5, White House Famous Names Collection, LBJ Library.
209. The vice presidential years were sheer misery: Multiple Johnson biographers and interviews with former staff members.
210. "I am like a wild animal": Nancy Dickerson, oral history.
210. Bess would sometimes find Lady Bird's stockings: Bess Abell, oral history, page 7.
210. In Washington, society columnists: Interview with Hope Riddings Miller.
210. "She knew what was going on.": Interview with Bess Abell.
210. In the first year of Kennedy's presidency: Bess Abell, oral history, pages 10–12.
211. "Never before has Texas beef": LBJ to Jacqueline Kennedy, Box 5, White House Famous Names Collection, LBJ Library.
212. Description of dinner party in Paris: Interview with Horace Busby.
213. "He was capable": Ibid.
213. "I would say that more than half of them": Helen Gahagan Douglas, oral history.

CHAPTER 11: LADY BIRD'S THIN LINE.

214. "If you don't do anything else for me": Bess Abell, oral history, page 24.
214. "You give so much happiness": Letter from Mrs. Johnson to Mrs. Kennedy, LBJ Library.
215. *The Death of a President*, Harper & Row, 1967.
215. On this particular day: Bess Abell, oral history, page 25.
216. "The two": Interview with CTJ.
216. In the transcript of Lady Bird's diary: This passage is from an audiotape of portions of Mrs. Johnson's dictated diary about the events of November 22, 1963, that was released by the LBJ Library in 1997. Portions of it were published in Mrs. Johnson's *A White House Diary* in 1970 by Holt, Rinehart and Winston.
217. a lavish party for the Johnsons: Virginia Durr, oral history.
217. "What really hurt Johnson with the public": Interview with George Reedy.
217. "The President told Yarborough": Interview with Nellie Connally.
218. This account of the assassination taken from multiple newspaper accounts, interview with Nellie Connally, and Mrs. Johnson's *A White House Diary*.
219. To this day, no one knows for sure: C. David Heymann, *A Woman Named Jackie*, page 400.
221. Luci never remembers a single incident: Interview with Luci Baines Johnson.
221. "I was proud of the way they reacted today.": Interview with Horace Busby.

221. "I want to find Mrs. Kennedy.": Lady Bird Johnson, *A White House Diary*.

221. "I never saw": Ibid.

222. Across the narrow hallway: Interview with Nellie Connally.

222. In fact, prior to the trip to Dallas: Interview with Robert Strauss.

222. "Every politician ought to be born a foundling": Interview with Luci Baines Johnson.

222. Lynda Bird, three years older than her sister: Nan Robertson, "Our New First Lady," *Saturday Evening Post*, February 8, 1964.

223. Kathleen Connally's death: John Connally, *In History's Shadow*, Chapter 8.

223. "I'm so sorry, Nellie," description of boarding *Air Force One*, the swearing-in and conversation with Mrs. Kennedy: Lady Bird Johnson, *A White House Diary*.

225. Conversation between Mrs. Johnson and Rose Kennedy: Audiotape November 22, 1963, 3:15 P.M., Texas time, LBJ Library.

226. "I have no statement": Interview with Liz Carpenter, various newspaper accounts, and Marie Smith, *The President's Lady*.

226. "Your daddy's all right": Feature story by Frances Spatz Leighton in the *Dallas Morning News*, February 1964.

227. "I can't watch those anymore . . .": Interview with Horace Busby.

228. "Oh, poor Bess, what you've been through!": Bess Abell, oral history.

228. "Everywhere I looked": Interview with CTJ.

228. "I hear Oswald has been killed": Lady Bird Johnson, *A White House Diary*.

228. After the funeral: Virginia Durr, oral history.

229. On November 26: Lady Bird Johnson, *A White House Diary*.

229. "Now that I think back on it": Mrs. Kennedy, oral history.

229. Liz Carpenter later described as "ghoulish": Liz Carpenter, oral history.

229. "thank you for walking": Jacqueline Kennedy to LBJ, Box 5, White House Famous Names Collection, LBJ Library.

230. Johnson's letter of December 1: Selection of letters between Mrs. Kennedy and the Johnson family: LBJ Library.

230. Transcript of December conversation between LBJ and Mrs. Kennedy: Audiotape, December 2, 1963, LBJ Library.

231. Meanwhile, Lady Bird struggled to figure out: Interview with Liz Carpenter and Lady Bird Johnson, *A White House Diary*.

232. She and Johnson quarreled: Interview with Luci Baines Johnson.

232. Like Lady Bird, Rayburn had not wanted Johnson: Interview with George Reedy.

233. "I wish you a happy arrival": From the letters between Mrs. Kennedy and the Johnson family, LBJ Library.

233. Audiotape conversation between LBJ and Mrs. Kennedy, 5:20 P.M., December 7, LBJ Library.

233. All conversations used in these pages are from the ones that LBJ secretly recorded from his first day in office through January 1969 on a Dictaphone system, and that have thus far been opened by the LBJ Library.

235. A few months later, Douglas spent the night: Michael Beschloss, *Taking Charge: The Johnson White House Tapes, 1963–1964*, page 268, note 5.

237. Throughout the winter: Interview with Robert Strauss.

CHAPTER 12: WHISTLING IN THE DARK

240. During a four-day, 1,628-mile: Office of the Press Secretary to Mrs. Johnson, news release, September 12, 1964.

240. "keeping it up": Lady Bird Johnson, *A White House Diary*.

240. "I knew the Civil Rights Act was right": Interview with Liz Carpenter.

240. "There are plenty of people": Opening speech of *Lady Bird Special*, October 6, 1964, Alexandria, Virginia.

241. Mrs. Ora Bryant: "The White Man Ain't Never Going to Let Us Vote," *New Republic*, October 24, 1964.

242. During the signing ceremony: Lady Bird Johson, *A White House Diary.*
242. "untold good": Ibid.
242. In an old photograph: Taylor Family Collection, Box No. 1, LBJ Library.
244. "I wonder": Lady Bird Johnson, *A White House Diary.*
244. "I don't think a white Southerner": Audiotape conversation between LBJ and Walter Jenkins, August 16, 1964, LBJ Library.
245. Lady Bird admired Jenkins's loyalty: Sam Houston Johnson, *My Brother Lyndon*, page 149.
245. "I don't": Audiotape recording of LBJ, August 26, LBJ Library.
246. The letter CTJ wrote to LBJ on August 25, 1964: Lady Bird Johnson, *A White House Diary.*
246. During the Democratic National Convention: Liz Carpenter, oral history, first interview, pages 10–18.
247. "You know": Liz Carpenter, oral history.
248. Ken O'Donnell, by then a special assistant: Interview with Bess Abell and Liz Carpenter.
248. However, Johnson seemed less enthusiastic: Audiotape conversation between CTJ and LBJ, March 10, 1964, LBJ Library.
249. Abell purchased large volumes: Entertainment—'64 Whistlestop, White House Social Files (Bess Abell's), Box 34, LBJ Library.
249. Lindy Boggs: Rally song of the Democrats, "Song of the Whistle Stop," ibid.
250. Description of train and menus: Ibid.
250. As Carpenter put it: Liz Carpenter, oral history, first interview, pages 10–18, and Carpenter, *Ruffles and Flourishes*, Chapter 14.
251. CTJ making calls to Southern governors: Ibid. and Lady Bird Johnson, *A White House Diary.*
252. The Secret Service received reports: Interviews with Liz Carpenter and Bess Abell.
252. Even the weather seemed to work against her: *Houston Post*, October 4, 1964.
252. Miraculously, two days later: *Houston Post*, October 6, 1964.
253. LBJ came on board: Maxine Cheshire, *Washington Post.*
253. "Sunshine and lots of friends": Copy of Mrs. Johnson's speech, Democratic National Committee Speeches—2, LBJ Library.
253. From the moment she got on the back of the train: Interview with Liz Carpenter.
254. When he disembarked from the train: Maxine Cheshire, *Washington Post.*
254. "Those first stops set the tone": Interview with Liz Carpenter and Liz Carpenter, oral history.
255. The secretaries wrote notes: White House Social Files, LBJ Library.
255. By mid-morning on that first day: Maxine Cheshire, *Washington Post.*
256. One was Ahoskie, North Carolina: Liz Carpenter, oral history.
256. One white Southern woman told her: Lady Bird Johnson, *A White House Diary.*
256. She posted a Dixie Dictionary: Liz Carpenter, *Ruffles and Flourishes*, page 156.
257. Connally placed a telephone call: Audiotape conversation between Connally and Dan Moore, September 24, 1964, LBJ Library.
257. South Carolina governor Donald Russell: Maxine Cheshire, *Washington Post.*
258. "She wanted": Liz Carpenter, oral history.
258. The advance team that had helped organize: From "The Report to the President and Mrs. Johnson on the Lady Bird Special," written by Mrs. Cecil E. Burney and furnished to author by her son, Frank B. Burney, an attorney in San Antonio.
259. Lady Bird arrived at the shopping center: Maxine Cheshire, *Washington Post*, and Isabelle Shelton, *Washington Star.*
259. At 9:40 P.M., LBJ placed a telephone call: Audiotape conversation between LBJ and CTJ and Lynda Johnson, LBJ Library.
260. "Greta Garbo complex": Liz Carpenter, oral history.
261. "When he would call": Liz Carpenter, oral history.
261. the *Atlanta Constitution* ran an editorial: *Atlanta Constitution*, October 8, 1964.
261. "It was a small way": Interview with Luci Baines Johnson.
261. "It's easy to make a lot of noise": Celestine Sibley, *Atlanta Constitution*, October 9, 1964.

261. Later that night: Interviews with Bess Abell and Liz Carpenter.
262. At noon on October 9: Maxine Cheshire, *Washington Post*, October 10, 1964.
262. "I was bringing roses anyway": Ibid.
262. "Don't you know the Goldwater people": Celestine Sibley, *Atlanta Constitution*, October 14, 1964.
262. Description of the crowd: *Washington Post*, October 10, 1964.
262. "You have brought to the depot": CTJ speech in New Orleans, Democratic National Committee—2, Box 203, LBJ Library.
263. "I was on the station platform": Interview with Katharine Graham.
263. Johnson's speech: Democratic National Committee—2, Box 203, LBJ Library, and multiple press accounts.
264. The following day, Max Freedman: *Atlanta Constitution*, October 14, 1964.
264. At about 10:30 A.M.: Liz Carpenter, oral history.
264. At 9:36 that night: Conversation between LBJ and Fortas, October 14, 1964, LBJ Library.
265. In New York, Reedy made the case: From previous audiotaped conversation.
266. "This could be the whole ballgame": Audiotaped conversation between LBJ and John Connally, October 14, 1964, LBJ Library.
266. The next morning, Carpenter arrived at 7:30: Liz Carpenter, oral history.
267. The conversation between LBJ and CTJ regarding Jenkins: Audiotape, 12:49 P.M., October 15, 1964, LBJ Library.
268. Carpenter wrote out a three-sentence statement: President, Personal Files—5, Lady Bird, LBJ Library.
269. Mrs. Kennedy not voting: Mrs. Kennedy, oral history.
269. On November 17, Lady Bird celebrated: Lady Bird Johnson, *A White House Diary*.

CHAPTER 13: PARADISE LOST

271. "so prissy, so slight": Sharon Francis, oral history, and interview with CTJ.
271. For instance, at one point in the spring of 1966: Lady Bird Johnson, *A White House Diary*.
271. "I have a kind of schizophrenic feeling": Interviews with Liz Carpenter, Nellie Connally, and others.
272. Description of inauguration: Lady Bird Johnson, *A White House Diary*.
273. "I just couldn't": Mrs. Kennedy's 1974 oral history.
273. Instead of trying to win over Jackie's friends: Multiple newspaper and magazine stories, including Frances Spatz Leighton, "LBJ's D.C.," *Washington Post* magazine, January 1964; "Lady Bird Gives Tour of White House," *Houston Chronicle*, January 1, 1964; Nan Robertson, "Our New First Lady," *Saturday Evening Post*, February 8, 1964.
274. The description of her first press conference and the trip to Wilkes-Barre: Lady Bird Johnson, *A White House Diary*.
275. "We were all thrilled": Interview with Helen Thomas
275. On this particular day: Sharon Francis, oral history, pages 7–8.
276. She tried to adapt the spirit of activism: "Report to the Nation: National Youth Conference on Natural Beauty and Conservation," June 26–29, 1966, LBJ Library.
276. By nature and habit: Interviews with family members and Edith Royal.
276. As First Lady, Lady Bird set out: Sharon Francis, oral history.
279. "She just wasn't comfortable": Interview with Liz Carpenter.
280. In Vietnam, as in every other crisis: Interview with George Reedy and oral histories, Sharon Francis and Bess Abell.
280. Bess Abell, Mrs. Johnson's social secretary: Bess Abell, oral history.
280. One such writer, John Hersey: Carl Sferrazza Anthony, *First Ladies*, Vol. 2, pages 133–34.
281. "I couldn't handle the war in Vietnam": Sharon Francis, oral history.
281. "Life is lived these days": Lady Bird Johnson, *A White House Diary*.
282. Johnson once explained to Nan Robertson: *Saturday Evening Post*, February 8, 1964.

283. "For some time I have been swimming upstream": Lady Bird Johnson, *A White House Diary.*
283. One night Johnson got up long after: E. Ernest Goldstein, "The Saint, the Son of a Bitch, and I," from *LBJ: To Know Him Better,* LBJ Library.
284. "Lyndon keeps talking": Lady Bird Johnson, *A White House Diary.*
284. There was no such peace in the White House: Interviews with George Reedy and other staff members and references to sibling rivalry in *Saturday Evening Post, Houston Post,* other press stories, and Lady Bird Johnson, *A White House Diary.*
285. "I was angry and struck out": Interview with Luci Baines Johnson.
285. Lady Bird described Luci as "uncomfortably intuitive": Lady Bird Johnson, *A White House Diary.*
285. Luci's decision to convert: Interviews with Luci Baines Johnson, Liz Carpenter, and Mrs. Johnson's diary.
286. Both Lady Bird and Johnson thought Luci was too young to marry: *Newsweek,* May 23, 1966, and description of wedding, *Newsweek,* August 1966.
286. "get out of the fishbowl": Interview with Luci Baines Johnson.
286. It was during this period that Lynda started dating George Hamilton: *New York Times,* January 2, 1966.
287. "He was extremely good for her": Interview with CTJ.
287. Hamilton introduced her to Hollywood hairdresser George Masters: *This Week* magazine, and other newspaper stories.
287. "Lynda is so smart": Frank Cormier, *LBJ, The Way He Was,* page 85.
288. "And now in a way it's daughter against daughter" and other Lady Bird thoughts: Mrs. Johnson's diary.
290. In late summer, Johnson summoned George Christian: Interview with George Christian.
291. Shortly after that, on June 21, 1967: Mrs. Johnson's diary.
292. "He was blowing": Interview with Jake Pickle.
294. "We should have": Interview with Liz Carpenter.
294. Robb was extremely gung ho: Liz Carpenter, *Ruffles and Flourishes,* page 129.
295. "You sure have made progress": Mrs. Johnson's diary.
295. Just a few days before Christmas: Interviews with George Christian and Horace Busby.
296. "Me," Lady Bird shrugged: Mrs. Johnson's diary.
296. "I just couldn't quit": Interview with George Christian.
296. Description of Women Doers luncheon: Liz Carpenter, oral history, and Mrs. Johnson's diary.
297. "What do you do about delinquent parents?": Remarks at First Lady's luncheon January 18, 1968, social files, Box 45, LBJ Library.
297. Is this a nightmare?": Mrs. Johnson's diary.
298. Telephone calls and initial reaction: Interview with Liz Carpenter, and *New York Times,* January 19, 1968, and *Washington Star,* January 20, 1968.
298. LBJ demanded an explanation: Liz Carpenter to the President, social files, Liz Carpenter, Box 45, LBJ Library.
299. After the New Hampshire primary: Interview with Horace Busby.
300. "Why do we have": Drew Pearson's article in *Look,* July 1968.
300. This account of the withdrawal is taken from Mrs. Johnson's diary, the White House daily logs, and interviews with Horace Busby and George Christian.

CHAPTER 14: HOME TO TEXAS

302. Four days later on April 4, 1968: Mrs. Johnson's diary.
303. That same night, Sharon Francis: Sharon Francis, oral history.
303. "Though I was right in the middle of it": Mrs. Johnson's diary.
304. "Sometimes there are no words": From the selection of letters between Mrs. Kennedy and the Johnson family, LBJ Library.
304. However, on *Air Force One:* Interview with Luci Baines Johnson.
305. "There was a definite line between them": Interview with Jim Hardin.

306. Description of Johnson in retirement: Multiple staff sources.
307. Still, he wanted her physically close to him: Bobby Baker with Larry L. King, *Wheeling and Dealing,* page 272.
307. "Bird, come here. Where are you?": Interviews with Jake Pickle and Luci Baines Johnson.
308. In her efforts to shield him: Interview with Darrell and Edith Royal.
308. Johnson's last golf game: Interview with Darrell Royal and Tom Frost, Jr.
309. Shortly thereafter, in June 1972: Interview with CTJ.
309. On the morning of January 22, 1973: Robert Dallek, *Flawed Giant,* pages 622–23.
310. "One to Mike": Interview with Mike Howard.
310. "Well": Ibid.
310. She had already telephoned several of his oldest friends: Interviews with Warren Woodward, Darrell Royal, Horace Busby, and Jake Pickle.

EPILOGUE: OUR LADY OF FLOWERS

312. "I seek to celebrate my glad release": Mrs. Johnson's diary.
312. "Work. Work. Work.": Associated Press, February 1973.
312. "Oh, wouldn't Lyndon have loved this?": Interviews with Horace Busby and others.
313. Encounter with Mrs. Carter at the LBJ Library: Interview with Robert Strauss.
314. In 1983: Interview with *Dallas Times Herald.*
314. In the next few years, she took each of her seven grandchildren: Interview with Lyndon Nugent.
314. To some degree, both daughters: Interview with Luci Baines Johnson.
314. Lynda, the shy White House bride: *Fort Worth Star-Telegram,* November 1, 1987, and multiple news stories.
315. "To think," she said: Interview with CTJ.

Acknowledgments

At the outset, I wish to acknowledge the circle of Johnson scholars and biographers for the documentation of the life of Lyndon Johnson and his family. The list includes Robert Caro, Robert Dallek, Doris Kearns Goodwin, Merle Miller, Joseph Califano, and many others. Within that group, I particularly thank Ronnie Dugger, my fellow Texan and friend, who first entertained me years ago with LBJ tales.

I also acknowledge my good friend, D. B. Hardeman, the former aide to Speaker of the House Sam Rayburn. I came to know D.B. in the late 1970s in San Antonio and in Washington before he died in 1981. He was a raconteur who both respected and admired Mrs. Johnson. Much of what he told me in conversation formed the thinking foundation for this book. I am also indebted to Maury Maverick, Jr., the civil rights lawyer and journalist, who has been my conscience and mentor for a quarter century.

At the Lyndon Baines Johnson Library in Austin, I owe thanks to Claudia Anderson, Linda Seelke, and other excellent archivists, as well as to Philip Scott, photo archivist. In Austin, I thank Bill Pugsley, an independent researcher, who helped me at critical times during the project, and provided much of the material in the whistlestop chapter. Thanks also to Diana Claitor, who found and copied most of the photographs in the book. In San Marcos, I thank Carol Parsonage, a history graduate student, for doing research about the 1952 flood in newspapers surrounding Johnson City. In San Antonio, I thank Tess Coody Anders for copy-reading the manuscript. In New York, I thank Cory Russell Leahy for the final read.

A number of friends sustained me in important ways. In particular, I owe a great debt to Linda Pace and Laurence Miller for giving me a place to work at ArtPace, a contemporary art foundation in San Antonio, and to the entire staff at ArtPace, who put up with my clutter with good cheer. In addition to Linda, I owe thanks to several other female friends—Kay Schanzer, Catherine Cooke, Cyndi Krier, Penelope Speier, and Mimi Swartz—for their warmth, support, and for being there when I needed them. For unraveling the mystery of my computer, I thank Kenneth Schwartzman.

I am grateful to my agent, Jim Hornfischer, who conceived of this project, and for my editor, Lisa Drew, whose penetrating knowledge, patience, and guidance helped bring the book to completion.

Finally, thanks go to my husband, Lucky Russell, and all our family—Cory, Kevin, Megan, Maury, and Tyler—for standing by me and sharing in the lessons that this book has taught us all.

Index

Index

Index

B
Johnson   Russell, Jan Jarboe.
R   Lady Bird.

DATE			

26.00